John Blaine Kerr

Biographical Dictionary of Well-Known British Columbians

John Blaine Kerr

Biographical Dictionary of Well-Known British Columbians

ISBN/EAN: 9783337030995

Printed in Europe, USA, Canada, Australia, Japan

Cover: Foto ©ninafisch / pixelio.de

More available books at **www.hansebooks.com**

Biographical Dictionary

—OF—

WELL-KNOWN

BRITISH COLUMBIANS

WITH A HISTORICAL SKETCH

BY J. B. KERR.

Vancouver, B. C.
PUBLISHED BY KERR & BEGG.

1890.

PREFACE.

The need of a work like the one here submitted to the public is especially manifest in British Columbia. Until a few years ago this province was cut off from the rest of the Dominion by what seemed an insuperable barrier, and communication was necessarily of a limited and unsatisfactory character. The result was that to the outside world, the history of the province and of the men who were guiding its affairs was almost entirely unknown. Since the construction of the Canadian Pacific Railway the condition of things in the Province has radically altered. The population is rapidly increasing by immigration from the East and the early settlers who underwent the storm and stress of pioneer life and made the new condition of things possible are rapidly passing away. If this book assists in preserving the names of some of these "old timers" it will not be valueless.

I desire to return thanks to those citizens of Victoria, Nanaimo and New Westminster who rendered me valuable assistance in collecting material for my historical sketch. Among the published books I made use of was William's directory for 1882, which contains a large amount of reliable information, carefully compiled and arranged, concerning early colonial history.

J. B. K.

INTRODUCTION.

In submitting the present volume to the public I make no apology for the briefness and imperfection of the historical sketch of the country with which the biographies are introduced. In a work of this character it would be impossible to place before the reader in exact and minute detail every gradation of the country's history from its condition as a wilderness to its present state as an important and enlightened province. This task will remain for the luminous and discriminating page of the gifted historian of the future who will possess unstinted means for obtaining his material and unlimited leisure for casting it.

There is none of the provinces of the Dominion, with the exception of Quebec, which offers such a large and interesting field to the historian as does British Columbia. From the beginning of the present century every change which has taken place in its condition has been strongly marked, and each period possesses an interest of a character separate and distinct from the others. In each, too, there is abundant material for historical work. This material is, however, yearly becoming less and may, if it is not collected without delay, be in a great measure lost. With the death of every time-honored agent of the Hudson's Bay Company, of course, valuable personal recollections and experiences entirely disappear. It is to be hoped, therefore, that while there is yet time some discerning writer who can judiciously arrange and forcibly present his narrative may enter this field and do for British Columbia what Mr. Parkham has done for French Canada. As it is at present there is no work containing a full and readable history of the country. Several volumes there are in which vivid and interesting sketches are given of certain periods but none presenting a satisfactory outline of the country's growth. There is, indeed, one book published by a most voluminous writer, named Hubert Howe Bancroft, which professes to be a history of British Columbia from the earliest period. It is, however, such a muddled mass of misstatements and misrepresentations that when one does, after much effort, break through the thick husk of rhetorical bombast in which the alleged facts are hidden, he finds the fruit utterly unsound. This writer, who is an American of most pronounced anti-British proclivities, has certainly obtained access to public records and private memoranda of a most valuable nature but the use, or rather mis-use, which he has made of his privileges and opportunities has been such that his "authorities" will in the majority of cases be found to be widely at variance with the statements with which he credits them. In addition to the untrustworthiness of his facts his book is written from that standpoint of antagonism to British institutions which characterizes the half-educated and bitterly-patriotic citizen of the American republic. This gentleman has "written up" (the expression is used advisedly as being the only one applicable to his style of work) the whole Pacific Coast of North America, and has presented the result of his "long historical pilgrimage from Darien to Alaska" in forty odd volumes. The arrangement of the whole work is so ingenious that without repeated reference to all the others a reader is unable intelligently to peruse any one of these volumes, and he is constantly experiencing the most remarkable transitions in time and space, of the many efforts of the writer's genius, and when they are placed side by side they fill a good sized book-case, it would be difficult to choose the one to which, for intrinisic worthlessness the palm should be awarded. If, however, there is one more than another which combines the quality of dullness with the quality of mendacity it is the volume on British Columbia. The facts it contains are indeed scanty, but they are sufficient for Mr. Bancroft's purpose. To the ordinary reader the book is an enigma. There is not even an attempt at chronological sequence in the arrangement of his facts. The matter is thrown together at hap-hazard and to the ingenuity of the reader is left the task of bringing some sort of order out of the chaotic mass. There is, too, throughout the whole volume a clearly defined impatience at treating of the subject at all, the writer's democratic instincts evidently rebelling against the prostitution of his pen to such ignoble uses as that of recording the events which have occurred in a British colony.

Among the number of books connected with British Columbia which I have thought it necessary to read is one entitled the "Story of Metlakathla" to which I shall make reference hereafter. The author of this work, who is also an American, quotes with evident relish one of the grossest misstatements of which Mr. Bancroft is guilty, and I shall, therefore, go to the trouble of citing it *in extenso* and then of giving the true version of the occurence. The following is Mr. Bancroft's version: "During the summer of 1850 a case occurred at Fort Rupert, while yet John Sebastian (Helmcken) wore ermine, which casts dark reproach, both upon the Hudson's Bay Company and the officers of the Imperial Government, and which tended in nowise to reconcile Blanchard to his anomalous position. The ship England, on her way from the southern coast to Fort Rupert for coals, stopped at Victoria for sailors, the vessel being short of hands. The California gold excitement was everywhere raging, and sailors willingly risked their lives to free themselves from service. From one of the Company's vessels, then lying at Victoria, three men deserted to the England, which then continued her way to Fort Rupert. Meanwhile notice was sent to Fort Rupert of the deserters, who thereupon became frightened, left the England and took to the woods, intending to join the vessel at another port. Indians were sent in pursuit with orders from Blenkinsop, then acting for the Company at Fort Rupert, to bring in the deserters dead or alive. Four days afterwards the Indians returned and claimed the reward, saying that they had killed them all. It was true. The sailors had been shot down in the forest by savages set upon them by an officer of the Hudson's Bay Company. Blenkinsop gave directions to have buried the bodies of the murdered men where they lay, and let the matter be hushed, but Muir insisted that they should be buried at the Fort, and it was done. Very naturally the colliers were furious. * * * * * * * * About a month after the murderous affair H. M. S. Dædalus, Captain Wellesley, arrived at Victoria, when the Governor went on board and proceeded at once to Fort Rupert. Now mark the course of justice pursued by the officers of the Imperial Government. Instead of proceeding against the instigators of the murder and arresting the officers of the Hudson's Bay Company, as they should have done, they direct the full force of their vengeance against the natives. Helmcken, the newly-fledged magistrate, cognizant of the whole affair, and well knowing who were the guilty persons, and what hand he himself had in it, goes to the Newittee Camp, twelve miles distant, and loudly demands the surrender of the murderers. The savages acknowledge the murder, but plead that they were only executing orders. Truer to themselves and to the right than were the white men, they refused to give up the perpetrators of the deed, but offered to give up the property paid them by the white men for the commission of the crime. This did not satisfy the European justice-dealers. Servants of the Hudson's Bay Company had been slain by order of the officer, of the Hudson's Bay Company. Some one must be punished; and as they did not wish to hang themselves, they must find victims among their instruments. As the magistrate was unable to accomplish their purpose, Wellesley sent a force, under Lieutenant Burton, in three boats of the Dædalus, against the Newittees. Finding their camp deserted, Burton destroyed the village and made a bonfire of all the property he could find. The following summer H. M. S. Daphne, Captain Fanshawe, arrived. Meanwhile the Newittees had rebuilt their village, supposing the white men satisfied with the injury already inflicted. One day, while holding a potlach, and being at peace, as they believed, with the white men, the Daphne's boats, under Lieutenant Lacy, crept into their harbor and announced their arrival by a discharge of musketry. Men, women and children were mercilessly cut down, persons innocent of any thought of wrong against their murderers, and their village again destroyed. Then the Daphne sailed away. Justice was satisfied; and Blenkinsop and the rest of them went about their work as usual."

Not only are the statements, as they are given above, untrue, but they bear *prima facie* evidence of deliberate malice. To any one at all conversant with the history of the Hudson's Bay Company in this country, the absurdity of the charge here made against Mr. Blenkinsop will be at once apparent. One of the first, or indeed the first, principle of the company's policy was to impress upon the natives a profound respect for the lives of its servants. It was upon this that the whole vast commercial system was built, and any divergence from it would have brought speedy disaster and ruin upon the corporation. Mr. Blenkinsop was a trusted servant of the company, in charge of a fort imperfectly garrisoned, and, that he should at such a juncture, when his own life might have been imperilled by any imprudence, have taken a step contrary and foreign to the well-known policy of the company, and offered a reward to the savages for the murder of his own servants, is supremely incredible. The true facts in connection with the whole affair are as follows, and are easy of verification even at the present time: During the summer of 1850 Mr. Blenkinsop was placed in charge of Fort Rupert in the absence of Capt. McNeil. There were at the time about thirty individuals within the pickets, all servants of the company, and a number of them miners, as a test of the coal seams at this place was then being made. In close proximity to the Fort was a villiage of Indians with a population of some three thousand. The news of the wonderful discovery of gold in California had been brought to the fort and had created considerable commotion. The miners of course became excited and wanted to get away. They refused to continue at work and claimed, as a ground for their conduct, that they were supplied with unsuitable food, and that there had been on the part of the company breaches of agreement committed. They refused, moreover, to submit to the discipline so necessary for the protection of the Fort and its inhabitants from surrounding tribes. The insubordination increased, and coming to the knowledge of Governor Blanchard he sent to Dr. Helmcken, the company's surgeon, stationed at Rupert, an acting commission of Justice of the Peace, and recommended him to appoint special constables. The men were called together, the proclamation was read, and volunteers to act as constables were asked for. The men, one and all, positively refused to serve. They would all sink or swim in the same boat, and they would not work for the company any longer. It so happened that Captain Dodd, of the Hudson's Bay Company's steamer Beaver, who brought and gave to Dr. Helmcken his commission as Justice, made complaint as soon as it had been read, that three of his men had deserted at Victoria in the barque England. The England, after the desertion of the men from the Beaver, had come to Fort Rupert for a cargo of coal destined for San Francisco, and was there then. Dr. Helmcken, in his capacity as Justice of the Peace, went on board the England, but found that the men, fearing capture, had left the ship as soon as the Beaver was sighted. In a couple of days afterwards the Beaver left, and as the men were no longer wanted, Dr. Helmcken told the Captain of the England to get his men on board as it was very dangerous for them to be prowling about the woods unprotected. One of the men only returned to the ship; the other two refusing to do this. This man becoming suspicious that his arrest was intended left again on the following day. The England was a source of much trouble and danger to the Fort at this time. The men and Indians got intoxicating liquor from her and this, together with the tales told by the crew of the riches in California, maddened the miners beyond measure with their imprisoned condition at Fort Rupert. The fort became anything but secure, with drunken Indians without and enraged miners within. The men made no secret of the fact that they would take the first opportunity which presented itself of leaving. The England, having nearly completed her cargo, one day it was found that all the miners had disappeared. Their whereabouts could not be discovered. They were not on board the England, and although the Captain and crew knew perfectly well where they were hidden they would not tell. The desertion of the men was, of course a great blow to the fort. By it the mining industry was brought to an end. Owing to this and other desertions, too, the gates of the fort were closed, and ingress and egress prevented. The Indians, of course, were only too well acquainted with the state of things within the fort, and as they were easily excited it became very questionable whether they would not make an attack on the fort or set it on fire. Mr. Blenkinsop and Dr. Helmcken had to keep watch and ward, and on more than one occasion Indians climbed to the top of the pickets and looked into the enclosure by way of bravado. The Indians, however, finally promised that if they found out where the deserters were they would let the officers at the fort know. At this time the England was ready to leave. One day the Indians brought word that three white men had been seen on an island not a great distance away. Knowing that these must be either miners or seamen, Mr. Blenkinsop despatched a canoe of Indians, with Old Whale, an Indian chief, in command. Whale was well acquainted and friendly with the miners. If he brought the men back safely he was to be rewarded. He returned empty, however, the men having left the island. A day or two after rumors became rife among the lodges that three men had been murdered by the Newittees, a tribe living thirty miles from Fort Rupert. The fort interpreter was sent to inquire into the truth or falsehood of the report and returned next day, having seen the deserting miners at Sucharto, near Newittee, from whom he learned that the murdered men were three sailors. The miners were waiting for the England to carry them away, and the sailors had been hiding in other places for a similar purpose. The latter had been supplied with food by the England, but no arms given to them. The Rupert Indians offered at once to go and make war on the Newittees, to avenge the murder, but their offer was declined. At this juncture Mr. Beardmore returned from Victoria, and immediately volunteered to go in search of the murdered men. The Newittees would not go with him, but directed him to the spot. On his way there he sighted the England at anchor off Sucharto, ready to take away the miners. Mr. Beardmore found the bodies and reported the discovery to Dr. Helmcken, who brought them to Fort Rupert. Here they were buried in the fort garden with Christian rites. During this time there was not a word of complaint against the officers at the fort, or a suggestion that these men had been murdered on account of rewards having been offered for their apprehension, but some one, as it subsequently transpired, wrote to Governor Blanchard informing him that rewards had been offered to the Indians to take and bring back these men dead or alive. How such a report originated is uncertain, as the only reward offered, as has before been mentioned, was the one to be given to Old Whale for every one of the deserters who was returned safe and sound. It is, however, surmised that a young man named Muir, who knew a little of Canadian French, was responsible for the report. In speaking to the Indians Mr. Blenkinsop was obliged to employ the aid of an interpreter, and in doing so he spoke French, the interpreter's native tongue. The French term for *each man*, which is, of course, *par tete*, struck on this young man's ear, and he construed it, whether wilfully or not, to mean "per head—dead or alive." This mistranslation at last got abroad among the men and matters grew worse at the fort for a time. They at length, however, found out the mistake and, as the England had gone beyond reach, things finally settled down into a hum-drum monotonous routine.

A month or so after the departure of the England H. M. S. Dædalus arrived at Fort Rupert with Governor Blanchard on board. When the Governor was placed in possession of the true facts of the case it was decided that Dr. Helmcken should go and demand the surrender of the murderers, in the usual manner. The doctor accordingly set off with an interpreter and half a dozen Indians for Newittee. On entering the harbor he was met by four or five hundred Indians, painted black, and armed with muskets, spears axes, and other weapons, and all making the usual hideous noise which they employ to strike terror into their enemies. Dr. Helmcken explained his mission to them from the canoe. The chief answered him that they would not and could not give up the murderers, but were willing to pay for the murdered men as many blankets, furs and other articles as might reasonably be demanded, this being their law and custom in such cases. Of course this was declined, and they were told that they were bringing great misery on themselves by not acceding to the demand of King George's law. When Dr. Helmcken returned and made known to Governor Blanchard and Captain Wellesley the decision of the Newittees chiefs, it was decided to send boats and men to seize the murderers or to punish the tribes. The boats arrived only to find a deserted village. The crew partly destroyed the village and returned without having seen a member of the tribe. Shortly after this the Daedalus left Fort Rupert and, when near Cape Scott, she was fired at, and a sailor slightly wounded. This may not, however, have been the work of the Newittees, but of some other Indians, who simply intended saluting the ship. The year following H. M. S. Daphne went up to punish the tribe, if they still refused to give up the murderers. On this occasion they were found in a new camp. They peremptorily refused the demands of the captain and accordingly the crew prepared to attack them. The Indians fired and wounded several of the sailors, who thereupon went at them. The Indians, however, fled to the thick woods in the rear, where they could not be followed. Only two Indians were killed in this skirmish. The village huts were then destroyed and the Daphne left. Governor Blanchard now ordered rewards to be offered for the delivery of the murderers. The Newittees by this time had quite enough, and fearing another attack they determined to make their peace by handing over the malefactors. They made an attempt to seize these men, but it was so clumsily done that in the scuffle a young chief was killed and another wounded. So the murderers were shot and their dead bodies brought to Mr. Blenkinsop at Fort Rupert, where they were buried. It is believed however, that one of the murderers escaped, and to make up the full number a slave was substituted. The reward offered by Governor Blanchard was asked for, but Mr. Blenkinsop declined to pay it. He gave the Indians, who had a right to the money, a letter to Governor Blanchard at Victoria. Whether it was ever delivered is unknown.

While the Daedalus was at Fort Rupert, Governor Blanchard held a court of inquiry, but after hearing the evidence he gave a very enigmatical decision. The fact was that in his first despatches to the Imperial Government, concerning the affair, which he had sent before he left Victoria, were based on *ex parte* statements, and when he came to enquire into the matter he found his error; an error, however, which he did not choose to acknowledge in view of the unfavorable light in which such an admission would undoubtedly have placed him. He made no complaints whatever of the conduct of Mr. Blenkinsop or Dr. Helmcken in the affair, and as Blanchard was inimical to the Hudson's Bay Company, he certainly would not have omitted to censure the officers of the company had there been any reasonable grounds so to do.

Now between these two accounts of the same occurrence it is left to the honest reader to judge which is the true one. It may be said that Mr. Bancroft's account was obtained from Muir, the man who is supposed to have written the letter which misled Governor Blanchard, and who has since died of disease of the brain. Mr. Bancroft made no attempt to verify the account, although there are men still living who were present at Fort Rupert during the whole trouble, and who could have set him right, not only on this, but on other matters. I may also say that I have sifted the matter thoroughly and give the facts as I found them. I would not have troubled the reader with this exposure of Mr. Bancroft's method of writing history, had I not, as I have said, found the account of this particular affair quoted elsewhere. The book, however, is full of such misrepresentations and, it will be admitted that when a writer allows his prejudices thus to warp his judgment and color his entire narrative, he simply shows his unfitness to write history.

Another book which I feel compelled to mention, owing to the fact that it has obtained in British Columbia a circulation far beyond its deserts, is that entitled "A Story of Metlakathla," by Henry S. Wellcome. This highly-colored romance is "dedicated to the cause of Justice, Truth and Humanity," and, as it is nothing more or less than a plea to the people of the United States for pecuniary assistance to a village of discontented Indians, the moral virtues which are thus called upon to become its sponsors are presumably those which have become so popular throughout the American Republic. This book tells "a story of outrage upon, and cruelty to, a civilized

Indian community on the part of the Dominion of Canada," and calls upon the people of the United States with its "government of the people, by the people and for the people, to save this stricken community from desperation, and perhaps from bloodshed." It contains, according to the author and the press of the Republic, materials for another Evangeline. It is not unlikely that in the hands of some dexterous versifier it may be so employed, and yet after all the labor of American genius has been expended upon it, the story will still retain about the same modicum of truth as Mr. Parkman has proved went to the manufacture of Mr. Longfellow's pretty poem. The history of Mr. William Duncan's labor among the Indian tribes about Fort Simpson is already fairly well-known, and it would therefore be unnecessary for me to attempt, had I space to do so, a narration of the seemingly impossible work which he undertook, the wonderful success he achieved, and the marvellous metamorphosis which he accomplished in the moral and social natures of the natives who came under his influence. He was sent out to British Columbia in the interest of the Church of England Missionary Society, and worked under their auspices for some twenty years, during which time he succeeded not only in converting and educating a great number of the most abandoned savages, but of founding an Indian village and establishing industries. Many men of note visited, at various times, his mission village, which had a population of about one thousand persons, and all bore testimony to the wonderful results of Mr. Duncan's labors. Mr. Duncan, however, impressed his people with such a profound regard and reverence for himself, and rendered himself so necessary to the spiritual and material life of the mission, that when it was decided to withdraw him and substitute another in his place, the natives rebelled and refused to submit themselves to the directions of their new spiritual guide. Mr. Duncan accordingly returned. The society now seeing the advanced stage of civilization to which the people of Metlakathla had attained, desired Mr. Duncan to conform his church more closely to the Episcopal form of government, and instructed him accordingly. He, however, refused to obey the commands of the organization which had so long maintained him in this field, and his people of course supported him in his difference with the society. The society then instructed the Bishop of Caledonia to take charge of the mission in their interests. This was done, and from this flowed all the trouble which subsequently occurred. A portion of the land attached to the mission was given to the society by the government, and a cry arose that this was a fraudulent seizure of Indian lands, although the Indians, it will be remembered, have no title to land in British Columbia. The Indians were told that they were being unjustly treated, and they took it so much to heart that when the government surveyors went north to survey the land they were prevented by the natives, which necessitated sending a warship to the spot. Mr. Duncan then went to Washington to see if he could obtain from the United States Government a strip of land in Alaska to which he could remove his people. He was successful in his mission and his people and he have been for some years living under the stars and stripes. Mr. Wellcome obtained all the material for his book from Mr. Duncan alone, and thus has only one side of the story. The whole matter, which might have been made plain, and lost none of its effect, even from Mr. Wellcome's uncompromisingly partisan standpoint, has been lengthened out to nearly 500 pages. The "filling in" consists of diatribes against the governments of the Dominion and the Province, the Church of England Missionary Society, the bishops and ministers of the church, residents of Victoria who were not disposed to reverence everything Mr. Duncan said and did, and all, in short, who took a different view of the matter from that taken by Mr. Duncan. These choice passages are relieved by panegyrics on Mr. Duncan, and by dissertations on law, morals, missionary work and the Indian question. The panacea prescribed for all the ills of the Metlakathlans is to settle them in Alaska under the mild and beneficent rule of the Washington Government. It is amusing when one reads this to think of the constant ill-treatment which the tribes in the United States have suffered at the hands of that government's officials, of the unconcealed villany with which they have been robbed of their lands, of the outrages which for years they have had to submit to, of the massacres which have repeatedly taken place, and the Indian wars which have made the name of the United States a by-word for their usage of the native races. The Metlakahtlan trouble could have been avoided by a little compromise on the part of Mr. Duncan and, after all, the society which had maintained him so long was not asking very much at his hands in desiring him to use a few church forms, which Mr. Duncan himself considered good in other than Indian churches. The land question, over which such a stir was made, and concerning which Mr. Wellcome whips himself into such a fury of virtuous indignation, he did not understand. It is nonsense to talk about an Indian title in British Columbia, at least on the coast. The aborigines never dreamed of tilling the land or of obtaining their food from it. The principal source from which they derived their living was the rivers, lakes, inlets, and the ocean itself. Animals and birds they also used, but the cultivation of the earth was beyond their conception. These same sources are still open to them, as they ever were, and the government sees that they are protected in their rights.

The geography of the Province is, since the construction of the transcontinental highway, fairly well known and it will be unnecessary here to do more than mention its chief features. British Columbia has the general shape of a parallelogram, is seven hundred and sixty eight miles long, five hundred miles broad, and contains a superficial area of three hundred and fifty thousand square miles. The Rocky Mountains, the great "backbone of the continent," form the eastern boundary, separating it from the remainder of Canada, and the Pacific Ocean bounds it on the west, save for a distance of about 300 miles to the extreme north, where the Alaska possessions of the United States interpose between it and the sea. Its southern limit is the forty-ninth parallel, which forms the international boundary line between the Province and the United States, and the northern is the sixtieth parallel. The general surface of the country is mountainous and broken, consisting of short mountain ranges, detached groups of mountains, elevated plateaus and many valleys of various extent. Running parallel with the Rocky Mountains, and in many places scarcely distinguishable from them, are masses of mountains, and along the coast lies a high range usually indicated as a continuation of the Cascades, but, in fact, a northern extension of the great Coast Range. Lying between these two, and extending as far north as latitude 55.30 degrees, is an irregular belt of elevated plateau. Beyond this the mountains, except those bordering the coast, decrease in height, and before the limit of the Province is reached the land has a gentle slope towards the Arctic Ocean, Peace river and other streams of the Arctic watershed finding their sources there. Such are the general features of the interior—high mountain ridges on the east and west, enclosing a high plateau, down the centre of which flows the Fraser river, its general course being south until almost to the international line, where it turns sharply to the west and enters the ocean. The other great streams of the interior are Thompson river, entering the Fraser from the east, and the Okanagan, Columbia, and Kootenay, the last two having very eccentric courses. The Columbia rises almost in the extreme southeastern corner, sweeps northerly around the upper end of the Selkirk Range, and then flow directly south between the Selkirk and Gold Mountains into the United States. The Kootenay has its source in the same region as the Columbia, makes a long sweep to the south, crossing the boundary line, and, returning again, discharges its waters into the Columbia. One peculiarity of this region is that nearly every stream of consequence has its origin in or passes through, one or more long, narrow lakes, consisting in many places of simply a broadening of the river, and at others a well defined lake of considerable area. Such are Shuswap Lake, whence flows the Thompson, and Lake Kamloops, through which the same stream passes; also Upper and Lower Columbia and Upper and Lower Arrow lakes along the course of the Columbia, and Lakes Kootenay and Okanagan, features of the streams thus christened. Lakes and water courses abound from one end of the Province to the other, many of them navigable by steamers of a light draught for great distances.

The coast line is the most wonderful in the world. The mountains border closely upon the sea, the shore being indented by a multitude of bays and inlets and fringed by countless small islands, between which run tortuous, but safe and navigable, channels. Outside of these, and protecting these inland channels for nearly the entire length of the coast, are a series of large islands, the greatest and most southerly of which is the Island of Vancouver, separated from the extreme northwestern portion of Washington Territory by the historical Straits of Juan de Fuca, through the center of which runs the international line. It is oblong in shape, extending northwesterly parallel with the mainland, from which it is separated by the narrow and island-dotted channel of the Gulf of Georgia, a distance of nearly 300 miles, and has a width varying from thirty to fifty miles. Its area of 12,000 square miles is heavily timbered and generally mountainous, the highest peaks attaining an altitude of from 6,000 to 9,000 feet.

As the immense yield of gold was, in the majority of instances, the magnet which for years subsequent to the founding of the colony of British Columbia attracted hither those who are now regarded as the fathers of the country and as the majority of these tried their fortunes at the mines for a greater or less period of time, it will not be out of place to describe briefly the methods pursued in working mining claims. The work of digging for gold was by no means of an easy character but on the contrary required arduous and persevering toil to be successful. All the processes of extracting the precious metal from the earth required water and with rare exceptions quick-silver. The following interesting description is from the pen of Commander R. C. Mayne, R. N. who in 1860 made a tour of the California gold fields and who both before and after that period visited the British Columbia mines. His book on that period of the colony is the most interesting extant and for accuracy and completeness of detail is unrivalled.

The first task of the miner attracted to a new gold country or district, by the report of its wealth, is "prospecting." For this purpose every miner, however light his equipment may otherwise be, carries with him a "pan" and a small quantity of quicksilver; the latter to be used only where the gold is very fine. Very little experience enables a miner to detect that "colour" of the earth which indicates the presence of the metallic sand in which gold is found. Wherever, as he travels through the new country, he sees this, he stops at once to wash a pan of dirt, and thus test its value. Although many diggings are found away from the bank of a stream, the river-sides are the places where gold is generally first looked for and worked. In saying this, of course I except the gold in quartz, of which I shall have to speak hereafter. The spots first searched are generally those upon the bank of a river where the deposit consists of a thick, stiff mud or clay, with stones. In some cases this is covered with sand, so that the surface has to be removed before the "pay dust" is revealed. All these workings on river-banks are called "bars," and are usually named after the prospector, or from some incident connected with their discovery.

When the prospector comes to dirt which looks as if it would pay, he unslings his pan from his back, and proceeds to test it.

This he effects by filling his pan with the earth, then squatting on the edge of the stream, he takes it by the rim, dipping it in the water, and giving it a kind of rotary motion stirring and kneading the contents occasionally until the whole is completely moistened. The larger stones are then thrown out, the edge of the pan canted upwards, and a continual flow of water made to pass through it until, the lighter portion of its contents being washed away, nothing but a few pebbles and specks of black metallic sand are left, among which the gold, if there is any, will be found. The rotary movement, by which the heavier pebbles and bits of gold are kept in the centre of the pan, and the lighter earth allowed to pass over its edge, requires considerable practice, and an unskillful prospector will perhaps pass by a place as not being worth working that an experienced hand will recognize as very rich. The specific gravity of the black sand being nearly equal to that of the gold, while wet, they cannot be at once separated, and the nuggets, if any, being taken out, the pan is laid in the sun or by a fire to dry. When dry the lighter particles of sand are blown away; or if the gold is very fine it is amalgamated with quicksilver. The miners know by practice how much gold in a pan will constitute a rich digging, and they usually express the value of the earth as "5," "10," or "15 cent dirt," meaning that each pan so washed will yield so much in money. Panning, it may be remarked, never gives the full value of the dirt, as may be imagined from the roughness of the process. If the gold should be in flakes, a good deal is likely to be lost in the process, as it will not then sink readily to the bottom of the pan, and is more likely to be washed away with the sand. In panning, as well as, indeed, in all the other primitive processes of washing gold, the superior specific gravity of this metal over others, except platinum, is the basis of operations; all depending upon its settling at the bottom of whatever vessel may chance to be used.

The "pan" is hardly ever used except for prospecting, so that the "rocker" or "cradle" may be described as the most primitive appliance used in gold-washing. In the winter of 1859, when I first went up the Fraser, the rocker was the general machine—the use of sluices not having then begun. It was used in California as early as 1848, being formed rudely of logs, or the trunk of a tree. And yet, ungainly as they were, they commanded, before saw-mills were established in the country, enormous prices.

The rocker, then, consists of a box 3½ to 4 feet long, about 2 feet wide, and 1½ deep. The top and one end of this box are open, and at the lower end the sides slope gradually until they reach the bottom. At its head is attached a closely jointed box with a sheet-iron bottom, pierced with holes sufficiently large to allow pebbles to pass through. This machine is provided with rockers like a child's cradle, while within cleets are placed to arrest the gold in its passage. One of the miners then, the cradle being placed by the water's edge, feeds it with earth, while another rocks and supplies it with water. The dirt to be washed is thrown into the upper iron box, and a continual stream of water being poured in, it is disintegrated, the gold and pebbles passing down to the bottom, where the water is allowed to carry the stones away, and the cleets arrest the precious metal.

When the gold is very fine I have seen a piece of cloth laid along the bottom box, covered with quicksilver to arrest the gold. When a party of miners work with rockers, they divide the labour of rocking, carrying water, if necessary, and digging equally among themselves. The rocker is the only apparatus that can be at all successfully worked single-handed; and rough as it appears and really is, I have seen men make 30 to 50 dollars a day with it, while far greater sums have been known to be realized by it. In these remarks I have assumed that my readers generally are aware that quicksilver arrests whatever gold passes over it, and, forming an amalgam with it, retains it until it is retorted from it. In washing gold, quicksilver has to be used always, except where the mineral is found very large and coarse. Even the earth is generally made to pass over some quicksilver before it escapes altogether, in order to preserve the finer particles. I may here mention that in a "sluice" of ordinary size 40 or 50 lbs. of quicksilver are used daily; in a rocker perhaps 8 or 10 lbs. Of course the same quicksilver can be used over and over again when the gold has been retorted from it.

The first improvement on the "rocker" was by the use of a machine called the "Long Tom." This, though common enough in California, I never saw used in British Columbia. It consists of a shallow trough, from 10 to 20 feet long, and 16 inches to 2 feet wide. One end is slightly turned up, shod with iron, and perforated like the sieve of a rocker. The trough is placed at an incline, sieve-end downwards. A stream of water is turned into the upper end of the Tom, and several hands supply it with earth, which finds its way to the sieve, carrying along with it the gold, which it washes or disintegrates in its passage. Immediately beneath the sieve a box is placed, in which are nailed cleets, or as they are more generally termed "Riffles," which catch the gold as in the rocker. When the gold is fine another box containing quicksilver is placed at the end of the riffle, to catch the gold which passes it.

A man always attends at the end to clear away the "tailings," or earth discharged from the machine, and also to stir up the earth in the Tom, and keep the sieve clear of stones, an iron rake being used for the purpose. By the use of the "Long Tom," rather than the cradle, a great saving is effected; the work being performed in a much more thorough manner. It is estimated in California that the Tom will wash ten times as much earth as a cradle, employing the same number of hands.

The next important method is "sluicing." This is by far the most commonly used both in British Columbia and California, employing, I suppose, one-half the mining population of both countries.

Sluicing is, moreover, an operation which can be carried on on any scale, from two or three men upon a river bar, to a rich company washing away an entire hill by the "Hydraulic" process. Whatever may be the scale of the operations, however, "sluicing" is necessarily connected with a system of "flumes," or wooden aqueducts of greater or less extent, either running along the back of a river-bar, and supplying the sluices at it, or cobwebbing and intersecting the whole country as in California. I have seen flumes on the Shady Creek Canal there, conveying an enormous stream of water across a deep ravine at the height of 100 to 200 feet.

"Sluice-boxes" are of various sizes, but generally from 2 to 3 feet long, by about the same width. These are fitted closely together at the ends, so as to form a continuous strongly-built trough of the required length, from 15 or 20 to several thousand feet, their make and strength depending entirely upon the work they have to do. I will here describe sluicing upon a moderate scale, as I found it in practice at Hill's Bar upon the Fraser during my visit there in 1858.

This bar was taken up in claims early in 1858, its size being then about 1½ mile, although it has since been much extended, the richness of the soil proving, I believe, greater as it is ascended. In this place, then, a flume was put up, carrying the water from a stream which descended the mountain at its southern end along the whole length of the bar, and behind those claims which were being worked. From this flume each miner led a sluice down towards the river; his sluice being placed at such an angle that the water would run through it with sufficient force to carry the earth, but not, of course, the gold with it. Its strength, indeed, is so regulated as to allow time for the riffles and quicksilver to catch the gold as it passes. The supply of water from the flume to each sluice is regulated by a gate in the side of the flume, which is raised for so much per inch. The price paid for water of course varies greatly with the cost of timber, engineering difficulties of making the flume, etc. It is ordinarily established by the miners, who meet and agree to pay any individual or company who may undertake the work a certain rateable rental for the water. Their construction, indeed, is one of the most profitable of colonial speculations. The flume I am now speaking of cost 7000 or 8000 dollars, and each miner paid a dollar an inch for water daily. Since that time it has become much cheaper, and the usual price is about 25 cents an inch, the width of the gate being 1 foot. The sluice-boxes here were very slight, about inch-plank, as the dirt which had to pass through them was not large. In the bottom of each box was a grating, made of strips of plank nailed crosswise to each other, but not attached to the box like the riffles. In the interstices of these gratings quicksilver is spread to catch the fine gold, the coarse being caught by the grating itself. The sluice is placed on tressels or legs, so as to raise it to the height convenient for shovelling the earth in; the water is then let on, and several men feed the sluice with earth from either side, while one or two with iron rakes stir it up or pull out any large stones which might break the grating.

Such is the working of ordinary sluices; but sluicing is also inseparable from the grandest of all mining operations—viz., "Hydraulic Mining." Hydraulic mining, as I witnessed it at Timbuctoo in California, is certainly a marvellous operation. A hill of moderate size, 200 to 300 feet high, may often be found to contain gold throughout its formation, but too thinly to repay cradle-washing, or even hand-sluicing, and not lying in any veins or streaks which could be worked by tunnelling or ground-sluicing.

A series of sluice-boxes are therefore constructed and put together, as described above; but in this case, instead of being of light timber, they are made of the stoutest board that can possibly be got, backed by cross-pieces, &c., so as to be of sufficient strength to allow the passage of any amount of earth and stones forced through them by a flood of water. The boxes are also made shorter and wider, being generally about 14 inches long by 3 to 4 feet wide—the bottoms, instead of the gratings spoken of above, being lined with wooden blocks like wood-pavement, for resisting the friction of the *debris* passing over it, the interstices being filled with quicksilver to catch the fine gold. The sluice, thus prepared, is firmly placed in a slanting position near the foot of the hill intended to be attacked.

To shovel a mass of several million tons of earth into these sluices would prove a tedious and profitless operation. In its stead therefore, hydraulic mining is called into play, by which the labour of many men is performed by water, and the hill worn down to the base by its agency. The operation consists of simply throwing an immense stream of water upon the side of the hill with hose and pipe as a fire engine plays upon a burning building. The water is led through gutta percha or canvas hoses, 4 to 6 inches in diameter, and is thrown from a considerable height above the scene of operations. It is consequently hurled with such force as to eat into the hill-side as if it were sugar. At the spot where I saw this working in operation to the greatest advantage they were using four horses, which they estimated as equal to the power of a hundred men with pick and shovel. There is more knowledge and skill required in this work than would at first sight be supposed necessary. The purpose of the man who directs the hose is to undermine the surface as well as wash away the face of the hill. He therefore directs the water at a likely spot until indications of a "cave-in" become apparent. Notice being given, the neighborhood is deserted. The earth far above cracks, and down comes all the face of the precipice with the noise of an avalanche. By this means a hill several hundred feet higher than the water could reach may easily be washed away.

The greatest difficulty connected with hydraulic work is to get a sufficient fall for the water—a considerable pressure being, of course necessary. At Timbuctoo, for instance, a large river flowed close by, but its waters at that point were quite useless from being too low; the consequence was, that a flume had to be led several miles, from a part of the river higher up, so as to gain the force required. Supplying water for this and similar mining purposes has, therefore, proved a very successful speculation in California. I am not able to give the exact length of the longest flumes constructed there, but I know that it has in some cases been found necessary to bring water from the Sierra Nevada, and to tap streams that have their rise there. It is not at all uncommon to bring it from a distance of 50 miles, and in some cases it has been conveyed as far again.

The expense of this is, of course, enormous, and it is in the ready supply of water at various levels, that the work of mining in British Columbia will be found so much more easy than in California. So scarce is it there, indeed, that it sometimes has been found cheaper to pack the earth on mules and carry it to the river-side than to bring the water to the gold-fields.

The difficulty of obtaining water in the early days of gold-digging in California gave rise to a very curious method of extracting the mineral, which, I believe, was only practised by the Mexicans. Two men would collect a heap of earth from some place containing grain-gold, and pound it as fine as possible. It was then placed in a large cloth, like a sheet, and winnowed—the breeze carrying away the dust, while the heavier gold fell back into the cloth. Bellows were sometimes used for this purpose also.

While upon this subject, I will take the opportunity of describing the most common appliance for raising water from a river for the use of a sluice on its bank. The machinery used is known as the "flutter-wheel," and the traveller in a mining country will see them erected in every conceivable manner and place. It is the same in principle and very similar in appearance to our common "undershot-wheel," consisting of a large wheel 20 to 30 feet in diameter, turned by the force of the current. The paddles are fitted with buckets made to fill themselves with water as they pass under the wheel, which they empty as they turn over into a trough placed convenient for the purpose and leading to the sluice. In a river with a rapid current, like the Fraser, they can be made to supply almost any quantity of water.

There is a kind of intermediate process between that which I have just described and tunnelling or "koyote-ing," partaking in a measure of both. This is called "ground-sluicing," and is quite distinct from "sluicing." The reader will better understand this process if I speak of "koyote-ing," and "ground-sluicing" together, the latter having become a substitute for the former.

As the miners in California began to gain experience in gold-seeking, they found that at a certain distance beneath the surface of the earth a layer of rock existed, on which the gold, by its superior specific gravity, had gradually settled. Experience soon taught the miner to discard the upper earth, which was comparatively valueless, and to seek for gold in the cracks or "pockets" of this bed-rock, or in the layer of earth or clay covering it. The depth of this rock is very various; sometimes it crops out at the surface, while at other times it is found 150 to 200 feet down. Where it is very deep, recourse must be had to regular shaft-sinking and tunnelling, as in a coal or copper mine; but when the rock is only 20 or 30 feet beneath the surface, tunnelling on a very small scale, known as "koyote-ing," from its fancied resemblance to the burrowing of the small wild-dog common to British Columbia and California, is adopted. These little tunnels are made to save the expense of shovelling off the 20 or 30 feet of earth that cover the "pay dirt" on the bed-rock, and their extraordinary number gives a very strange appearance to those parts of the country which have been thoroughly "koyote-ed." I have seen a hill completely honeycombed with these burrows, carried through and through it, and interlacing in every possible direction. So rich is their formation, however, that after they have been deserted by the koyote-ers they are still found worth working. I remember looking at one in the Yuba county in California which appeared so completely riddled that the pressure of a child's foot would have brought it down. Upon my expressing my conviction that anyhow that seemed worked out, a miner standing by at once corrected me. "Worked out, sir?" he said—"not a bit of it! If you come in six months, you'll not see any hill there at all, sir. A company are going to bring the water to play upon it in a few days." "Will it pay well, do you suppose?" "All pays about here, sir," was the quick reply; "they'll take a hundred dollars each a-day."

The Koyote tunnels are only made sufficiently high for the workman to sit upright in them. They are generally carried through somewhat stiffish clay, and are propped and supported with wooden posts, but, as may be imagined in the case of such small apertures extending for so great a length as some of them do, they are very unsafe. Not unfrequently they "cave in" without the slightest warning. Sometimes, too, the earth settles down upon the bed-rock so slowly and silently, that the poor victims are buried alive unknown to their companions without.

The danger of this work and its inefficiency for extracting the gold, much of which was lost in these dark holes, gave rise, as the agency of water became more appreciated, to "ground-sluicing." This consists in directing a heavy stream of water upon the bank which is to be removed, and, with the aid of pick and shovel, washing the natural surface away and bringing the "pay-streak" next the bed-rock into view.

Before proceeding to the subject of quartz-crushing, it will be well perhaps to give the reader some further idea of the great extent of those mining operations which, begun by a few adventurers, have become a regularly organized system, carried on by wealthy and powerful companies. As a striking monument of their courage and the extent of their resources, I would instance the fact of their having diverted large rivers from their channels so as to lay their beds dry for mining purposes. This has been done at nearly every bend or shallow in the numerous streams of California, and will doubtless be imitated in Columbia ere long. The largest of these operations that I ever saw was near Auburn, a large town in Placer county, on the American river.

Sometimes the water can be brought in a strongly-built flume from above, and carried by a long box over the old bed of the river; at other times a regular canal has to be made and dams constructed upon a very large scale. The result is that the bed of the river is laid dry, when its every crevice and pocket is carefully searched for the gold which the water has generally brought down from the bases of the hills and the bars higher up the stream. These operations are frequently so extensive as to occupy several successive seasons before the whole is worked, and to employ hundreds of laborers besides the individuals composing the company, who usually in such an enterprise number fifty or sixty. Sometimes the premature approach of the rainy season, and consequent freshets, carry away the whole of the works in a night. These works occasionally yield immense returns, and it is not unfrequently found, on renewing them after the rainy season, that fresh deposits of gold have taken place, almost equal in value to the first. On the other hand, no amount of judgment can select with any degree of certainty a favourable spot for "jamming" or turning a river, and, after months of hard labour, the bed when laid bare may prove entirely destitute of gold deposits. The long space of still water below a series of rapids will sometimes be found in one spot to contain pounds of gold, while in another the workers who have selected that portion of the river above the rapids will find themselves in the paying place.

All gold operations, indeed, depend very much upon chance for success. No one can ever calculate with any degree of certainty on the run of the "lode" underground, or in the "pay streak" near the surface. Thus it is ever a lottery. As an instance of this on a large scale, I remember when I was at Grass Valley, "Nevada county," going to see the working at the "Black Bridge" tunnel there. The first shaft for this tunnel was sunk five years before my visit, and up to that time nothing had been taken, though it had been constantly worked and was nearly 20,000 feet long. It was commenced in 1855 by a company, who sunk a shaft nearly 250 feet, to strike, as they hoped and expected, a lode from the opposite side of the valley. The original company consisted of five men, and in the course of the five years some of them gave up and others joined, part of them working at other digging to get money for provisions, tools, &c,, to keep their firm going. At length, just before my visit, all the original projectors, and about three sets of others who had joined at different periods, gave the enterprise up as hopeless after carrying it, as I have said, nearly four miles. A new company then took possession of it and summoned the miners of the valley to a consultation. The meeting decided that they had not gone deep enough, and the shaft was accordingly sunk 50 feet lower, when the gold was at once struck. I tried to ascertain what had been expended upon this tunnel, but it had passed through so many hands that it was impossible even to estimate it. The gentleman who showed me over it, and who was an Englishman and the principal man of Grass Valley (Mr. Attwood), said it would cost the new company 12,000 or 14,000 dollars before they took out anything that would repay them. The recklessness with which money is risked and the apparent unconcern with which a man loses a large fortune, and the millionaire of to-day becomes a hired labourer to-morrow, is one of the most striking characteristics of the American in these Western states. It is owing in a great degree to the mere accident which gold-working is. The effect of this upon society is of course most injurious. The poor miner, hobbling along the street of San Francisco or Sacramento trying to borrow—for their are no beggars in California—money enough to take him back to the mines from which ague or rheumatism have driven him a few months before, knows that a lucky hit may enable him in a very short time to take the place of the gentleman who passes by him in his carriage, and whose capital is very probably floating about in schemes, the failure of which will as rapidly reduce him to the streets, or send him back again to the mines as a labourer. The spirit, too, with which these changes of fortune are borne is wonderful. I travelled once in California with a man who was on his way to the mines to commence work as a labourer for the third time. He told me his story readily: it was simple enough. He had twice made what he thought would enrich him for life, and twice it had gone in unlucky speculations. An Englishman under these circumstances would probably have been greatly depressed: not so my fellow-traveller. He talked away through the journey cheerfully, describing the country as we passed through it, speaking of the past without anything like regret, and calmly hopeful for the future.

LIST OF ILLUSTRATIONS.

Sir James Douglas .... Frontispiece.

Barnard, F. J.	66
Bate Mark	74
Beaven, Hon. Robert	96
Begbie, Sir Matthew Baillie	28
Bole, Judge	106
Brighouse, S.	112
Clute, J. S.	126
Corbould, G. E.	130
Cornwall, Hon. C. F.	56
Cunningham, Robert	134
Cunningham, Thomas	140
Davie, Hon. Theo.	160
Dickinson, Robert	168
Douglas, Benjamin	144
Dunsmuir, Hon. Robert	152
Earle, Thomas	156
Edmonds, H. V.	162
English, M. M.	170
Ewen, Alex	176
Fisher, I. B.	182
Grant, John	188
Helmcken, Hon. J. S.	194
Hendry, John	202
Horne, J. W.	208
Innis, J. H.	214
Irving, John	220
Laidlaw, J. A.	228

Macaulay, W. J.	234
Marvin, E. B.	240
McBride, Arthur H.	244
McInnis, Hon. T. R.	250
Nelson, Hon. Hugh	36
Oppenheimer David	258
Pooley, Hon. Charles E.	264
Prior, E. G.	270
Robson, Hon. John	42
Scoullar, E. S.	276
Shakespeare, N.	282
Townsend, W. B.	290
Turner, Hon. J. H.	48
Vernon, Hon. F. G.	60
Weiler, John	300

DICTIONARY.

HISTORICAL SKETCH.

Half a century ago that portion of the British possessions in North America, now known in its relation to the Canadian Confederation as the Province of British Columbia, was a wild and trackless region peopled by fierce and hostile savages whose barbarous empire was only broken here and there at distant intervals in the boundless forest by a few scattered trading posts, which the resistless energy of the Anglo-Saxon had succeeded in establishing and maintaining for the purpose of commerce with the natives. To the civilized world the country was as if she did not exist. Her harbors and streams, her mountains and valleys were unvisited save by the hunter; and the hardy mariner, who ventured into her waters, was in continual dread of the perils which might await him and against which he could not provide in an unexplored and unknown ocean.

To-day her shores are dotted with populous cities and thriving towns, and her waters are covered with a thousand sails bringing the products of distant lands in exchange for those of her virginal soil. The fame of her inexhaustible wealth and her salubrious climate has attracted to her the enterprising and ambitious spirits of two continents, while from the advantages of her situation, commercially and politically, she has become a matter of Imperial concern.

Her history during these fifty years is one of especial interest, not alone on account of the many and seemingly antagonistic forces which have co-operated in her settlement and development, but also for the happy conditions which, established during the early portion of this period, made the colonization of the country by the civilized races and all the beneficial results following in its train, a matter of easy and frictionless accomplishment.

It has been remarked that England, more than any other nation, has ever exercised humanity in her dealing with primitive races who were being dispossessed of their lands. It is beyond question that no other Empire has been able to accomplish so many bloodless victories in extending her territories and her civilizing influences, and it is doubtful if within the catalogue of Britain's colonial possessions there is a parallel to the quiet and effectual redemption from savagery of British Columbia. Indeed, from the time that the white man, in the capacity of a simple trader, obtained a permanent foothold in the country to the present, when all danger of any uprising has forever passed away, there has never been any serious or combined effort on the part of the primitive tribes to eject him. Not only this, but it may without exaggeration be said that throughout the entire period of early occupation attempts at outrage, or even acts of injustice or dishonest dealing on the part of the natives were of rare occurrence; and this at a time, when, but a handful, separated by hundreds of miles, possessing scanty facilities of communication, and with but little means of defense against a vigorous or sustained attack, the early settlers might easily have been exterminated.

By one familiar with the history of the subjugation of the southern portion of this continent,—a history replete with fraud and rapine and murder, the usual concomitants of avarice and lust and ambition—an explanation of the happy condition of things which obtained here is naturally looked for. The explanation lies in the character of the early occupants, and the attitude which from the beginning of their intercourse they assumed towards the natives.

They were indeed a wonderful class of men, those early fur traders, and viewed by the light of the present day seem almost to have been specially designed by Providence to pave the way for the introduction into this country of Christian civilization. By their unflinching courage, inflexible honesty, and resolute forbearance in their daily intercourse with the native, they quickly won his respect and confidence and established with him relations of truth and justice. These sentiments, early planted and industriously cherished, have ever since continued to flourish and to bear fruit. It is to this policy of humanity and justice that, while we have seen during the last twenty years other lands, and especially the neighboring Republic, disturbed by massacres and outrages on the part of their Indian populations, and by wars in which thousands of valuable lives have been sacrificed, there has been nothing but peace and harmony in our own country.

In my sketch of the country's history I shall therefore go back to a period anterior to colonial rule, and briefly review the progress of events from the time the agents of the Hudson's Bay Company first crossed the mountains in search of new hunting grounds to the time that the discovery of gold made it advisable for the Imperial Government to raise the Mainland to the dignity of a colony; and I shall first speak of New Caledonia, by which appellation the Mainland was then known, as it was here that the company's agents first established themselves.

NEW CALEDONIA, 1800 TO 1843.

It was towards the close of the last century and late in its own history that the Hudson's Bay Company, eager to precede rival organizations in the field, pushed its outposts from the valley of the Saskatchewan across the Rocky Mountains. The Peace River Pass had been previously traversed by that famous explorer Alexander Mackenzie, when he made his then perilous trip to the Pacific ocean in 1792-3, and it was by the same route that the agents of the Hudson's Bay Company first penetrated into British Columbia. The country's rugged and mountainous character, diversified by delightful valleys, and the similarity of its climate reminded these adventurous wanderers, the majority of whom where of Scotch birth, of their native land, and they bestowed on the region the name of New Caledonia—a name which it continued to bear for over half a century. The fur traders, however, did not waste much time on sentimental considerations of the country's picturesqueness and beauty. Their minds were engrossed by thoughts of business, and they found immediate employment in making themselves secure against the dangers which everywhere threatened them. When this had been accomplished their next task was the initiation of the natives into the mysteries of traffic.

As New Caledonia was simply a game preserve, leased to the Hudson's Bay Company, and as the private transactions of that company have in themselves nothing of historical value, this sketch will necessarily be limited to a brief description of the fort life of the traders, the relations which existed between them and the natives, and the permanent results which accrued from the good understanding which they established.

It did not come within the scope of their design to attempt the elevation of the mental or moral character of the Indian population, except in so far as it tended to the betterment of the fur trade. The servants of the company knew by experience that the less the aboriginal races were brought into contact with civilizing influences and the longer they were permitted to retain their primitive habits and natural instincts, the better hunters they were likely to be. The fur trader, therefore, having an eye simply to his own profit wisely abstained from any attempt to introduce the arts of civilized communities.

On entering a new region the first task which lay before the adventurers was the construction of a fort within which they intrenched themselves, and where was stored the year's supply of goods, which was to be employed in the purchase of furs. The location of a trading post was always a matter of deep consideration. It was necessary, of course, that between it and headquarters the means of communication and the facilities for the transmission of supplies should be reasonably good. As the water system of the country was very largely utilized in travel, the trading posts were usually situated on some navigable river or lake, which communicated with other bodies of water, and afforded the speediest and safest means known of reaching the seaboard. The site of a fort, usually a cleared space of over one hundred yards square, was enclosed by stout wooden pickets from ten to fifteen inches in diameter sunk in the ground and rising about twenty feet above it. At corners diagonally opposite, and raised above the tops of the palisades, two wooden bastions were so placed as to command the surrounding country. In each of these bastions several large guns, ranging between six and twelve-pounders, were mounted. Within the palisades were built the store houses, work shops and quarters of the company's servants, and as a rule so arranged as to form an inner square. Here it was within these narrow limits that the trader confined himself and passed weary days which often crept into weeks of unchanging monotony. Here he experienced his triumphs and reverses, went through his routine of daily labor, made his bargains with the Indians and learnt the great lesson of endurance. His only relief consisted in occasional trips from one post to another, or perhaps an expedition to an as yet unvisited part of the country. In the estimation of the savages the forts were the storehouses of priceless treasures, where they could exchange their furs for all that was most desirable, and they soon came to regard the erection of a trading post within convenient distance as a boon conferred upon them by the white man—a boon the white man was only too willing to confer, if business justified it.

Many years elapsed after trade was opened with the natives of British Columbia before the Hudson's Bay Company was able to place its business in this country on a perfect systematic footing. But as its operations extended, and its establishments grew in number, the country was divided into departments, each department possessing its compliments of forts, and each having a chief post to which subordinate forts sent the result of each season's business. These departmental capitals in turn transmitted the furs to headquarters, situated subsequent to 1810 on the Columbia River. From here they were sent overland to Lachine for shipment to London.

The system of government to which the company's servants were subject was a most reasonable and perfect one. All who aspired to command had first to serve, and a long term of apprenticeship was required before every promotion. The highest officers had passed through every grade and knew thoroughly every detail of the business. The entire country was subject to the command of one man, who occupied the position of chief factor, and who was directly amenable to the jurisdiction of the Governor, resident in Canada. Next in dignity to the chief factor was the chief trader, who was usually in charge of some important fort. The chief clerk ranked third, and was either entrusted with the management of a minor fort, or sent on expeditions through the country. Inferior to the chief clerks were the subordinate and apprenticed clerks, who were learning the business, and who were prospective traders and factors. There were also a great many mechanics and laborers in the company's employ, none of whom, however, were eligible to fill the higher offices in the gift of the corporation.

Their fort life and training was largely answerable for the mental and moral character of the early Hudson's Bay traders. The majority of young men who entered the service were possessed of good natural abilities and bodily health and strength, and in the discharge of their duties to the company these gifts were strengthened and developed to the utmost. From the time a youth entered the service as an apprenticed clerk he was under the most rigid discipline, and taught that self-reliance, honesty and assiduity in the company's business were the highest of moral qualities, and those in the practice of which his material welfare was most likely to be advanced. His existence amid the solitude of the mountains and the forest was calculated to impress him with the fact of his own individual weakness and the dangers to which he was continually exposed, and to avoid which he had ever to be on the alert, developed within him the principles of thoughtfulness and resolution.

As it was necessary for the company's business that absolute truth should be the basis of all dealings with the savages, the trader early came to guard his words with caution, and never say what he did not mean, nor promise what he did not intend to fulfill. It was part of his duty carefully to study the Indian character, and this study was of incalculable benefit to him in his future career. The natives he found were possessed of no small amount of shrewdness, quick to see through subterfuges, and suspicious and resentful when once wronged or deceived. He speedily perceived also that moral courage was, in the estimation of the savages, regarded equally with physical fearlessness as necessary to the character of a leader. Acting on the knowledge thus gained the trader in his dealings with the Indians was truthful and just, and gained at once their respect and confidence. At the same time, however, that the company's agents sedulously cultivated the friendship and good will of the natives, they closely inquired into the relations of the various tribes, noted their rivalries and jealousies, and kept alive all those differences which were calculated to prevent a good understanding among them. By this means all possibility of a general union of the tribes was prevented, and among the warring and jealous elements the agents of the company held the balance of power.

On this basis of justice, toleration and tact, it was that the power of the Hudson's Bay Company was built up in British Columbia, and the considerate observer will admit that the fruits of the system have amply proven the wisdom of its adoption.

Until 1821 the Hudson's Bay Company did not possess an undisputed monopoly of the fur trade on the Pacific slope. The comparatively young Northwest Company had for many years been cutting into the business of the older organization, and the keen competition which had resulted had not only reduced the profits of the trade, but had in some respects demoralized it. In the Red River district, to the east of the Rocky Mountains, this rivalry had terminated in bloodshed, and while it did not in New Caledonia reach this extreme point, there was enough reckless bidding by the agents of both companies to alarm a sensitive Montreal or London stockholder.

In 1821, however, the two companies were consolidated under the name of the Hudson's Bay Company, and in the same year the united company was given a twenty-one year's monopoly of trade in the territory stretching from the Columbia River to the Russian boundary of Alaska. Astoria, situated at the mouth of the Columbia, which had been established in 1810 by John Jacob Astor, became the headquarters of the company on the Pacific coast. Besides Astoria there were two permanent establishments on the coast, and about fifteen in the interior. The majority of the company's forts were at this time situated in what are now know as the Omineca and Cariboo districts, with Fort St. James, on Stuart Lake, as their central point. At this post Chief Factor Ogden, then in charge of this district, made his headquarters. Eighty miles in a north easterly direction was Fort McLeod, on Lake McLeod, where Chief Trader Tod ruled, and sixty miles, in a south easterly direction, was Fort George, on the Fraser River. A number of minor posts also sent their furs to Fort St. James. Farther down the River Fraser, the next post of importance was Fort Alexandria, situated about one hundred miles from Fort George. To the south east of this, on the Kamloops River, was Fort Kamloops, the capital of what was known as the Thompson River district. Near the mouth of the Fraser was Fort Langley, and away up on the north coast was Fort Simpson. All of these posts, and their subordinate establishments, yielded large annual returns. Besides the business done by the permanent forts, migratory expeditions were yearly dispatched to districts in which no permanent establishments as yet existed, and along the coast the company's steamers, Beaver and Cadboro, every year did a large trade.

With the consummation of the union the Hudson's Bay Company became absolute rulers over an extent of territory greater by one-third than that of Europe and exercised supreme civil and criminal jurisdiction over the greater portion of this enormous region. Their system of communication was complete and extended in an unbroken chain from the Atlantic to the Pacific ocean. A consideration of these facts will give the reader an idea of the energy and enterprise of this ambitious corporation and the perfect system it necessarily employed in the successful management of so great a possession. After the union of the two companies, operations were continued with renewed confidence, on a more extensive scale and with a success that surprised the most sanguine anticipations of the directors.

The year 1824 marked an epoch in the affairs of the company west of the Rocky Mountains, and also in the history of British Columbia, as it was in that year John McLoughlin came from the east to take charge and brought with him James Douglas, then a young man of nineteen years, who was to play such an important part in the subsequent history of the country. McLoughlin had been chosen to fill the position of chief factor on the Pacific coast, on account of his superior knowledge of the Indian character and his keen business instincts coupled with a large spirit of enterprise. He had until the consolidation of the two companies been in the service of the Northwest Company and had been stationed at Fort William on Lake Superior, where Douglas, then in the same service, was employed as one of his clerks. McLoughlin became attached to his youthful subordinate and not only induced him to remain in the company's service after the union had been consummated but took him along with him when he was transferred to New Caledonia. McLoughlin came to his new field of labor possessing the fullest confidence of his company and with power to make whatever changes suggested themselves to him as wise. His first action, after a careful survey of the country, was the removal of headquarters from Astoria to a site farther up the Columbia river near the mouth of the Willamette. To his new foundation he gave the name of Fort Vancouver, which continued to be the central depot for the Pacific District until 1849. McLoughlin as far as possible encouraged the cultivation of the land in the immediate neighborhood of forts and the result was before many years agriculture began to assume importance. Not only were the company's own establishments thus kept in supplies but at no distant date large quantities of grain and dairy produce were disposed of at profitable rates to the Russians resident in Alaska. Douglas crossed the mountains in company with James Connolly and wintered in Fort St. James where the following year he took command. For several seasons he was kept at outposts and sent on expeditions by which means he was enabled to gain a knowledge of the country, its inhabitants and their language, and being a close observer and a ready student, he not only mastered the dialects of the natives but obtained such an accurate knowledge of the domain as stood him in good stead throughout his subsequent career. During this time he established several forts and among them Fort Connolly on Bear Lake. He was then summoned to headquarters where he became second in command.

In this vast domain, then, the Hudson's Bay Company continued to build forts, explore trails, cultivate their farms, drive an extensive trade in furs and in every way enrich the pockets and swell the importance of those who were fortunate enough to possess stock in this commercial corporation. Everything favored and furthered their aims. Men fitted by temperament and intelligence, had the management of the company's affairs in the country, the native races had been won over not only to peace but in most cases to ardent friendship and as yet the idea of colonizing the country had not suggested itself to the civilized races. Three ships owned by the company made annual trips from England to the chief fort with supplies which were distributed twice every year.

From the date of the consolidation of the two companies until the year 1839 there was no disturbing element from the outer world to question the traders' perfect possession. Mutterings there had been in the United States and much babble of the Republic's ownership by right of purchase as far north as parallel of latitude 54° 40" but as it only ended in bluster the traders paid little heed to it. In the year 1839, however, appeared the first signs of what was eventually to destroy the monopoly and practically terminate the fur trading business of the company on the Pacific coast. The immigrant found his way to Oregon and began to settle on its fertile lands. The earliest of these enemies of the fur trade were in most cases destitute and starving, and the company's agents, although they saw the danger of further invasion were compelled by their sense of humanity to give food and assistance to these destitute wanderers. The assistance thus supplied, as was to be expected, only aggravated the evil and thereafter the tide of immigration continued to increase. The London managers were made acquainted with this condition of affairs and also with the fact that substantial sympathy had been extended to the suffering settler. They did not, however, look at the matter in the light in which it presented itself to their agents on the Pacific coast. As they were not familiar with the causes which impelled the immigrant to Oregon and had not the advantage of a personal acquaintance with the extreme destitution which appealed to the humanity of the traders they were inclined to blame the chief of the department on the Pacific for encouraging, when he should not even have permitted settlement on their hunting preserves. Their suspicions were aroused against McLoughlin and from this time they continued to watch with a jealous eye his attitude towards the immigrant. McLoughlin was unaware of the offense he had given and being of a kindly disposition continued his good offices to the unfortunates and thus laid himself yet more under the displeasure of his superiors. These suspicions of the managers were, however, kept dark while McLoughlin's services seemed indispensable and so during six years the pioneer settlers had the benefit of his advice and assistance.

If, however, the southern border of its Empire was thus being threatened the company was enlarging its northern domain. In 1839 a strip of the Alaskan coast was leased at a yearly rental of $2,000 and in the following spring formal possession was taken by Douglas who placed a man in charge at Fort Stikeen which had been a Russian post. He then held a conference with the Russian Governor, Etholin, during which certain matters of trade were arranged. He also decided to build another post on the newly acquired territory and Fort Taco on the Taco river came into existence. The following three years were not marked by any event of importance save the assassination, in 1841, of John McLoughlin, Jr., at Fort Stikeen. The returns from the different departments during this period were in excess of those of any previous period and if the company were not occupied in making history it was because they found it more to their interest to confine themselves strictly to the barter in furs.

VANCOUVER ISLAND TO 1858.

Down to this time no settlement nor any attempt at permanent settlement had been made on Vancouver Island and its existence even seems to have excited no interest in the minds of the adventurous men who had covered the mainland with their forts. A combination of circumstances now, however, conspired to render it desirable for occupation. The rush of agricultural settlers from the East to Oregon and the doubt which existed as to where the dividing line between the United States and British territory would fall made the site of the headquarters on the Columbia river in every respect one of questionable advantage. It was more than desirable—it was necessary that the company's chief station should be situated on British soil and as far as possible removed from civilized settlements. These and many minor reasons pressed on the minds of the company's chief agents the need of at least having in readiness a well established place of business to which they could remove their headquarters at short notice. The erection of a fort on the seaboard was accordingly, after mature consideration, decided upon, and as the selection of the site required prudence and judgment and a large knowledge of the bays and harbors of the country Douglas was deputed to take the matter in hand. After carefully balancing the advantages of a number of different points he chose that on which the city of Victoria now stands. In his selection he was influenced by the good harborage afforded and the ease and quickness with which it could be reached from most of the posts on the mainland as well as by the quality of the soil in the immediate neighborhood and by its timber.

The history of Vancouver Island previous to this time is a record of a few fights in its waters between European vessels for the right to possession and of a few conferences between inferior plenipotentiaries with the same object in view interlarded by a number of massacres of each party by the native inhabitants. The discovery of the Island was the result of a search for that chimera of the mariner of the 16th and 17th centuries—a north west passage between the Atlantic and Pacific oceans. In this vain quest the shores of the Pacific were eagerly explored and the Spaniards, then the foremost adventurers in the New World, dispatched many expeditions northward. Boisterous seas and the cold climate, however, retarded discovery and the hostile attitude of the native tribes damped the enthusiasm of the sailors. The first European who is recorded to have visited these waters was a Greek pilot named Apostolos Valerianos, known to his fellow sailors as Juan de Fuca. He discovered the straits which now bear his name and sailed some distance up them. He was confident that he had found the long sought for channel but was unable to push his investigations owing to his capture shortly after by an English freebooter and the consequent loss of all he possessed. Some years subsequent the story of his discovery became current and was by many believed to be true but little or no effort was made to verify it until the voyage of Captain Cook in 1778, almost two centuries later. Captain Cook was unable to find the channel as indicated by Fuca and unhesitatingly pronounced the tale a fiction. Some ten years later, however, an English naval captain named Meares re-discovered the straits and sailed up them about thirty miles.

Shortly after this date a number of Spanish vessels anchored at Nootka Sound and the country (they did not then know it was an island) was taken possession of in the name of the King of Spain. With all the arrogance which has ever characterized the procedure of that Power on this continent, absolute ownership as far north as the 60th degree of latitude was laid claim to and in enforcing this claim frequent outrages were committed on English vessels visiting these parts. The matter was brought to the attention of both governments and nearly precipitated a war. This calamity, however, was averted by the timely humility of Spain who promised to make restitution of the vessels and goods seized and indemnify the owners for losses. What is known as the Nootka Convention was held in 1790 in which England and Spain came to an understanding regarding the territory north of California, and to adjudge the amount of indemnification due by Spain Captain Vancouver, of the English navy and Bodega Y. Quadra a Spanish officer were sent hither by their respective governments. In addition to this official business Vancouver had instructions to explore the coast and report to the home authorities. In doing so he discovered the insular character of the country, having sailed around it. The island thus discovered was given the name Quadra and Vancouver Island and so appears on many of the early maps. The Spaniards not long after this abandoned their post at Nootka and gradually withdrew from this part of the coast. With the settlement of this dispute all interest in the Island seems to have died out and until the time that James Douglas decided on building Fort Victoria or Camosun as the post was first named, the primitive inhabitants had remained in undisturbed possession.

At the same time that a fort on the southern part of Vancouver Island had been resolved on, it was also decided to abandon the posts Taco and McLoughlin and to transfer their men and supplies and whatever else they possessed of value to the new establishment. In consequence of this Douglas had only fifteen men with him when he arrived from Fort Vancouver in March 1843 to commence building operations at Camosun. This number, however, was increased to fifty by the addition of those from the northern stations. The work was now pushed forward with rapidity under the supervision of Douglas. The tribe of Indians native to the locality, the Songhies, expressed their satisfaction at the establishment of a fort on their territory and offered their assistance, and surrounding tribes were attracted to the spot by the novelty of the proceeding. With the exception of a few attempts at pilfering which in most cases were defeated no trouble was given by the natives. Their good behavior was probably owing, however, in a large measure to the fact that the workmen were armed to the teeth and kept guard night and day to prevent any hostile manifestations. After seven months of unflagging labor Douglas declared the new fort in a defensible state and prepared to take his departure. He appointed Charles Ross to the command of the fort with Roderick Finlayson as his assistant and giving general directions for their guidance returned to Fort Vancouver.

Thus Victoria rose into being forty-seven years ago as a palisaded fort of one hundred yards square enclosing eight log houses and garrisoned by two dozen men. Douglas' parting exhortation to his lieutenants to be zealous and thrifty and accomplish the largest possible results with the smallest possible means was acted upon to the letter. The men in charge regarded their management of the fort as a crucial test of their ability and were determined that their work should be such as would not admit of failure. As soon as it was possible to do so the work of clearing land for agricultural purposes was commenced as it was intended that next year the fort should be self sustaining. In the spring of 1844, Mr. Ross, the chief officer died and Mr. Finlayson took his place. By this time considerable land had been cleared, cattle had been brought from the company's establishments on Puget Sound and a small dairy farm started. This year was marked by the only attempt on the part of the Indians to occasion trouble at Fort Victoria. The traders missed a number of cattle from their herd and after careful enquiry fastened the guilt of stealing them on the natives. When reparation was demanded the aborigines became threatening and even went so far as to make an attack on the fort. They were easily beaten off, however, and frightened by an exhibition of the powers of the big guns. On the same day that they made their attempt they also brought to the gates of the fort the full value of the stolen cattle and sued for peace.

By rigid economy, industry, ingenuity in turning almost everything to account, devising new means of surmounting difficulties and by tact in the management of the Indians the young post was very shortly able to take care of itself and it did so to the admiration of even the exacting Douglas. In 1845 the name Camosun which it had borne until this time was dropped and that of Albert, in honor of the Prince Consort, was substituted. The year following another change took place and Fort Albert became Fort Victoria under which designation it has since continued to flourish. In accordance with the intentions of the Hudson's Bay Company Victoria was pushed rapidly forward in importance and almost immediately became recognised as the second depot on the Pacific Coast. The ships from England were ordered to sail directly to that port and after depositing there the supplies for distribution among the coast establishments to proceed to Fort Vancouver. In founding Victoria the company had it within the horizon of their hopes that it should become a redezvous for whalers—a business which at that time was rapidly assuming large proportions. It seemed at first as if this hope would be fulfilled and for several years whaling vessels did drop anchor in its harbor but it was finally found that the Hawaiian Islands offered a more convenient port of call and Victoria accordingly lost this trade.

While these events were taking place in Vancouver Island and the foundation of a future capital was being thus modestly laid, a question, the settlement of which was big with results for Victoria, was exercising the minds of men in the greater world. The question as to where the line of boundary between Her Majesty's dominions and the territory of the United States should fall was assuming threatening importance and for a time it appeared more than likely, especially in view of the hostile and unreasoning stand taken by the American people or at least those who undertook to speak for them, that over it the two nations would be plunged into war. The people of the Republic, as has ever been their custom in their dealings with England, put forward most monstrous and unjust claims and trusted to bluster and chicanery to carry their point. They asserted a right of possession to the territory as far north as Alaska and throughout the entire Republic rang the cry "54° 40' or fight." But a popular cry no matter with what enthusiasm it may be shouted or how much effect it may have in determining matters of internal economy, especially in a country where mob-law is supreme, fortunately is of little avail in settling matters of international importance. The English Government, it must be confessed, did not take the firm stand which it should have done at this time. The fact was, the British ministers, who did not think the territory worth fighting for, seemed only anxious to get out of the difficulty with as good grace as possible. This lukewarmness when the time for settlement arrived cost this country dear and robbed her of a vast deal of territory. The Home Government, indeed, sent out a special commission of enquiry, consisting of two engineers named Warre and Vavasour to report on the value of the country and these gentlemen arrived at Fort Vancouver in 1845 having come overland by way of York Factory. H. M. S. America, Captain Gordon, also arrived at Victoria in 1845 and during the next year quite a number of naval vessels followed. The officers in command of most of these ships had instructions to report to the Home Government on the same matter —the value of the territory. As the majority of these gentlemen were men whose opinions on questions with which they were most intimately acquainted would have been of little value, nothing, plainly, was to be expected from them on a matter concerning which they were profoundly ignorant and on which they had neither the energy nor inclination to inform themselves. Their reports it is needless to say were unanimously to the effect that the country was not worth a battle and this view of the case received the confirmation of the managers of the Hudson's Bay Company. Under these circumstances and with the politicians of the United States keenly alive to the desirability of acquiring all the territory they could on the continent it is not to be wondered at, that matters were so badly managed and so much was yielded by Britain when by the treaty of 1846 the 49th parallel of latitude was agreed upon by the two nations as the line dividing their dominions. The settlement of the boundary question could not but open up a large prospect of future greatness to Victoria, which now became the principal station of the company on British territory west of the Rocky mountains. Improvements went on rapidly around the fort and by the time it had been three years in existence one hundred and sixty acres of land had been cleared and placed under cultivation. At the end of 1847 double that amount had been tilled and two dairies each possessing seventy milch cows were in operation. Thus matters progressed with the infant city and its trade increased so rapidly that very soon the picketed enclosure was not of sufficient size to accommodate the business done and it had, therefore, to be enlarged.

As it was now the avowed intention of the company to remove the headquarters from Fort Vancouver as soon as a route to the interior by way of the Fraser River had been opened up, the work of exploration in this connection was at once begun. Mr. A. C. Anderson, who had charge of Fort Alexandria, was entrusted with this work and early in 1846 he set out from Fort Kamloops with five men to survey the country from that point to Fort Langley. He did not meet with much success on his downward journey but was more fortunate when returning and the result of his labor was the adoption of a route from Langley by way of the Quequealla river and Lake Nicola to Kamloops from whence the trails to the interior were reasonably well known. 1847 he made another survey but without further success and his route of the previous year was in the main adopted and has since become the wagon road to the south-eastern interior. Anderson's explorations were conducted in the face of a considerable amount of Indian hostility, which, however, was not openly displayed but exhausted itself in attempts to misguide and discourage him in his undertaking. Notwithstanding this, his determination to succeed, and the fidelity of several native servants enabled him to defeat the machinations of the savages. This enmity on the part of the Indians, while it did not come to a head or adversely affect the company's interests, was indicative of a restless feeling which at this time possessed the tribes of the interior and which during 1864 found vent in an attempted uprising of the united Shuswap peoples. The attempt was defeated by the address and courage of chief trader Tod who was in charge of the Kamloops station and steps were at once taken to remove any cause which tended to dissatisfy the natives with the rule of the corporation. Consequent upon the success of Anderson's survey and the necessity that arose for a resting place on the new route between Kamloops and Langley, Fort Yale was established in 1848 on the Fraser and in the year following Fort Hope, a short distance farther down the river, came into existence.

The Hudson's Bay Company was now at the zenith of its prosperity on the Pacific coast and Douglas was at the head of its affairs in name as well as in fact, McLoughlin having retired from the service in 1845. The company's license of trade had been renewed in 1838 for a second term of twenty-one years and would not, therefore, expire until 1859. The country had been thoroughly well explored from a fur trader's point of view and posts established wherever business warranted. These establishments amounted in all to thirty-nine and were all of them doing profitable businesses. In 1849 the time had come when, in the opinion of the management, the headquarters could be removed from Fort Vancouver with advantage and accordingly in that year Douglas placed Mr. Dugald McTavish in command on the Columbia and, accompanied by Chief Factor Ogden, removed to Fort Victoria.

But if this period saw the realization of the company's largest hopes on the Pacific it was also fruitful in causes which ultimately led to the destruction of the fur trade. Chief among these causes were the tide of immigration which began to flow from the east into Oregon; the fact recently come to light that coal beds existed on Vancouver Island, and the discovery in 1848 of gold in California.

1. The first of these, namely the rapid settlement of the American territory had attracted the attention of English statesmen and the question naturally arose in their minds why the adjacent dominion of Britain should not be utilized as a colonization ground for their overplus population. The idea had no sooner been entertained than

it received expression in parliament. It chanced, however, that the same idea had suggested itself to the managers of the monopoly who were ever awake to what affected their interests and they regarded it from a stand-point directly opposite to that taken by those who brought the matter before parliament. None saw more clearly than they that the colonization of the country was simply a matter of time and while they did not apprehend any trouble for years to come, they considered it as well to be prepared against all contingencies. They, therefore, without delay, set themselves to solve the problem how best to reconcile the colonization of the country with their own interests. Their cogitations took the form of an application to parliament asking that they be granted the privilege of colonizing the country. This solution of the question was a highly ingenious one as it meant, when analyzed, that the company would have it within their power to retard or assist settlement as suited them best. The application was made in 1847 and in the form it first took somewhat startled the Government by its magnificent proportions. The proposal was that the company should undertake the government and colonization of all the territories belonging to the crown in North America and should receive a grant accordingly. It was quickly seen, however, that such a proposition would not be entertained and it was accordingly withdrawn and after several modifications and the substitution of Vancouver Island for British North America was again presented. This request the Government was not averse to granting and a charter was placed before Parliament in 1848, which, although it met with strong opposition was finally carried. By the terms of this grant which was consummated on January 13th, 1849, the company was given the Island "with the royalties of its seas, and all the mines belonging to it, subject only to the domination of the British Crown and a yearly rental of seven shillings. The company was to settle upon the Island within five years a colony of British subjects; and to dispose of land for purposes of colonization at reasonable prices, retaining of all the moneys secured from such source as well as from coal and other minerals, ten per cent., and applying towards public improvements upon the Island, the remaining nine-tenths. Such lands as might be necessary for a naval station, and for other government establishments, were to be reserved; and the company should every two years report to the Government the number of colonists settled on the Island, and the lands sold. If at the expiration of five years no settlement should have been made, the grant should be forfeited; and if at the expiration of the company's license of exclusive trade with the Indians in 1859 the Government should so elect it might recover the Island from the company on the payment of such sums of money as had been actually expended by them in colonization. Except during hostilities between Great Britain and any foreign power, the company should defray all expenses of all civil and military establishments for the government and protection of the Island."

2. The existence of coal on the Island had, as early as 1835, been brought to the attention of the traders by the tribe inhabiting the district about Beaver Harbor, but as the company had little need for it themselves, and no market in which to sell it, they made no use of their discovery. With that caution, however, for which they were remarkable, they said nothing about the matter, and until 1845 the outside world was in ignorance of the hidden wealth which the country possessed. In that year the engineers Warre and Vavasour, in their report to the Home authorities, mentioned the fact of the existence of this mineral, both on the Island and on the Mainland, and in the following year the steam-sloop Cormorant, of the Royal Navy, loaded some sixty-five tons at Beaver Harbor. It was not till a couple of years after this that the company decided on working the mine. Early in 1849 an expedition was sent north and a post, to which was given the name Fort Rupert, erected at Beaver Harbor. A practical miner named Muir was brought out from Scotland, also proper mining machinery, and everything got in readiness for a thorough test. Muir began work without delay and, notwithstanding the hostility of the natives, succeeded in making a sufficient test to convince him that the seams at this point were not valuable enough to pay the working. During the same year, however, the Douglas seam, situated near what is now the City of Nanaimo, had been discovered by Chief Facter McKay, and Muir abandoned Fort Rupert and removed his machinery to the new field where his test was successful beyond anticipation. Accordingly in 1852 a fort was built at this spot which has since grown into a city. The work progressed so well that before the end of two years two thousand tons had been shipped to California where it brought $28 per ton.

3. In the spring of 1848 a rumor of the existence of gold in California flashed over this continent, and in the following year occurred the great rush to the auriferous regions. This discovery, while not immediately affecting the company's fur business, inaugurated a new state of affairs at Victoria, and gave the traders a novel commodity for which to barter their goods. Fort Victoria was at that time the nearest point outside of San Francisco where miners could obtain their outfits, and many of them preferred wintering here to wasting the result of their labor in the gambling hells of California. The first that was seen of the miners at Fort Victoria was in 1849, when a large number of them arrived direct from the gold fields. Finlayson at first supposed them to be pirates and prepared to give them a warm reception, but discovering his mistake entered into converse with them and finally took their gold in exchange for goods. The report of the vast wealth to be got with little trouble spread like wildfire through the company's forts, and many of the servants deserted for the mines. With the exception of the loss of some of their men, however, the traders were in no way disturbed and continued in happy unconsciousness of the fact that the same magnet which had drawn such a mass of struggling humanity to California, lay embedded in the soil of their own territory, and would in a brief decade of years draw the same eager thousands to British Columbia.

At the end of these twenty-eight years of undisturbed and undisputed occupation by the Hudson's Bay Company the country still retained all its primitive characteristics. A considerable number of trading posts had indeed been added to those already in existence before the beginning of that period, and on the Island Forts Rupert and Nanaimo had been established as coaling stations. This industry was, however, yet in its infancy, and these posts accordingly had not begun to assume even the importance of villages. The whole territory was simply a vast wilderness threaded by a few trails that were distinguishable only by the practiced eye of the hunter or the savage. Victoria indeed existed, and notwithstanding the fact that it was not only the capital but was, as far as civilized man was concerned, the whole country, and that to the shrewd observer it had a considerable future before it, it was still nothing but a large palisaded fort. Over this immense hunting forest then the word of the Chief Factor was law, and no Norman Conqueror's mandates were more respectfully listened to or more implicitly obeyed. He was law-maker and judge, and from his decision there was no appeal. With the country so firmly in the grasp of a monopoly, whose interests were so largely concerned in keeping it in its savage condition, it will be easily understood how its colonization could be retarded, and how difficult it would be in the face of the company's opposition, always prudently directed, for the Imperial Government to have its intentions carried out in regard to a colony situated at a distance of eight thousand miles. We shall see how the first representative of the Government to Vancouver Island was confronted with this opposition, how insuperable he found it and how, after a struggle of nearly two years, he abandoned his post in despair.

It was shortly after the charter of the Hudson's Bay Company had been confirmed by Parliament, that the Imperial Cabinet signified its intention of appointing a Governor to look after the interests of Her Majesty's subjects on Vancouver Island, and the company's management in London was asked to suggest the name of a suitable man to fill the position. With numerous reasons attached for his choice, one of which was that he would serve without remuneration, Sir John Pelly, then at the head of the company's affairs in London, submitted the name of James Douglas, Chief Factor on the Pacific coast. The company's nominee, however, was rejected, and Richard Blanchard, a lawyer, was appointed instead. Blanchard accepted the position without salary and immediately sailed for the seat of his government, which he reached on March 10th. 1850. He was not long in discovering that the honor to be derived from the incumbency of this high official position was on a par with its emoluments. His presence was regarded by the company's agents, then the only white men on the Island, as a joke, none the less good that their politeness did not permit them to smile too broadly. Indeed, from the time Blanchard landed on the Island till the time he left it in chagrin, he had not so much power as the untaxed denizen of the forest. In addition to his powerlessness he had from first to last numberless inconveniences, vexations and discomforts to submit to, besides paying handsomely for his maintenance. He found on his arrival at Victoria that no residence had been prepared for him and so, after reading his commission, he returned on board the Government vessel in which he had come and visited various points on the coast as far north as Fort Rupert. He then returned to Victoria and was given a room in the fort while a house was being prepared for him outside the pickets. With the exception of one visit north in September, 1850, to enquire into some trouble at Fort Rupert, Blanchard remained at Victoria till his departure for England on September 1st, 1851. During this whole period his administration consisted in giving orders, which were disregarded, and writing despatches to the Home Authorities, in which he complained of the actions of the Hudson's Bay Company's officers. The fact was Blanchard's position was a most anomalous one and it would have been impossible for the most forcible man to have asserted himself in the circumstances in which he was placed. As before stated the company's officers and servants where the only white men in the colony, and they regarded the appointment of Blanchard as an attempted interference with their control of the Island. This they were not disposed to submit to, and made the fact unpleasantly plain to Her Majesty's representative. Blanchard was not deficient in courage and he fought the monopoly till the contest became too heavy a drain on his pocket as well as his pride. He then succumbed to the inevitable.

Meanwhile the first effort at colonization had been made. In March, 1850, the ship Norman Morrison, Captain Wishart in command, arrived at Esquimalt with eighty emigrants aboard. On this vessel came out as medical officer to the company Dr. John Sabastian Helmcken, so well known in the country's subsequent history. As the majority of these emigrants had been engaged to work in the company's coal mines, this apparent attempt to induce settlement had little meaning. Indeed it cannot be said that the settlement of the Island progressed with even reasonable success under the company's regime; in fact if any genuine efforts at all were made in the direction of colonization they proved unsuccessful. Nor was this to be wondered at when the terms offered to intending settlers are considered. In conformity with the terms of their charter the company immediately after the grant was confirmed had issued a prospectus and advertised for colonists. In the prospectus the price of land was fixed at one pound an acre, and for every hundred acres purchased at this price, the investor was obliged to bring at his own expense three families or six single persons. It will thus be readily seen that only a person of means was able to take advantage of the company's offer to leave a comfortable home in the old land and come to the wilds of British Columbia to hew a fortune out of the forest. At the same time that the company was building this wall of high terms against settlers, land was being sold in Washington Territory at one dollar an acre. In addition to this the settler was completely in the power of the monopoly. All his supplies he had to purchase from the company's agents, and at the prices they demanded, and to them alone could he look for a market for his crops. Besides that he came directly into competition with the traders, who were themselves the largest farmers on the Island.

The result of all this was what the company had intended—the discouragement of colonization. Of the unfortunate men who did come out during the first year the majority, after a few months, abandoned their lands for the gold fields, and those who remained were at incessant war with the company and continually imploring Parliament to abridge its powers. To the wretched settler everything seemed to play into the hands of the monopoly, and the very fact that some abandoned their farms in despair and went to the gold fields, was given by the company, and accepted by the Government as a reasonable excuse for the failure to colonize. The weakness of this pretext was apparent to all familiar with the facts, and it was well known that after the subsidence of the excitement in California, many who had left the mines would have been only too willing to take up land and settle on Vancouver Island under British rule, but were repelled by the exorbitant terms which they were required to subscribe to.

Previous to his departure from the colony Governor Blanchard appointed a Provisional Council, composed of James Douglas, James Cooper and John Tod, to carry on the administration. In September of 1851 James Douglas was made Governor, and in the following November took the oath of office, and Roderick Finlayson was appointed to the vacant seat at the Council Board. Douglas, in accepting office, stipulated for a salary, and £800 per annum was granted. Now that Her Majesty and the monopoly were represented by the same person the government of the country was conducted harmoniously enough, and the ever discontented colonists alone refused to join in the general satisfaction.

In 1852 Victoria was laid out into streets, the boundaries of the town then being the harbor on the west, the present Government street on the east, Johnson street on the north, and the fort on the south. At the close of 1853 there were 450 white men on the Island, 300 of whom where at Victoria, 125 at Nanaimo, and the remainder at Fort Rupert. Up to this time 19,807 acres of land had been applied for, 10,172 being for the Hudson's Bay Company, 2,374 for the Puget Sound Company, and the rest for private individuals. In 1853 the increase in population pointed to the necessity of a judicial functionary, and David Cameron was appointed Chief Justice of the Island, which appointment was confirmed by the Home Government. There had previous to this been no judiciary, nor in fact any constabulary, with the exception of a volunteer force of mounted men to keep the Indians in check.

As the five years' term drew towards its close the company again became anxious about their charter. They began to fear that if some efforts sufficient to hoodwink the Government were not made in the direction of colonization trouble might ensue. Accordingly they released some of the ten thousand acres of reserve land they held in the vicinity of Fort Victoria, and ordered a number of their servants to become settlers, and to bring out their families to the Island. Many of the officers also purchased wild lands at the fixed price of one pound per acre, to give color to their proceedings. The agents of the company, resident on the Island, however, no longer shared the anxiety of the management. The majority of them had become land holders, and they saw plainly that for themselves there was more to be gained by the settlement of the Island than in the continuation of the fur trade, and they were not averse to seeing the government of the Island pass out of the hands of the monopoly. Moreover, Douglas' dual position as Governor and Chief Factor gave satisfaction neither to the colonists nor to the agents of the company subordinate to him, and therefore when the settlers' petition to Parliament was prepared, asking that the company's grant be not renewed at the expiration of the five years' term, and that the Island be taken under the immediate management of the Imperial Government, it was signed, not only by the colonists themselves, but also by the highest officials of the company then on the Island, with the exception of Douglas himself. The petition, among other things, asked that a Governor and subordinate functionaries be appointed and paid by the Home Government; that courts of justice be established; that the executive council be separated from the legislative;

that the house of assembly consist of nine members, to be elected every three years; that the election franchise, now enjoyed only by persons holding twenty acres of land, be extended so as to include persons occupying houses or paying rent to the extent of ten pounds per annum, or owning farm lands to the extent of ten pounds, or city lands to the value of twenty pounds, and that the price of public lands be reduced to ten shillings an acre payable in five annual installments, at the rate of five per cent. per annum. Notwithstanding this petiton, supported as it was by a number of prominent members of the Imperial House, the company's charter was renewed for another five years.

In Blanchard's commission a clause existed empowering him to establish a representative assembly, with whose advice, and that of his council, he should govern the colony. Blanchard had not acted on his power in this respect, owing to the fact that there were not at that time men on the Island, outside the company's officials, who were qualified to act as representatives. In 1856, however, the English Government decided that matters were now far enough advanced in the colony for the establishment of representative government. Douglas was accordingly instructed to call an assembly and he at once summoned a meeting of his council to consider the matter. As a result of their deliberations a proclamation was issued on June 16th, 1856, dividing the Island into four electoral districts, and appointing to each its number of representatives. The districts were as follows: Victoria, with three members; Esquimalt and Metchosin, with two members; Nanaimo, with one member, and Sooke with one member. The property qualification for voters was twenty acres, or more, of freehold land, and that for representatives £300, or more, in freehold estate. Writs were issued and made returnable on August 4th. On this day then the first election on Vancouver Island was held, and representatives were elected without any disturbance. In Victoria there was that day, as there has been on every similar occasion since, a very spirited contest. Five candidates here offered themselves for election, but in the other constituencies the nominees went in by acclamation. The members returned were: John F. Kennedy, Nanaimo; John Muir, Sooke; J. S. Helmcken and Thomas Skinner, Esquimalt; J. D. Pemberton, Joseph Yates and E. E. Langford, Victoria District. This first assembly met in August and elected J. S. Helmcken speaker. After listening to the

Governor's address the assembly considered the validity of Langford's election, which was disputed, and unseated him. J. W. McKay was chosen in his place. The labors of this assembly were not very onerous, consisting chiefly in finding ways and means for carrying on the government, whose requirements were as yet inconsiderable, and in the performance of their duties they received the assistance and guidance of the Governor. Even at this early stage of the country's history a strong dislike was manifested on all hands to anything like taxation, and for the first few years the revenue was chiefly derived from licenses imposed on liquor dealers. This assembly continued to meet annually till 1859, when its four years lease of life expired. During this period the judiciary was placed on a sound footing and properly constituted officers were appointed to carry out the orders of the court. Throughout the Island Justices of the Peace were appointed, and the machinery of law set to work in civilized fashion.

As the years between 1855 and 1859 slipped by, the question of the charter again presented itself to the minds of the company's management. They no longer, however, felt the same anxiety in regard to it which had disturbed them in the past, having prepared themselves against its abrogation, should such be the Government's decision. Indeed, several of the largest shareholders considered a further tenure of power as of doubtful advantage, and were therefore opposed to accepting a renewal of the grant. It was evident to all that the Island could no longer be held for strictly trading purposes, and the company, with its large parcels of land at Victoria, could not now lose by its colonization. Besides this it had been stipulated in the company's agreement with the Government, that upon its relinquishment of the charter it was to be repaid for the outlay which the attempt to colonize the Island had cost it. This sum amounted to the handsome figure of £80,000. In the House of Commons too there was a strong feeling against the monopoly, and the government was aware that the termination of existing relations between the company and the colony would be popular.

In 1857 therefore, when the company inquired what action the Government intended taking in the matter, the question was laid before Parliament and a select committee of nineteen members was appointed to consider the state of those British North American possessions which were under the administration of the Hudson's Bay Company, or over which they held license to trade. The Governor-General of Canada was notified of the appointment of this committee, and Chief Justice Drake was commissioned by the Canadian Government to watch proceedings in its interest. The Parliament of Canada also appointed a committee to make investigations. After sitting for six months, and examining twenty-four witnesses, the committee decided that the connection of the Hudson's Bay Company with Vancouver Island should be terminated, and means provided for extending the colony over the whole or any portion of the Mainland.

When the committee reported the result of their enquiry to Parliament in 1858 its recommendations were adopted, and the government of Vancouver Island was ordered to be taken out of the hands of the company as soon as the charter should expire. James Douglas was offered the position of Governor of the colony, on condition of his severing his connection with the Hudson's Bay Company, which he accepted, disposing of his interest therein and forever bidding adieu to the corporation he had served so long and well. In the meantime, in consequence of the discovery of gold on the Fraser and Thompson Rivers, and the enormous rush of people to that region, it had been deemed advisable to take measures for the government of the Mainland, and New Caledonia was raised into a colony, under the name of British Columbia. Of this colony Douglas was appointed Governor, as well as of Vancouver Island. Some months subsequent to this the company's license of exclusive trade on the Mainland was revoked, and the territory west of the Rocky Mountains was forever rid of a monopoly which had seen and survived its day of usefulness.

Before leaving this period to enter upon what may be called the history of the colony proper, it will be necessary to relate the particulars of a dispute arising out of the boundary question which for a time assumed quite threatening proportions. The treaty of 1846 was in one or two particulars somewhat loosely drawn up owing in a measure to the lack of exact knowledge of the hydrography of the country, and as might have been expected, the people of the United States as soon as they saw it was to their advantage so to do set themselves to work to override a clause, the intention of which was unmistakeable. The treaty in fixing the line of boundary from the mainland to the Pacific ocean provides that the navigation of the channel south of the 49th parallel of latitude shall remain free and open to both parties and that this line as continued west from the mainland shall, when it reaches the middle of the channel separating Vancouver Island from the continent, pass southerly through the middle of said channel and of Fuca straits.

Now, there are two channels leading into the straits of Fuca one only of which, Rosario, was known to navigators at the time the treaty was made, and there is not the slightest doubt but that it was intended by those who drew up the treaty that this was to be the dividing line between the possessions of the two nations. This interpretation of the treaty was not questioned for nearly ten years subsequent to the settlement of the boundary question and during all that time the Hudson's Bay Company had been utilizing the largest and best of the islands west of this channel as a farm for the raising of stock. About 1850, a second channel known as Haro, considerably to the west of Rosario channel, and deeper and wider, and in some respects more convenient for ocean vessels was discovered and the Americans at once leapt to the conclusion that this should have been the channel indicated in the treaty. The idea was highly pleasing to them as it meant if adopted that they would come into possession of some very fine islands, one of which, San Juan, was especially valuable, not alone on account of its fertility but also because it was the key to the Gulf of Georgia. Their minds were no sooner made up on this point than they began to resort to their usual arts of bluster and chicanery, for the accomplishment of their design. In 1850 accordingly the legislature of Oregon proceeded to organize these islands into a district, attached to that territory. Of course after this official proceeding on the part of the Americans, and as the Hudson's Bay Company was in quiet possession of San Juan, and had no intention of yielding it up, trouble was sure to follow, and it came. The difficulty began when early in 1854 J. N. Ebey, collector of customs for Puget Sound, attempted to levy dues on a quantity of stock placed on the island by the Hudson's Bay Company. The company's clerk in charge on the island, John Griffin, promptly refused to acknowledge Ebey's right to collect such dues, and acquainted Governor Douglas with the pretentions of the American official. Douglas, accompanied by the Victoria collector of customs, Mr. Sankster, went over to San Juan Island to look

into the matter. Sankster ordered Ebey to quit the Island, and threatened to arrest all Americans in future found navigating the waters west of Rosario Channel. Ebey, however, was not to be frightened and, while he was unable to levy the dues he claimed, he replied that he would leave a deputy collector on the island who would do his duty. A deputy was accordingly sworn in who faithfully assessed the company's property, but who magnanimously refrained from enforcing collections. In March of the following year, however, the Sheriff of Whatcom county seized and sold a number of sheep belonging to the company and, for his timerity, was promptly censured by his Government, which gave orders that those living on the island should not be interfered with till the matter had been considered by the two Governments. After this the United States officials contented themselves with simply valuing the property on the island. In 1856-7 commissioners were appointed by the two powers to examine thoroughly into the matter for the purpose of coming to some amicable understanding. Captains Provost and Richards, of the Royal Navy, were deputed by Britain, and Archibald Campbell and Lieut. Parke by the Republic. After two years of consideration the commissioners could not agree, and their labor proved barren of results. In 1859 matters were brought to a crisis by an American squatter on the island, named Cutter, shooting a hog belonging to the Hudson's Bay Company, and refusing to pay for the same. Cutter being threatened with arrest by the British authorities appealed to General Harney, commander of the Military Department of Oregon. Harney, who was a bellicose "patriot," immediately sent a company of militia to the island to take possession of it for the United States. This action on the part of the American officials created surprise and indignation at Victoria, and Douglas immediately sent Major DeCourcy to the island as stipendary magistrate. Two gun-boats were also dispatched to prevent the landing of more American troops. Notwithstanding this, however, reinforcements were sent by General Harney and were permitted to land. The Americans now threatened that any attempt on the part of the British to land troops would occasion a collision. Captain Provost suggested a joint occupation of the island till the boundary question was settled, but this was rejected. A correspondence then ensued between Douglas and Harney in which the former made an effort to arrange matters until the Governments of the respective powers should have come to some understanding. All his overtures, however, were rejected by Harney, and indeed throughout the entire trouble the Americans conducted themselves with a swaggering impudence strongly in contrast to the courteous forbearance of the British officers. Affairs began to look so warlike that General Scott was sent by President Buchanan to enquire fully into the conduct of General Harney and examine the reasons for his action. Scott proposed a joint occupation of the island, but this was rejected by Douglas, who urged the withdrawal of the American troops promising that the naval force should also be removed, and assuring Scott that there was no intention of dislodging the troops in possession without orders from the Home Government. Scott accepted the proposition on these conditions and withdrew all but one company of infantry. Harney was shortly afterwards censured by his own Government and relieved of his command. In 1860 a proposal was made by the English Government that the question be left to arbitration, and one of three powers was suggested as arbitrator: Denmark, Belgium or the Republic of Switzerland. It is probable that the question might have been settled then, but for the outbreak of the civil war in the United States. From that time till 1868 nothing more was heard of the matter, but during that period Americans were quietly settling on the island and making homes for themselves. During 1869 two efforts were made by England to have this matter adjusted, and agreements were intered into by American officials to submit the question to arbitration, but on each occasion the agreement was nullified by the United States Senate. The matter remained in this state till 1871, when England sent five commissioners to Washington, and a treaty was negotiated whereby the question was referred to the Emperor of Germany for arbitration. In 1872 the matter was decided, and in the estimation of all just men on both sides, who were at all conversant with the case, most unjustly so, in favor of the United States.

THE COLONY OF BRITISH COLUMBIA.

The golden auspices under which the colony of British Columbia came into existence fittingly presaged the illustrious destiny which all thinking men now recognize is reserved for her. The fitful light which played around her morning has indeed passed away, but it has been succeeded by the strong, steady glow of human industry and human progress, and beneath these happy rays a wealth more beneficial in its influence than that extracted from gold mines has been developed. And even the precious metal, the existence of which in her soil first attracted the attention of the world to her shores, has been but superficially touched upon, that which lies hidden in her mountains offering a larger reward to systematic labor than ever did her pactolean streams to the rough miner of early days.

The existence of gold in British Columbia had been known to the Hudson's Bay traders long previous to the rush of 1858. As early as 1852 the Queen Charlotte Islands and Skeena River had been prospected, but without successful results, although indications were everywhere abundant. In 1856 and 1857 Chief Trader McLean, then stationed at Kamloops, had obtained considerable quantities from Indians, and in the latter year he had transmitted three hundred ounces to Victoria. Two American prospectors, named McDonald and Adams, had also mined on the Thompson River in 1857, and had collected a large quantity of dust. On their way to California McDonald killed Adams, secured the gold and displayed it at Olympia. The story told by McDonald was verified and the news thus conveyed shot like a flame through Oregon and California and kindled hope and desire in the hearts of thousands.

Governor Douglas learning of the ferment which the reports had occasioned understood what the result would be, and in anticipation of a rush issued a proclamation in December, 1857, forbidding all persons to dig or disturb the earth or search for gold until authorized on that behalf by Her Majesty's Colonial Government, and he imposed a license of ten shillings a month, afterwards increased to five dollars, by virtue of which persons would be permitted to mine within certain prescribed limits. Early next year he stationed H. M. S. Satelite at the mouth of the River Fraser to prevent the entry of persons who did not possess the necessary license. Besides this he taxed the supplies of the miners, and every boat which entered the Fraser paid a toll of from six to twelve dollars. Douglas' expectations were not disappointed. The excitement throughout California was greater than that of '49 and it was confidently asserted on every hand that the deposits in the River Fraser were richer than had ever been found in the Golden State. The excitement, however, was not confined to California. The story of the golden streams had spread from state to state and country to country, and was canvassed in Europe and Australia almost as eagerly as it was in America. Early in 1858 the stream of immigration began to flow. Hundreds of eager fortune seekers came from Europe, thousands from Eastern America, and tens of thousands from California. Sailing vessels and steamers, good, bad and indifferent, daily left San Francisco crowded beyond their capacity with human freight, and stages carried those to Puget Sound who could not get away quickly enough by water. The exodus from California was unprecedented. It was estimated that over thirty-five thousand left San Francisco during the year. Business in California was at a standstill, and the injury done to its commerce was incalculable. The newspapers tried to stem the tide, but without avail, and a baseless rumor had more effect on the public mind than the monitions of reason and experience.

It was on the 25th of April, 1858, that the first contingent of fortune seekers arrived at Victoria on board the steamer Commodore from San Francisco, and during the succeeding fortnight two thousand others followed. Steamers and sailing vessels entirely new to these waters daily entered the harbor at Victoria with hundreds of men, attracted from all quarters of the globe. After landing their passengers these vessels returned whence they came to spread exaggerated reports of the country's richness and thereby increase the excitement and the tide of migration. It is estimated that by the twentieth of June fourteen thousand eight hundred men had embarked for the mines. All this volume of immigration flowed through Victoria in consequence of Governor Douglas' refusal to grant permits and mining licenses elsewhere. The result of this was that Victoria became within the short space of a month a populous city, the inhabitants of which in great part lived under canvas. Of the thousands who constituted this population not more than one in a hundred had any intention of remaining in Victoria. The desire of all was to get as speedily as possible to the mines, and every day's delay seemed to place them so much farther away from their anticipated fortune. Notwithstanding their impatience, however, the majority of them were doomed to delay, owing to the insufficiency of the steamboat service from Victoria to the mines. The Hudson's Bay Company had the monopoly of this service, the American steamers being excluded from the river, and as the company's vessels were neither large enough nor numerous enough to accommodate the enormous crowds, thousands had to await their opportunity with what grace they could, or else discover some independent means of getting across the gulf. Early in the month of May some rendered foolhardy by their eagerness decided to cross the gulf in skiffs, and the example of these infecting others, many risked themselves in small boats—which, in the majority of cases, were of their own construction, and were therefore unseaworthy—on unknown and treacherous waters. As might have been expected numbers were never again heard of.

Several efforts were made by the American steamship companies to establish on Puget Sound a rival town to Victoria, the intention being to cut a trail from this point to the mines on the Fraser. It was believed at this time that the river was not navigable by ocean vessels, and the prospects of an overland route were therefore reasonably good. These considerations led to the establishment of Whatcom, at which all the American steamers began to land their passengers, after having first called at Victoria for the necessary mining permits, and for a time this place made rapid progress. The cutting of a trail was also begun, but was abandoned as soon as it was discovered that ships could ascend the Fraser as far as Langley. This discovery also terminated Whatcom's existence for the time being. In June Governor Douglas removed the restrictions against American vessels and allowed them to go up the river on payment of a royalty for each trip. This gave all the transportation facilities required, and by the end of July nearly all the miners had left Victoria. Both banks of the river were speedily lined with eager adventurers, and wherever dust was found in paying quantities a stampede was made to the spot and the ground staked off into claims. These spots were called bars, and many of them have become historical from the quantities of the metal which they yielded, and by the associations which cluster around them. The first paying bar above Langley was Maria, and between this and Yale there were twenty others, from all of which diggers were taking large amounts of money. Hill bar was the last and richest before reaching Yale, and here during the Summer of 1858 were congregated many of the old California experts, among whom could be counted not a few of the wild and abandoned characters who had made unsavory reputations in the Golden State. As bases from which supplies were distributed to the miners, Langley, Hope, Yale, Lytton and Lillooet, rapidly rose into populous towns with thriving businesses. As the bars below Yale became filled the intrepid prospectors forced their way northward over the Little Canyon and up to the mouth of the Anderson River. In this stretch thirteen bars were located from all of which the miners extracted on the average $15 a day to the man. Boston Bar, at the mouth of the Anderson River, was especially rich, and indeed it seemed to the adventurers that the farther north they went the more abundant and more valuable the "finds" became. This fact led the more daring to push forward in the face of all difficulties and privations. There were already miners as high up the river as the forks of the Thompson, who had penetrated thither by way of the Columbia River and who, since April, had been obtaining large returns, although working in the very teeth of starvation. This point was as far north as the miners got in 1858. There was, of course, a small number of the more adventurous who prospected as far up as the Quesnelle, but Winter closed in before they were able to accomplish anything beyond finding the indications everywhere excellent. On the Fraser below the Thompson, and on the Thompson itself, however, work during this year was pursued with zeal, and a great portion of the river gravel was sifted by the miners.

Of the twenty-two thousand who went to the Fraser River in 1858 all but about four thousand left before the middle of Summer. This immense exodus was owing to the seemingly inaccessable character of the country, together with the discouraging fact that the bars from which the gold was to be taken could not be got at on account of the high water till after midsummer. Notwithstanding this great defection, however, the diggings were still overcrowded. A question too, which pressed itself on the minds of all, but especially of those who remained, was how supplies were to be transported beyond Yale. The river navigation rendered transportation to Yale comparatively easy, but to get provisions above the canyons in sufficient quantities to meet the demand puzzled the ingenuity of the most anxious. The first men who had crossed had carried supplies on their backs, but these, of course, would not last long, and when they were exhausted it was necessary to obtain more. This difficulty occasioned great distress during the Summer, and as far up as the forks of the Thompson the miners were almost starving. So extreme indeed was the destitution that the servants of the Hudson's Bay Company, stationed at the forks of the Thompson, were reduced to living on berries. During the Summer a limited quantity of food had been brought in by way of the Columbia River, but as it was quickly consumed none of it reached the men on the Fraser, who had to supply themselves in a very inefficient manner by crossing the canyon and re-crossing it with supplies on their backs. How long this condition of affairs would have lasted had Governor Douglas not taken it upon himself to solve the difficulty can only be guessed at, but it is certain that the development of the Cariboo region would have been delayed. When Douglas paid his visit of inspection to the mining region in the Summer he saw the absolute need there was of at once cutting a trail that would be reasonably secure and easy, as hundreds of miners who desired to push north were deterred by the difficulties and dangers attending the journey, and the privations which awaited them at its termination. After due consideration he decided to take advantage of the chain of lakes of which Harrison is the first and Seton the last on the journey north. With portages built between these lakes a tolerably easy route of seventy miles in length would be given the miner from the time he left the Fraser at the confluence of the Harrison River till he again reached the Fraser at Lillooet. Douglas placed his plan before a body of miners and made an arrangement with them whereby they undertook to build the portages. The route came to be known as the Harrison-Lillooet road and proved satisfactory for the purpose it was intended to serve. Men in thousands passed over the road and supplies in comparative abundance reached the Thompson River in the Autumn. Beyond Yale, of course, everything in the form of food brought a price never before dreamed of. A pound of beans sold for a dollar and other articles were on a like scale. Douglas became aware during his journey of a strong feeling of discontent among the Indians. They were indignant that their territory should have been so despotically appropriated by the white man and the yellow metal, esteemed so valuable, extracted and taken away without any equivalent being offered the original owners of the soil. This gloomy mood of the natives was intensified to fury by the reckless and brutal manner in which some of the worst of the old California miners treated them. Douglas did what he could to soothe their ruffled tempers and they listened to his admonitions with the respectful attention they always accorded him, but they failed to be convinced that they should not resort to violence. The Governor appointed several justices of the peace while on his journey and gave general directions for the guidance of those to whom he looked to keep order. At most of the bars rules and regulations of a stringent character, especially as regards the treatment of Indians, had been adopted by the miners themselves, and, everything considered, a wonderful state of orderliness prevailed all along the river. Notwithstanding this, however, there were a few who committed acts calculated to inflame the worst passions of the natives, and besides this the outrages during the early part of the summer could neither be forgotten nor forgiven. In the latter part of July a number of bodies of white men were found on the banks of the river mutilated beyond recognition. Murders were reported almost daily till at length the miners became roused to the alarming state of affairs and held a meeting at Yale. A large number of men were enrolled and an expedition dispatched up the river to overawe the Indians. The expedition was fortunately successful, the tribes as far as the forks of the Thompson entered into a treaty of peace with the whites and the miners returned to their claims which they had abandoned in terror. In October another influx of fortune seekers took place in consequence of the success of the prospectors on the Thompson. There were now about ten thousand miners distributed along the river, two thousand of whom were above the Little Canyon. When the winter of 1858 closed in the transformation which had taken place in the country along the River Fraser as high up as the Thompson, was marvellous beyond measure. In the space of eight months a country had been populated, towns had sprung into existence and

HON. HUGH NELSON.

a colony had been established. Difficulties, which in this age can be only partially appreciated by those even best acquainted with the country, were overcome. To give a life-like picture of what the early prospectors had to contend with, would be next to impossible, and if given, would hardly be credited. To the appalling ruggedness of the country, which everywhere offered a stern resistance to their advance, were added the daily companionship of famine and the hostility of enraged Indians. Their heroism, if such it can be called, although of a venal character, was worthy of admiration, and was useful in paving the way for another and a better order of things.

Early in the spring of 1859 the human stream again began to flow to the north and in larger volume than the year previous. It lasted unabated throughout the summer, and reports were being constantly brought down concerning the richness of the upper country. By November the Quesnelle had been reached, and between the Thompson and this point there were twelve bars, at each of which hundreds of men were employed and obtaining excellent results. During this year mining was still practically confined to the Fraser and Thompson, although some of the pioneer prospectors had found their way to the Cariboo country. Road building was pushed forward with commendable zeal, and indeed Governor Douglas showed a determination that the country should be developed as rapidly as possible, and every facility which it was in his power to grant should be given to the miners. In the summer of 1860 the streams of Cariboo attracted the attention of prospectors, and during this and next year a rush thither was made. There the miners of British Columbia found the highest realization of their dreams. There they built camps and washed millions worth of gold from Keethley, Lowhee, Antler and Williams Creeks. Before this time, however, changes had taken place in the government of the country, of which some account will have to be given here.

On the 25th of August, 1858, the Imperial Parliament passed an act to provide for the government of British Columbia, by which name for the future should be known that territory between the United States boundary on the south and the Naas River on the north, and between the Rocky Mountains and the Pacific ocean, including all the islands adjacent thereto, except Vancouver Island. A townsite, to which was given the name of Darby, was surveyed by Mr. Pemberton, the Colonial Surveyor, and laid out into lots. This, the proposed capital, was situated about three miles below the old Hudson's Bay trading post, Langley, and here on the 17th of November Mr. Douglas, who had accepted the position of Governor of the new colony, was sworn in by Chief Justice Begbee. The following week a large number of lots in the new town were sold and aggregated $68,000. Thus before the end of the year the new colony was fairly launched and everything pointed out for it a bright and prosperous career. In fulfillment of the promise made by the Imperial authorities to send out an officer of engineers in command of a body of sappers and miners to survey the country and build roads, Col. Richard Clement Moody arrived at Victoria on the 25th of December with a force of one hundred and fifty men. Col. Moody also held the position of Chief Commissioner of Lands and Works, and was authorized to administer the government of the colony in the event of the Governor's absence or incapacity. Moody was a man of large experience and possessed of a shrewd, practical judgment and a strong, resolute will. He was, therefore, a most suitable man to direct at this time the destinies of the young colony. His first important official act after arriving was to remove the capital of the colony. He objected to Darby because it was difficult of approach by sea-going vessels, and also because the Hudson's Bay Company had ten square miles of land in reserve adjoining it. After careful examination and mature consideration he chose the site on which New Westminster now stands as the seat of government for the colony, and no sooner had he decided than the work of clearing the land to admit of the erection of government buildings was begun. To the new metropolis was given the name of Queensborough. Those who had invested their money in lots in Darby, when it was declared the capital, were allowed the equivalent of their purchases in Queensborough property. Col. Moody took up his residence here and the town began to take form under his ever watchful eye. Early next year a revenue officer was stationed at this town and it was declared the port of entry for British Columbia. The town increased with marvellous rapidity and by the end of 1859 its existence as a commercial centre was assured. In the summer of 1860 it had made such strides that the inhabitants petitioned for the privilege of incorporating their town under the name of New Westminster, appointing municipal officers and taxing themselves. A measure embodying these requests was proclaimed on the 16th of July, 1860. In the meantime Moody had with untiring zeal been urging forward whatever was calculated to develope and build up the colony, and in his efforts he was strongly seconded by the leading citizens of New Westminster, many of whom have since continued to take a prominent part in guiding the destinies of the country. The building of roads and other public works was prosecuted with activity, and the interest of the colony, from a mining standpoint, was especially regarded with concern. During this period the attention of immigrants had not been confined entirely to gold digging and trading. The riches of the country in other respects had not escaped the observing eye of the intelligent adventurer. The inexhaustible wealth of valuable timber, the rivers, lakes and inlets teeming with magnificent fish of almost every description, and the hidden deposits of coal, began to receive some of the attention which they deserved. The fertile valley of the Fraser also attracted the agriculturist. It is to these industries and to the men who engaged in them that the country owes in a great measure its position to-day. Among the vast throng of unthinking miners which rushed into the country during 1858-59 and '60, were many, especially those from Eastern Canada and Britain, who, while they were attracted to British Columbia by the reports of its riches, did not come like the majority with the intention of making their "pile" rapidly and returning whence they came. They desired to make homes for themselves and prosper with the country which they would give their best energies to develope and build up. Many of these men did not go to the mines at all, but set themselves the task of wresting from the soil or hewing from the forest treasures more abiding than gold. Before the end of 1863 a small cannery was in operation on the River Fraser and here and there a saw mill was being erected.

In the Winter of 1863 a legislative council was organized under a royal order, and held its first sitting on January 21st, 1864. The council consisted of fourteen members, five of whom were elected and the rest appointed. Governor Douglas opened the first session of the Council. The following members were present: Hon. Henry P. P. Crease, Attorney-General; Hon. Wymond O. Hamley, Collector of Customs; Hon. Charles W. Franks, Treasurer; Chartres Brew, Magistrate of New Westminster; Peter O'Reiley, Magistrate Cariboo East; E. H. Saunders, Magistrate Yale; H. M. Ball, Magistrate Lytton; J. A. R. Homer, New Westminster; Robert J. Smith, Hope, Yale and Lytton; Henry Holbrook, Douglas and Lillooet; James Orr, Cariboo East; Walter S. Black, Cariboo West. In his address to the Council Governor Douglas urged upon that body the necessity for vigorous prosecution of public works, and stated that with a view to increase immigration and encourage settlement, he had thrown open public lands to actual settlers on the most liberal terms. After recommending appropriations for special purposes, he submitted the revenue and expenditure for the last year, the former amounting to $110,000, and the latter to $192,860, leaving a large deficit, most of which, however, was covered by bonds and loans to the amount of $65,000. Throughout the session the Council displayed a commendable desire to act in concert with the Governor in his efforts for the development of the colony and voted such supplies as enabled him to push forward the work without being embarrassed for want of funds. During this period law had been administered throughout the colony under the active supervision of Chief Justice Begbie, and so prompt were his movements and so certain and unfailing his justice that crime was apparently unknown in the whole Mainland. In the early part of the period Governor Douglas, as stated, had appointed justices of the peace at the mining camps, and while in general these officials did good work and assisted greatly in maintaining order, occasionally some circumstance would arise, the developments of which betrayed their ignorance of legal procedure, or their inability to enforce their commands. One such case was that in which Ned McGowan, a man still remembered by most of the pioneers of '58, played so conspicuous a part. A very vivid description of the circumstance is given in a book written by Commander Mayne, of the Royal Navy, who at this time was attached to H. M. S. Satelite, then stationed at the mouth of the River Fraser to prevent the entry of miners without passports. The account is somewhat long, but as it contains not only a picture of the occurrence itself, of which Mayne was an eye witness, but also an interesting description of travel on the river, I make no apology for the extract.

"The rumor of another outbreak, not at Victoria, but at Yale, up the Fraser River, arrived to disturb, not altogether unpleasantly, the monotony of our winter life in Esquimalt Harbor. Intelligence had been sent down the river to Victoria that some miners had made a disturbance at Yale, and that Col. Moody had, immediately upon being informed of it, started from Langley for the scene of action with the engineers stationed there, which, numbering 25 men, had just arrived in the colony. The Governor considered it desirable at once to strengthen his hands. Fort Yale, ninety miles up the Fraser, was one of the stations to which some of these miners who were anxious to remain near their claims on the upper bars, so as to commence work directly the season opened,—or to whom, for sundry delicate private reasons, the delights of San Francisco were not obtainable,—flocked to pass the winter. The climate of Yale was milder than that of the Upper Fraser, which induced a great number of men having claims north of it to come down and pass some months there, while others working on the bars near Yale were wont to spend their Sundays and holidays in the town. Among them, pre-eminent for certain social qualities which had rendered him generally obnoxious to the laws of whatever country he had favored with his presence, was a certain Edward McGowan. This individual had spent some time in California, where he had become very notorious, and had been honored with the especial enmity of the "vigilance committee" of San Francisco. Nor without good cause. He had, I believe, had the misfortune to kill several of his comrades in those little personal encounters which one sees reported so frequently in the American newspapers under the head of "shooting" or "cutting affairs." The act for which the vigilance committee of San Francisco doomed him to the gallows was killing a man in cold blood in the streets of that city who knew too much of his antecedents. McGowan of course denied this, and always asserted that he had shot his foe in self-defence: but there is little doubt that the view which the vigilance committee took of the matter was the correct one. As an instance of universal suffrage, it may be mentioned that this man at one time filled the office of a judge in California; and quite recently, when, after shooting at a man at Hill's Bar, whom, luckily, he missed, he escaped across the frontier into American territory, he has been elected to the House of Representatives of one of the border states that lie east of the Rocky Mountains. This worthy has given his adventures to the world in the shape of an autobiography, published some five years since, and written with considerable spirit. The story told in it of his hairbreadth escapes from the clutches of the vigilance committee is extremely exciting. Its agents pursued him with such rancor that, after with the greatest difficulty he had escaped to a steamer starting for Victoria, he was recognized, fired at, and a bullet sent through the lappel of his coat.

That such a man as this was known to be at Hill's Bar, some two miles below Yale, where he had a very rich claim, and to have with him, and under his influence, a strong party of followers bold and lawless as himself, might well give the authorities serious concern. Upon the news, therefore, being sent down of McGowan's having created a disturbance, the Governor requested Capt. Prevost to send a party to aid the Colonel. The 'Plumper' was the only vessel available for this service, and accordingly we embarked a party of marines and blue-jackets, under Lieutenant Gooch, from the 'Satelite,' and started at once for the scene of action.

Upon arriving at Langley we found that Colonel Moody had taken the 'Enterprise,' the only steamer then on the river capable of going farther up it than Langley, and had pushed on to Yale with twenty-five of the engineers under the command of Captain Grant, R.E. As the field-piece we had brought with us must have been parted with had the men been sent on, there being no other way of despatching them except in canoes, it was considered advisable to keep them on board the 'Plumper' at Langley, and that a messenger should at once follow and overtake Colonel Moody. This service devolved upon me, and I received orders to proceed up the river with despatches from Captain Richards informing the Colonel of the presence of the force at Langley, and to bring back his instructions.

Mr. Yale, the Hudson's Bay Company's officer at Langley, undertook to provide a canoe and crew for the journey, and my own preparations were soon made—a blanket, frock and trowsers, a couple of rugs, two or three pipes, plenty of tobacco, tea, coffee, some meat and bread, a frying-pan and saucepan, completing my outfit. At this time canoe-travelling was quite new to me, and, familiar

HON. JOHN ROBSON.

as it has since become, I quite well remember the curious sensations with which this my first journey of the kind was commenced. It was mid-winter, the snow lay several inches thick upon the ground; the latest reports from up the river spoke of much ice about and below Fort Hope, so that I was by no means sorry to avail myself of the offer of Mr. Lewis, of the Hudson's Bay Company, who had accompanied the 'Plumper' to Langley as pilot, to be my companion. Mr. Yale had selected a good canoe and nine stout paddlers, four half-breeds and five Indians, and when I landed from the ship a few minutes before eleven they were waiting on the beach, dressed in their best blankets, with large streamers of bright red, blue and yellow ribbons, in which they delight so much, flying from their caps. Mr. Yale had previously harangued them, and presented them with these streamers by way of impressing them with the importance of the service in which they were engaged. Seating ourselves in the canoe as comfortably as we could, away we started, the frail bark flying over the smooth water, and the crew singing at the top of their wild, shrill voices, their particolored decorations streaming in the bitter winter wind.

The North American Indians, and, indeed, the Canadians as well, paddle much more steadily when they sing. They keep splendid time, and, by way of accompaniment, bring the handles of their paddles sharply against the gunwale of the canoe. In singing their custom is—and the greatest stickler for etiquette among us will find himself outdone by the Indian's respect for whatever habit or fashion may have dictated—for the steersman to sing, the crew taking up the chorus. Although I have frequently tried to induce one of the others to start a song, with the view of testing the strength of their social habit in this respect, I have never succeeded unless supported in my request by the steersman. This post of honor is usually conferred upon the senior of the party, unless the owner of the canoe happens to form one of the crew when he takes the seat by virtue of his interest in it. Next in position and importance to the steersman are the pair of paddles who sit immediately behind the passengers; then come the two forward hands, who have a great deal to do with the management of the canoe in keeping it clear of blocks of floating ice, or the snags which often appear suddenly under its bows, and preventing the current from spinning it round and swamping it, which, but for the keen look-out they keep and their dexterity in the use of the paddles, would often happen in such swift and treacherous currents as those of North American rivers.

We paddled along quickly until five o'clock, when we stopped for supper, and, landing, made tea. This meal over, we started again and held on steadily all night. If the journey by day was strange and somewhat exciting, how much more so did it become when night set in! Wet, cold, and tired, we rolled ourselves up in our rugs, and in time fell into a broken sleep, lulled by the monotonous rap of the paddles upon the gunwale of the canoe, the rippling sound of the water against its sides, the song of the men now rising loud and shrill, now sinking into a low, drowsy hum. Ever and anon roused by a louder shout from the paddlers in the bow, we started up to find the canoe sweeping by some boat moored to the shore, or the miner's watch-fire, from which an indistinct figure would rise, gaze at us wonderingly as we passed howling by, and sometimes shout to us loudly in reply. We might well startle such of the miners as saw or heard us. Whenever we passed a fire, or a boat drawn up ashore, or moored to the trees by the beach, in which miners might be sleeping, the Indians would commence singing at the top of their voices; and we often saw sleepers start up, in wonder, no doubt, who could be travelling on the river at night at such a season,—and in some fear, perhaps, for several murders had lately been committed, which were attributed, rightly or wrongly, to Indian agency. And, indeed, as we swept by a watch-fire near enough for its glare to light up the dark figures straining at their hard work, and their wild, swarthy faces, with the long, bright ribbons, streaming behind them,—we might well give a shock to some wearied sleeper roused abruptly from dreams of home, or some rich claim which was to make his fortune, by the wild Indian boat-chant.

Most of our journey lay close along the shore, where, of course, the current was less rapid and advantage could be taken of the numerous eddies that set in near the banks. Our chief man was quite well acquainted with the river's navigation, having been for years in the Hudson's Bay Company's employ. When we came to a rapid, or it was necessary to cross the river from one bank to the other, by one consent the singing would cease, the paddlers' breath be husbanded to better purpose, and every muscle strained to force the canoe over the present difficulty. At such times when any greater exertion was necessary, or a more formidable obstacle than usual seemed on the point of being mastered, the Indians would give a loud prolonged shout, terminating in a shriller key, and dash their paddles into the boiling water with still fiercer vehemence. There can be few stranger sensations than that which we felt many times that night, when after paddling so steadily alongshore that we had fallen fast asleep, we were awoke suddenly by a heavy lurch of the canoe, and found the water rushing in over the gunwale, and the boat almost swamped by the fierce exertions of the paddlers, and tearing broadside down rather than across the rapid river, until with a shout it was run ashore on the opposite bank, and the excited rowers rested a few minutes to regain their breath before again paddling up the quieter water by the shore.

Next morning, about four o'clock, we landed for a short spell of rest, and, clearing away the snow, lit a fire and lay round it for a couple of hours. At the end of that time we picked ourselves up, still with cold, and breakfasted, and by half-past seven were under weigh again and paddling up the river, the Indians, to all appearance, as lively and unwearied as if they had slept the whole night through. I cannot say the same for their passengers. It was very cold, a sensation which we both tried in vain to get rid of by taking an occasional turn at the paddles; and the few snatches of short, disturbed sleep we had managed to obtain had left us very much fatigued. The novelty of the situation, too, in my case had worn away, and I confess that the second night of my journey was one of unmitigated discomfort and weariness. Upon the second morning we rested a little longer by our watch-fire, Myhu-pu-pu, the head man of the party, assuring us that we had plenty of time to reach Hope before nightfall. But Myhu-pu-pu was wrong: night fell while we were still some miles below the fort. About three in the afternoon we had boarded the 'Enterprise' and learnt that she had been three days in the ice, and had only got out of it indeed the previous morning, and that Colonel Moody had not, therefore, been able to reach Hope until that day. We had reason to congratulate ourselves upon our good fortune, as we had only met some floating ice and been nowhere in very serious danger from it, although once or twice we had narrowly escaped being swamped by floating blocks. But as we proceeded we found the river more and more swollen, the ice thicker and in greater quantities, and despite all the efforts of the crew, darkness set in while we were yet some miles short of our destination. On we pushed, however, and I had fallen asleep, when I was suddenly awakened by a sharp crack almost under my head. The canoe had struck a rock in crossing a rapid in the river, at a spot now known as Cornish Bar, but then called Murderer's Bar, from a murder that had taken place there, and she was stove in unmistakeably.

Thanks to the courage and skill of the elder of the crew, we were extricated from our perilous predicament. Leaping on to the rock, against which the full force of the current was driving the canoe, they lifted her off without a moment's hesitation, and the other rowers shooting her ashore, we all jumped out and ran her up upon the snow. Of course everything was wet, ourselves included; but we were too grateful for our narrow escape to heed this trifling inconvenience. Meanwhile the men, whose courage and readiness had preserved us, were still upon the rock, the current sweeping by up to their knees and threatening to carry them away. The canoe being hastily repaired and veered down to them by a rope, they too were brought safely ashore. Then arose the question, how were we to be got to Fort Hope that night? It was a serious one, not admitting of a very easy solution. To get the canoe afloat again was soon found impossible, as she was split fore and aft, and it was ultimately determined to leave two of the Indians in charge of it while the rest of us tried to make the trail, which was known to pass near this spot to the Fort. I have since that night walked that trail when it was as pretty and pleasant a summer evening's stroll as any one would wish to enjoy; but on this occasion, with two or three feet of snow upon it, and three or four feet more ready to receive us on either side if a false step was made, that three-mile walk to Hope was very hard work while it lasted. It was worse for my companion (Mr. Lewis), for in crossing a river by a fallen tree, which served as a bridge, his foot gave way and he slipped in, drenching his frozen clothes and limbs afresh. Fortunately, however, it was not very deep, and he was fished out, and we reached the Fort without further accident.

Since the time of which I am now writing the old Hudson's Bay Fort has been pulled down, and a more commodious one erected in its stead. The officer in charge of it had only one chamber to serve for both sitting and bed room; and late at night into this and the presence of Colonel Moody, Captain Grant, Mr. Begbie and the Hudson's Bay Company's officers, gathered round the fire, we made our way, looking, I dare say, pitiable objects enough. With the ready kindness which I never failed to meet with from the Company's officers in British Columbia, Mr. Ogilvy soon equipped both of us in suits of dry clothes and seated us before a hot supper.

In a subsequent chapter I shall have occasion to speak more fully of "bars;" but as the word occurs frequently in this book, I may here say that all those places where gold is found and worked on a river's bank are called by that name. This term has become the recognised one, and is not mere miner's slang; all proclamations referring to gold-extracting, etc., being addressed to the "mining bars" of such and such a district.

Bars are formed simply by a deposit of heaps of detritus at various bends of a river flowing through accumulations of irrupted rock, and between mountains whose sides have been broken down by former great convulsions. The rushing river tears away mass after mass of this rock and gravel, and, carrying on a natural combination of the "sluicing" and "crushing" processes, deposits the gold, with its ever-accompanying black metallic sand and a certain quantity of common earth, at intervals along its banks, carrying most of the lighter sand, etc., out to its mouth, there to form sandbanks and flats. It will be easily understood, therefore, that these bars are formed at every place where there is or has been anything to catch the drift as it comes down. But what is somewhat curious is the very different value of the deposit at various bars, or even parts of the same bar, some being very rich, others very poor, even where they are close together; and this happens not in the vertical section, which would be to some extent intelligible, but at an equal distance under the surface. One part of a bar may "give out," while another part will be worth working 20 feet deeper.

Thus all bars are formed in the same way, even although the rivers which deposited some of them have long since ceased to flow, or been diverted into other channels, causing what are termed "dry diggings," of which I shall speak hereafter. Very rich bars are often covered with sand, mud, etc., for, in some instances, several hundred feet. In California some of the richest diggings now worked are the beds of old rivers, quite dry, often running in very different directions to those of the present streams, and occurring from 100 to 300 feet below what is now the surface of the earth.

The Commissioner was, when I reported myself, rather surprised with the promptitude with which his requisition for troops had been met by the Governor, and perhaps a little embarrassed. His impression now was that the reports which had reached him at Yale and hurried him hither had been greatly exaggerated, and from the accounts which had since reached him he had the best reason to believe that the feeling of the mining population at Yale and elsewhere had been grossly misrepresented. However, he said that he had decided on proceeding next day to Yale with Mr. Begbie only, leaving Captain Grant and his party of engineers at Hope; and he desired me to accompany him, so that if, upon his arrival at Yale, the presence of troops should be found necessary, I might return to Hope with orders to that effect; and it was also determined that Mr. Lewis should take the canoe back to Langley as soon as it was repaired, and tell Captain Richards of my arrival and detention.

Next morning, therefore, we started, and reached Yale at three. The town was perfectly quiet, and the Colonel was received upon his entrance with the most vociferous cheering and every sign of respect and loyalty. Upon the way up we stopped at several of the bars, and made enquiries which satisfied us that the miners were doing very well, although they complained that the snow had for some days past kept them from working. The river scenery between these two ports was beautiful even at this season of the year. The distance is only fifteen miles, but the strength of the current is so great that in the winter five or six hours are consumed in the journey, and in the summer—when the stream is swollen by the melting snow—double that time is often taken. The only streams of any size that feed the Fraser for this distance are the Swal-lach-Coom, which flows into it some few miles below Yale, and the Que-que-alla, which

HON. J. H. TURNER.

runs into it two miles above Hope. The Que-que-alla is a considerable stream, dividing into two branches further in, and contains numbers of trout. The mountains on either side are from three to four thousand feet high, and are composed almost entirely of plutonic rocks and at their base is found the "drift" in which the gold is contained.

As I have already said, Fort Yale presented the most peaceful aspect imaginable. The day after our arrival happening to be Sunday, Colonel Moody performed the service in the Court House. It was the first time this had ever happened in Yale, and the thirty or forty miners who attended formed a most orderly and attentive congregation. After church, the difficulty which brought us here was investigated, and the magistrate at Hill's Bar, the principal bar on this part of the river, lying a mile below Yale, was suspended from his functions. A very few words will suffice to explain it. At Hill's Bar there was a resident magistrate, who was one of the miners though superior to most of them in position and acquirements; and at Yale two others—one who was shortly afterwards proved guilty of some rascality and discharged; the other, an honest man enough, but altogether unfit, from temperament and social position, for the discharge of his duties. These three dignitaries were not upon the best terms with one another, and two of them claimed a certain case and prisoner as belonging each to his own district, and disputed the right of adjudicating upon them to such a degree that, one having possession of the culprit's body, and refusing to give it up to his colleague, the other went to the extent of swearing in special constables to his aid, and removing the prisoner by force of arms to his jurisdiction at Hill's Bar. Among these special constables, and very probably among the instigators of the squabble, Mr. Edward McGowan figured conspicuously; and it was the outraged magistrate's report, that this worthy had been prison-breaking in his district, that gave it to the authorities at Langley and Victoria so serious an aspect. However, upon investigating the matter, he was found to have acted, if with indiscreet zeal, yet not illegally, and no charge was preferred against him on that account. But the same afternoon, while Colonel Moody, representing the majesty of the law, was still at Yale, Mr. McGowan outraged it unmistakably by committing an unprovoked assault. This, coupled with sundry other suspicious circumstances, caused Colonel Moody to think that

McGowan's friends and admirers would, if provoked, break into serious insubordination; and he at once instructed me to drop down the river to Hope and Langley, and order up the engineers, marines and bluejackets left at those places.

The utmost precaution was taken about my journey. Mr. Allard, the Hudson's Bay Company's officer at Yale, was instructed to have a small canoe launched unseen by the miners, who, it was thought, might endeavor to stop me, as they no doubt easily could have done. The darkness was waited for, and, the canoe being launched and dropped about half a mile down the river, Mr. Allard came to the house for me, and led me to it along the river's bank. As we dropped down the stream I was afraid even to light a pipe lest we should be stopped at Hill's Bar. Absurd as all this now seems—especially as I heard on my return that the miners knew perfectly well of my starting—it was not without its use at the time. The promptitude with which Captain Grant appeared on the spot with the engineers at daylight next morning astonished the miners a good deal, and it need not be assumed that, because they apologized and paid their fines, they would have done so equally had coercion not been threatened.

Reaching Hope at half-past eight that night, I very much astonished Captain Grant by telling him that he was to start for Yale at once, and, landing his men below Hill's Bar on the opposite side of the river, to march thence to Yale. Having given these instructions I embarked in the canoe once again, and about midnight—spinning down the Fraser being a very different matter to struggling up against its current—reached the "Enterprise" which was to convey me to Langley, and bring the men there up. Here a slight delay took place, as the steamer could not be got ready to start until daybreak; but away we went the instant dawn broke, and reached Langley in the afternoon of the following day, where, the "Enterprise" having wooded, every one was got aboard, and we were struggling up against the current by six p.m., reaching Smess River by nine or ten that night, and Cornish Bar by 8:30 the following night.

There the "Enterprise's" further progress was effectually barred, and, taking a canoe again, I made my way to Hope, where I found that further instructions had come from the Colonel to the effect that the blue-jackets were to remain there and only the marines to go on to Yale. So things were looking less martial, and I was not surprised, on pushing forward to Yale next morning, to find that the short campaign was at an end, and the peace, which had hardly been disturbed, restored. Mr. McGowan, after enjoying the sensation he had caused, paid the Commissioner a formal visit, and, after making a very gentlemanlike apology for the hasty blow which had disturbed the peace of British Columbia, and entering into an elaborate and, I believe, successful defence of his previous conduct in the squabble of the rival judges, committed himself frankly into the hands of justice. What could be done with such a frank, entertaining rascal? Justice herself could not press hardly for her dues in such a case. He was fined for the assault, exonerated from all previous misdemeanours, and next day, upon Hill's Bar being visited by Mr. Begbie, (the Chief Justice) and myself, he conducted us over the diggings, washed some "dirt" to show us the process, and invited us to a collation in his hut, where we drank champagne with some twelve or fifteen of his Californian mining friends. And, whatever opinion the vigilance committee of San Francisco might entertain of these gentlemen, I, speaking as I found them, can only say that, all things considered, I have rarely lunched with a better-spoken, pleasanter party. The word "miner" to many unacquainted with the gold-fields conveys an impression similar, perhaps, to that of "navvy." But among them may often be found men who, by birth and education are qualified to hold their own in the most civilised community in Europe. Here, for instance, I was entertained in the hut of a man who—by virtue of his rascality, no doubt—had been selected to fill the office of judge among his fellows in California; while one of his neighbors had taken his degree at an American University, and may since, for aught I know, have edited a Greek play and been made a bishop. I remember afterwards travelling with two men, who, meeting casually, recognised one another as old schoolfellows and class-men. Neither was in the least surprised at the other's condition, although one was a well-to-do surgeon with a very remunerative practice, and the other was an "express" man, penniless, and carrying letters some 130 or 140 miles for a subsistence."

Such occurrences as the above were, however, confined entirely to the early days of the colony's existence. When Chief Justice

Begbie had once made fully known the fact that he was at the head of the judicial system, and it did not take him long to accomplish this, disorderliness became as rare in the mining camps as in the capital of the country. In 1864 Mr. Douglas' term of office expired, and, as the people both of the Island and the mainland had petitioned the Imperial authorities to appoint a governor for each colony, Frederick Seymour was sent to British Columbia as his successor. The colony certainly did not gain by the change. Mr. Seymour, while personally a most estimable gentleman, was wanting in that firmness of character and capacity for business so requisite in a ruler of a young and energetic community. The hesitancy, however, which marked his administrative acts, was counterbalanced by the vigor and enterprise of the leading men of the Province, and thus the progress of the state was fortunately not hampered by the deficiencies of the Governor. Three days after Mr. Seymour's arrival at New Westminster came the news of the Chilkotin massacre, in which thirteen men, employed in cutting a trail from Bute Inlet towards Alexandria, were slaughtered by natives. The party at work on the trail numbered seventeen in all and only five escaped. When the news reached New Westminster and Victoria hundreds of men volunteered for service in suppressing the Indians and bringing the guilty ones to justice. Following this outbreak came the news, three weeks later, of the capture by the same Indians of a pack train *en route* from Bentinck Arm to Fort Alexandria, and the murder of three of the men in charge. A force of volunteers and marines was immediately despatched to the scene of these outrages and several of the bloodthirsty savages were caught and hanged. In October Governor Seymour dissolved the legislative council and a new election took place. In 1865 the question of uniting the two colonies of Vancouver Island and British Columbia was agitated, and in 1866 consolidation took place, the executive government and legislature of British Columbia being extended over the Island and the number of members of the Legislative Council being increased to twenty three. Mr. Seymour became Governor of the united colony and retained the position until his death in 1869.

The History of Vancouver Island, between the years 1859 and 1866, is marked by rapid settlement and development, especially in and about the City of Victoria. Everywhere building operations were carried on and it is estimated that in 1862 fifteen hundred substantial structures had been erected where two years previous the forest had stood. In 1861 the white population of Victoria was 3,500, and in 1863 it had increased to 6,000, and that not counting the large number of miners who yearly wintered there. In 1862 the city was incorporated with six councillors and a mayor, the latter office being filled in that year by Mr. Thomas Harris.

The existence of the first Legislative Assembly terminated in 1859, and a new election took place. The representation had been increased to thirteen, and the members returned, with the constituencies, were: Victoria City, J. H. Cary, S. Franklin; Victoria District, H. P. P. Crease, W. F. Tolmie, A. Waddington; Esquimalt Town, G. T. Gordon; Esquimalt District, J. S. Helmcken, James Cooper; Lake District, G. F. Foster; Sooke District, W. J. Macdonald; Saanich District, John Coles; Salt Spring District, J. J. Southgate; Nanaimo District, A. R. Green. In 1863 Mr. Douglas' term as Governor of the Island expired, and he signified his desire of retiring from public life. His successor was appointed in the person of Captain Kennedy, and Mr. Douglas was rewarded for his services to the crown by the distinction of Knighthood. The people of the Island also testified their high regard for his personal character and administrative abilities by the presentation of largely signed addresses and by banqueting him. Kennedy held the Governorship until 1866, when the union of the colonies abolished his office. By the Act of Union, which was proclaimed on November 17th, it was provided that the Legislative Council should consist of twenty-three members. In 1868, at the urgent solicitation of the colonists of both the Island and the Mainland, the capital was transferred from New Westminster to Victoria and has since continued there.

With the consolidation of the two colonies British Columbia's outlook was of the most bright and hopeful character. Her immense resources had been recognized by the world. Her mineral wealth was being developed as rapidly as the character of the country would admit. Her vast tracks of unsurpassed agricultural lands were being settled upon by intelligent and industrious farmers. Her riches in timber and fish were attracting the attention of capitalists, and already mills were in operation and supplying distant markets. Roads were being opened up in all directions, and towns were arising. Well edited newspapers were published at Victoria and New Westminster, a system of education existed in the more thickly populated districts, and throughout the entire colony the power of the law was supreme. In the two leading cities the value of land was rapidly increasing, commodious hotels had been built for the accommodation of the travelling public, banking houses were doing large businesses, and everywhere signs of prosperity were visible. Between the years 1861 and 1865 the excitement over discoveries of immense deposits of gold in Cariboo continued without cessation. During the latter part of 1859 prospectors had pushed their way along the Quesnelle and Swift Rivers and reported the existence, in abundance, of coarser gold than previously found. In 1860 the riches of the number of creeks now famous in the mining history of the country were demonstrated, and when, early in 1861, reports were confirmed of the great wealth of Antler Creek, a rush for that region at once took place. Before the close of the summer all the streams tributary to the rivers of Cariboo had been explored and in the beds of nearly all wonderful deposits were found to exist. The effect of these discoveries was beneficial to the whole colony, and gave a fresh impetus to business on the coast. During 1861 over three million dollars were taken out of Keithley, Harvey, Antler, Lowhee and Cunningham Creeks, and in 1862, with the fresh influx of miners and the further development of the country, this amount was greatly increased. By the end of 1862 as many as five thousand miners were distributed over about sixty miles of country. In 1862 Williams and Lightning Creeks, the former the richest of all the streams of Cariboo, were discovered, and the excitement among the miners was intensified by the amount of gold which they yielded. The system of mining pursued in the Cariboo region was different to that on the Fraser, owing to the fact that whereas on the Fraser the dust lay practically on the surface, in the streams of Cariboo it was many feet below the river bed. Shafts, pumps, and hoisting machinery, had therefore to be employed here, and large sums had often to be expended in the development of a claim. In the great majority of instances, however, the returns warranted any reasonable outlay. It was not an uncommon thing for men to make four or five hundred dollars per day, and many made a great deal more. At various times as much as $600, and even as high as $900, were taken out of Williams Creek in a single pan. Large fortunes were thus made very rapidly, and it is estimated that one-third of those who went early in 1860 came out with handsome fortunes, and another third with moderate means. By the end of 1867 over twenty-five million dollars had been shipped from the entire region. A number of towns sprang up during the period between 1861 and 1865, but as they were in most instances situated at some largely paying claim they declined with the claim. Barkerville, on Williams Creek, became recognized as the centre of the mining region, and increased rapidly in population and has since continued to be the capital of the Cariboo country.

In 1863 some excitement was occasioned by the reported discovery of rich diggings on the Kootenay River, and a large number of miners, including not a few fifty-eighters, went to the scene of the reported "finds." By the end of the year about one thousand men were distributed along the river, and were making wages averaging from three to fifty dollars each. During the next year prospectors reached Big Bend, on the Columbia River, and early in the succeeding spring reports were carried to Victoria that discoveries equal to those of Cariboo had been made at this point. These reports were readily believed and a rush thither accordingly took place during the next year. A considerable amount of money was taken out during this and the following year, but nothing was found comparable to the richness of Cariboo. Big Bend was, fortunately, of such easy access that provisions could be brought into the camps in abundance and the miners were, therefore, able to live cheaply. Had this not been the case it would have been impossible for the large number of people, who, during 1866 and 1867 thronged there, to have existed. While some of the claims "panned out" richly the majority of the prospectors got little or nothing and left the mines considerably poorer in pocket than they were on reaching them. These men, of course, had nothing favorable to say of the country and their reports were instrumental in calming the excitement. One drawback to the ordinary prospector in the Big Bend country was that the better claims were not as shallow as had been supposed but required machinery and much labor of an expensive nature which only those having money could afford to pay for. However, those who were in a position to expend considerable sums in opening up good claims made large returns.

During the first two years of mining on the Columbia a considerable number of people lost their lives on the river through their ignorance of the dangerous rapids which exist in many places and especially at Dallis des Morts, which received its lugubrious name from the extreme danger there was in passing it. In one instance a boat filled with twenty-five men was capsized here and twenty of the passengers drowned. Until 1875 mining was carried on here by a number of white men but the majority of diggers were Chinamen many of whom are still making fair wages at the same place. Simultaneous with the discoveries on the Columbia the opulence of Omineca began to be unfolded, and Artic, Vitell's, Manson and Germansen creeks gave further assurance of the golden character of the British Columbian streams. And pushing further north prospectors found in the Stikeen River, in Cassiar, yet another mining field which, during 1874 and 1875, yielded good returns for the labor expended on it.

HON. CLEMENT F. CORNWALL.

THE PROVINCE of BRITISH COLUMBIA.

The question of confederation with the Dominion became a living issue in the colony in 1867. It was first brought to the front by the leading men on the Mainland, who were unanimously in favor of it, and it also found many advocates in Victoria. During the session of 1867 it was brought up in the Legislative Council, when a resolution was unanimously adopted requesting Governor Seymour "to take measures without delay to secure the admission of British Columbia into the confederation on fair and equitable terms." No action in conformity with the expressed wish of the Council, however, was taken by the executive, and in consequence, when the House met in the following year, the question was in the same condition that it had been the session previous. The opinion of the members of the Government had during the twelvemonth entirely changed, and when the matter was again brought forward it met with overwhelming opposition. In consequence of this action of the Executive Council and its supporters, agitation outside the Legislature was resorted to, and the people of the country were called upon to express their views on the question. On the 21st of May, 1868, a large meeting was held in Smith's hall in the city of Victoria and an organization known as the Confederation League was formed for the purpose of furthering confederation. James Trimble, Mayor of Victoria, was made President, and Captain E. Stamp, Dr. I. W. Powell and J. F. McCreight, first, second and third Vice-Presidents; Robert Beaven, Recording Secretary; J. G. Norris, Financial Secretary, and George Pearkes, R. Wallace, C. Gowan, M. W. Gibbs, Amor DeCosmos and George Fox, the Executive Committee. The League began with a membership of one hundred in Victoria, and branches were organized at many places on the Mainland and at several places on the Island. The work of the active members of the organization brought out the arguments and energy of the opposition element, and quite a heated discussion took place through the newspapers. Dr. Helmcken was recognized as the champion of the anti-federationists, and he wrote many telling articles on the question, which did not fail to have their effect. On September 14th at Yale a convention of the League was held, at which most of the leading men of the colony were present, and a committee composed of Hon. Amor DeCosmos, Messrs. McMillan, Wallace and Norris, of Victoria; Hon. John Robson, of New Westminster; and Hon. Hugh Nelson, of Burrard Inlet, was appointed to carry out the objects of the convention. At the meeting of the Legislature of 1869 the question was again brought forward and again the Government showed its power by carrying the following adverse resolution: "That this Council, impressed with the conviction that under existing circumstances the confederation of this colony with the Dominion of Canada would be undesirable, even if practicable, urge upon Her Majesty's Government not to take any steps towards the present consummation of such union."

Next day a protest against the passage of this resolution was entered by the Mainland members, Messrs. Carrall, Robson, Havelock, Walkem and Humphreys, who stated that they had been returned as federationists, and must place on record their disapproval of the action of the Government. At this time there was considerable talk about annexation to the United States, and a petition, circulated and signed chiefly by American residents, was presented to the President praying for admission to the Union. While there was no desire on the part of any number of genuine British subjects for other than British rule, some of the anti-federationists used the annexation cry for political reasons. In June of 1869 Governor Seymour died at Victoria, and Anthony Musgrove was appointed to the vacant position. Governor Musgrove's instructions were to bring about confederation as speedily as possible in conformity with the Imperial policy, and with what was now clearly recognized as the desire of the great majority of the people of British Columbia. Governor Musgrove was admirably fitted for the work of reconciling the opposing elements, and his efforts were easily successful. In his inaugural address he said that Her Majesty's Government had no desire to urge confederation with the Dominion against the wishes of the people of British Columbia, but he expressed the conviction that under certain conditions the colony might derive substantial benefit from the Union. A scheme embodying such conditions he had, with the advice of his Executive, prepared and would submit for the consideration of the Council. The resolutions were passed and a delegation, comprised of Hon. J. S. Hehucken, Hon. Joseph W. Trutch and Hon. R. W. W. Carrall, were sent to Ottawa to arrange with the Dominion Government the terms of confederation. In the session of 1871 the report of the Privy Council of Canada upon the matter was laid before the Legislature and the terms were accepted. An address was therefore passed to Her Majesty praying for admission to the Dominion in accordance with the provisions of the British North America Act of 1867. By the Terms of Union, Canada was made liable for the debts and obligations of the Colony of British Columbia. The liabilities of the provinces then constituting the Dominion, being greatly in excess of those of British Columbia, the latter was to be entitled to interest at the rate of five per cent. per annum on the difference between her debt and that of Nova Scotia and New Brunswick, pro ratio of their population. A subsidy of $35,000 a year for the support of her Government and Legislature were to be paid, together with a grant of eighty cents per capita of the population, then estimated at 60,000, such grant to increase with the number of inhabitants till that number should have reached 400,000, after which the grant would not further be increased. The Federal Government was to provide a fortnightly mail service between Victoria and San Francisco by steamer, and twice a week between Victoria and Olympia. The Dominion was to defray all charges which, according to the British North America Act, pertain to the general Government, and pension those whose positions and emoluments would be affected by the change. The province was to be represented in the Senate of the Dominion by three members, and in the Commons by six, this representation to be increased according to the growth of the population. The Government of Canada undertook to secure the commencement, simultaneously, within two years from the date of the Union of the construction of a railway from the Pacific towards the Rocky Mountains, and from such point as might be selected east of the Rocky Mountains towards the Pacific, to connect the seaboard of British Columbia with the railroad system of Canada, and further to secure the completion of such railway within ten years from the date of the Union. The Government of British Columbia agreed to convey to the Dominion Government, in trust, to be appropriated in such manner as the Dominion Government might deem advisable in furtherance of the construction of the said railway, a similar extent of the public lands along the line of railway throughout its entire length in British Columbia, not to exceed, however, twenty miles on each side of said line, as might be appropriated for the same purpose by the Dominion Government from public lands in the North West Territories and the Province of Manitoba. In consideration of the land to be so conveyed in aid of the construction of the said railway, the Dominion Government agreed to pay to British Columbia from the date of the Union the sum of $100,000 per annum, in half-yearly payments, in advance. The Dominion Government also guaranteed the interest for ten years from the date of the completion of the work at the rate of five per cent. per annum on such sum, not exceeding £100,000 sterling, as might be required for the construction of a first-class graving-dock at Esquimalt. The Indians were taken under the care of the Federal Government. These terms took effect on the 20th of July, 1871, and on the 14th of February the Constitution Act was passed abolishing the Legislative Council and substituting in its stead a Legislative Assembly, to be elected once in four years, and to consist of twenty-five members chosen by twelve electoral districts.

That condition in the terms of confederation which was regarded as the most important and the one, the fulfillment of which alone could bind the new Province to the Dominion, was, of course, the construction of a line of railway from the Atlantic to the Pacific ocean. The value of such a railway had before this time suggested itself to the minds of both Imperial and Colonial statesmen, but the magnitude of the project to the majority of men was an absolute demonstration of the impossibility of its accomplishment. There were, however, a few dreamers, as they were termed, who clung tenaciously to the opinion that in order to preserve to England her possessions on the Pacific an interoceanic system of communication would have to be built. When the construction of the road was, by the terms of union, agreed upon, neither the Dominion nor Provincial authorities had any accurate knowledge of the difficulties which would have to be surmounted, but as it lay with the Dominion to accept or reject British Columbia with the railway as a necessary part of the conditions of federation, the Macdonald ministry took the chances of being able, with what aid they could obtain from the Home Government and English capitalists, to carry out the project. Their ultimate success is one of the marvels of the age.

HON. FORBES VERNON.

Hon. Joseph W. Trutch was appointed Lieutenant-Governor of the new Province, and under the new constitution the first election for members of the Legislative Assembly of British Columbia took place in October, 1871. To that Assembly the following members were returned: Cariboo—Hon. George A. Walkem, Joseph Hunter, Cornelius Booth; Comox—John Ash, M.D.; Cowichan—Wm. Smithe, John Paton Booth; Esquimalt—A. Rocke Robertson Henry Cogan; Kootenay—John Andrew Mara, Charles Todd; Lillooet—Andrew F. Jamieson, T. B. Humphreys; Nanaimo—John Robson; New Westminster City—Henry Holbrook; New Westminster District—Joseph Charles Hughes, Wm. Armstrong; Victoria City—Robert Beaven, John Foster McCreight, Simeon Duck, James Trimble, M.D.; Victoria District—Amor DeCosmos, Arthur Bunster; Yale—Robert Smith, James Robinson, Charles A. Semlin. The Assembly met on the 15th of February, 1872, and Mr. J. F. McCreight was called upon to form a Cabinet. He accepted the task and his Ministry consisted of A. Rocke Robertson, Provincial Secretary; Henry Holbrook, Chief Commissioner of Lands and Works, and Geo. A. Walkem, Minister of Finance, the Premier himself taking office as Attorney-General. During the existence of this Government the permanent civil list, created by the last Council of the colony, and amounting to $78,346.25, was abolished, and for the future it was decided that bills should be brought in yearly for defraying this expense. The Canadian Tariff was adopted by the Assembly, and the system of education altered and placed on a better footing. Early next session the Government was defeated on a want of confidence motion, and Mr DeCosmos formed a coaliton Cabinet, composed of Messrs. Walkem, Beaven, Ash and Armstrong. This Government continued till the 13th of February, 1872, when, in consequence of the abolition of dual representation, Mr. DeCosmos resigned his seat in the Assembly and retained that in the House of Commons. Mr. Walkem then took the Premiership, the members of the DeCosmos Ministry still retaining office. In 1873 the Pacific Railway question began to give trouble, and continued until 1880 to occupy the closest attention of each succeeding Government. Immediately after the ratification of the terms of union the work of exploration and survey began, but at the expiration of the time for the commencement of construction, namely, on the 1st of July, 1873, only such exploratory surveys had been made in

British Columbia as were required to determine the direction in which the experimental surveys should be carried on. In 1872, in the House of Commons, Sir George E. Cartier introduced a bill by which it was proposed to grant a subsidy of $30,000,000, together with fifty million acres of land, for the construction of a railway from Lake Nipissing to the Pacific coast. The Government was authorized to come to an agreement with a single company for the construction of the entire line, provided that such company possessed a capital of $10,000,000, of which ten per cent. must be deposited with the Receiver-General. The bill met with the approval of Parliament and a charter was given to an amalgamated company, with Sir Hugh Allan as its head, and among its members some of the wealthiest men of Victoria. Sir Hugh Allan then went to London to borrow the money necessary to carry out the undertaking. In this, however, he failed of success. To enter on a description of the trouble which at this time occurred in Dominion politics over the sale of the charter to the Allan company would be useless. Every school-boy knows the history of the Pacific scandal. The Macdonald Government was defeated and an administration was formed by Hon. Alexander Mackenzie. Previous to this change in the management of affairs, however, the Government of British Columbia had been notified that Esquimalt had been selected as the terminus of the railway, and the subsequent alteration in this respect continued to be a fruitful source of bitterness and contention. When Mr. Mackenzie came into power he refused to comply with the terms made by the preceding Government, and sent a lawyer named Edgar to British Columbia to negotiate new terms. Mr. Edgar's mission was, however, unsuccessful, owing to the fact that he had come without proper credentials; and on his recall Lieut.-Governor Trutch complained to the Imperial Government that a breach of contract had been committed by the Federal authorities in failing to carry out the terms of confederation.

In 1874 Mr. MacKenzie introduced his Pacific Railway Bill by which the line was divided into four sections; the first extending from lake Nipissing to the west end of lake Superior; the second from lake Superior to Red River, in Manitoba; the third from Red River to some point between Fort Edmonton and the Rocky Mountains; the fourth from the western terminus of the third section to some point in British Columbia. The Government was to be at liberty to divide any of these sections into sub-sections, and might at its discretion construct the line or any part of it as a public work. The MacKenzie Government declined to accept Esquimalt as the terminus of the railway, and made other alterations in the plans of construction, which did not satisfy the Provincial legislators, who made another appeal to the Imperial authorities. Matters between the two Governments went from bad to worse and a rupture seemed imminent. In June 1874, when feeling ran highest, Earl Carnarvon consented to arbitrate between the two parties and the terms known as the "Carnarvon terms" were accepted by both the Dominion and Provincial Governments. The immediate construction of a railway on Vancouver Island, from Esquimalt to Nanaimo was one of the clauses of this agreement, but when a Bill for this purpose was brought into the Dominion Parliament it was defeated by a majority of the Senate. Consequent upon this further delay arose and increased complaints from British Columbia. Her Majesty was again memorialized of the breach of faith on the part of the federal authorities and separation was loudly threatened. It was at this time that Lord Dufferin, then Governor-General of the Dominion, paid his memorable visit to the Pacific Province for the purpose of seeing what he could do to allay the discontent which existed. His Excellency's efforts were certainly not without good results. He brought into play all those happy gifts with which he is so plentifully endowed and left a lasting impression of his personal accomplishments and genial traits as well as appreciably mitigating the acerbity of the Provincial temper. His anxiety for a settlement of the trouble did not, however, seem to be shared by the Dominion Cabinet, and the opportunity which certainly offered itself at that time of coming to a good understanding was permitted, through the dilatoriness and incapacity of his ministers, to slip by. Matters continued to grow worse and relations more strained till 1878, when a petition was forwarded to the Queen asking that the Province be permitted to withdraw from the union, unless the Carnarvon terms were carried out before the first of May. There was also some talk of annexation, but this was confined to the American residents at Victoria. It was fortunate for all parties concerned that at this juncture a change took place in the Federal administration. At the general election of 1878 the MacKenzie Government was defeated and when the House assembled Sir John Macdonald was again called to the head of affairs. The desire he displayed to carry through the gigantic project restored confidence throughout the province and the determination evinced by the Walkem-Beaven Government that no rest should be permitted the Federal authorities till the work was begun, met with general approbation. A definite pledge was given on the 26th of April, 1878, that the work of construction in British Columbia would be begun that season and pushed vigorously. Sir John Macdonald's Government was, however, apparently unwilling to acquiesce in the selection of the Fraser River Route made by its predecessor, and surveyors were sent out to look for a northern route. The search, however, was fruitless of results, and Mr. MacKenzie's selection was finally adopted, with Port Moody on Burrard Inlet as the terminal point. The Government at once awarded the contract for the construction of the line from Emory's Bar to Savona to Mr. Onderdonk, and early next season work was commenced on this section and pushed forward with wonderful energy. The Provincial Government, however, was not satisfied with this. They desired to see the work on the section between Emory's Bar and Port Moody and also the line on the Island begun, and in 1880 Hon. Amor De Cosmos, M.P., was authorized to press this matter and the loss to the Province by delay upon the Federal authorities. He did so, but failing to obtain any reply of a satisfactory nature, he was commissioned by the Provincial Legislature in 1881 to go to London and present a petition upon the subject to the Queen. The result of his efforts here consisted in an opinion offered by the Secretary of State, Earl Kimberley, as a basis for a settlement of the whole question. The basis proposed by Kimberley were: the construction of a light line of railway from Esquimalt to Nanaimo; the extension without delay of the line to Port Moody; and the grant of reasonable compensation in money for the failure to complete the work within the term of ten years, as specified in the conditions of union. During this time the work of construction above Emory's Bar was being pressed forward. From the beginning of the work in 1880 there had been a small army of over seven thousand men steadily employed. This portion of the line presented difficulties unequalled in the history of railway building on this continent and it is estimated that in some parts as much as $300,000 per mile was expended on it. Several tunnels were bored at an enormous outlay and the construction of the cantaliver bridge across the Fraser below Lytton was a marvellous feat of engineering workmanship.

Meanwhile in strictly local politics changes had taken place. In the general election of 1875 the Province returned a majority against Mr. Walkem's Government, and Hon. A. C. Elliott formed an administration consisting of F. G. Vernon, T. B. Humphreys, E. Brown and A. E. B. Davie. When the Ministers returned to the country for re-election Mr. Davie was defeated. This Government existed for two and a half years. In 1878 it introduced a measure for a re-distribution of seats and an increase of the number of representatives to thirty-five. The Bill was thrown out, and an appeal was made to the country with the result that the Elliott party were defeated. Mr. Walkem was again called upon to form a Cabinet, and Messrs Beaven, Hett and Humphreys joined him in the Government. It was during this administration that the Province took such a determined stand on the question of constructing the Canadian Pacific Railway without further delay, and there is no doubt that the resolute attitude of the Legislature at that time had a great deal to do with the subsequent energy displayed by the Dominion Government in this respect. During this Government's existence, also, the construction of the Dry Dock at Esquimalt was begun. In 1882 Mr. Walkem was elevated to the bench and Hon. Robert Beaven became premier. The opposition, however, carried a majority of the constituencies at the election which ensued a few months later, and Hon. Wm. Smithe formed a Cabinet composed of Hon. A. E. B. Davie, Hon. John Robson and M. W. T. Drake. In the first year of this administration the Settlement Act was passed, by which all questions between the Province and the Dominion were finally disposed of. By this Act a subsidy of $750,000 was given by the Dominion Government for the construction of the Island Railway. This, together with a most liberal grant of land from the Provincial Government, was sufficient inducement to capitalists to undertake the project, and a Company, of which Mr. Robert Dunsmuir was the head, obtained the charter for the line, which was to extend from Esquimalt to Nanaimo. The work was begun at once and was completed before the time specified in the contract. It is possible that in the near future this Railway will be extended to the extreme north of the Island, and there is little doubt that had Hon. Robert Dunsmuir lived the work would have been begun during the present year. During this time work on the construction of the Canadian Pacific Railway was being pushed forward with unremitting vigor, and early in 1885 the line was complete from Montreal to Port Moody, the last rail having been laid at Eagle Pass. Contrary to the expectations of a great many persons who invested their money in property at Port Moody, the terminus of the line was changed to Coal Harbor, on which the City of Vancouver now stands. This was in consequence of the insufficient accommodation afforded at Port Moody for shipping purposes. At Coal Harbor not only was there unlimited accommodation in this respect, but the Inlet at this point was so broad and deep, and so completely land locked, that it afforded a harborage for vessels second to none on the coast.

With the completion of this mighty work—this national transcontinental highway—a new era dawned for British Columbia; new blood and fresh energy was infused into the body politic and the possibilities of successful development became less uncertain and less difficult of accomplishment. Along the line of railway, at favorable points, the nuclei of future towns were laid during the period of construction, many of which have already become places of some importance and must, with the continued settlement of the Province, attain large proportions. Business on the coast increased at once, and the population of the cities doubled in a few months. Among the thousands who crowded into the country immediately after the completion of the railway were many of the shrewdest men of the east. A majority of these remained in Vancouver, the terminus of the railway, a town whose growth and prosperity have been unexampled in the history of Canadian cities. From a village of two hundred persons in 1886 it has become a city of eighteen thousand in 1890. On the 14th of June, 1886, the town, then rapidly progressing, was completely destroyed by fire and three thousand people were left without a shelter, but with that energy which has since marked its existence, the inhabitants set to work to erect better structures on the sites of their ruined dwellings. When the nature of the British Columbia forests are considered, and it is remembered that the site of the now handsome City of Vancouver was three years ago covered with dense underbrush and mighty trees, the energy displayed by the inhabitants will be regarded as little less than marvellous. In 1887 the railway was extended from Port Moody to Vancouver, and a line of steamships was provided to run from the terminus of the route to Japan and China. The advantages of

F. J. BARNARD.

this route to and from Australia, India and China, over the American lines are easily apparent, and there is little doubt they will commend themselves to the commercial world. While the stimulus imparted by the completion of the through line of railway was largely confined for the first year to the cities, where fortunes were made very rapidly, it did not, fortunately for the immediate future of the Province, exhaust itself here. The agricultural districts began to fill up rapidly, or at least those districts where the farmer saw he would have a convenient market for his produce. The rich valley of the Fraser River, where already many settlements existed, especially attracted the agriculturist. The salmon industry, which had already attained large proportions, gained a larger market, and the exhaustless wealth of timber induced the capitalist to place his money where a return in proportion to the judgment exercised in the outlay was assured. An impetus was given to quartz mining, which as yet had been attempted on a very limited scale, and the mountains once more became the haunt of prospectors. As soon as it was placed beyond a doubt that the Canadian Pacific Railway was to be built local companies were formed for the construction of lines which would further open up the country. In 1883 the New Westminster Southern road, which will very soon be an accomplished fact, was projected, and a company was incorporated to build it. The Fraser River Railway Company was also incorporated, and the Columbia and Kootenay Railway Company. In 1885, also, a company was formed for the purpose of building the Shuswap and Okanagan Railway, to connect with the Canadian Pacific Railway, and open up the Okanagan and Spallumcheen valley. This district, which contains, perhaps, for mixed farming, and especially for wheat growing, the finest land in the Dominion, was very little known at that time, (and indeed this may be said of a great portion of the country), and the efforts of the projectors of this railway were met with opposition, both in the local and Dominion Parliaments. The persistent labor, however, of one or two men, who knew the value to the Province of settling and developing this tract of country, finally triumphed over the adverse stand taken by the legislature, and this year will see the commencement of this line.

The Province as she now exists is among the most promising and valuable members of confederation, and her people are fully alive to the greatness of their possession. Their representatives in the local and federal parliaments are men of ripe experience and large acquaintance with the country's possibilities and requirements, and whose personal interests are bound up with the welfare and progress of the Province. The representation in both Houses, which has remained as it was fixed at confederation, will be immediately increased in proportion to the increase in population.

In its efforts to advance the material prosperity of the Province, the Government has not lost sight of that which alone can support through a period of generations the stability of the state. It has ever since the date of Confederation been the especial care of each succeeding Government to make the most liberal provisions for educational purposes, and to create a school system which should be second to none on the continent. Hon. Mr. Beaven devoted, during the period of his administration, a great deal of thought to this question, and the educational system as it exists to-day is partly his workmanship. During the past four years Hon. John Robson. Premier and Provincial Secretary, has taken charge of this department of the Government and, with the assistance of the Educational Superintendent, Mr. S. D. Pope, has made a great many improvements of much value, and got the system into the most perfect and admirable working order. To-day there is not in the whole Province a community which has not easy access to all the advantages which this system of free public education affords. The system of British Columbia combines many of the excellencies of that of Ontario, as well as those of the maritime provinces. The most conspicuous differences between the system of British Columbia and that of Ontario, are that the former is strictly non-sectarian and provides more liberally than the latter, inasmuch as not only are school sites and school buildings paid for directly from the Provincial treasury, but the salaries of the teachers and all incidental expenses connected with the operation of the schools are paid from the same source. As an evidence of the increasing prosperity of the country at large it may be stated that provision has been made for the salaries of nearly 200 teachers, amounting to $150,000, and school buildings amounting to $50,000. There are at present four high schools in the province, one in each of the four principal cities, viz.: Victoria, Vancouver, New Westminster, and Nanaimo. Each of these schools is well equipped with efficient teachers. There are also throughout the province eleven graded schools, four ward schools and one hundred and ten rural schools. The high schools are fed from the graded and rural schools. The course of study prescribed in the rural and graded schools embraces besides the elementary branches some of the more advanced departments in mathematics and natural science. The growth of the schools since the period of Confederation has been great indeed, as will be at once apparent by glancing over the following comparative statement taken from the last annual report of the Superintendent:

Year.	Number of School Districts.	Aggregate Enrolment.	Expenditure for Education Proper.
1872-73	25	1,028	$ 36,763 77
1873-74	37	1,245	35,287 59
1874-75	41	1,403	34,822 28
1875-76	41	1,685	44,506 11
1876-77	42	1,998	47,129 63
1877-78	45	2,198	43,334 01
1878-79	45	2,301	22,110 70
1879-80	47	2,462	47,006 10
1880-81	48	2,571	46,960 68
1881-82	50	2,653	49,268 63
1882-83	59	2,693	50,850 63
1883-84	67	3,420	66,655 15
1884-85	76	4,027	71,151 52
1885-86	86	4,471	79,527 56
1886-87	95	5,345	88,521 08
1887-88	104	6,372	99,902 04
1888-89	109	6,796	108,190 59

Mr. Pope, the provincial superintendent, is keenly alive to the importance of stimulating, by every possible means, the pupils to study and thereby awakening in them a thirst for learning, and his efforts have met with an abundant success. The annual examinations for the granting of certificates to teachers are of a stringent character and the standard of efficiency is quite equal to that of any other province and certainly superior to most. The examinations are held simultaneously at Kamloops and Victoria by a Board of Examiners appointed by the Lieutenant-Governor to assist the superintendent. Graduates from other provinces are exempt in British

Columbia from examinations in other than professional subjects. Every graduate is required, however, to satisfy the examiners that he has a good knowledge of the art of teaching and school management as well as being thoroughly versed in the regulations and school law of the province. While the system of education is strictly non-sectarian it is an instruction to the teacher that the highest morality should be inculcated. The crowning point of the public school system of the province of British Columbia will be reached by the establishment of a university, legislation for which was a portion of the work of the local parliament at its recent session. A normal school for the training of teachers will be an appendage to the university.

Among the subjects which, in this necessarily brief and imperfect outline, I have left untouched, are the Indian question and the progress of missionary work among the native tribes. As I have stated previously there has been little difficulty in the management of the Indians from the earliest time, and the few tragic occurences which took place during the early days of mining history were the result not so much of native hostility to the presence of the white intruder as of that spirit of arrogance and wanton cruelty which actuated the more abandoned adventurers from California in their dealings with the aboriginal inhabitants. The natives had, through a long course of years of intimate business relations with the Hudson's Bay Company's agents, been led to repose confidence in the trader, and this confidence they would also have given to the miner, as they have since to the settler, had they not been outraged by the treatment they received. Since that period, however, under the just and kindly care of the Government they have lived contented and peaceful lives. The condition of a great number of the natives throughout British Columbia to-day is a proof of what can be accomplished among savage peoples by civilizing influences properly employed. They have, in a large measure, except in the northern portion of the Province, accepted the white man's mode of living, and thousands of them are industrious citizens. Through the upper country many of them have taken to farming and cattle raising, and have prospered side by side with the white settlers. In British Columbia the Indian title to land has, under colonial or provincial rule, never been conceded, and to the world at large, especially to the English world, this may savor of injustice. But when the primitive condition of the tribes here is considered, and it is remembered that all the modes of obtaining their food employed before they were disturbed in their wilds by the Europeans, are still as much open to them as in their most savage days, the loss of their lands, which they never cultivated, it will be admitted, cannot be considered as a hardship. The restrictions imposed upon the other inhabitants, in regard to hunting and fishing, are not intended to apply to the Indians, and they therefore have, at all seasons of the year, the same absolute freedom their forefathers possessed in obtaining their food supply. Of late years they have displayed a commendable desire to educate their children and acquire the knowledge which has given the white man his power.

The earliest missionaries in British Columbia, as elsewhere on this coast, and one might say on this continent, were the agents of the Jesuite order. In 1843, when James Douglas first landed at Camosun to establish the fort there, a Jesuit father accompanied him, and previous to this time a number of agents of the same order had been all along the coast as far up as Fort Simpson. These indefatigable men, although courting death at every turn, and persevering undauntedly in their mission among the savages, do not seem to have accomplished much beyond inspiring the natives with a respect for their persons, and baptising indiscriminately large numbers of savages totally ignorant of the meaning attached to the ceremony to which they passively submitted, or indeed, of the most elementary principles of the religion into which they had just been received. The same order also established missions in the interior among the Kootenay tribes, in the Okanagan district and in the Chilkotin country. In the year 1858 Mr. Wm. Duncan, who established the celebrated mission at Metlakahtla, arrived at Victoria as the agent of the London Church Missionary Society. He was a man of indomitable will, who regarded himself as having received a divine call to the work. He went about his labors in a practical level-headed manner, and the success which attended him almost from the beginning was beyond all expectation. Having thoroughly mastered the language of the tribe he delivered his message to them in their own tongue. He settled among them as one of themselves and, after obtaining an influence over them, he started various industries. Thus, at the same time that he ministered to their spiritual needs he broke up their tribal system and taught them handicraft trades. In short he raised them in the material as well as spiritual scale of humanity. His mission has been attended with greater success than any on this continent, and might be taken by the church as an example of what can be done by adopting the same system which he pursued. A large number of other agents were sent out by the same society and following these came regularly appointed ministers of the various denominations. The Hudson's Bay Company from the first gave every assistance possible to these Christian teachers without respect to their creed. From the year 1858 the city of Victoria was well supplied with ministers of the gospel, who, while they did not face the sufferings and danger experienced by those who ventured among the savages, had nothing of the studious ease enjoyed by the clergy of the present day. Among earliest and most zealous workers in the cause of religion in the Province were Rev. Bishop Cridge, of Victoria, and Rev. E. Robson, now stationed at Vancouver.

Among the present population of British Columbia is a large number of Chinamen and here as in California the question of how to deal with this class of immigrants has for the past ten years exercised the minds of those having at heart the best interests of the province. With the excitement over the discovery of gold in 1858 hundreds of these Asiatics crowded into the country with the European adventurers and spread themselves along the Fraser and Thompson rivers. They were regarded with aversion not only by the whites but by the Indians, but as in this country "sufferance is the badge of all their race" they were content to put up with contumely so long as they were not subjected to personal violence. They were excellent miners, possessing more patience and no less skill in the work than their white co-laborers, and being able to subsist on less food and that of a coarser kind they often found excellent claims which had been passed over by the others in their impatience to push further north where, it was reported, coarser gold existed in great abundance, and obtainable with no greater labor than on the lower parts of the River Fraser. During the trouble with the Indians in the early part of 1858 it was suspected that the Chinese were in league with the natives, were fomenting the rage of the savages and wherever possible supplying them ammunition for their intended struggle with the white miners. In 1861 there were between fifteen hundred and two thousand

Chinese in and about Yale alone and there must have been nearly an equal number throughout the rest of the province. Their presence or their number did not at this time nor for nearly twenty years afterwards attract the thoughtful attention of the people. It was at Victoria, where their labor was brought into competition with that of white men, that the baneful effect of their presence was first clearly recognised and almost immediately an agitation for their exclusion from the province was begun. The representatives of the city in the Dominion parliament urged the government to pass restrictive legislation, and the people of Victoria organized an anti-Chinese league the object of which was to keep alive the agitation till such legislation had been accomplished. As was to be expected the administration demurred at carrying out the full wishes of the province but in 1884, by persistent effort, a bill was obtained imposing a tax of fifty dollars on every Chinaman entering the country. Previous to this, however, the work of construction on the Canadian Pacific Railway had been commenced and thousands of coolies were brought into the country and employed by the contractors. At one time as many as six thousand five hundred of these Chinese laborers were at work on the different sections in the province. There is little doubt but that the people of British Columbia are unanimous on the Chinese question and if it lay with the province to determine its settlement there would be no further immigration of this race. Those at present in the province are engaged in almost every business and are the very worst class of citizens which a country could possess. Not only do they compete with male but also with female workers and in every instance they sell their labor at a price which would not provide the white man with food. Whatever locality they live in becomes at once a pollution where every imaginable disease is fostered and where every vice is nourished. Whatever respect they have for the law is simply the offspring of fear and as they know no rule of morality they are capable of any crime against society. Wherever possible they avoid the payment of taxes and they are amongst the most expert and successful smugglers on the coast. The eastern provinces have not experienced their baneful influence and are therefore unable to thoroughly understand or appreciate the vital necessity there was for British Columbia ridding itself at least in part of this blight upon the country's prosperity.

During the past three years the destiny of the Province has been shaped by the Davie and Robson Governments, and the marked progress it has made has been largely owing to their wise and liberal administrations. In 1889 Hon. A. E. B. Davie, the Premier, died, and Hon. John Robson was called upon to form a Ministry. Since he has been at the head of affairs he has made it his chief endeavor to induce the settlement of agriculturists in the country, and for this purpose public lands have been thrown open on the most liberal terms, and every assistance afforded to intending settlers. Industries also have been cherished, and provision on a large scale made for survey and exploration of those portions of the Province concerning which as yet little knowledge of an exact nature has been obtained. In view of the new footing on which the relations between Japan and Canada have been placed by the construction of the railway and the steamship service, a Japanese Consul has been appointed to look after the interest of that country. For this office one of the most distinguished subjects of His Japanese Majesty has been chosen in the person of Mr. Fukashi Sugimura, a scion of the titled military class of that country. Mr. Sugimura, previous to his mission to British Columbia, spent many years of his life in the foreign service of his government. During the revolutionary war in Japan, in 1866, he entered himself as a volunteer and saw active service. In 1871 he went to Tokio, where he spent three years in the study of Chinese sciences and international law. He then accompanied the Japanese army to Formosa, when that island was invaded, and spent the greater portion of the year there. During the civil war of 1877, in Japan, Mr. Sugimura contributed a series of articles from the seat of war to the Yokohama "Daily News," and at the termination of the war he assumed the editorship of the same paper. In 1880 he was appointed a member of the Consulate at Pusan in Corea, and in 1882 became an attache of Legation at Corea. In July of that year an attack was made by the Coreans on the Japanese Legation, and fourteen persons, including officials, students and servants, were slaughtered. Other twenty-four, including the ambassador and Mr. Sugimura, escaped in a junk, and after two days on the ocean they were rescued by the British man-of-war, "Flying Fish." In September of the same year Mr. Sugimara was appointed to the position of Vice-Consul at Themulpo. In 1886 he was made Secretary of Legation at Corea, where he

MARK BATE.

stayed as Charge d'Affairs about seven months. On his return from Corea he acted as Secretary to the Foreign Department till May, 1889, when he came to Vancouver as Consul. Mr. Sugimura is the first consul appointed to a British City. He is a most energetic man and thoroughly adapted to the position which he at present fills.

With the business enterprise for which her people have already made themselves known, with the great natural advantages of her situation, her unexcelled climate and her immense resources, British Columbia cannot fail to fulfil the hopes which her children have formed for her future. At the present time there is a great deal of contention among all the cities north of San Francisco as to which shall stand second to her in commercial importance, and the struggle has done not a little to build up very rapidly the ports on Puget Sound. The foundations of these towns are, however, in many respects, insecure, and the energy which is undoubtedly expended is to a very large extent mis-applied. In British Columbia the activity of the people has been naturally called forth in taking advantage of the wealth with which she abounds. Within her borders is none of that feverish excitement which is so prevalent elsewhere on the coast, and which must necessarily be followed by a state of weakness and collapse. British Columbia is content to proceed with caution, feeling confident that with her own strength added to that of the vast country east of the Rocky Mountains, the issues of the future are with her.

BIOGRAPHICAL SKETCHES.

Abbott, Harry Braithwaite, (Vancouver), son of Rev. Joseph and Harriet Elizabeth Abbott, was born at Abbotsford, Eastern Townships, on June 14th, 1829. His father, who was a graduate of Glasgow University, was sent to Canada by the Society for the Propagation of the Gospel. Mr. Abbott was educated at the high school in Montreal, and subsequently at McGill University. He early displayed a taste for mechanics, and this study he cultivated energetically. In 1847 he received an appointment on the engineering staff of the St. Lawrence and Atlantic (now Grand Trunk) Railway, under Col. C. S. Gzowski, the chief engineer, and was connected with this enterprise till the completion of the line. He was then appointed resident engineer of one of the divisions. In 1857 he, in conjunction with Messrs. Cortland & Freer, took a contract for the maintenance of way of 150 miles of the Grand Trunk Railway. When this contract expired he and Mr. Freer leased the Riviere du Loup section of the G. T. R., which they opened up and conducted with success for one year, after which they took charge of the Carleton and Grenville Railway, in which they had a large interest, and which they remained in charge of till its purchase by the Ottawa River Navigation Company. In 1864 Mr. Abbott assumed the managing directorship and filled the position of chief engineer of the Brockville and Ottawa Railway, and in 1872 he built the Carletonplace and Ottawa branch of the Canada Central Railway. He then held till 1873 the presidency and managing directorship of the Brockville and Ottawa Railway, and managing directorship of the Canada Central. In 1874, in conjunction with Mr. Duncan Macdonald, he constructed a section of the Occidental Railway between Montreal and Ottawa, including the bridges across the Black River and Riviere du Chine. In 1876 he organized the Eastern Extension Railway Company, and was appointed chief engineer and manager of construction. He next year re-assumed the managing directorship of the Brockville and Ottawa and Canada Central

Railways. He retained this position for a year, resigning it to again take charge of the Eastern Extension Railway. In 1882 he was appointed manager of construction of the Sault Ste. Marie branch of the Canadian Pacific Railway, and after completing this work he became manager of construction of the main line west from Sudbury. After completing his division in May, 1885, he laid an additional 75 miles of track. He had charge of this division during the time of the Riel rebellion in the North West Territories, and made all the arrangements for the transmission of troops from the eastern provinces to the seat of the trouble. He was subsequently appointed supervising engineer of the Canadian Pacific Railway, and in 1886 was offered and accepted the appointment of General Superintendent of the Canadian Pacific Railway in British Columbia. In March, 1885, the last spike was driven in the presence of Mr. Abbott, and on July 3rd, 1886, the first train was run from Donald to the terminus on the seaboard, Mr. Abbott being on board in formal charge. In politics Mr. Abbott has always been a strong and consistent Conservative. He stood for the House of Commons for Brockville in 1872 in the interests of his party, but, owing to the fact that during the progress of the campaign he was prostrated with a dangerous illness and could not therefore give his personal attention to the election, he was defeated. During the *Trent* affair he assisted in raising a battalion of infantry in Argenteuil, of which he was gazetted major. He married Margaret Amelia, daughter of Judge Sicotte. In religion Mr. Abbott is an adherent of the Episcopal Church.

Abrams, James Atkinson, (Nanaimo), was born at Napanee, Lennox county, Ontario, on the 11th of November, 1844. He is the second son of Isaiah Abrams, factor of the Sir Richard Cartwright estate. He was educated at the Napanee academy and after leaving school was apprenticed to Stants, Sager & Madden, a firm of tanners at his native place. He remained five years with this firm and in 1862 he left Napanee and went to New York where he spent two years working at his trade. In 1864 he came to the Pacific coast by way of Panama and landed in San Francisco after a thirty-seven days' voyage. He lived for three years in California, working in tanning establishments in San Francisco, Santa Cruz and other towns. In 1867 he came to British Columbia landing in

Victoria with thirty-seven cents in his pocket. He remained in Victoria till 1876 during which period he was foreman in the Rock Bay tannery and afterwards in the Belmont tannery. In 1876 he went to Nanaimo where he started a general store on Commercial street and where he has lived continuously since. In 1878 Mr. Abrams stood as a candidate for the Nanaimo district for the local legislature in the interests of the Walkem Government against Mr. D. W. Gordon, the present member for the Commons. Mr. Abrams was elected by fifteen of a majority. In 1882 he was urged to stand again but refused to do so as he found that his large business made too great demands on his time to permit of his attending to public affairs. In march, 1886, he opened a business in Vancouver in partnership with Mr. McLean, under the firm title of Abrams & McLean, still continuing his business in Nanaimo. In June of the same year the great fire which destroyed the town swept this store and stock out of existence and left them poorer by $16,000. In 1888 Mr. Abrams sold his business in Nanaimo and in the same year his Vancouver partner bought out his share of the business in Vancouver. Mr. Abrams had thus time once more to interest himself in politics and during 1889 he served the city in the council. He refused, however, to stand for the mayoralty. Mr. Abrams is a Justice of the Peace for British Columbia and is president of the Nanaimo tanning company. He has large interests both on the Island and Mainland and is anxious for the development of the province. He is a member of the Masonic body and has occupied the position of Senior Warden in that order; he is also a member of the Ancient Order of United Workmen. He was married on December 11th, 1878, to Miss Georgina Wenborn.

Ackerman, Sheron, Contractor, (New Westminster), was born in Alleghany county, New York, on the 29th of March, 1850. He is the second son of Urastus B. and Annis Bennett Ackerman. His family were among the earliest settlers in New York state having established themselves there before the revolutionary war in which the then living representatives took an active part. Mr. Ackerman's grandfather was a prominent figure in New York during the early part of the century and in the war of 1812 he saw active service. Shortly after Mr. Ackerman's birth his parents removed to Iowa where his father carried on business as a farmer and contractor.

Here he attended school until he reached the age of fifteen years when he began to learn the trade of carpentering. In 1866 the family again removed, this time to Minnesota. Here for ten years Mr. Ackerman followed the trade and during this period he married Miss Agustine Nobles. In 1876 he left Minnesota and went to Kansas where he was engaged in farming for five years. He did not find this life congenial, however, and in the spring of 1881 he went to California where he started business as a contractor. In 1883 he removed to Seattle where he remained for a short time and from which place, in consequence of the representations of his father and brothers who were settled at New Westminster, he came to British Columbia. Since that time he and his brothers have been in the building and contracting business and have been markedly successful. Mr. Ackerman is about to abandon the contracting business and establish a sash and door factory at New Westminster. He is a member of the order of Knights of Pythias and Chancellor Commander of that society. He is holding his second term as chief of the fire department.

Alexander, Richard Henry, (Vancouver), eldest son of James and Eliza Alexander was born at Edinburgh, Scotland, on March 26th 1844. His paternal ancestors came originally from near Stirling and his mother was a member of the well-known border family, the Scots. Mr. Alexander's elementary education was obtained at the Edinburgh academy. In 1855, when he had reached the age of eleven, his parents removed to Canada taking him along with them. The family settled in Toronto and Mr. Alexander's education was continued at the Upper Canada college. He remained at this institution till the Model Grammar school was established, the principalship of which Mr. G. R. R. Cockburn, now member of parliament for Centre Toronto, was brought from Scotland to fill. Mr. Alexander's name was second on the roll of the new school. He carried off several scholarships at this school and graduated in the spring of 1860, being then in his 17th year. A few months later he matriculated at the University of Toronto taking honors in classics. It was his intention to have completed an Arts course at the university and after graduating to have entered on the study of medicine. His calculations in this direction, however, were all overthrown by the death of his mother and the determination of his father to return to

Scotland. Mr. Alexander decided to remain in Canada and resolved to abandon his academic studies and at once begin the work of making his way in life. He obtained a position in the milling office of Mr. W. P. (now Sir W. P.) Howland, at Waterdown near Hamilton. He remained here about a year, leaving at the end of this time to take a position at Meaford in the business of Mr. W. B. Taylor, wheat merchant. In the Spring of 1862 there was quite an excitement in Ontario over the discovery of gold in Cariboo and the Saskatchewan valley and a great deal of talk about organizing parties to go overland to the mines. The people in the east did not then possess a very accurate knowledge of the geography of north western Canada and the distance between these two localities was not regarded as very great. Several of Mr. Alexander's old schoolmates had announced their intention of joining any party which might be formed and as he himself had been pondering deeply over the matter he decided that he also would make one of such an expedition. At length a large party was formed in Toronto and on the 3rd of April, (St. George's day), a start was made on the passage across the continent. Mr. Alexander's immediate friends with whom he shared his tent were two sons of an old country gentleman named Hancock, a brother of professor Hinds and a young barrister named Carpenter. The party travelled by way of St. Paul and after leaving this point directed their course towards Fort Garry. They sailed down the Red River from Georgetown on the first steamer ever placed on that route. It took them six days to accomplish the journey but owing to the social qualities of the passengers the time was anything but tedious. One of the passengers on this trip was the present Archbishop Tache, who, on a visit to the Pacific province last summer, met and remembered Mr. Alexander, after a lapse of nearly twenty years, from having made this trip with him. When the party reached Fort Garry Mr. Alexander and his friends pitched their tent on what is now Main street. At this point the party split up and took different routes. The one with which Mr. Alexander and his friends remained struck due west and crossed the Assiniboine at Fort Ellis, and the south branch of the Saskatchewan at Clarke's Crossing. From here they journeyed on to Fort Edmonton through plains hitherto almost unvisited by white men and still teeming with herds of buffalos and all imaginable species of wild game. On reaching Edmonton another split occurred in the party

(7)

and about twenty-two, of whom Mr. Alexander was one, started for the mountains. They had considerable trouble in crossing the Athabasca but succeeded without any fatality. They entered British Columbia by the Yellowhead pass and up the valley of the Miette. At length they reached a stream flowing westward which proved to be the Fraser. They then hollowed out canoes and came down the river to the mouth of the Quesnelle. On the way Mr. Alexander's friend, Carpenter, with whom he had travelled all the way from Toronto, was drowned in the first canyon. When the party arrived at the mines they found everything frozen up and the majority of them went down the country to New Westminster, which place they reached bankrupt in pocket and expectation. Here Mr. Alexander found any number of people in his own position. He found educated men, accustomed all their lives to the comforts of civilization, engaged in the roughest work of pioneer life. It was these men who laid the foundation on which has been erected the present province of British Columbia. The first work at which Mr. Alexander engaged was chopping cordwood, near New Westminster, and during this period he lived principally on flour, bacon, tea and tobacco. After continuing at this work for some time he got a position in the office of Mr. (now Hon.) John Robson who was conducting the *British Columbian*. Here he remained for some months but in the Spring of 1863 went to Cariboo, engaging as a packer. He mined for a time on William's Creek but in the Autumn returned to Victoria without having had any success and during the winter he worked as a 'longshoresman on the Hudson's Bay Company's wharf. In 1864 he obtained a situation in a wholesale warehouse on Wharf street where he remained till 1870, when he came to Burrard Inlet to take charge of the store at Hasting's saw mill. At this time Captain Raymur was the manager of the mill. The shores of Burrard Inlet wore their fringes of primeval pine and the whitemen who dwelt there could be counted on one's fingers. Shortly after his arrival the company signified its sense of the value of Mr. Alexander's services by promoting him to the position of accountant and on the death of Captain Raymur he was appointed manager. Since that time Mr. Alexander has resided continuously on Burrard Inlet in the position of manager of Hasting's mill. He has been a Justice of the Peace for the province for a long term of years and was a member of the first Granville school Board. When the city of Vancouver was incorporated Mr. Alexander, who possessed large interests in the city, ran for the position of Mayor and was defeated by a small majority. He was a member of the councils for 1887 and 1888 and has for two years past been a member of the Board of Park Commissioners. At the present time he is president of the Pilot Board and also of the Board of Trade of Vancouver. He has very large interests in the district and is keenly concerned in its progress. He is a member of the Masonic body and of the Ancient Order of United Workmen. He married Miss Emma Tammage and has four children.

Anderson, George William, M. P. P., (for Victoria district), farmer, was born May 20th, 1836, at Wooton, near Dorking, Surrey, England. Is the eldest son of John and Amelia La Mott Anderson. Attended school at Dorking until fourteen years old when he was withdrawn to assist his father in the management of his farm. He remained on the farm for a year after which he was apprenticed to the bakery business. For three years he worked at his trade in England and in 1854 he came to America. He resided in New York for two years working at his business and then moved west to Dubuque, Iowa, where he opened out for himself. His business in Dubuque prospered and he remained there for eight years, during which period he married Miss Mary O'Connell, daughter of James O'Connell, merchant, of that town. In the spring of 1864 he sold his business and began speculating in brood mares which were bringing good prices in the California market. Early in the summer he crossed the plains with a large herd of young stock which he disposed of when he reached the coast at excellent prices. He then settled in Grass Valley and again went into the bakery business. In 1869 he disposed of his business at Grass Valley and came to British Columbia where he purchased Ferndale farm, in Lake District, on which he now resides. During 1869 and '70 he made several business trips to California but decided to permanently establish himself at Victoria. He accordingly opened a bakery business here which he personally conducted, at the same time carrying on his farming operations by hired help. Both ventures were eminently successful. In 1882 Mr. Anderson disposed of his business in Victoria and took up his residence on his farm, his chief object in living in the city, the education of his children, having been accomplished. In 1887 he stood for Victoria district as a candidate for the local legislature in the interest of the Smythe Government and was elected with Mr. Robert F. John as colleague. In provincial politics Mr. Anderson is a supporter of the Robson Government, believing that its members have at heart the best interests of the country and that their policy is far-seeing and wise. In Dominion politics he is a Liberal Conservative and an upholder of the Macdonald administration. He is an ardent Imperial Federationist, feeling confident that the great scheme will yet be carried out but that with the colonies will lie the task of making it practicable. On this and other questions affecting the Empire Mr. Anderson occasionally contributes articles to the English press, among the journals for which he writes being the "Colonies and India." Mr. Anderson is a member of the Independent Order of Oddfellows and also of the Foresters. In religion he is an adherent of the Episcopal church.

Andrew, John Alexander, Cashier Hudson's Bay Company, (Victoria), was born at Wallair, Madras Presidency, on the 7th April, 1840. He is the eldest son of the late Dr. Patrick Alexander Andrew, of the Hon. East India Company, Madras establishment. His ancestors for generations were faithful and distinguished servants of the same Hon. Company and some of them have been mentioned with distinction in the history of India. In 1852, at the age of twelve years Mr. Andrew was sent home with his brother Walter and his sisters Annie and Jane to England and remained there for a few years at school until his mother and four brothers arrived from India after his father's death at Secunderabad of cholera. The family then went to Ireland and resided at Port Arlington, Queen's county, until 1859, in November of which year (being tired of waiting for his nomination to a cadetship in the Hon. East India Company's service, so many of the orphans from the Indian mutiny having to be provided for) Mr. Andrew started out to seek his fortune in British Columbia in company with his friend Fitzherbert Despard. Their intention was to have gone to London, Ontario, but shortly before leaving England their plans were changed. When their outfit was pretty well under way Mr. Andrew chanced one day to bring a book from the library with a newspaper covering on it. This paper contained an account of the new country of British Columbia and gave a glowing description of the colony written by Rev. John Garrett, Bishop Hill's commissary, and by Mr. Donald Fraser of the Hudson's Bay Company. After reading these accounts they completely changed their plans and in November of 1859 they (Mr. Andrew and Mr. Despard), set out from Liverpool in the barque Kathleen to seek their fortunes in the new country flowing with milk and honey. They stopped at Honolulu for about a month, leaving there on the 12th of April, 1860, and arriving at Victoria on the 12th of May. They were rather disappointed, expecting to have been put ashore on some beach instead of landing on a wharf in a small town. They had brought with them every imaginable article required in a wilderness—pistols, bowie-knives, pots, pans, crockery, nails for fencing, and so on. They had come to farm. In June, 1860, they went to Salt Spring Island and took up a pre-emption claim of two hundred acres. They soon found, however, that they were totally unfit to "tackle" the rough soil and returned to Victoria in 1851 completely "strapped" having spent the little money they had travelling back and forth to Victoria. For a few months Mr. Andrew taught Indian school with Rev. A. C. Garrett and then entered the office of Mr. John James Cochrane, C. E., and land agent. He remained with Mr. Cochrane till 1862 when he "took the gold fever" and started off to Cariboo with two friends, going by the Harrison-Lillooet route. There was no wagon road in those days and accordingly they had over a month's rough tramp before they reached their destination. Mr. Andrew fell ill before getting to Keithley's creek and was left there by his companions. He managed, however, in a short time to make his way to William's creek, reaching it in the condition known in the mining vocabulary, as "busted." The years of 1862 and '63 were those of the great rush and much destitution prevailed. About one month was sufficient for Mr. Andrew after which he started down the county. He was completely destitute and alone and was compelled to live on berries during the greater part of his journey. At Lillooet he remained a short time with a friend and recuperated and then worked his way down to Harrison. At Harrison he obtained money enough to pay his way down to New Westminster where he obtained employment in a general store. He soon left this, however, and returned once more to Victoria. During the autumn and winter of 1862 and spring of 1863 he made a living at miscellaneous work and saved enough to take him up to Cariboo a second time—on his way stopping and working at Wright's road (the Cariboo wagon road). This season soon after arriving at Richfield he obtained employment with Mr. George Hunter Cary, the Attorney General, as his clerk at $10 per day. He retained this position for a short time and then went mining in a gulch which supplied the Black Jack tunnel with water power. After digging out quite a hole here they washed up and found only a nugget worth $16.25 and a little fine gold. After striving in vain to find the spot from which the nugget came they had to abandon the claim. Mr. Andrew then went back to the Attorney General's office and worked with him till the fall when he returned to Victoria. Upon arriving here he entered the office of Mr. George Dennis, solicitor, where he worked till the Leech River excitement broke out when he at once packed up and started for the diggings. He did not remain there long, however, and when he returned to Victoria he entered the office of Messrs. Elliott & Stuart, the brewers, where he remained till he accepted a position in the Hudson's Bay Company's service on the 18th of February, 1875. On the 12th of September, 1882, he married Miss Helen Kate, the youngest daughter of the late Richard Woods, Esquire, at that time Sheriff of Vancouver island.

Armstrong, Francis Patrick, (Golden), son of Hon. James Armstrong, C.M.G., Chief Justice of St. Lucia and Tobago, W. I., was born in Sorel, Province of Quebec, in 1862. He was educated in Montreal, and on leaving school entered the employ of the harbor commissioners of that city. While engaged in this occupation he obtained his thorough knowledge of the steamboat business. He came to British Columbia with the first exploring party under Major Rogers, and took up land on the Columbia Lakes. He was the first to engage in freighting by row boat on the Upper Columbia. In 1886 he built the steamer Duchess, which continued to make her runs till 1888, when, owing to the large increase of freight and traffic, he discarded her and built two others, a large one, to which he gave the name of his former vessel, the Duchess, and a smaller one, which he called the Marion, both commodious and beautifully furnished and fitted. In 1890 he found that in order to accommodate his growing business he would have to increase his fleet and he accordingly built the new light draught steamer, the Pert. His business is growing steadily and especially in summer his vessels are crowded with tourists. The trip over this route from Golden to

Windermere and return occupies three days, and, from the exceptional grandeur and beauty of the scenery, is one of the most delightful in the world. Captain Armstrong has confined his attention to milling and steamboating and has not troubled himself with politics. In January, 1890, he married Miss Barber, of Montreal. In religion he is an adherent of the Church of England.

Armstong, Joseph Charles, Manager of the New Westminster Telephone Company (New Westminster), is the third son of Captain William Armstrong who emigrated from county Caven, Ireland, towards the close of the last century and settled in Durham county, Ontario. Mr. Armstrong was born in April, 1837, and received his early education at Millbrook, then the chief town of the county of Durham. In 1851 when fourteen years of age he removed with his parents to California, and in Grass Valley where the family located Mr. Armstrong finished his school days. When the excitement over the discovery of gold in British Columbia broke out the family left Grass Valley and came to the Fraser river, settling at Langley. In 1861 Mr. Armstrong and his brother George went to Cariboo and during this year they mined on Antler creek but did not meet with much success. The following spring they took up claims on William's creek and here they were rewarded for their perseverance by exceptionally large returns. In the following year Mr. Armstrong left Cariboo and came to New Westminster where he engaged in business pursuits. In 1866 when the Big Bend excitement broke out Mr. Armstrong was among the first to go to the new field. He was unsuccessful here, however, and returned to New Westminster. In 1868 he again went to the Cariboo region where fortune once more smiled on him. In company with a number of other miners he owned and worked the celebrated Minnehaha claim on Musquito creek which paid its proprietors so handsomely. Mr. Armstrong remained in Cariboo till 1869 when he left the gold fields for good although not disposing entirely of his interests in them. During his mining career he suffered all the privations, and hardships incident to the life of the prospector for gold. Three times he footed it from Yale to Cariboo and back again, packing his blankets with him and once he made the journey to Big Bend, then more difficult of access than even Cariboo. Mr. Armstrong located and was the original proprietor of Harrison Hot

Springs and he still retains a large proprietory interest in them. The springs were originally covered by the waters of the lake and the task of separating them was regarded as next to impossible. Mr. Armstrong, however, by rejecting the advice of engineers and the warnings of his friends solved the difficulty by running a cut, constructed on a principle of his own, between the lake and the springs. Since 1869 he has resided at New Westminster and has been actively interested in almost every enterprise calculated to benefit the city and develope the province. For nine consecutive years from 1870 to 1878 inclusive he was a member of the city council. He has always taken a strong interest in provincial and dominion politics but has hitherto refused to stand for parliament. In 1885 he was married to Miss Freeze, of California.

Armstrong, Richard Wallace, Barrister, (New Westminster), was born at Strathroy, Ontario, on the 12th of March, 1858. His father, William H. Armstrong, is a native of Sligo, Ireland, and his mother, Elizabeth Armstrong, a Canadian of English parentage. Mr. Armstrong received his elementary education at his native town and then matriculated at Toronto university. In Toronto he studied at the college of pharmacy with the intention of following the business of chemist and druggist. He took his degree of Bachelor-of-Arts at Victoria college, Cobourg, and then decided to abandon pharmacy and enter on the study of law. He entered at Osgoode Hall, Toronto, where he took his barristership at the expiration of three years. Shortly after this, in 1883, he came to British Columbia and entered on the practice of his profession at Victoria. Here he remained for six months when he accepted the office of District Registrar of titles for the district of New Westminster. He filled this position for five and a half years after which he resigned to go into active practice again at the bar. Since that time he has been the senior partner in the firm of Armstrong & Eckstein and has been recognised as one of the leading lawyers of the province. Owing to the fact that during the largest part of the time he has been in British Columbia he has been an official of the government, he has not taken an active interest in the politics of the country. Mr. Armstrong is a shareholder in several mines and has also invested money in many other enterprises. Mr. Armstrong is an adherent of the Anglican church.

Armstrong, Hon. William James, Sheriff of the county of Westminster, is a native Canadian, having been born in the county of Durham, Ontario, on the 31st of October, 1826. He is a son of Captain William Armstrong who emigrated from county Caven, Ireland, towards the close of the last century and settled on a farm near Millbrook in Ontario. During Mr. Armstrong's youth the school system of Upper Canada was not on the excellent footing it now is and in the rural districts the children of the settlers had very few advantages in the way of education. The consequence was Mr. Armstrong had in a very large measure to educate himself. He attended the school in his native township till he had fully mastered the elementary branches of learning which only were taught and he then assisted his father in the management of the farm till 1852 when the family left Ontario and went to California where they settled in Grass Valley. Here Mr. Armstrong was engaged with his father and brother in mining till 1858 when the family came to British Columbia and took up their residence at Langley. In March of 1859 Mr. Armstrong built a house at New Westminster, then known as Queensborough, which had been selected by Col. Moody as the capital of the colony. This was the first house erected in the new town and Mr. Armstrong was the first citizen. He opened a general store and continued in business uninterruptedly till 1873. When the first municipal council was elected in 1860 he was chosen as one of that body and remained in the council continuously till 1873. In 1869 he was selected by the council as its president and also in 1870. Mr. Armstrong took an active part in bringing about confederation and after the consummation of the union he was elected to represent the District of Westminster in the provincial legislature. In 1873 when the McCreight Government was defeated and the De Cosmos Government came into power Mr. Armstrong joined t Cabinet as Minister of Finance and Agriculture and retained this office till 1876 when his party was defeated. He continued an active worker on the opposition benches till 1879. During the session of this year a deadlock occurred and the government was about to appeal to the country without having passed the estimates. Mr. Armstrong seeing the effect which this action would have on the provincial credit arranged a meeting between three representatives from each party and brought about an understanding whereby supplies were voted for the conduct of public business. In the general elections of 1879 Mr. Armstrong stood as a candidate for the city of New Westminster but was defeated, largely in consequence of his inability to make a personal canvas owing to the draughts on his time in attending to his large business interests. In the bye-elections of 1881, however, he again offered himself as a candidate for the city and was returned by an overwhelming majority. Towards the close of the session of this year Hon. Robert Beaven was called upon to form a ministery and Mr. Armstrong accepted a port-folio as Provincial Secretary. In the general election of 1882 Mr. Armstrong was again returned as representative of New Westminster but his party was in the minority in the House and he accordingly took his seat on the opposition benches. In 1883 the shrievalty of Westminster county fell vacant and the position was offered to and accepted by Mr. Armstrong. The House thus lost one of its most able and energetic members and one who looked more to the interests of the country than of those party. Since his retirement from political life he has been urged time and again to stand for the dominion and provincial parliaments but has declined. In 1867 Mr. Armstrong built a flour mill, the first in the province, at New Westminster and carried it on until 1871, and in 1876 he established a saw mill which he continued to conduct till 1882. He has been connected with most of the enterprises which have since 1860 had for their object the benefit and development of the country and has especially interested himself in the district of Westminster. Previous to confederation the colonial government signified its appreciation for Mr. Armstrong as a public spirited citizen by appointing him a Justice of the Peace. He is a member of the Oddfellows' society and was the first in New Westminster to hold the position of Noble Grand in that order. In 1861 he married Miss Ladner, a native of Cornwall, England. In religion Mr. Armstrong is an adherent to the Episcopal church.

Ashwell, George Randall, (Chilliwhack), born at Henlow, Bedfordshire, England, on the 17th December, 1835. He is the   Mary Ashwell, of Henlow, where his family have resided for generations. He was educated at his native town, and before he had reached the age of twenty-one he left England to seek his fortune in the new world. He first went to Ontario, where he followed the business of a carpenter for five years, residing during this period at Toronto, Guelph and Dunville. Early in 1860, during the period of the gold excitement, he left the east and came to British Columbia by way of Panama. He arrived in Victoria in April, 1860, and shortly afterwards settled at New Westminster, the capital of the new colony. He did not go to the mines, but remained at Wesminster, where he worked for one year as a carpenter, and then went into the hardware and furniture business with Mr. Thomas Cunningham. In 1862 the business was divided, and Mr. Ashwell carried on the furniture branch for a few years, selling out at length to Withrow & Tilley. After a residence of ten years in New Westminster Mr. Ashwell removed to Chilliwhack and opened a general business, which he has since carried on. For several years Mr. Ashwell was postmaster at Chilliwhack, and for two years occupied the position of warden of the municipality. For several years he was justice of the peace for Westminster district. He has not interested himself actively in politics, but is a Reformer. He is a strong advocate of temperance principles, and a consistent member of the temperance society. He was married in 1865 to Sarah Ann Webb, of Manton, Bedfordshire, England. In religion he is an adherent to the Methodist Church.

Barnard, Francis Jones, born February 18th, 1829, died July 10th, 1889. Direct lineal descendant of Francis Barnard, who settled in Deerfield, Mass., prior to 1642, and who is mentioned in the Hartford records of that date as one of the select men of that town. Mr. Barnard was born in the city of Quebec, and was brought up to the hardware business. His father died when he was twelve was of age, and he was compelled to earn a living for his mother and her young family. He married Ellen Stillman, of Quebec, in 1853, and in 1855 he moved to Toronto, Ont., where he engaged in business. Meeting with reverses he emigrated to British Columbia in the spring of 1859, leaving his wife and children in Toronto. He travelled via Panama to San Francisco as a third class steerage passenger in order to save the few dollars he possessed, and endured all the discomforts that steerage passengers from New York to San Francisco in those days were subjected to—filthy quarters, bad food, and brutal treatment. He arrived at Victoria with crowds of other gold seekers when the Fraser river excitement was at its height. He proceeded at once to Yale where he landed with a five dollar gold piece in his pocket—all the money he had in the world. He earned his first few dollars by carrying cordwood to the town on his back, and then sawing and splitting it. Subsequently he staked-off a claim, made a few dollars out of it, and then sold it. During the summer he secured the position of constable of Yale, and while in the discharge of his duties it fell to his lot to take two prisoners to New Westminster, going down the river in a canoe. He remained at Hope over night and while there one of the prisoners succeeded in slipping his hand-cuffs and attempted to murder his guard. Mr. Barnard was aroused by the prisoner trying to take the pistol out of his holster for the purpose of shooting him. He grappled with the fellow and succeeded in recapturing him. In 1860 Mr. Barnard was engaged as purser on the steamer Yale. This vessel was built by the merchants of Yale to navigate the Fraser river to that point; steamboats to that date not having attempted to stem the current above Hope. Having also made some money during the summer building, in conjunction with Captain Powers, (now of Moodyville), the trail up the Fraser river to Boston bar, Mr. Barnard sent to Toronto for his wife and two young children, who arrived in Victoria in December and crossed the gulf on the steamboat Yale. The same steamer was blown up during her next trip, just below Hope, and the captain, fireman and others killed. The purser, Mr. Barnard, who was sitting at the dining table, was thrown out and fell on the guards of the steamer and was rescued by Indians. After this Mr. Barnard took a contract from the government for clearing, grading and stumping Douglas street in Yale, a work which he satisfactorily completed. In the autumn of 1860 he first began the express business, laying the foundation for Barnard's Express, now the British Columbia Express Co., by carrying letters and papers on his back, and travelling on foot from Yale to Cariboo, a distance of 380 miles, or 760 the round trip, which he did entirely on foot. He received two dollars for every letter he carried and sold newspapers in the Cariboo mines at one dollar a piece. During the winter of 1861-2 he made trips between New Westminster and Yale, a distance of 200 miles. In 1862 Mr. Barnard established a pony express, which meant that he led a horse, with the express goods packed on the animals back, between Yale and Barkerville, connecting at Yale with Messrs. Dietz and Nelson, (now Governor Nelson), who carried on the business between Victoria and Yale. Gold was being taken out of Williams creek in large quantities, and was entrusted by the miners for transport to Victoria to the well-known expressman, who several time during the season of 1862 made his trip of 760 miles walking and leading his horse, and who, only through courage, vigilance, unwonted pluck, perseverance and energy, accomplished the perilous journey and avoided being robbed. The Victoria wagon road from Yale to Cariboo, which the government commenced in 1862, being completed to Soda Creek, some 240 miles above Yale, Mr. Barnard, with the small capital he had accumulated, and backed by parties who realized the stuff he was composed of, established Barnard's Express and Stage Line, equipping the road with 14-passenger six-horse coaches, all driven by "crack whips." The rush to the mines was so great in this year that the enterprising and energetic proprietor, through the carriage of passengers, freight, letters, papers, and gold dust, met with excellent returns for his outlay, and in 1864 extended his business and increased his stock, securing the contract at a very remunerative price for carrying the mails. He also, having won the confidence of the banks, induced the government to disband the gold escort and entrust the carriage of all gold dust to him, employing an armed messenger to protect it. In 1866 Barnard bought out Dietz and Nelson, and extended his business to Victoria, thus doing the whole business between Victoria and Barkerville. He moved his family to Victoria from Yale in 1868, where he continued to reside to the date of his death. In 1870, with characteristic enterprise, Mr. Barnard, associated with Mr. J. C. Beedy, of VanWinkle, attempted to place road steamers on the Cariboo wagon road, and securing from the legislature an exclusive right to run them for one year, he went to Scotland, and, purchasing six, brought them, with engineers, to the country at an enormous cost. After several attempts and heavy pecuniary losses, the steamers were found not adapted to the roads of this colony, and Mr. Barnard met with his first set-back since his arrival on the Pacific coast. The road steamers, save two, were sent back to Scotland, as well as the engineers, except Mr. Andrew Gray, (now of Spratt & Gray), and Mr. J. McArthur, (now of the Albion Iron Works. Notwithstanding his very heavy losses Mr. Barnard continued to carry on his express and staging business, and in 1874 obtained, unfortunately for himself, the contract for building part of the trans-continental telegraph line. His section extended from Fort Edmonton to Cache creek, a distance of about 700 miles. This contract Mr. Barnard was never permitted to finish, the route being twice changed by the government, and although steamboats, pack trains and supplies, as well as wire and other material, had been purchased, work was suspended for four years, until 1878, and Mr. Barnard kept out of his money for that time. In 1878 the new government came into power, and perceiving the foolishness of building and clearing the right of way for a telegraph line and railway before the road was located, cancelled the contract, leaving Mr. Barnard with a large claim for damages against the government, which has not yet been finally settled. The worry and anxiety from this broke up Mr. Barnard's fine constitution, which had stood all the trials, exposure and fatigue incident to pioneer life,—trials and fatigues, which in his case were far beyond the ordinary, and, perhaps, unparalleled in the colony. In the fall of 1880 he met with his first stroke of paralysis, which left him an invalid until his death on the 10th of July, 1889. From 1880, until his death, his interests, which were large and scattered throughout the Province, including stock raising, steamboating, staging and mining, were looked after by Mr. Frank S. Barnard, now M. P. for Cariboo. In 1866 Mr. Barnard was first returned to the legislature for Yale, which he continued to represent until 1870. He was one of the prime movers and fathers of confederation in this Province, and, together with Hon. John Robson, (now premier), Hon. Mr. Nelson, the late Dr. Carrall, (senator), fought the battle against great odds on the Mainland, and in the legislature, and on the stump, and through the interior. Just before confederation was adopted by the legislature of British Columbia, after it had been virtually secured, Mr. Barnard resigned, as he was interested in a private bill coming before the House, and although always active in politics and recognized as a power on the Mainland, being engaged in business, he did not seek re-election until 1879. In this year he was elected by a large majority to represent the Yale-Kootenay district in the House of Commons, and continued through two parliaments to retain the confidence of his constituents. On account of ill health he did not seek re-election at the general election in 1887—and for the same reason declined a senatorship in 1888. He left three children, F. S. Barnard, M. P., Alice, wife of J. A. Mara, M. P., and George Henry Mara, law student, Victoria.

Barnard, Frank Hillman, M. P., (Victoria), eldest son of the late Francis Jones Barnard, was born on May 16th, 1856, at Toronto, Ontario. He came with his mother to British Columbia in 1860, where his father had preceded them by one year. He was educated at the Collegiate School, Victoria, from 1866 to 1870, and subsequently at Hellmuth College, London, Ont. He returned to British Columbia in 1873, and for seven years assisted his father in his business, filling different positions of trust. In 1880 he was appointed manager of the B. C. Express Company, which position he occupied till 1888, when he resigned and successfully contested Cariboo district for the House of Commons. Mr. Barnard has large interests both on the Island of Vancouver and on the Mainland, and is vitally concerned therefore in the rapid settlement and development of the country. He is president and a large shareholder in the Victoria Transfer Co., and also in the Vancouver Transfer Co. He is a director and secretary of the Vancouver Improvement Co., and a director of the Hastings Saw Mill Co.; of the B. C. Milling and Mining Co., and of the Selkirk Mining and Smelting Co. He was a member of the Victoria City Council for 1886 and 1887. In politics Mr. Barnard is a liberal conservative and a supporter of Sir John Macdonald's administration, and as a member of parliament he has worked hard and successfully in the interests of the Province. In 1883 he was married to Miss Martha Amelia Sophia, daughter of Joseph Loewen, of Victoria. Residence Duval Cottage, Victoria. Member of Union Club, Victoria, and Rideau Club, Ottawa.

Batchelor, Owen Salusbury, son of Rev. Frederick Batchelor, M. A., Oxon, born at Calstock, England, June 1st, 1864. Educated at Tavistock grammar school, Devonshire, England. Previous to his arrival in British Columbia in 1885, Mr. Batchelor was engaged in cattle ranching in Colorado and California and settled shortly after coming to this Province at Salmon Lake in the Nicola division of Yale district. He has confined himself exclusively to stock raising since 1882, and is one of the largest ranchers in the Province, being the owner of two farms near Salmon lake. He also manages the estate of Mr. Hewitt Bostock, at Ducks, on the South Thompson River, near Kamloops. He fills the office of postmaster at Ducks. Mr. Batchelor is an adherent of the Episcopal chuch and a member of the Odd Fellows' Order.

Bate, Mark, (Nanaimo), youngest son of the late Thomas Bate, who was a partner in the widely-known firm of manufacturers in iron, Bramale, Cochrane & Co., Woodside, Worcestershire, England, Was born at Birmingham, Warwickshire, on December 11th, 1837. Educated at Dudley grammar school, Worcestershire, and at the age of seventeen left school to engage with his father's firm. He remained in this business for two years, obtaining a thorough knowledge of mercantile pursuits, and in 1856, left England on the Princess Royal for Vancouver Island, coming to the new colony by way of Cape Horn. He landed at Victoria in January, 1857, and went direct to Nanaimo, where he was employed in the offices of the Hudson's Bay Company. He reached Nanaimo on the 1st of February, and has lived there continuously since that date. The present handsome town was then a small collection of rude huts, inhabited by a handful of people, and Mr. Bate has therefore in his long residence of thirty-three years marked every gradation in the progress of his adopted city. By careful attention to business and assiduity in the company's interests, Mr. Bate rose rapidly in the service, and was appointed accountant and cashier at Nanaimo. This position he continued to hold till 1869, when the Nanaimo Coal Company's mines were purchased by the Vancouver Coal Mining and Land Company, and Mr. Bate was offered and accepted the position of manager of the new company. This position he continued to fill till 1884. The City of Nanaimo was incorporated in 1874, and at the election for the first council, in 1875, Mr. Bate stood for the mayoralty against the late Mr. James Harvey, and was elected by a sweeping majority. During the succeeding five years he was re-elected by acclamation. He declined the nomination for 1880, but in the following year the citizens insisted that he should consent to guide the affairs of the municipality, and he was returned without opposition. In 1883 he again accepted the nomination, and was elected by a vote double that of his opponent. In 1885 he was again opposed and again returned by a large majority, and from that time he has sat continuously in the mayor's chair till 1890, the present year, when he refused to allow his name to be placed in nomination. During these eleven terms in which he was at the head of affairs, Nanaimo made remarkable progress, and the wisdom and energy of Mr. Bate's government are attested by the present condition of the city. In 1887, when it was doubtful if he would accept the

HON. ROBERT BEAVEN.

nomination, a requisition, signed by nine-tenths of the voters, was presented to him, and in the following year he was made the recipient of a magnificent address from the citizens accompanied by a gold watch, gold headed cane and a silver tea set. During his incumbency of the mayoralty Mr. Bate received all the Governor-Generals who have visited British Columbia since confederation His monetary interests are almost exclusively confined to the district, but he takes a pride in the Province at large, and regards with pleasure all evidences of progress and development. He, however, looks upon his own city with especial favor, and considers that she has resources which not only guarantee her permanent prosperity, but assure her a position second to none in the Province. Mr. Bate was married in 1859 to Sarah Ann Cartwright, of Worcestershire, England, and has a family of five sons and five daughters. He at present holds the position of assessor of the district. He was appointed the first justice of the peace in the district of Nanaimo, receiving his commission in 1873. He was the first chairman of the Board of Education of Nanaimo, and has been continuously connected with and interested in the school system since 1865. He was for many years president of the Nanaimo Library Institute, and is the government nominee on the Hospital Board. He is a member of the Masonic Order and Past Deputy Grand Master; Past District Chief of the the Order of Foresters; Past Noble Grand of the Oddfellows; Past Noble Arch of the Druids; Past Commander of the American Legion of Honor; Master Workman of the Ancient Order of United Workmen. In religion Mr. Bate is an adherent of the Episcopal Church.

Beaven, Hon. Robert, M. P. P. for Victoria city, (Victoria), was born at Leigh, Staffordshire, England, on 28th January, 1836. He is the son of the late Rev. James Beaven, D. D., who occupied the chair of metaphysics and ethics in the university of Toronto and who had filled the professorship of divinity in King's college, Toronto, previous to the time that that institution was merged in the university. Mr. Beaven received his education at the Upper Canada College, Toronto, where he graduated. After a period he decided to visit British Columbia, where the gold excitement was then at its height. He left Toronto with four companions and journeyed by way of Panama and San Francisco to Victoria. A few years afterwards he with two others left Lowhee Creek, Cariboo, the day before Christmas, on foot, carrying only some gold dust. They travelled by the wagon road, breaking a trail part of the way through the snow, to Yale. There they procured a canoe and by pulling it over the ice and and using it in the open parts of the Fraser river reached New Westminster after an adventurous trip of nearly five hundred miles. He then paid a visit to eastern Canada where he married Miss Susan Libbald Ritchie, the daughter of the Rev. Canon Ritchie, M.A., of Georgina, Ontario, and returned during the following summer to Victoria, which he has since made his home and where some years later he went into business. The first time he came prominently before the public was during the agitation in 1868 for confederation with the Dominion. He took an active part in the organization of the Confederate League of which he was made secretary. After the consummation of the union Mr. Beaven stood as a candidate for the first legislative assembly and was elected in October, 1871, for the city of Victoria. He has ever since represented the same constituency in the House and is the only member who has retained a seat continuously since confederation. His constituents have thus shown their confidence in him and their appreciation of his services. He has been elected seven times in the city of Victoria. Mr. Beaven was appointed Chief Commissioner of Lands and Works on 24th December, 1872. He held that office until 27th January, 1876. He was appointed Minister of Finance and Agriculture on 27th June, 1878, and held that port-folio until 29th February, 1883. During a portion of this period he was the Premier and Chief Commissioner of Lands and Works. In May, 1873, he was appointed a Gold Commissioner. He was a member of the De Cosmos Government, the first and second Walkem Governments, and was the Premier when His Excellency the Governor-General, the Marquis of Lorne, and Her Royal Highness the Princess Louise, visited the province in 1882. He is now the leader of the opposition in the provincial legislature. These governments had many very important questions to deal with, notably, the trans-continental railway question, resulting in the construction of the Canadian Pacific Railway. By the terms of confederation Canada agreed to commence construction of this railway in the province on or before the 20th July, 1873, and connect the seaboard of British Columbia with the railway system of Canada on or before the 20th

July, 1881. The repeated failure on the part of the Dominion Government to commence the work in the Pacific province caused endless trouble to its government and people, which nearly culminated in the withdrawal of the province from the union. Matters came to a climax in 1879, the Walkem-Beaven Government being then in power. The legislature was kept in session three months, resulting in a sitting with closed doors to consider the policy the provincial government had adopted in dealing with the question. To the credit of all parties in the legislature it is to be chronicled that the action then taken was unanimous, all the members uniting in their support of the stand taken by the Provincial Government. This unanimity resulted in the Legislature obtaining, on the 26th of April, 1879, a definite pledge "that the Canadian Government was determined to commence the construction in British Columbia that season and press it vigorously." The Dominion Government in some degree carried out this pledge by awarding contracts upon the Mainland for the construction of the railway from Emory Bar, Fraser River, to Savona, but the sections between Emory and Burrard Inlet, and Esquimalt and Nanaimo, were not commenced. Consequently in 1880 the Hon. A. DeCosmos, M. P., was authorized to press upon the Dominion authorities the importance of extending the railway on the Mainland, and of their carrying out their agreement to build the Island section of the Canadian Pacific Railway, and to point out the advantage to be gained therefrom, as well as the serious injury the Province had sustained by the withdrawal from settlement and sale for over seven years of the extensive area of valuable land along the east coast of Vancouver Island. Failing to obtain anything satisfactory from Sir John Macdonald's Government, Mr. DeCosmos was appointed by vote of the Assembly in 1881 the special agent and delegate to London to present a petition upon the subject to the Queen. The Secretary of State, Earl Kimberley, gave it as his opinion that the extension of the railway from Emory to Burrard Inlet; the construction from Nanaimo to Esquimalt; and the grant of reasonable compensation in money for the failure to complete the railway by the 20th July, 1881, as specified in the Conditions of Union, would offer a fair basis for the settlement of the whole question. Sir John Macdonald informed Lord Kimberley that the Dominion Government would at once construct the railway on the Mainland from Emory to Port Moody, Burrard Inlet, and that the

Canadian Pacific Railway Syndicate had been urged and were considering the question of construction between Nanaimo and Esquimalt, and as soon as that question was finally decided and disposed of, his government would be ready to submit a proposal to parliament with reference to compensation for delay. This was the position of the railway question when Mr. Beaven resigned office. On the 4th July, 1886, the first overland railway train reached Port Moody. The construction of a graving dock at Esquimalt was another large question for a province sparsely populated. The government obtained a grant of $250,000 for this dock, (in lieu of the terms of union), payable as the work progressed, and a bonus of $250,000 from the Imperial Government, payable upon completion of the dock. Mr. Beaven, as Chief Commissioner of Lands and Works, first entered into an agreement with Messrs. Kinippie & Morris, Engineers for the Greenock Graving Dock, to do all the engineering, for a fixed sum of £6,500. He subsequently let the first contract in 1875 to Messrs. Hayward & Jenkinson, of Victoria, and was a member of the government which awarded Contract No. 3 for the main portion of this work to Messrs. F. B. McNamee & Co., of Montreal, Canada. The dock did not progress satisfactorily, and on 12th April, 1882, the contractors stopped work. Mr. Beaven took possession, on behalf of the government, of the unfinished dock on the 27th June, 1882. It was decided to carry on the contract by day labor until such time as the engineers could prepare tenders for its construction. This was done, the tenders for the caisson were to be sent in by the 30th January, 1883, and for the main work by the 15th February, 1883. In consequence of an adverse vote in the legislature, Mr. Beaven's Government resigned on the 29th January, 1883, and the management devolved on the Smithe administration, who entered into negotiations with the Dominion Government to sell the dock to Canada; in the mean time they carried it on by day labor. On the 24th August, 1883, the dock was formally taken over by the Dominion authorities, and completed by Messrs. Larken & Connolly, of St. Catherines, Ontario, in 1887. The Government of the Dominion have received the Imperial subsidy of $250,000, and own this valuable graving dock. In addition to these important subjects the governments with which he has been connected went largely into a system of exploration, and into making the Province generally fit for settlement, by the survey

of land, by opening trunk and branch highways, by enacting liberal
land and mining laws, and by disseminating reliable information
about the Province and its resources. The principal laws of the
Province had their origin during this period. The policy which
established that the Supreme Court of British Columbia was a
Provincial Court, and subject to Provincial legislation, and the pen-
sioning and retirement from the county court bench of gentlemen
who were not barristers; the addition of two supreme and county
court judges to the bench were advocated and carried to a successful issue. While the Province generally was being developed, the
City of Victoria largely benefitted by the legislation carried to a
successful issue by the government mentioned. The acts guaranteeing the bonds of the city issued for the construction of the water
works was passed in 1873 and 1874. The act transferring to incorporated cities for their own use the revenue which was formerly
collected for provincial purposes by the government in cities from
trade and liquor licenses, owes its origin to Mr. Beaven. The act
abolishing dual taxation upon real estate in municipalities was
passed by the legislature in 1878 upon the recommendation of the
Walkem Government, and the largely extended municipal powers
have their origin mainly through Mr. Beaven's efforts. The free
non-sectarian system of education, advocated by him when first a
candidate for parliamentary honors, has been a live factor in educating the youth, and bringing population into the Province. The
legislature made its first grant for the erection of the brick school
buildings on Yates and View streets when he was Chief Commissioner of Lands and Works. Many of the principal schools throughout the Province were also then erected and established. Several
important measures owe their origin to this gentleman as a private
member, viz.: The law stamp act; the act limiting the fees payable on the estates of deceased persons; the first general municipal
act of the Province and the municipal act, 1889, (part of which is,
however, consolidated); the game protection acts, 1878 and 1880;
the act extending the rights of property to married women; the
amended ballot act of 1877; the companies act. 1878; The act of
1881 exempting the members of the volunteer fire department from
jury duty. When visiting Toronto years ago he spoke of a railway
traversing British territory and terminating on the Pacific, but was
looked upon no doubt as a visionary enthusiastic. He has since

had the satisfaction to meet his friends, who reached the Pacific coast in a few days by rail, travelling in Pullman cars across the "sea of mountain." Mr. Beaven advocated for years a railway from the Atlantic to the Pacific, with its terminus at Esquimalt, V. I., at the same time admitting that under the Terms of Union with Canada, as accepted by British Columbia, the Government of Canada had the undoubted right to terminate the railway anywhere upon the seaboard of British Columbia. It was not until 1873, when the Dominion Government, after due deliberation, declared by an Order in Council passed under parliamentary authority, that Esquimalt was the terminus, that Vancouver Island became entitled to it. He opposed the Settlement Act, introduced in the legislature by the Smithe Government in 1883, which was claimed by its promoters would satisfactorily settle all questions between the Province and Dominion, and contended that its passage would place the land on Vancouver Island, which had been reserved in 1873 to aid in the construction of Canada's national railway, together with most valuable and extensive coal measures, timber and minerals, in the hands of a semi-foreign corporation, to the disadvantage of the Canadian Pacific, and predicted that it would result in the Canadian Pacific being obliged to make their final terminus at Burrard Inlet, instead of at Esquimalt. He considers to-day that the so-called Settlement Act was a great blunder, and its baneful consequences far-reaching, but recognizes that the Statute was approved by a majority in the Legislature and cannot now be recalled. He places great value on Burrard Inlet as a harbor for a terminus of a railway on the Mainland, but considered that the Canadian Pacific Railway Syndicate made an error in not promptly accepting the offer made to them in 1881, as regards the railway on the east coast of Vancouver Island, between Nanaimo and Esquimalt, thus securing a line which would be remunerative from its completion; the immensely valuable coal, mineral and timber lands, which had been reserved for years; and a terminus for their railway on the harbor of Esquimalt. He is a warm advocate of British Columbia as a whole; he expresses great gratification at seeing cities springing up and growing throughout the Province; the land occupied by settlers; and industrial enterprises being established. He considers the building and opening of the Northern Pacific Railway to Puget Sound, U. S. A., in 1883, and the subsequent opening of our own national line, the Canadian Pacific, in 1886 in British Columbia, Canada, have practically created a new era, and been the principal aids to prosperity.

Begbie, Sir Matthew Baillie, eldest son of the late Col. T. S. Begbie, of the 44th Foot, was born in 1819, and educated at St. Peter's College, Cambridge, where he took the degree of B.A. in 1841 and A.M. in 1844. He was called to the Bar at Lincoln's Inn in 1844, and practised his profession in England till 1858, when he was sent out as Judge of the Colony of British Columbia—immediately after its creation by act of parliament of the same year. His appointment was made by Sir Edward Bulwer Lytton, (afterwards Lord Lytton), on the nomination of Sir Hugh McC. Cairns, (afterwards Earl Cairns). Vancouver Island was then a colony with a court of its own; British Columbia being entirely continental. In 1866 the Colony of Vancouver Island was merged in that of British Columbia, and Mr. Begbie received the designation of Chief Justice of the Mainland. On the departure of Chief Justice Needham Mr. Begbie became Chief Justice of British Columbia. In this position he has since remained, the court, by virtue of the B. N. A. Act of 1867, continuing unchanged when British Columbia joined the Dominion in 1871. The wisdom of the Imperial Government's choice in the person of Mr. Begbie was at once apparent from the fearless manner in which the law was administered and the respect in which Mr. Begbie's court was held. At that time the whole country was of course swarming with adventurers in search of gold, and no small percentage of the population were old miners who had contracted lawless habits in the camps of California and were accustomed to guide their conduct according to the impulse of the moment—an impulse usually misdirected. In the tumultuous race after gold the worst passions of the human breast usually obtain sway, and it was owing to Mr. Begbie's wise and firm administration of the law that the individual found it desirable to keep those passions in check. Indeed, that the page of colonial history in British Columbia is so free from crime and bloodshed, was very largely due to Mr. Begbie's efforts. In 1871 the distinction of knighthood was conferred on Mr. Begbie.

Begg, Alexander, (Victoria), was born in the parish of Walten Caithness-shire, Scotland, on May 7th, 1825. He is a son of Andrew and Jane Taylor Begg, of Walten. Mr. Begg received his early education at a private school at Backlass, Dunn, taught by William Campbell, a teacher of considerable note. Subsequently he attended the Normal School at Edinburgh, where he received a teachers diploma. In 1846 he emigrated to Canada, where he taught school for a time in the townships of West Huntingdon and Madoc, and afterwards at Oshawa. He then, in conjunction with Mr. J. E. McMillan, published the *Messenger*, the first paper in Bowmanville. After a couple of years he disposed of his interests at Bowmanville and started the *Sentinel* at Brighton. Subsequently he published the Trenton *Advocate*. He shortly afterwards abandoned this business, and paid a visit to his native land. Returning to Canada he was appointed on the customs staff at Morrisburg, and in 1869 was promoted to be Collector of Customs and Inspector of Inland Revenue for the North West Territories, and accompanied Hon. Wm. McDougall and staff as far as Pembina, when they were compelled to return by the advance of the half-breeds under Riel. Mr. Begg subsequently accepted the position of Emigration Commissioner in Scotland for the Ontario Government, and was remarkably successful in this work. When he returned to Canada he settled a temperance colony at Parry Sound, and while there became editor and proprietor of the Muskoka *Herald*, and subsequently commenced the publication of the *Canadian Lumberman*. In 1881 he went to the Northwest by way of Chicago, St. Paul and Bismarck as the correspondent of the Toronto *Mail*. Next year Mr. Begg returned to the North West and established a sheep ranch at Dunbow, at the confluence of High River with Bow River. For some years past Mr. Begg has acted as special emigration commissioner for the British Columbia Government to arrange for the settlement of Crofter fishermen on the western shores of Vancouver Island, and in this capacity has made several trips to the old country and placed before a special committee of the Imperial Parliament a plan for carrying the scheme out. He has met with much success and there is little doubt that before long a large number of this excellent class of colonists will be settled in this Province.

Bell, Robert B., (New Westminster), was born at Campbletown, Argyleshire, Scotland, August 6th, 1850. He received his education at Shanden Grammar School on the Gareloch, and served his apprenticeship to the carpentry and building trades in Helensburgh, Scotland. He left Scotland and came to Canada in 1870 and lived some nine years in the North West Territories, arriving in this province three years ago, 1887. Mr. Bell has resided in New Westminster since that time, following his trade of contractor and builder, in which he has been very successful. He has manifested his belief in the future prosperity and greatness of the Province by investing largely in property and centering all his interests here. Mr. Bell is married and has eight children. He is a Presbyterian in religion and a Liberal in politics.

Bodwell, Ebenezer Vining. Born 30th April, 1827, died 18th October, 1889. Mr. E. V. Bodwell who, during the last three years of his life, was a resident of Vancouver, and who was one of its most enterprising and respected citizens, was born in the township of Nissouri, county Middlesex, Ontario. He was descended from United Empire Loyalist stock, and throughout his life he remained faithful by his attachment to his country and by his high ideal of personal honor to the traditions of his house. Shortly after his birth his family removed from Nissouri to the township of Dereham, county of Oxford, where they settled on a farm. Here Mr. Bodwell received his elementary education. He was then sent to Madison where he attended the State University of Wisconsin. After graduating he returned and for a few years resided on the farm with his father. At the age of 23 years he was appointed clerk of Dereham, and subsequently became treasurer. He was then elected one of the township councillors and finally reeve. During his incumbency of this office he was elected on the County Council Board, and filled the position of warden of Oxford. The incumbency of this position brought him prominently before the people, and his large ability as an administrator became recognized. He was an ardent politician and a strong Liberal, and among members of his party was regarded as a future standard-bearer in his county where his influence was very great. When the late Sir Francis Hincks wrested Oxford from the Van Sittarts he found in Mr. Bodwell a leal and loyal co-worker in the cause of reform. In 1857 the deceased was instrumental in introducing the late Dr. Skeffington Connor to stand for South Oxford, which then became, and has since continued to be the stronghold of Liberalism in Western Ontario. Dr. Connor was elected by a majority of one after a very keen contest. In 1861 Dr. Connor was re-elected. His death in 1862 caused a vacancy in the constituency. The Sandfield McDonald-Sicotte Government was then in power. The supporters of that government selected Mr. Bodwell as the Liberal candidate for the vacancy in Oxford, whilst a wing of the Liberal party and the Conservatives pitched upon the late Hon. George Brown as their standard bearer. The contest was a keen, close one, resulting in a victory for Mr. Brown, who held the seat until the general election in 1867, when Mr. Bodwell was elected by acclamation. In 1872 Mr. Bodwell was again re-elected by acclamation. His constituency at this period contained 21,675 voters. The Pacific Scandal affair in 1873 resulted in another general election in 1874, when Mr. Bodwell was opposed by Dr. Thrall, Conservative, but the veteran Liberal again carried the constituency by a vote of 981 against 223. In 1875 Mr. Bodwell received the appointment of Superintendent of the Welland Canal, which position he occupied until 1879, when he was transferred to British Columbia as accountant for the Dominion Government in connection with the construction of the Canadian Pacific Railway and the administration of Dominion lands under Sir Joseph Trutch. His headquarters were in Victoria till 1887, when he removed to Vancouver where he had invested largely in property. By the citizens of Vancouver he was regarded as an acquisition to the community, and efforts were made to induce him to allow of his name being put in nomination for the mayoralty of the city for 1888, and again for 1889. Notwithstanding the fact that on each occasion the other candidates offered to retire, and thus put him in by acclamation, Mr. Bodwell refused the proffered honor. As a private citizen, however, he did a great deal for Vancouver, and his advise on questions of importance affecting the city was always freely given, and almost invariably acted on. He was a member of the Board of Trade, and at the time of his death was president of that institution. He was a prominent member of the Baptist denomination. During the latter years of his life Mr. Bodwell's health was very poor, and it was while in search of a change of air that he died. He was on a pleasure excursion with Mr. R. Marpole, superintendent of the Pacific division of the Canadian Pacific Railway, and while at Morely, N. W. T., on the evening of October 18th, he passed quietly away.

JUDGE BOLE.

Bole, His Honor Judge W. Norman. Judge Bole is descended from an old Surrey family who settled in Ireland in 1520, and on the maternal side from the Campbell's, a branch of which clan settled in the North of Ireland under James the First's plantation scheme. But like most of those who can claim similar ancestry, the Bole family can now fairly claim to be more Irish than the Irish themselves. Eldest son of the late John Bole, Esq., of Lakefield, Mayo, for many years Clerk of the Crown and Peace for that county, besides filling several other public offices of importance, and Elizabeth Jane Campbell—Judge Bole was born at Castlebar on 6th December, 1848, and was educated partly by private tuition and partly at Santry public school. He succeeded his father as Deputy Clerk of the Crown for Mayo, and after serving his time to the late Neal Davis, Clerk of the Peace for Mayo, he passed his final examination fourth on list, being five marks less than gold medalist, in 1873. In 1877 he settled at New Westminster, being the first lawyer who permanently settled on the Mainland of British Columbia, and immediately after was admitted to practise, and entered upon a lucrative business. Married 26th February, 1881, Florence Blanchard, only daughter of Major John Haning Coulthard, J. P., of New Westminster; was called to the Bar of British Columbia in 1878; was made Queen's Counsel 27th May, 1887; was a bencher of the Law Society; is a Justice of the Peace and Stipendary Magistrate for the entire Province; was director and president of the Royal Columbian Hospital for over four years; was lieutenant in Seymour Field Battery of Artillery from 1879 to 1882, and served as captain of No. 1 Battery, B. C. Brigade of Artillery, from 1884 to 1887; is a director of the New Westminster and Southern Railway Company, and was chairman of the Hastings Sawmill Company when that company with the Royal City Planing Mills Company amalgamated as the B. C. Lumber Company; was solicitor of the Bank of British Columbia from the time that bank opened in New Westminster till his elevation to the Bench; is president of the New Westminster Rifle Association; was returned at general election of 1886, as member for New Westminster by a large majority; was appointed Judge of the County Court of New Westminster 19th September, 1889. Judge Bole has, since his arrival in New Westminster, always taken, and still takes, a warm and active interest in every matter which tended to the advancement of the

Province and New Westminster in particular—and has the strongest faith in the future greatness of his adopted country, his favorite motto being: No matter where we come from, we are now British Columbians.

Bossi, Carlo. (Victoria), son of Viencenzo Bossi, grain merchant of Porto Ceresio, Lombardy, was born November 26th, 1826. At the age of twelve years he was apprenticed to a marble cutter in his native place and worked at his trade till 1850, when he emigrated to America. He remained in New York for four years, and then removed to San Francisco. In both places he worked at his trade, but engaged in mining as well in California. In April, 1858, he arrived in Victoria on the steamer Commodore, and was thus one of the first who came to British Columbia during the first year of the excitement over the discovery of gold on the Fraser. He did not go to the mines, however, but remained in Victoria, where he obtained employment with James Vignolo, a general merchant at that place. After eight months in Victoria Mr. Bossi removed to Fort Langley, where he opened a general business. As, however, Langley did not give immediate promise of going ahead, Mr. Bossi, at the end of six months, returned to Victoria and opened a general store on Johnson street. His business prospered, and in 1868 he opened a grocery establishment on Yates street. In 1875 he retired from commercial life, having disposed of both his businesses. In 1868 he married Petronilla Medana. He is a member of the Pioneer Society.

Bouchier, Francis, born in Devonshire, England, in 1855. Educated there, and, after having travelled for some years and visited most of the colonial possessions of Great Britain, he settled in 1885 in Victoria, British Columbia. He is senior partner in the firm of Bouchier, Croft and Mallette, real estate brokers, and partner in the firm of C. E. Mallette & Co., of Port Angeles. He is among the shrewdest business men of the Pacific coast, and has, by energy and foresight, built up one of the largest businesses in the Province. Mr. Bouchier has not heretofore taken any active part in politics.

Braden, John. (Victoria), second son of the late Wm. Braden, of Liverpool, England, was born June 18th, 1841, at Liverpool. He was educated at his native town and then apprenticed to the plumbing trade, being the first apprentice of the firm of which Sir David Radcliffe was the head. Mr. Braden left England in 1871, and, after spending two years on Puget Sound, came to British Columbia. In February, 1873, he went to the Stickeen country, intending as soon as the spring opened to begin prospecting. He travelled north on dog sleighs, and on the way from Deas Creek to the Cariboo camp rescued two men, John Smith and Robert Williams, who were in a starving condition, and who must inevitably have perished had it not been for the assistance he rendered them. While at the mouth of Big Canyon, Buck's Bar, he and his companion, Wm. Jeffrey, with the assistance of Mr. Braden's dog, Rover, succeeded in repulsing the attack of a number of Indians who attempted to rob them. In 1875 he established a plumbing business in Victoria in partnership with Mr. John Stewart. In 1883 the firm dissolved, and Mr. Braden carried on the business himself till 1887, when he was joined by Mr. Leonard Stamford, since which time they have done in the gas, steam and sanitary engineering business. Mr. Braden was a trustee on the School Board from 1883 till 1886, and a member of the City Council for Yates Street Ward during the years 1885 and 1887. He is an active politician and a strong Conservative. He is interested in a number of enterprises which have for their object the opening up of the Province. Among these is the Salt Spring Mining Company, of which he is president. Mr. Braden married Miss Loveland, eldest daughter of Mr. William Loveland, of Northampton, England.

Bray, Marshal Bidwell, (Nanaimo), eldest son of Ezra Bray, farmer, of Halton county, Ontario, was born at Oakville, on August 30th, 1840. Mr. Bray is of United Empire Loyalist stock. His family originally settled in New Jersey, but after the termination of the war of independence they removed to Canada, and located in Halton county, Ontario, where some representatives still live. Mr. Bray was educated at Oakville grammar school, and having completed his studies at the age of eighteen years, he subsequently assisted his father in the management of the farm. In 1862 during the Cariboo excitement he left Ontario and came to British Columbia. On his arrival he went direct to the mines and remained in that region till 1876. During that period he mined on most of the now famous creeks of Cariboo, as, Williams, Antler, Lightning and Grouse. He was in the main unsuccessful in his prospects, for while he "washed out" a great deal of gold, he lost it again in further efforts. In 1876 he went to Cassiar where he mined during the summer, and where he had pretty fair luck, finally, however, working his claim out. In the autumn of 1876 he went to Nanaimo where he obtained a position with the Vancouver Coal Company. He continued in this till 1878, when he accepted an engagement in the business of Mr. Jas. Abrams, which he held till 1880, when he was appointed government agent, which position he now holds. He took considerable part in politics till his appointment as agent, since which time he has not actively interested himself in this direction. He was married on October 8th, 1883, to Miss Sarah Randle, of Nanaimo, and has two sons. Besides his position as government agent Mr. Bray is registrar of the Supreme and County Courts, mining recorder, and is also a director of the Nanaimo Telephone Company. In religion he is a member of the Episcopal Church.

Brewer, Charles, (Okanagan), son of late Josiah Brewer, 5th, of Litchfield, was born at Fairport, Maine, on September 1831. Educated at Rockland, Maine, and studied the science of navigation with the intention of pursuing a sea-faring life. After completing his studies, however, he went to California, where he engaged in mining till 1866, when he came to British Columbia. After coming to this Province he first went to the Big Bend mines in the Kootenay district where he was fairly successful, and where he remained for two years. At the expiration of that time he moved to Okanagan, where he has since been engaged in farming and stock raising. In 1873 he built a grist mill near Vernon, and in 1883 a saw mill, which latter enterprise he is still interested in. In 1876 he filled the position of superintendent of roads for his district. He has always been interested in the progress of education in the Province, and has for many years been a trustee of the school board.

Brighouse, Sam, fifth son of Samuel and Hannah Brighouse, was born at Lindley, Huddersfield, Yorkshire, England, on the 13th of January, 1836. His paternal ancestors have for generations been residents of Huddersfield, and have filled important offices in the gift of the crown and the people. His great grand-father was sheriff of that county, and his father, who was a large farmer, was parish overseer, and occupied a position on the board of poor-law guardians. His mother's family, the Mortons, originally Scotch, had, in the latter part of the sixteenth century settled at Lindley, where they subsequently established the pottery industry, for which that place is so well-known, and which the family still control. Mr. Brighouse was educated in his native town, and at the age of eighteen years took charge of his father's farm, which he continued to manage until he left England. He had not himself formed any definite plan of coming to America, as, for a young man, he was prospering very well at home, but in consequence of a promise previously made to his cousin, John Morton, he decided to try his fortune in the new world. At this time the fame of British Columbia was being sounded throughout England, and the cousins determined to come to this country. Accordingly on the 8th of May, 1862, they took shipping from Milford Haven for New York in the Great Eastern. From New York they went to San Francisco via Panama, and from there came to British Columbia, going direct to New Westminster, which they reached about the last of June, 1862. After remaining here a few days they went to the Cariboo region, by the Harrison-Lillooet route. They only remained at the mines one month, owing to the inclement character of the season and the fact that all the good claims were taken up. They returned to New Westminster in October, having completed the round journey on foot, and on the 4th of November they came over to the shores of Burrard Inlet, where Vancouver City now stands, and where they had, in conjunction with Mr. William Hailstone, purchased five hundred and fifty acres of land. Here the three partners passed the winter, having erected a log house and a small barn. During the wet season they worked industriously at clearing their land. The parcel of land which they then purchased is now known on the plan of Vancouver townsite as 185. Their house was the first white habitation erected on the shores of Burrard Inlet, and Mr. Brighouse has therefore a clear claim to the title of "oldest inhabitant." They lived on good terms with the Indians and only once, and that shortly after they had come, was there any attempt on the part of the Indians to commit theft. On this occasion they complained to Col. Moody, who sent for Capilano, the chief of the tribe at this place, and insisted on the stolen articles being returned. Capilano promised to have restitution made, and was as good as his word. Mr. Brighouse brought the first cooking-stove to the shores of the Inlet, carrying it in on his back. Shortly after settling in their log house he and Mr. Hailstone began the work of cutting a trail across the peninsula, from where the Sunnyside Hotel now stands to False Creek, and this they accomplished before the beginning of the next summer. In the spring of 1862 the partners put in a crop of vegetables. During the summer of the same year they leased a large parcel of land on the Fraser River, where the McLaren-Ross mill now stands, and farmed this in conjunction with their own ranch. In the autumn of 1864 Mr. Brighouse, who had examined the farming country in the Fraser valley, and had forseen how valuable it must become, purchased six-hundred and ninety-seven acres on Lulu Island, in what is now the most thickly settled portion of the farming country. His land included the site on which the town hall now stands, which the municipality purchased from him. At the time he acquired this estate there were no white settlers on the island. In 1864 he and his partners in the Burrard Inlet property leased their farm, and Messrs. Morton and Hailstone went to California. Mr. Brighouse, however, remained in British Columbia and continued his farming pursuits with ever-increasing success. In 1866 he bought another property called Rose Hill, near New Westminster, and this he made into a dairy farm. This, and the Lulu Island farm, he continued to conduct simultaneously from that time till 1881. In 1867 his lease of the land where the McLaren-Ross mill stands, ran out, and he did not renew it, having as much of his own property on his hands as he could conveniently manage. He found that the dairy farm at Rose Hill and his Lulu Island farm were running admirably together, and he accordingly expended money largely in improving them. In 1870 his barn on Lulu Island, the largest on the river, was burned with the entire crop. When he had fairly got the land under cultivation he went pretty largely into stock raising and was especially anxious to increase the quality of the farm cattle in this country, and did not a little in this direction by the purchase of thoroughbreds. Mr. Brighouse served in the second council of Lulu Island, having been appointed by that body to fill the place of a member who had gone to Canada. He had been requested previously to stand for the council and had refused, and now only accepted the position at the solicitation of the councillors. During 1869 and 1870 Mr. Brighouse was one of the active

SAM. BRIGHOUSE.

workers for confederation with the Dominion, but he opposed the adoption of the Dominion tariff. In 1881 he leased his farms on the Fraser and returned to his property on the Inlet. He found that the persons to whom the land had been leased had departed some time before, the Indians having burned their barns and stables. Shortly prior to this two hundred acres of this property had been sold, so that there now remained among the three partners three hundred and fifty acres. Mr. Brighouse immediately began the work of clearing the land, and let contracts for that purpose. He felt confident that the Canadian Pacific Railway would be extended from Port Moody, and he realized how valuable the property had become. When the extension of the line was decided upon, they gave one-third of their land to the company, according to agreement, and the work of cutting the balance into lots and building streets through it was at once proceeded with. With Mr. Brighouse's immense interests in Vancouver it goes without saying that he has ever been keenly interested in the city's progress and welfare. He was one of the most active workers in obtaining the first charter, and in 1887 he was elected by acclamation to represent ward one in the City Council and accepted the position of acting chairman of the Board of Works. He also sat in the council during the following year and filled the chairmanships of the same committees as during the year previous. Mr. Brighouse was recognized as one of the most energetic and broadest minded members of the council, and it was largely through his efforts as chairman of the Board of Works that the city is in the good condition it is to-day. He lost heavily in the great fire which destroyed the city in 1886, but instead of repining went to work to restore his ruined buildings. Mr. Brighouse has paid two visits to his native land since coming to British Columbia, once in 1874, when he remained one year, and again in 1887, when he was absent three months. He is a member of the St. George's Society and an adherent of the Episcopal church.

Brown, John Cunningham. (New Westminster), son of the late Robert Campbell Brown, of Belfast, Ireland, and grandson of Robert Ewing Brown, of Erinville, Isle of Man, was born at Fermoy, Ireland, in 1844, and educated at the Royal Academy, Belfast. In 1861 he entered Queen's College there with a view to the study of medicine, but in May, of the following year, he accompanied an elder brother to British Columbia, landing in Victoria in July, 1862. Shortly afterwards he went to the Stickeen mines, returning to Victoria in October, and in the following March he went to New Westminster. There, after a few years, he entered the newspaper business, beginning at the foot of the ladder, and working "at the case" in New Westminster and Victoria until the end of 1871, when he established the *Herald*, now the *British Columbian*, which he conducted until 1880, when he sold out on being appointed postmaster, which position he still holds. In 1887 Mr. Brown married Miss Kate E., fourth daughter of Mr. Wm. Clarkson, of New Westminster. With the exception of some two years, spent in Victoria, Mr. Brown has resided continuously in New Westminster ever since his arrival in British Columbia. He was a member of the first volunteer rifle company of that place, and was connected with the volunteer, and later with the militia, force for about eighteen years. Between 1871 and 1880 he occupied numerous public positions, as president or secretary of various local boards, but has never been a candidate for any political office. He is at present Mayor of New Westminster, President of the Mainland Association of that place, and also of the executive for the district, Honorary President of the New Westminster Lacrosse Club, President of the New Westminster Sabbath School Association, and Chairman of the Board of School Trustees. He is a member of the Presbyterian Church, and has been for a number of years an elder of St. Andrew's, New Westminster, and the superintendent of its Sabbath school.

Burgess, John Pope, (Victoria), was born in Somersetshire, England, on July 2nd, 1839. While a child his parents emigrated to Canada and settled at Kingston, Ontario, and there Mr. Burgess received his education at the common and grammar schools. At the age of 15 he apprenticed himself to the carpentering trade. In 1862 he left Ontario and came to British Columbia via Panama, reaching Victoria in May. He went direct to the mines on the Fraser River, and during the next few years he staked off a number of claims between Yale and Williams Lake. He did not expend much labor on them, however, his time being occupied chiefly in putting up buildings. In 1869 he went to the Omineca District where he opened a store and dealt in miners' supplies. In the autumn of this year he returned to Victoria and in the following spring went to Cariboo, where he took charge of the Lane and Kurtz Mining Company, of which Mr. Robert Brown was local manager. In the autumn of 1871 he again returned to Victoria and being satisfied with his mining experiences he began business as a builder and contractor. In 1885 he took a trip east, visiting his old home and the principal cities of the eastern States and Canada. On December 29th, 1886, he married Miss Sarah Jane Yale Bailey. Mr. Burgess has been solicited to stand for both the Municipal Council and Provincial Legislature, but has refused.

Calbick, John Alloway, (New Westminster), second son of John Calbick, farmer, of Clinton Ontario, was born at Brantford on August 18th, 1837. His parents were both of Irish birth and came to Canada in 1830 and finally settled, when Mr. Calbick was four years of age, in Goderich township in what was known as the "Queen's Forest." His father was one of those resolute settlers in Western Ontario whose labor and self-sacrifice left such a rich heritage to the present generation. Mr. Calbick attended the county school and after acquiring what knowledge could be gained there he assisted his father on the farm and remained with him till he had reached the age of twenty-three years. In 1860 he left Ontario and came to British Columbia which he reached after fifty days of a wearisome journey by way of Panama. He went direct to New Westminster and landed without a dollar in his pocket. During the latter part of 1860 gold had been discovered in the Similkameen country and in the following spring the Government began the construction of a road from Hope to this place. Mr. Calbick was employed at this work and continued at it till the autumn. In 1862, with eight others, he started from New Westminster for the Cariboo gold fields each man having sixty-five pounds, chiefly food, on his back. They began their march on the 1st of May and after a toilsome journey afoot, of thirty days, they reached Williams Creek. During the early part of the summer there was a great scarcity of food at the mines and much suffering in consequence. Mr. Calbick paid as high as $1.25 a pound for flour and $1.50 for beans. During this summer he, in conjunction with a Mr. Holt, took a contract to build a court house. This work occupied them two weeks. They had to haul the logs for its construction from the mountain sides with ropes, with much danger to themselves. They accomplished the work without mishap, however, and put up the building so solidly that it is yet standing and was up till a year ago used for the purpose for which it was constructed. After this Mr. Calbick prospected on Jack of Clubs creek, spending his time and money without meeting with success, and in the autumn returned to New Westminster poorer than when he left. He had reason, however, to congratulate himself that he got down in safety as the party he was with were searched for by Indians, whose intention was murder and robbery. During that autumn the same Indians had murdered eight returning miners, and as this fact was widely known Mr. Calbick's party were on the lookout constantly and saved themselves simply by their vigilance. Indians were not the only highwaymen who lay in wait for returning miners. White men also were engaged at this work and in the summer of 1862 had murdered three Jews and created so much alarm that miners rode to and from camp with their firearms in their hands ready to shoot the first person they met who showed signs of hostility. In the spring of 1863 the Government took action in the matter, cleared these desperadoes from the road and hung five Indians. Matters then grew better. During the succeeding winter Mr. Calbick worked in the lumber woods and made about $200, and with this amount ahead he concluded to make another venture at the mines. He got a couple of pack horses and freighting them with 250 pounds apiece he started for the mines by way of the Yale-Hope route. During this journey he lost one of his horses and in the search for it succeeded in losing himself. He was unable to find the road and had it not been for the sagacity of his horse which could not be whipped to take the direction he desired it to take, and to which he finally gave the rein, he would assuredly have perished among the hills. He found matters very much improved over the previous year. The government waggon road had been completed as far as Soda Creek and was being pushed with all energy. In consequence of the improved condition of affairs food in Cariboo was very much cheaper than the year previous. Mr. Calbick during 1863 mined on Jack of Clubs Creek again and in the Fall returned to New Westminster "broke." From this time till the spring of 1866 he took contracts in the lumber woods. The Big Bend excitement, however, broke out in 1866 and the white population of New Westminster and its neighborhood became fevered with a desire to be off to the diggings. Mr. Calbick was not yet tired of the search for the yellow metal and accordingly was among the first who took the road. The party he was with footed it to Savona's Ferry from which place they took a canoe to the head of Shuswap lake. They then footed it again from Seymour across the Gold range and down to the diggings. At French Creek they found the snow so deep on the ground that it was impossible to accomplish anything and after a two weeks stay they returned, going down the Columbia and passing over Death rapids the day before the catastrophe to the Victoria party in which so many were drowned. Mr. Calbick got back to New Westminster having lost all the money he took with him. He now sold what property he had in British Columbia and went to California, settling in Nevada city where he lived for four years. During this time he worked up a large business as contractor. His health, however, was extremely poor, and during 1869 he took a trip back to Canada to see if the voyage by sea would do him good. When he came back from his trip without having recovered his doctors advised him to return permanently to Ontario. He accordingly did so, settling at Goderich not far from his old home. He followed the building trade here for six years with decided success and also during that time got rid of his illness. In December, 1876, Mr. Calbick returned to San Francisco, where he intended settling, but finding business very dull came on to British Columbia and took up his residence again at New Westminster after an absence of eleven years. He established a contracting and building business which he has conducted continuously since. Mr. Calbick has been twice married. His first wife, nee Miss Lydia Church, died in 1868, in California. In 1871 Mr Calbick married Miss Martha Ratcliffe, of Goderich, Ontario. Mr. Calbick has always taken a keen interest in politics and is a strong supporter of Sir John A. Macdonald's Government. He served the city of New Westminster for six years at the Council Board and has for twelve years been a member of the School Board. He is especially interested in the question of education and desires to see the system in British Columbia made as perfect as possible. He is a member of the Order of Oddfellows and has passed through all the chairs. He is an adherent of the Methodist church.

Campbell, Francis, (Victoria), a pioneer of the Province and the Pacific coast, was born in Beragh, Tyrone, Ireland, February

2nd, 1832, his family left Londonderry for America, arrived in Philadelphia, July 10th, 1834. In 1843 they moved west to Burlington, Iowa, where his relatives still live. In October, 1852, Mr. Campbell left Burlington and went to California, where he mined in California until the Fraser river gold excitement of 1858 broke out. On the 27th of June of that year he married Miss Margaret Morrow, of Cavan, Ireland, and the next morning they took the stage for San Francisco. They remained in San Francisco about two weeks waiting news from the Fraser. They got started at length and arrived in Victoria, August 3rd, 1858. In November, Mr. Campbell and his wife left for Derby, or New Langley, on the Fraser river, about 15 miles above Westminster, where they had bought a lot. In Febuary, 1859, in company with Mr. Chas. McK. Smith, late of the "*Standard*" newspaper, Mr. Campbell went to Pitt river to hunt for water power for a saw mill. They could not find anything there and they returned to Derby. On April 4th, 1859, Mr. Campbell left Derby for Bridge river, but on arriving at Lytton he found the miners returning. He then went up the Thompson about 25 miles and found fine gold but nothing to pay. He returned to Lytton and from there to Derby. In May he moved down to "Queensboro" (New Westminster. In July, in company with Mr. Sewell P. Moody, Mr. Campbell went to the San Juan Island war, but it turned out a fizzle and he returned to Victoria in February, 1861. On returning to Victoria he worked at his trade as a carpenter and joiner for about 18 months, when he went into the tobacco business, where he still remains.

Campbell, John, (Revelstoke), physician and mining expert, was born in Alleghany county, Pennsylvania, on December 23rd, 1843, his father being of Scotch and his mother of Irish origin. Mr. Campbell was first educated in Pennsylvania, and afterwards at the Medical College of Ohio, Cincinnati, and graduated at Bellevue Hospital Medical College, New York City. He then engaged in the practice of medicine for some years in Alleghany City and also in Pittsburg, Penn., but latterly has been occupied entirely in mining enterprises and speculation, especially those of smelting and reducing gold and silver ores in Colorado and California. He has also seen military service, having served in the United States army for three years, during the greater part of which period he was with the 17th army corps, (south west), principally under General McPherson. On receiving his discharge Mr. Campbell was acting lieutenant of artillery. He has, however, served in all branches of the service. In 1872 he was appointed general manager of the American Hydro-Carbon Gas Company, continuing several years in that position, and was at a later period general manager of the American Hydro-Carbon and Water Gas Company. Mr. Campbell was also president and manager of the Campbell Mining and Reducing Company, of New York. Desiring to examine mining properties in this Province, Mr. Campbell came to British Columbia in 1886 and settled at Revelstoke, and since that date has examined most of the mines in that part of the interior. In March, 1889, he was appointed general manager of the Kootenay (B. C.) Smelting and Trading Syndicate, (Limited), and since that time has attended to the management of the company's business at Revelstoke. It may be said that the first class smelting and sampling works at the latter place owe their origin almost entirely to the efforts of Mr. Campbell, who has done considerable work in opening up and developing the mines near that locality. He has never been an applicant for any public office, though he was elected city physician when in the City of Alleghany, and drafted the health by-laws for the municipality. Mr. Campbell is a Presbyterian, and was married in 1870. He is still connected with the Grand Army of the Republic.

Campbell, Lewis, (Kamloops), was born 20th September, 1831, in Guernsey county, Ohio, U. S. A. His father was an extensive farmer residing latterly near Baltimore, Maryland. Mr. Campbell received his education at Huntington, Indiana. During his residence in the States he carried on the trade of a cooper. On his arrival in British Columbia in 1858 Mr. Campbell settled on the South Thompson River some twelve miles above Kamloops. He avoided being drawn into the vortex of the rush after gold, but followed the occupation of a packer, doing an extensive business in that line from Yale to Cariboo till 1865. Since that date he has pursued the calling of a stock-raiser and farmer on a large ranch owned by him near Kamloops and at the place where he first settled on his arrival in British Columbia. Mr. Campbell is married and has seven children. He is a member of the Presbyterian church and is connected with the Ancient Order of Oddfellows and the Pioneer and Caledonian Societies. He is largely interested in Kamloops city property and various other speculations. In 1874 he drove 150 head of cattle to Cassiar and was the first man who shipped cattle from the Upper country to Victoria.

Cannell, Edmund Y., (Kamloops), is one of the oldest settlers in British Columbia, and especially of the interior, having arrived in Yale in May, 1861, on the Flying Dutchman. He had passed the previous winter in Victoria, but being desirous of getting to the mines left that place as soon as the spring opened. He remained in Yale only one day, and then started for Lillooet, which he reached after a rough journey. Here he spent six weeks cutting logs for Cadwaller & Co.'s saw mill. In conjunction with Mr. Archie Michael he then purchased a young steer, which they trained to pack goods, and having loaded this animal with a complete miners' outfit, they started for Cariboo. On the way they fell in with a mule train and travelled in company with it to the Forks of the Quesnelle. They proceded through Keithley's and Antler Creek on their way to Williams Creek, which was their objective point. Here Mr. Michael opened a butcher shop and made beef of the steer, obtaining 50 cts. a pound for it. Mr. Cannell worked in the mines off and on for five years without, however, having much success. In the autumn of 1863 he wintered in Kamloops and returned to Cariboo in the spring. For twelve years he engaged at teaming on the Cariboo road, and in 1880, during the Canadian Pacific Railway construction, he conducted a butcher business in Yale. Since that time he has been engaged in the hotel business—two years at Chapman's Bar and four years at Kamloops.

Carne, Frederick, Jr., son of Frederick and Harriet Carne, was born August 18th, 1856, at Burealstone, Devonshire, Eng. In 1864 he came to British Columbia with his parents, who settled at Victoria. Here Mr. Carne went to school till he reached the age of fifteen. Since that time he has been continuously in business in Victoria. In 1883 he, in conjunction with Mr. Munsie, opened the grocery business the firm now conducts. Mr. Carne is also engaged with Mr. Munsie and Mr. A. J. Bechtel in the sealing business, and with these gentlemen has three schooners on the water. Two of their vessels have been seized by the United States revenue cutter, one, the Caroline, in 1886, which was loaded with all her cargo, and the Pathfinder, in 1889, which they recovered, the captain bringing her to Victoria with the prize crew on board. Mr. Carne is a member of the Order of Foresters. In 1885 he married Miss Agnes Gowan, of Victoria.

Chandler, William Sutton, (East Wellington), eldest son of R. J. Chandler, coal merchant, of San Francisco, was born at San Francisco on January 18th, 1858. He received his primary education in his native city, and was then sent to Fredericksburg, Hesse Darmstadt, Germany. He remained here and in other parts of Germany for four years, when he returned to America. While in Germany he studied the sciences of geology and engineering with especial zeal and on his return he prospected through Mexico, Oregon, Washington, Arizona and Vancouver Island, and was subsequently stationed at Wellington Carbonate in the Cascade Range for two years. He was then transferred by his company to East Wellington and given the task of opening up the mine there. This he accomplished, sinking the two shafts which are at present producing largely. Mr. Chandler has resided at East Wellington continuously. He is now in negotiations with the owners of coal lands in the neighborhood of the present mine, with a view to purchasing them. On the 2nd of August, 1882, Mr. Chandler married Miss Nellie Irving, daughter of the late Captain William Irving. He is a member of the American Legion of Honor, of the Ancient Order of United Workmen, and in religion is a Presbyterian.

Cherry, John Brisco, (New Westminster), solicitor, son of the late R. W. Cherry, solicitor, of Waterford, Ireland. Was born August 1st, 1845, at Waterford. Educated at Trinity College, Dublin, where he graduated in arts in 1876. Was admitted a solicitor of the High Court of Ireland in Easter term, 1876. Practiced for ten years in Waterford and Dublin, and came to British Columbia in June, 1887. Admitted a member of the British Columbia Law Society in July, 1889. Married Miss Isabella Chambers, daughter of Mr. John Chambers, of County Armagh, Ireland. Is a Conservative in politics.

Chisholm, Donald, born, 1822, died, April 5th, 1890. Mr. Chisholm was, at the time of his death, a member of the Federal

Parliament for New Westminster District. His parents came from Inverness-shire, Scotland, in the early part of the present century, and settled on the Lower South river of the county of Antigonish, Nova Scotia. After having received a good education Mr. Chisholm began life as a teacher, but very soon abandoned this profession. In 1849 he left his native place and started for the California gold fields with a party of twenty-three prospectors. While there he helped to frame the mining laws which still exist in the Golden State. He met with indifferent success in California, and after a few years he returned to Canada and settled in Ontario, where he engaged in the wheat trade. He speculated largely during the Crimean war, and with the proclamation of peace he was left with thousands of bushels on his hands. The proclamation came three weeks too soon or he would have gained great wealth by his venture. After this experience Mr. Chisholm came out to British Columbia in 1858, and there is scarcely a prominent line of business peculiar to this country which he has not since engaged in. He first settled in Hope, and in the year 1860 was elected by the people of that district as a delegate to a convention held in New Westminster to frame and present to the Imperial Government a petition praying for the establment of a measure of government for the Mainland of British Columbia, which was then simply administered by Governor Douglas, of Vancouver Island. This convention in New Westminster was his first appearance as a public man. In the year 1860 Mr. Chisholm was one of the party who went to the Big Bend of the Columbia river prospecting for gold and other minerals. During that trip he nearly lost his life. In crossing the McCullough Creek on a snow bridge when the melting of the mountain snow formed a torrent the bridge gave way and he was let down into the torrent and carried by the current half a mile in the ice cold water, and was rescued by a small party of miners in an unconscious condition. He went to Cariboo in 1862, where he mined for some time. Afterwards in the Kootenay District he was for years engaged both in the lumbering and mining industries. For some time he was foreman of the famous Cherry Creek silver mine. It was Donald Chisholm who took Major-General Selby Smith and staff through the mountains to Hope on his pack train, when that distinguished officer first visited British Columbia. In the year 1874 he came to New Westminster, and from that time onward resided on the Coast, where his honor and wealth increased with his years. Shortly after settling at the Royal City he invested in the property and business belonging to Mr. Fred. Woodcock, and established a wholesale and retail liquor business and a flour and feed business in connection therewith on Front street. He also purchased property at Ladner's Landing, and started the hotel and store now owned and conducted by Mr. Thos. McNeely. He also became a partner in the Delta Canning Company, whose history is well known. He afterwards invested, in company with Mr. Brewer, in a large tract of land in what is now the City of Vancouver, above where the smelter is located, and also in an estate at Hastings, and in blocks of property which are now in the centre of the City of New Westminster. The government early showed its confidence in Mr. Chisholm by appointing him a constable during the trouble at Yale and Hill's Bar, in the early days on the Fraser River. When mining in California Mr. Chisholm also practiced medicine, and many a miner owed his life to "Doc" Chisholm's therapeutic skill. He also practiced during the cholera epidemic. Mr. Chisholm brought the Price Brothers to Westminster to be tried for the wanton murder of an Indian, through whole bands of hostile redskins, and surrounded by almost insuperable difficulties and frightful dangers. In partnership with Mr. Daniel Mills he owned one of the most beautiful farms on Salt Spring Island, if not in the Province. Physically, Donald Chisholm was a magnificent specimen of the British Columbia pioneer; he was possessed of herculean strength, and had the reputation of being the strongest man in the Province—no light thing when the population was almost entirely composed of strong, able-bodied men. He stood six feet four and a half inches in his stockings, and in energy, strength and courage was truly a modern Ajax Telamon. For several years Mr. Chisholm was President of the New Westminster Board of Trade. He was first returned to Parliament at the general election of 1887 as a supporter of the Liberal Conservative administration of Sir John Macdonald.

Clark, Robert. (Vancouver), second son of James and Anna McGouch Clark, was born in Patrick, parish of Govan, Lanarkshire, Scotland, on September 17th, 1845. His people, on the paternal side, were originally from Sutherlandshire, while his mother's family had lived for generations on the border. Mr. Clark was educated at Old Kilpatrick, in Dumbartonshire, at the parish school, and at the age of fourteen was apprenticed to the grocery business in Dumbarton and served the required three years time. He was then apprenticed to the trade of shipwright with the firm of Denny & Rankin, of Dumbarton. This firm failed before his time was up and he completed his articles with the well known firm of Peter Denny & Brothers. He remained at Dumbarton for two years working at his trade, and during 1869 and 1870, he worked on the Tyne, in England. He returned to Scotland in Christmas of the latter year, and on the 2nd of May, 1861, he left Glasgow on the steamship Patrick for Canada. He went direct to Toronto where he worked at his trade for three months, and then engaged with Captain Dick to work on the construction of some Government steamers, which were being built at Fort Francis, at which place he put in the winter. This was the first experience he had had of backwoods life in Canada, and one that he will never entirely forget. In addition to the suffering which he endured from privation and exposure, he nearly lost his life in an accident in which his hand was almost cut in two. That he did not lose his hand was owing to the skill of an Indian who bound and poulticed the wound. In the following spring he with five companions started down Rainy river in an open boat, on their way to Winnipeg. When they reached the Lake of the Woods they found it covered with ice, although it was then the month of May. They had accordingly to abandon their boat and walk across the lake, carrying their supplies and outfit on their backs. They ran short of provisions and had to pack muskrats in case of absolute need. When they reached the government station at North West Angle they had been without food for eighteen hours. One of the party, who had contracted rheumatism, was laid up here, while the others pursued their way over the prairie, on which the snow was still tolerably deep. Mr. Clark wore a pair of high heeled boots he had purchased before leaving Toronto, and in these his feet became so sore that he was finally obliged to discard them, and for the next sixty miles he walked through snow and brush in his bare feet. When they finally reached Winnipeg the whole party was in such a condition of exhaustion that they were laid up for a fortnight. Mr. Clark remained in Manitoba till 1870. In the winter of 1872-3 he was engaged at Broken Head river, south shore of Lake Winnipeg, where he assisted in the construction of the steamer Prince Rupert, owned by Mr. Peter McArthur. In the spring he went to Lake Manitoba and built the hull of the first steamer built for trade on that lake. He was in Winnipeg during the next winter, and in the spring went to Grand Forks to nurse his brother who was lying ill there. While at Grand Forks he was engaged on the construction of the steamer Colville built by the Red River Transportation Co. In July of 1875, he and his brother left for San Francisco, which they reached in August. After a three months stay they came to British Columbia and settled in Victoria, where Mr. Clark followed his trade till the following March. During this period building operations had been very active, but owing to the disagreement at this time over the terms of the Canadian Pacific Railway, business now became somewhat dull. Mr. Clark then went to Seattle and afterwards to the Skeena river where he assisted in the construction of the steamer Alexander. He subsequently took a trip to Alaska and then worked in Astoria for three months, after which he returned to Victoria and continued at his trade till the autumn of 1879. In the spring of 1880, he and Mr. Gilmore formed a partnership and opened a dry goods business at Nanaimo. In consequence of the dullness accasioned by the strike of the coal miners, the firm moved their business to Yale in 1881. They had only been three months in Yale when they were burned out by the big fire there. They continued business in Yale till the spring of 1886, when they removed to Vancouver and established themselves there on the 5th of April. In March, 1890, the firm dissolved and Mr. Clark continued the business himself. Mr. Clark has taken no active part in politics but has been prominent in municipal matters in Vancouver. He was elected a member of the council for 1888 and again for 1889, and was one of the most far-sighted and enterprising men on the board. He is a member of the Knights of Pythias and was first Vice-Chancellor of the Order in Vancouver, and has passed through the various offices. He is a member of the St. Andrews and Caledonian Society and has been president of that body. He is a member of the Vancouver Board of Trade, and was for two years a member of the council of that organization. In religion Mr. Clark is a Presbyterian and in Dominion politics a Liberal.

Clay, Samuel Alfred, (Victoria), born at Derby, England, on December 13th, 1832. Educated at Derby. Left school at the age of 15 years and was apprenticed to a clothier and outfitter in his native town. He remained at this business for fourteen years when, in consequence of the glowing accounts published in the English press regarding British Columbia, he left England and came to this country, landing at Victoria in October, 1861, after sailing around Cape Horn. The condition of the country did not fulfil his expectations, but he decided to make the best of it. He first tried his fortune at mining, but proving unsuccessful he purchased a sloop and spent some time sailing between the Island and Mainland, transporting freight. In 1863 he, with others, went prospecting in the Similkameen country, where they endured great privations without being successful in their search. After this Mr. Clay mined for four years in Cariboo, and his labors there were partially successful. He made considerable money on Antler Creek and along Bear River. He then went to Omineca where he mined for one season without, however, making anything. Upon leaving Omineca he went to Victoria, where he established the business which he still conducts. His commercial venture proved very successful, and a few years later he opened a branch business at Elgin, which has also proved a paying investment. Mr. Clay has large investments in Victoria and the district and is interested in the progress of the Province. He has been solicited to stand as a candidate for the City Council and also for the Legislature, but has steadily declined on account of the demands his own business make on his time.

Clute, John Stillwell. (New Westminster), second son of J. S. Clute, of Kingston, Ontario, was born on June 15th, 1840, at Kingston. He is of United Empire Loyalist stock, his paternal ancestors having settled in New York in the early part of the last century. During the revolution his great grandfather took part on the loyalist side and after the termination of hostilities the family removed to Canada and settled near Kingston. When the rebellion of 1837, headed by William Lyon Mackenzie, broke out, Mr. Clute's father was in arms on behalf of the Government. Mr. Clute received his elementary education at Kingston, and when ten years of age removed to Picton with his father, who had been appointed the customs officer at that port. He completed his education at the

J. S. CLUTE.

county grammar school at Picton, and then took a position in a drug store with the intention of ultimately studying medicine. After a year's acquaintance with this business he decided to abandon it, and went to Port Hope, where he entered the clothing establishment of his brother-in-law. He remained here for two years, after which he returned to Picton for a short time and then went to Texas, where he filled the position of secretary to the Texas Telegraph Company, of which his brother was general superintendent. He was here during the outbreak of the civil war in the United States. In the summer of 1861 he returned to Picton where he remained till March of 1862, when he left Ontario to come to British Columbia. After remaining in Victoria for a time he joined a mining party going to the Quesnelle, but after reaching the mines he saw plainly the condition of things and concluded to return to New Westminster. Here he secured a position in a general store which he retained till the autumn of 1863, when he formed a partnership with Mr. Major and opened a clothing and boot and shoe business, on Columbia street. He conducted this business till the Autumn of 1870, when he disposed of his interest, retaining his property in the city, however, and went to Sedoia, Missouri, for the purpose of entering into business with his brother. He stayed there till March, 1875, when he returned to New Westminster and opened a general business, which he conducted till August, 1878, when he was appointed sub-collector of customs, and stationed at New Westminster, which was then an outpost of Victoria. In 1880 New Westminster was made an independent customs port and Mr. Clute was appointed collector, which position he still continues to fill. Previous to his appointment on the customs staff Mr. Clute always took an active interest in politics, Dominion, Provincial and Municipal. He was one of the most active workers for confederation during the agitation of 1869 and 1870. He served the City of New Westminster at the council board for a number of years, and in 1867 was president of that body. He is a firm believer in the future greatness of the Province, and in New Westminster District as the most important part of the country. He is a member of the Masonic Order and Grand Master of British Columbia. He is also a member of the Ancient Order of United Workmen. In June, 1866, he was married to Miss Jenny Clarkson, daughter of Mr. William Clarkson, of Vancouver. Mr. Clute is an adherent of the Presbyterian Church.

Coldwell, Charles Augustus Latrobe, (Vancouver), was born in the city of St. John, N. B., on June 4th, 1844, his parents being of Irish and French descent. He was educated at St. Andrew's High School and during his early life studied for the ministry, and later on for the profession of civil engineer. Previous to his arrival in British Columbia, he was engaged in civil engineering and railroad construction in his native province. In March, 1862, Mr. Coldwell arrived in British Columbia, and went directly to Cariboo, where for many years he endured all the hardships incident to early pioneer life, and met with varied success. He has travelled at different times from San Diego to British Columbia, visiting most of the mining camps en route, some of which were quite celebrated in their day. He was in Montana during the stirring mining days, just after the discovery of gold in that region, and saw many thrilling scenes in the time of the "Vigilance Committee." Much has been written about those pioneer days of long ago, but it conveys only a vague idea of the actual reality,—a wild region peopled by men of free and generous hospitality, but only too willing to resent an affront (perhaps but trivial) with the ever-ready Colt revolver or Bowie knife. For many years Mr. Coldwell was Superintendent of the "Hasting Saw Mill Co." and was also, under the late Capt. Ramer, inspector of spars for the same firm. He was one of the first Aldermen of Vancouver city, and Chairman of the Board of Works. Mr. Coldwell was also requested to allow himself to be nominated for Mayor, but declined the honor. In 1888 and 1889 he represented the Province at the Toronto exhibition, and in the fall of the latter year was appointed Registrar of the County Court of New Westminster, holden at Vancouver, which position he resigned in June, 1890. In politics he is a supporter of the present government, and is a member of the Ancient Order of United Workmen, the Knights of Pythias, and the Independent Order of Foresters. He is married, and is an adherent of the Episcopal Church.

Cooper, Hugh M. M.D., (New Westminster), was born in Toronto in 1840. His father, a native of county Antrim, Ireland, came to Canada in 1835 and in 1837 married Christina Muttart, of Prince Edward Island. Dr. Cooper received his elementary education in Toronto and then entered Trinity College, where he studied five terms, leaving with his degree of Bachelor of Arts. Simultaneously with his study at Toronto he gained a practical acquaintance with medicine by working with Dr. J Bovell and walking the hospital. During the civil war in the United States Dr. Cooper practised on the field as a surgeon. In 1886 he graduated from the school of hydropathy in New York, of which Dr. Ivall was the head. From this time till 1870 he practised his profession as a hydropathist. In 1870 he was ordained by the Church of England to carry on a materialistic controversy, and this commission he held till 1880, practising his profession as a physician during the same time. In 1881 he removed to Saginaw City, Michigan, where he devoted his time entirely to medical work. In 1882 he graduated in the regular school of allopathy, and in 1883 he came to British Columbia and settled in New Westminster where he has since remained and where he has a large and increasing practice. Dr. Cooper since his arrival in the Province has been interested in the development of the mineral resources of the country. His extensive professional work has made it impossible for him to leave New Westminster in person, but he has expended his money freely in sending prospecting parties to the interior. He was one of the company interested in the first effort to open up the Nicola mines. Dr. Cooper is a member of the Ancient Order of Foresters; of the Ancient Order of Odd Fellows; of the Royal Black Knights and the Orange Order. In 1889 he married Mrs. Galbraith, of New Westminster. In religion he is an adherent of the Episcopal Church.

Corbould, Gordon Edward, (New Westminster), barrister and solicitor, was born at Toronto on November 2nd, 1848. He is the youngest son of Charles Corbould, who came from England and settled near Toronto and who, at the age of 91 years, is still living Orillia, Ontario. Mr. Corbould was educated at Upper Canada College, Toronto, and after graduating there was articled as a law student in the office of Crooks, Kingsmill and Cattanch, and subsequently studied with J. D. Edgar. He was called to the bar of Ontario in 1871, and then formed a partnership with Messrs. Edgar & Fenton, the firm title being Edgar, Fenton & Corbould. They opened an office at Orillia, and of this office Mr. Corbould took personal charge, residing in Orillia for that purpose. He practised here till 1878, when in consequence of ill-health he was forced to abandon his practice for a period. He went to England where he remained for about two years, during which time he was married to Miss Arabella Almond, fourth daughter of Major Downe of the 1st Madras Fusileers. In the spring of 1880 he came to British Columbia and opened an office at New Westminster. He was called to the bar of British Columbia in May, 1882, and the following year he formed a partnership with Mr. McColl. Mr. Corbould is one of the ablest lawyers in the Province and has one of the most extensive practices. He has been identified with most of the large enterprises which have had birth in New Westminster for the past ten years, and is a leader of opinion in politics, though he has only once entered the field as a candidate, when he was defeated for the local legislature by Mr. Thomas Cunningham. He has been solicited repeatedly to stand for the Commons, but has heretofore refused. He is a member of the Board of Trustees of the Royal Columbian Hospital, and for several years was chairman of the Board. He is one of the provisional directors of the Coquitlam Water Works Company, of the New Westminster Southern Railway Company, and of a number of other enterprises. He is a member of the Military School of Toronto, where he took a first and second class certificate. He is one of the Executive Committee of the New Westminster Synod, and solicitor for the Synod and for the Bank of Montreal. He is a warden of the English Church, a member of the Masonic fraternity, and of the Ancient Order of United Workmen.

Cornwall, Hon. Clement Francis, (Ashcroft), was born at Ashcroft, county of Gloucester, England, in 1836. His family can lay claim to high rank among the "untitled nobility" peculiar to the British Isles; both his father, the Revd. Alan Gardner Cornwall and his mother Caroline, daughter of Thomas Kingscote, Esq., Gloucestershire, being able to trace their descent in an unbroken line from the time of the conquest in A. D. 1066. Mr. Cornwall received his primary education at private schools and afterwards became a member of the Magdalene College, Cambridge, from which he graduated in 1858, taking the degree of Bachelor of Arts. Prior to his departure from England he was called to the Bar by the Hon. Society of the Inner Temple, London, in 1852, arriving in British Columbia the same year. Mr. Cornwall, after reaching the new colony first visited the mining districts but took no active part in

G. E. CORBOULD.

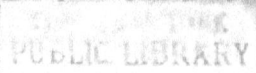

mining enterprises, devoting his efforts principally to stock raising and his profession, and spending seasons at Wild Horse, Kootenay, French Creek and Big Bend as a practising barrister. In the year 1864 when the first Legislative Assembly was created Mr. Cornwall was one of its most prominent and energetic members as representative of the Hope-Yale-Lytton district and occupied a similiar position in subsequent years being one of its members in the session of 1871 when the province joined the Canadian confederation. Immediately after confederation, Mr. Cornwall was appointed a member of the Canadian Senate, and continued such till 1881, when he accepted the Lieutenant-Governorship of British Columbia. He occupied the position till 1886. In 1864 Mr. Cornwall was appointed a Justice of the Peace for the province which he accepted, serving in that capacity till April, 1885. From that time till 17th September, 1889 Mr. Cornwall was solely engaged in rural pursuits, at which date he was elevated to the bench as Judge of the County Court of Cariboo, receiving the appointment of Stipendiary Magistrate in October of the same year. Mr. Cornwall is a member of the numerous agricultural and pioneer societies which have for their object the development and prosperity of the province, and is also a member of the the Dominion Council of Agriculture. Except such periods as were occupied in attending to political and official duties necessitated by his numerous appointments Mr. Cornwall spent most of his time in the arduous pursuits and healthful pleasures of a country life. In connection with his brother, Mr. Henry P. Cornwall, he has been the largest and most successful stock raiser in the province and has contributed in no small degree to its agricultural prosperity. Their stock has for years been famed throughout the district for its excellence. Mr. Cornwall has always been enthusiastically fond of all kind of field sports, for which the British nation is so celebrated, and for twenty years at Ashcroft kept a pack of foxhounds which came from the most noted kennels in England, principally those of His Grace the Duke of Beaufort. The hounds showed wonderful sport and helped greatly to relieve the monotony of country life. For many years also the principal race meetings of the province were held at Ashcroft. In these Mr. Cornwall took a prominent part and at present he is president of the British Columbia Jockey Club. Although possessing exceptional abilities and with an education which fitted him rather for highly civilized surroundings Mr. Cornwall's proclivities as a sportsman are such that he does not regret having exchanged the graces and comforts of life in England for the stirring though ardous pursuits of a pioneer in a new land. Mr. Cornwall is a member of the Church of England and in 1871 married Charlotte, daughter of the Rev'd A. G. Pemberton, Vicar of Kensal Green, London England.

Cowan, George, M.P.P., (Cariboo), was born in the county of Leeds, Ontario, on June 25th, 1831. Eldest son of James and Maria Cowan, of Leeds County, where his father was engaged in farming. Was educated at his native place, and at the age of twenty went to Australia, whither he was attracted by the gold fields. He settled in the Colony of Victoria, where he remained for seven years, during which time he was engaged in both quartz and placer mining. He met with more than average success in Australia, and in 1859 he returned to Canada. After visiting his old home he settled in Ontario, with the intention of living there, but in the spring of 1862 the report of the discovery of immense gold deposits in Cariboo attracted him to British Columbia. He landed in Victoria in June of that year and went direct to the mines. He staked out claims at different times on Williams, Grouse, Antler, and other celebrated creeks, and met with considerable success. With all the ardor of an old and experienced miner he pursued his quest after the precious metal, and lost most of what he had made in further prospecting. He has continued in Cariboo since that time and has been extensively engaged in both quartz and placer mining, and has expended a great deal of money in the work of development. During a bye-election in 1877 he contested the riding, which he now represents, against the Hon. A. E. B. Davie, and was successful. He has since that time sat continuously in the legislature of the Province. As a member he has labored in the best interests of the Province, and especially of his own district, fully believing that she possesses the golden key to provincial greatness. In Federal politics he is a supporter of the Macdonald administration, being convinced that that Government has pursued and is pursuing the wisest course for the Dominion. In religion Mr. Cowan is a member of the Presbyterian Church.

Crease, Hon. Henry Pering Pellew. (Victoria), was born in England in 1825, and educated at Clare College, Cambridge, where he graduated as Bachelor of Arts in 1847. Entered as a student-at-law in the Middle Temple, London, and called to the bar in 1849. Practised his profession in England till 1858, when he came to British Columbia. Elected a member of the Legislative Assembly of Vancouver Island in March, 1860, as representative for Victoria district. Occupied his seat for two sessions till January, 1862, when he resigned. Appointed the first Attorney-General of the colony of British Columbia in April 1864, and occupied that position till May 1870, when he was appointed a Judge of the Supreme Court of British Columbia. He was one of the commission which in 1871, compiled and published a new edition of the laws of British Columbia. In 1874, he, in conjunction with Chief Justice Begbie and Mr. Justice Gray, formed a commission to enquire into the Texada matter. In 1877 he was one of a commission which consolidated the public general statutes of British Columbia. He married a daughter of the late Dr. John Lindley, F.R.S., Professor of Botany at University College, London, England.

Creighton, J. W., (Lasqueti Island), born in 1853, at Hayton Castle, (the ancestral seat) in Nottinghamshire, England. He left home in 1875, and went to the Cape of Good Hope, South Africa, with a half formed intention of engaging in ostrich farming. He spent five months in South Africa hunting, and saw that continent up as far as Transvaal. He then went to Adelaide, South Australia and from there, after a few months, to New South Wales. While there he went over a considerable portion of the country, with the intention of engaging in sheep farming, but not finding what he desired he went to Queensland. He landed at Rockhampton and rode on horse back four hundred miles inland to Barcoo river. Here he spent six months on a station which possessed eleven hundred square miles of land and two hundred and fifty thousand sheep. After this six months of colonial experience, Mr. Creighton took up a station of his own. Here he remained until he was laid up with rheumatism, contracted from exposure during wet weather. To get rid of this the doctors ordered him to the hot sulphur lakes of New Zealand. He accordingly disposed of his station and went to New Zealand, where he remained for nine months bathing in the hot lakes, which were destroyed about five years ago by a volcanic eruption. He completely recovered and left New Zealand on a trading schooner for Samoa, and from there he went to Auckland, from which place he took the steamer for Honolulu. He remained in the Sandwich Islands three months and then went to San Francisco. He spent nine months in California, hunting and camping out in the foot hills of the Sierra Navada mountains. He then passed into Oregon, and through the Willamette valley to Portland and then up the Columbia to Walla Walla. From there he rode to the borders of Idaho with the intention of going into stock raising. He found, however, that the laws were framed to prevent large ranches being taken up. He then passed over into British Columbia by way of the big bend of the Columbia, and came down the valley of the Fraser. After remaining for a time at Victoria he established himself on Lasqueti Island and started the sheep ranch he at present possesses.

Croft, Henry, M. P. P., (Victoria), a member of the ancient Saxon family of Croft, of Herefordshire, England, which settled in that county prior to the reign of Edward the Confessor. Mr. Croft was born in Sydney, New South Wales, on January 15th, 1856. In 1849 he was sent to England, educated at Rugby school and afterwards entered the profession of civil engineering. He was engaged in superintending engineering works in England, and in 1879 left England for Sydney, where he entered the service of the government of New South Wales. He was engaged for three years as as inspecting engineer and superintended several works of magnitude. He then returned to England and afterwards visited British Columbia where he engaged extensively in the lumber business, carrying on an export as well as local business. In July, 1885, he married Mary Jean, daughter of the late Hon. Robert Dunsmuir. In 1887 he was elected by acclamation to represent the District of Cowichan in the local Parliament, his colleague at the time being the then Premier, the Hon. Wm. Smythe. Mr. Croft fully believes that every endeavor ought to be made to develope the latent resources of the Province whose wealth in forests, minerals and fisheries is incalculable, and he has shown this belief by investing largely in industries which are calculated to advance the prosperity of the Province. In politics Mr. Croft is a Conservative.

ROBERT CUNNINGHAM.

He is a member, both, of the Institute of Civil Engineers and the Institute of Mechanical Engineers, of England. At the last general election he was again returned to the Provincial Legislature as representative of Cowichan district.

Cunningham, Robert, (Skeena), second son of the late George Cunningham, who was an extensive farmer in the north of Ireland, was born in 1837 in the county of Tyrone, Ireland. He received his elementary education at his native place, and at the age of 18 years entered Islington College, the Church of England Missionary Society's College at London. He pursued his studies there for three years, when in 1862 he was sent to British Columbia by the society as a lay teacher. He arrived at Victoria on the 26th of September and remained there till the following March, assisting Rev. Mr. Cridge and studying the native language. He then went north to the Metlakahtla Mission where he worked in conjunction with Mr. Duncan. After two years arduous labor in this field, Mr. Cunningham abandoned missionary work and entered the service of the Hudson's Bay Company. He continued in the employ of this company for five years, two years of which were spent in charge of a post on the Naas River and three years in charge of a post at Fort Simpson. In 1869 the Hudson Bay Company sent Mr. Cunningham and Mr. Manson to explore a route from Stikeen river to Dease's Lake. They accomplished the work successfully and with remarkable quickness, and were the first white men who traversed this portion of the country. While at Dease they camped at the mouth of Dease Creek, and Mr. Cunningham in examining the gravel came to the conclusion that it contained gold. When he returned he unfolded his discovery to a number of miners who, on his representations, determined to prospect it. Mr. Cunningham accordingly gave them a sketch of the route to the lake and the bearings of the compass by which they were enabled to reach the spot indicated. Mr. Cunningham's predictions were found to be correct, the miner's finding gold in good paying quantities. This was the first of the gold digging in Cassiar. About this time Mr. Cunningham applied to the company for increased renumeration for his services. The company not wishing to lose so valuable an employee offered him a gratuity but this he refused and in the autumn of 1869 he resigned his position. In the following spring he formed a partnership with Mr. Hankin and began a forwarding and commission business, dealing in miner's and general supplies, and sending goods to the Omineca, at the mouth of the Skeena river, and built a store at Woodcock's Landing. Their business prospered so well that in a short time Mr. Hankin went to Hazleton, at the headquarters of the Skeena river and opened a branch business. After he had been a year at Woodcock's Landing, Mr. Cunningham abandoned his claim there and pre-empted what is now the town site of Port Essington. The firm of Cunningham & Hankin continued to do business at Port Essington and Hazleton for about six years, at the end of which time the partnership was dissolved, Mr. Cunningham retaining the Port Essington branch of the business and Mr. Hankin the Hazleton branch. About this time Mr. McAllister built a saw mill at Port Essington and built the steamer Alexander. The Hudson's Bay Company also seeing the amount of business to be done there, came seeking a site for a store, and notwithstanding the fact that the company had all along been doing all they could to injure his business, Mr. Cunningham furnished them with land on which to build. The company accordingly began business in opposition to him with the avowed intention of detroying his trade. They had superior advantages bringing their own goods in and refusing to carry his freight, except at abnormally high prices. Nevertheless after a bitter struggle of five years duration the company abandoned the fight and withdrew from the field after having sacrificed about $5,000.00. About this time Mr. Cunningham's attention was turned to the salmon fishing on the Skeena river. In 1880 Mr. Neal started the Inverness Cannery, and Mr. Cunningham in the year following established a saltery under the name of the "Skeena Packing Company." In 1882 Mr. Cunningham established his present canning business and has since conducted it. It is the largest establishment on the Skeena and is fitted up in the most approved manner. His brand of canned salmon, the diamond "C," is well known in America and Europe. Last year his returns from his business netted him over $100,000,00. In 1883 he built a saw mill at Port Essington. In 1889 Mr. Cunningham established a business at the Forks of the Skeena, where there will in time be a town as there is a fine farming country about it. Mr. Cunningham has two tugs on the water, the Muriel and the Cariboo Fly. He is a member of the Masonic Order.

Cunningham, Thomas, M.P., (New Westminster), was born in the Province of Ulster, Ireland, April 12th, 1837. His ancestors were prominent in Irish affairs during 1667-8-9, one of them having command of the ships that relieved the beleagured inhabitants of Londonderry. Mr. Cunningham was brought up in the country and has always evinced a strong predilection for country life and pursuits. He emigrated to Canada in 1853 and after a year's residence in that country, at Kingston, Ont., he made a tour of France, Bermuda, Cuba, and the Southern States, returning to Kingston in 1855, where he remained until the discovery of gold in British Columbia. He came to the coast in April, 1859. On reaching California the discouraging reports he heard of British Columbia induced him to remain two months in that state. He finally came to Victoria in July, 1859. He remained there until the following spring and then tried his luck at Cariboo, walking all the way from Port Douglas to Antler Creek, carrying 90 lbs. of food besides blankets, tools and rocker iron. After trying the mines he settled in New Westminster, in the autumn of 1861, and went into business the next year, dealing in stoves and hardware. He bought out the Vancouver Coal Co., in 1864 and carried on that business in Nanaimo until 1867. He was elected to the House of Assembly of Vancouver Island, and cast his vote for the union of the two colonies. He removed to Oregon in 1867 and remained in that state till 1882, and carried on a mercantile and manufacturing business during that time. For ten years he manufactured wagons, carriages, and agricultural implements. This business he abandoned when the Central Pacific Railway rendered competition with eastern manufacturers impossible. He lost heavily by the failure of the Northern Pacific Railway Company, and finally returned to New Westminster in 1882 resuming there his old business as a hardware merchant. His tastes led him to lay out and complete what are now known as Pelham Gardens in 1885 for the culture of fruit and cattle raising. Pelham Gardens are the finest in the Dominion. He took the first prize for fruits over all Canada at the last Toronto Exhibition (1889). His entire attention is now devoted to fruit growing and Jersey cattle breeding. He was elected to represent New Westminster city in 1889 in the Provincial Legislature. He was a member of the Westminster Municipal Council in 1864 and again in 1889, and had charge of the Queen's park operations during the latter year. He was the first to take up the question of establishing an agricultural exhibition in Westminster, and it was owing to his unflagging efforts that the British Columbia Provincial Agricultural Society, of which he is president, came into existence and to his untiring zeal it is that it owes its present flourishing condition. To no one so much as to him does Westminster district owe her present deserved reputation as one of the finest agricultural countries in the world. Mr. Cunningham is one of the shrewdest business men of the country, and has the energy and resolution to carry through what enterprises he undertakes. He is among British Columbia's best citizens. Mr. Cunningham married Miss E. A. Woodman and has five children.

Curtis, David Samuel, (New Westminster), son of Samuel Curtis, of Tirconnel, Elgin County, Ontario. Born at Tirconnel on January 1st, 1856. Attended the public school until 1871, when he engaged as a clerk in a drug business at Dresden, it being his intention to learn this business. He remained here for one year and then went to Chatham, where he attended the Central School. After graduating there he returned to Dresden and studied his business as a druggist with Dr. Clarke of that place. In the autumn of 1874 he came to British Columbia over the Union Pacific line of railway, and settled at once in New Westminster. Here he continued the study of his profession. In 1883 he opened the business he now has, in conjunction with Dr. Clarke, and after three years bought out his partner's interest. Since that time he has conducted the business himself. In 1881 he was elected a member of the City Council, for St. Patrick's Ward, and has sat at that Board almost continuously since. In the election for municipal representatives for 1889, when ward divisions did not exist, Mr. Curtis headed the poll with fifteen candidates in the field. During all the years he was in the Council he filled the position of chairman of the Finance Committee. For two years he was secretary of the Board of Trade of New Westminster. Mr. Curtis is one of the most prominent and successful merchants of the Royal City, and is recognized on all hands as a coming man in politics. He is a supporter of the Robson Government and in Federal politics a Liberal Conservative. He is a member of the Methodist Church and President of the Y.M.C.A. In 1884 he married Miss Harriet Cunningham, daughter of the late John Cunningham, of Kingston, Ontario.

Davie, Hon. Alexander Edmund Batson, born November, 1848, died July 31st, 1889. Mr. Davie, who at the time of his decease occupied the position of Premier of the Province, was born in Somersetshire, and educated at Silcoates College, near Wakefield, in Yorkshire. His father, John Chapman Davie, who for some years practised his profession as a surgeon, in Merton, England, came to British Columbia with his family in 1862. Mr. Davie studied for the legal profession, and in 1868 was admitted an attorney of the Province and called to the bar in 1873. From 1862 to 1874 he filled the office of law clerk to the Provincial Assembly. In 1875 he stood for the Legislature, for the district of Cariboo and was returned, but on his accepting office as Provincial Secretary in 1877, and returning to his constituency for re-election he was defeated. He was a successful candidate for Lillooet in the general elections of 1882, and when the government of Hon. Robert Beaven was defeated, Mr. Davie accepted office in the Smythe administration as Attorney-General. On the death of Mr. Smythe in 1887, Mr. Davie succeeded as Premier. In 1883 he was appointed a Q. C., and subsequently elected a bencher of the Law Society. On the 3rd of December, 1874, Mr. Davie married Constance Langford, third daughter of T. O. Skinner, Esq., of Farleigh, near Maple Bay. In Dominion politics he was a Conservative.

Davie, Hon. Theodore, Q.C., was born in Brixton, Surrey, England, on the 22nd March, 1852. His father, John Chapman Davie, of Lyme Regis, Dorsetshire, England, was a surgical practitioner, and at the time of his decease a member of the Legislative Assembly of British Columbia. Mr. Davie received his elementary education in England, which country he left early in life, and soon after his arrival in this Province, in 1867, commenced studying law at Victoria. From 1874 to 1878 Mr. Davie resided in Cassiar District and practiced law there about three years. Mr. Davie has represented the Capital City since the general election of 1882, being returned the second time in 1886 at the general elections. In August, 1889, Mr. Davie was appointed Attorney-General of the Province, thereby vacating his seat, to which he was re-elected during the same month. On the 14th of January, 1884, he married Alice Mary, daughter of Gregory York, Esq. In religion Mr. Davie is a Roman Catholic.

Davie, John Chapman, M.D., (Victoria), is the son of the late Hon. John Chapman Davie, M.R.C.S., L.S.A., who practiced his profession in Merton, Surrey, England, and afterwards in Victoria, B. C. Dr. Davie was born March 22nd, 1845, in Wells, Somersetshire, England, and educated in Silcoates College near Wakefield, under tuition of Rev. Dr. Beyoglass, L.L.D. He came to British Columbia with his father in 1862 by way of Panama and, after remaining in Victoria for a year, went to San Francisco, where he entered the university of that city. Here he remained for three years studying medicine. Among the professors whose lecturers he attended were Drs. H. H. Ireland and L. C. Lane, both of whom had continental reputations, and who subsequently distinguished themselves by founding colleges. Dr. Davie returned to Victoria where he practised in conjunction with his father. He has remained in Victoria continuously since. Is a memeber of the Provincial Medical Council, of which he has been president. Is a member of the Odd Fellows Order. Has not taken any active part in politics.

Davis, Lewis Thomas, M. D., C. M., (Nanaimo), son of Wm. Davis, Portland, Maine, U. S. A., general traffic manager of the Grand Trunk Railway, was born at Portland, July 4th, 1862. His parents are both of Welsh birth, his paternal ancestors having lived at Cirencester for centuries. His father was the first of the family to leave the old country. Dr. Davis received his elementary education at his native city and was then sent to Trinity College, at Port Hope, Ontario. From there he matriculated into Queen's University, Kingston. He entered the medical department and remained there four years graduating in 1883. Shortly after taking his degree he removed to lower California and settled at Redwood City, where he practised his profession for seven months, at the end of which time he came to British Columbia and took up his residence at Nanaimo. He formed a partnership with the late Dr. Cluness, medical officer for the Vancouver Coal Company. This partnership continued for two and a half years, when it was dissolved by mutual consent, and Dr. Davis has since conducted his practice singly. His practice is one of the most extensive in the Province. He is surgeon to the Nanaimo hospital; physician and surgeon to the Marine department for the port of Nanaimo, and

THOMAS CUNNINGHAM.

Departure Bay; surgeon to the Nanaimo jail, and holds several positions as medical examiner in different lodges. He is examiner for the New York Equitable and Sun Mutual Life Assurance Companies; the Citizens' Life Insurance Company, of Montreal, and several others. He is a member of the British Columbia Medical Council. He is a member of the Masonic Order, the American Legion of Honor, the Knights of Pythias, the Ancient Order of Druids, and the Ancient Order of United Workmen. In August, 1887, he married Miss Raynard, daughter of the late Rev. Mr. Raynard, Rector of the Episcopal Church, at Nanaimo, and lately at South Saanich, where he died.

De Cosmos, Hon. Amor, (Victoria), one of the most prominent figures in the early political history of British Columbia, the leader in the battle for responsible government, and in the agitation for confederation with the Dominion of Canada, was born at Windsor, Nova Scotia, and educated there and in Halifax. In 1852 he went to California and in 1858 came to British Columbia and settled in Victoria, where shortly after his arrival he founded the *British Colonist* newspaper which he owned and edited till 1863. In 1863 he was first elected a member of the Legislative Assembly of Vancouver Island, to represent the city of Victoria, and continued to represent the same constituency in this assembly, and, after the union of the two colonies, in the Legislative council of British Columbia till confederation. He was elected a member of the first Legislative Assembly of the Province, and was premier and president of the executive council from December 1872 to February 1874, when he resigned to stand for the House of Commons. He represented Victoria in the Federal Parliament till 1882 when, in the general elections of that year, he was defeated at the polls. Since that time Mr. De Cosmos has not taken an active interest in politics. In 1870 he founded the *Daily Standard*, and owned and edited it till 1874. In 1873-4 he was sent to London, England, as special commissioner of the Provincial Government, to lay before the Imperial authorities, the grievances of the Province in the matter of the Canadian Pacific Railway. Mr. De Cosmos is a Liberal in politics, and while in the House of Commons was a member of the Reform party.

Dewdney, Walter, (Vernon), was born in Devonshire, England, and educated with a view to fitting him for a military career. As a young man, however, he determined to seek his fortune in a new country, and accordingly came to British Columbia. Like the majority of others who came here at an early period, he went to the mines, but did not meet with much success. After following various pursuits he accepted the position of Government Agent and Gold Commissioner, and during the period of the construction of the Canadian Pacific Railway was stationed at Yale. He was subsequently transferred to Vernon, where he now resides. He is a member of the Ancient Order of United Workmen.

Dick, Archibald, (Nanaimo), was born at Kilmarnock, Ayrshire, on December 25th, 1842. His father, James Dick, was a miner. Mr. Dick received his education at Dreghorn, and in 1865 came with his family to British Columbia. The journey was made in the ship "Countess of Fife" and by way of Cape Horn. The family went direct to Nanaimo, where they settled, and Mr. Dick was engaged at the mines till 1870, when he went to Cariboo where he became interested in several gold claims. He remained in Cariboo for three years developing these claims, but he did not have much success. He then returned to Nanaimo where he again became connected with the Vancouver mines till he was offered and accepted the managership of the Baynes Sound Co's. mines. He remained in this position till the mines shut down. He subsequently bored the South Wellington estate and when Mr. Prior resigned the position of government inspector of coal mines, Mr. Dick was appointed to the post. Mr. Dick is a member of the Order of Oddfellows, and of the Presbyterian church. On January 1st, 1879, he married Elizabeth Clara Westwood.

Dickinson, Robert, born in 1836, died November 2nd, 1889. The name of the late Robert Dickinson was associated perhaps more than that of any other man, with the growth and progress of the city of New Westminster. He had resided in it almost from its foundation, and during thirty years of citizenship had labored as zealously in the interest of the community as in his own. During ten terms he occupied the office of chief magistrate, and was regarded with such respect and confidence by the citizens, that there was no office in their gift which he could not have had, by signifying his desire. Mr. Dickinson was born in Liverpool, England, was educated there, and in 1859, when twenty-three years of age, came to British Columbia and settled in New Westminster, where he resided continuously till his decease. The first municipal council met in 1860, and in 1861 Mr. Dickinson was elected a councillor, and again in 1862. In 1863 he was again elected councillor and chosen as president of the council, which office he filled for that year. He was elected and served as a member of the council thereafter for the years 1864, 1867, 1869, 1872 and 1873. In January of 1874, Mr. Dickinson was elected mayor of Westminster, being the second mayor of the city. In December, of 1874, he was elected to represent the city in the Legislative Assembly of the Province, and served for one term. Subsequently Mr. Dickinson was honored with the mayoralty of the city, and filled that office acceptably for the years 1874, 1880, 1881, 1883, and for the five following years consecutively. For over a quarter of a century Mr. Dickinson had been a Justice of the Peace for New Westminster city. He was also connected with the New Westminster Rifles from 1865 to 1869, in the capacity of ensign, retiring retaining rank. In addition to his arduous services in connection with the city council, Mr. Dickinson was a member of the Board of Trade from its organization, and a member of the council of that board for some time. The deceased had been for many years a member of Holy Trinity church, and had taken an active interest in its work. He was also a member of the Ancient Order of United Workmen. In 1860 Mr. Dickinson married Miss Harris, at New Westminster. In politics he was a consistent Conservative.

Dodd, William, (Yale), was born 4th of April, 1837, at Matfen, in the county of Northumberland, England, where his ancestors had resided for more than a century. Mr. Dodd went to school at Matfen and Wittington and received a thorough business education. Before leaving England he held a position in a manufacturer's office on the Tyne for over ten years. In 1862 Mr. Dodd arrived in British Columbia, settled at William's Creek, Cariboo, and spent over nine years at the mines, meeting however, with no success. From January, 1873 till October, 1885 he was agent for the British Columbia Express Company at Yale, and on January 16th, 1886, was appointed government agent at Yale, which position he still fills. On June 29th, 1878, he was married to Miss C. Lewis McCall. He is an adherent of the Church of England.

Douglas, Benjamin, (New Westminster), was born at Huntington, P. Q., May 6th, 1838. He was educated in his native town and subsequently served his apprenticeship to his trade. His father was for many years collector for Port St. Francis, and was an intimate friend of Mr. John Arthur Roebuck, afterwards member for Sheffield. Mr. Douglas arrived on this coast in 1862, and after residing in California a short time, came to British Columbia in the autumn of 1862, during the gold excitement. He landed in New Westminster in 1863, and shortly afterwards went to Cariboo and staid there a year. Mr. Douglas next lived in Victoria working at his trade, and then went over to Puget Sound and conducted a logging camp returning afterwards to Victoria. In 1866 he went to Yale and remained in that town until 1884 when he came to Westminster, where he has resided and carried on business since. Mr. Douglas has always been a Liberal-Conservative in politics, and is a Protestant. He is married and has six children. Mr. Douglas was a member of Westminster City Council during the years 1885 and 1886. He is a member of the Masonic fraternity.

Douglas, Sir James, K. C. B., born in May, 1803, at Jamaica, West India, died August 2nd, 1877, at Victoria, British Columbia. The history of the life of Sir James Douglas is identical with the history of British Columbia till 1865, and it may be said that it was from the wisdom and firmness of his administration as Chief Factor of the Hudson Bay Company, and subsequently as Governor of the colony, that the rapid growth of later years became possible. For twenty years his authority as absolute ruler over the immense area which constitutes the present Province of British Columbia was undisputed, and the impartial reviewers of his public actions during that period admit his statesmanlike qualities, his fidelity to duty, his uprightness and impartial justice. His father was a member of the noble Scotch family of Douglas and his mother was a Creole. After some years at school in Scotland he was entered as an apprentice clerk at the age of sixteen in the service of the North West Company, and stationed at Fort William under John McLoughlin. When the Hudson's Bay and North West Companies

BENJAMIN DOUGLAS.

were consolidated, Douglas was induced to remain in the new service, and when McLoughlin was transferred west of the Rocky Mountains to take charge of New Caledonia, Douglas was sent with him. A warm friendship existed between the Chief Factor and his young subordinate, and Douglas accordingly did not lack such advice and assistance as it was possible to give him. In such circumstances as he was thrown, however, native ability and inherent force of character were the essentials of success, and without them favor from a superior was of little avail in pushing a man to the front. From the time Douglas arrived on the Pacific coast, in 1824 he was practically at the head of the company's business, and while McLoughlin was nominally his superior, Douglas was not only the mind which conceived but the hand which carried into effect all the enterprises of the company. He was thoroughly familiar with all the branches of the business and as an accountant had no superior in the service. On his arrival in New Caledonia he set himself without delay to study the conditions of the country, its geography and hydrography, and the languages and characteristics of the various tribes of natives with whom he would have business dealings. He spent four years in the interior of New Caledonia, a portion of the time on Stewart lake, and during this period he founded several forts and had a number of encounters with the savages in which his prudence, address and courage made him feared and respected by the natives. During this time also, he was married to the daughter of John Connolly, who was stationed at Fort St. James. When Douglas went to headquarters at Fort Vancouver, in 1828, he took the position of accountant in the office and was made a chief trader. He improved and simplified the system of accounts employed, and placed the clerical work on a clear and understandable basis. In 1830 he was made chief factor and from that time he took personal charge of all important expeditions, made annual visits of inspection to the various posts, and selected sites and superintended the establishing of new stations. In this work he continued till 1845, when the retirement of McLoughlin placed him in name, as well as in fact, at the head of the company's business on the Pacific coast. As he was a shrewd observer and close student, these expeditions gave him opportunity for enlarging and perfecting his knowledge of the country and its inhabitants, and it was not long till he was regarded as having an

(11)

intimate acquaintance with every crevice on the coast. In 1840 he made a trip to Alaska and took over for his company the strip of that territory leased from the Russians. He also built Fort Tako on Tako river. In 1843 he established Fort Victoria, which has since grown into a large and beautiful city, and during the succeeding years the new station grew and flourished under his fostering care. After the settlement of the boundary question, Douglas, now at the head of the service, determined to transfer his headquarters to the new fort, and after making careful preparation, acccomplished the change in 1849. In September, 1851, Douglas was appointed Governor of the colony of Vancouver Island, and continued to hold that office till 1863. During the greater portion of this time he united in himself almost all the offices required for the conduct of the public affairs. In 1858 he was appointed Governor of the newly created colony of British Columbia, and thus filled a dual position until his retirement from public life in 1864, when he was knighted. During that year he paid a visit to the Mother Country and subsequently till the time of his death lived in private life. Governor Douglas was a man of irreproachable character and made such an impression on those with whom he came into contact, that men of the most opposite views, unite in extolling his virtues and his ability. He was a man born to command, but was full of charity and as generous as he was brave. The citizens of British Columbia raised an obelisk to his memory which stands in front of the house of parliament in Victoria.

Drake. Hon. Montague William Tyrwhitt. (Victoria), a Justice of the Supreme Court of British Columbia, is descended from a very old English family, the Tyrwhitt Drakes, of Shardilves, Bucks. Mr. Justice Drake was born at Kings Walls, Hertfordshire, England, in 1830, and was educated at the Charter House School. He was admitted as a solicitor and attorney-at-law, to the Superior Courts in England in 1851. He came to British Columbia in 1863, and settled in Victoria. He took an active part in public affairs shortly after his arrival, and he was elected a member of the Legislative Council of British Columbia, as representative for Victoria in 1868 and sat in the house till 1870. He was a member of the Board of Education for British Columbia from 1872 to 1879. In 1877 he was elected Mayor of the City of Victoria, and at the general election of 1882 he was returned to the Legislative Assembly to represent Victoria He was president of the Executive Council from January 26th, 1883 to October, 1884. Mr. Drake was called to the bar of British Columbia in 1877, was appointed a Q. C. on the 21st of September, 1883, and was elevated to the Bench in 1889. He is a bencher of the British Columbia Law Society. He married Miss Tolmie, of Ardersin, Invernessshire, Scotland.

Draper, James Nelson, (New Westminster), was born in Woodstock, New Brunswick, on October 9th, 1834, his father Isaac Draper, who was a farmer, having settled in New Brunswick in the early part of the present century. Mr. Draper was educated at Carleton Grammar School and King's College and after completing his studies passed a few years in St. John. In 1858 he came to British Columbia and engaged in the lumber trade. He was the first settler in the Royal City and soon after his arrival there, spent three days trying to discover the mouth of the Fraser river. In 1859 he went to Puget Sound where he engaged extensively in the lumber trade, not returning to New Westminster till 1876. Mr. Draper is harbor master of the Royal city, secretary of the woollen mills (in which he has an interest) and is a well-known and much respected citizen. On 17th March, 1862, he married Miss Vickery, of New Brunswick. He is an adherent of the Church of England.

Duck, Simeon. M. P. P., (Victoria), born at St. Catharines, Ontario, on December 1st, 1834. His parents were both of English birth, and his father was engaged in farming near St. Catharines, where Mr. Duck was educated. He left Ontario in the spring of 1859, and came by way of Panama to British Columbia. He arrived at Victoria on July 21st and went direct to the Fraser river mines. He took up a claim at Hills Bar which he worked during the summer without much success however, and in the autumn he returned to Victoria, where he established a wagon and carriage factory. He built the first wagon ever made in Victoria, which was purchased and used by Mr. F. J. Barnard for his express business between Yale and Cariboo. Business did not at first flourish with Mr. Duck, owing to the little demand there was for vehicles of any kind, but he continued at it without being discouraged and finally when the Government road was built through to the Cariboo mines the demand for wagons became considerable, and was supplied almost entirely by Mr. Duck. Mr. Duck took an active interest in the agitation for confederation with the Dominion and after this had been affected he stood for the city of Victoria as a candidate, in the first general election, for the local Legislature and was elected as a supporter of the McCreight government. At the next general election Mr. Duck again stood for Victoria but was defeated. In 1877 he took a trip to Ontario, and while he was in the east the elections for the third parliament took place. In 1882 Mr. Duck was again returned by the electors of Victoria to the local assembly as an independent. The Beaven government was defeated immediately after the meeting of the House, and Mr. Smythe formed an administration. This government introduced what is known as the settlement bill and in this measure they received the support of Mr. Duck. In 1885 Mr. Duck accepted office in the Smythe cabinet as Finance Minister, which he held till the dissolution of the House in 1886. At the general election of this year he was defeated in his candidature. A bye-election took place in the following year in consequence of Mr. Prior's resignation of his seat to stand for the Commons, and Mr. Duck was again returned as a supporter of the Davie government. In 1865 Mr. Duck married Mrs. Sarah Miller, of Victoria. Mr. Duck is a member of the Masonic fraternity, and at one time filled the office of Grand Master of British Columbia. He is a member of the Ancient Order of United Workmen, and was for years a member of the Victoria Volunteer Fire Brigade and filled all the different offices in the brigade.

Duncan, William Chalmers. (Cowichan), was born in the township of Sarnia, county of Lambton, Ontario, on October 18th, 1836. He is of Highland Scotch descent, his people having, in 1779, moved from the north and settled in the town of Hamilton, twelve miles from Glasgow. In 1820 his grandfather emigrated to Canada and settled in Lanark, where his mother's people also settled in the following year. His father and mother were married in 1825 and lived in Lanark for ten years, when they removed to Sarnia county where Mr. Duncan was born. He was educated at his native place by Ebenezer Watson who established a school there. At that time everything was in a very primitive condition and educational facilities were extremely limited. Mr. Duncan, at an early age, worked with his brothers in clearing the farm of timber, but during the winter and in summer evenings he attended school. He remained on the farm till 1862, when, in company with his brother James, he left Ontario for British Columbia, being attracted hither by the excitement over the discovery of gold. They came by way of Panama and arrived at Victoria on the 11th of May. During that summer Mr. Duncan worked on the wagon road between Yale and Lytton, while his brother went to the Cariboo mines. His brother took up what afterward proved to be one of the richest claims in Cariboo, and abandoned it as worthless, on the advice of an old miner. During the next year both brothers worked on the wagon road between Yale and Lytton, building bridges and constructing kerbing, and in the autumn Mr. Duncan went to Cariboo, leaving his brother who had made considerable money and had decided to return to eastern Canada. Mr. Duncan found a great deal of suffering and destitution in Cariboo, and the place over-crowded, when the difficulty of getting supplies in, were considered. He got the work of building a bridge across the Cottonwood river and when he had completed this he put up some buildings on Smith & Ryder's ranch. During the winter he drove a team for Smith & Ryder, from the mouth of the Quesnelle to the mines, bringing in goods to the camps. During this time he brought a boiler, weighing 1,500 pounds, from Fort Alexandria to the mines driving it in on his sleigh over the mule train. In the spring he started out prospecting, and located a claim on Stewart's creek. After carrying his supplies over the mountains on his back for a distance of twelve miles, to his claim and then working down to bed rock he found that it was barren, and abandoned it. He then went to Lightning creek and formed a company of Canadians to work a claim which he had prospected. They sunk a shaft thirty-seven feet, and during the whole summer they labored with energy. It cost them considerable money, and as everything was at that time exceedingly expensive, they ran short of funds, and decided to abandon the claim till the following spring. The company did not reform, and the claim was afterwards taken up and developed by another company, which made a great deal of money out of it. Mr.

Duncan returned to Victoria and found the Leech river excitement in full blast. In that year he took up the farm on which he at present resides, and in the spring of 1865 he went to work to clear it. His outfit consisted of a cross-cut saw, a frying pan, and a billy, and he was without a dollar in his pocket. He obtained credit, however, and succeeded in securing a contract from Drinkwater Bros., by which he made money sufficient to pay off his debts, and procure necessaries. During that year he cleared six acres on his farm and had one acre under cultivation. In January of 1866, he heard of the reported discoveries at Big Bend and determined to try his fortune once more at the mines. He accordingly went to Victoria, and succeeded in getting passage across the Gulf in the steamer Enterprise. A short distance above Langley the vessel got stuck in the ice and the passengers, most of whom were on the same errand as Mr. Duncan, were put ashore. The passengers started up the river bank on foot and when beyond Sumas, got lost in a snow storm, and during the night made only two miles on their journey. They finally reached Chilliwhack, and from there worked their way up the Fraser, which was one moving mass of ice. They were confined at the hotel, at the mouth of Harrison river, for three days by a blizzard. They finally started again with an Indian guide although there was three feet of snow on the ground. During the next five days they toiled on through almost insurmountable difficulties, sleeping at night wherever they could find shelter. On the fifth night they reached Yale where after resting they joined a party of about forty-five going to the mines. Their journey as far as Spuzzum was one of extreme danger, but was safely accomplished, and when they got into the flat country beyond, they found the snow lying four feet on the level. They pushed on however, and after two days and a half of hard travelling, with very little to eat, they reached Lytton. After leaving Lytton their path lay along the side of the mountains, and they were in imminent peril from falling rocks and snow slides. The party had by this time separated, the smaller number, with whom Mr. Duncan was, being ahead of the main body. The party he was with accomplished this part of the journey in safety, but the rear party lost one man, who was killed by a falling rock, and whom they buried at Spence's bridge. They pushed on to Kamloops, which they were compelled to reach by a roundabout way, owing to the lake being frozen over.

At Kamloops, Mr. Duncan was engaged by the Hudson's Bay Company to work on the construction of a steamer to be built for the navigation of Shuswap lake. Those engaged for the work started from Kamloops with the thermometer registering about 40 degrees below zero, and after two days and a half's journey, during which they camped out at nights, they reached their objective point. Here they found that no house had been prepared for them according to promise and they had to set too and erect one themselves. Mr. Duncan worked here for thirty days, getting $75.00 per month and his board. He then started, once more, for the mines. Before setting out he and his companions constructed hand sleighs, which they loaded with about 200 pounds of provisions each. It took them four days to reach Seymour, which they found to be quite a flourishing place, and where they remained for a week constructing toboggans, at which work Mr. Duncan made five dollars per day. Another start was made, the party now numbering about twenty, all having toboggans well stocked with provisions. The snow was very heavy and to increase their discomfort the rain began to descend in torrents. After two days of hard travel they reached Kerby's Landing. They were now compelled to cross a small range of hills which divided them from the plains of Big Bend. They took advantage of a dry creek bed running down from the mountain and began to ascend by it. They found the snow too soft however, and after a day's hard work, without much result, they built a shelter and camped for three days. During that time frost set in and they were able to proceed. It took them four days to reach the summit, a distance of fourteen miles. The descent on the other side, however, did not take them more than a few hours, as, at the suggestion of Mr. Duncan, they came down the greater portion of it on their toboggans. When they got into camp, Mr. Duncan and three others secured a claim on McCulloch's creek. They went to work, as soon as the weather would permit, and sank a shaft, put in water wheels and all the necessary appliances for separating the gold from the earth. They toiled all summer, and when they came out of the shaft in October after reaching bed rock, they had not made a dollar. They made about $14 each, by cleaning up a surface digging, and started down the country by the way they had come. They had a rough journey back and when after many days of hard travelling, with blistered feet they reached Boston Bar, Mr. Duncan was able to borrow a little money to take him to Victoria. During the greater part of the following winter he was laid up in Victoria with mountain fever. In the spring he returned to his farm. He was without money and in order to make some he took a contract to supply wood to a steamer, and during the autumn while at work he cut his foot badly and was laid up. Things looked very blue at this time, but he had friends who insisted on looking after him. One of these was Rev. Mr. Reece, the Episcopalian clergyman, who invited Mr. Duncan to stay with him during his illness and would take no refusal. While here Mr. Duncan became delirious with the pain from his foot, which grew so bad that he had to be sent to Victoria. Here he was place in the hands of the doctors and had an operation performed on his foot. In the spring of 1867 he returned to his farm and again began the work of clearing it. During the next three years he continued at this and succeeded in making sufficient money to keep him going, by taking contracts to build bridges, barns and other works of a similiar character. In 1870 he had a considerable number of acres free from timber and stumps, and in this year he purchased two young heifers, the nucleus of his future herds. In three years time he had twenty head of cattle, and from this out everything went smoothly. In 1875, Mr. Duncan married Miss Sarah Ann Ingram, daughter of the late Thomas Ingram, of Donegal, Ireland. In Dominion politics, Mr. Duncan is a Liberal, and in Provincial a supporter of the opposition. He has always taken an active interest in public affairs and especially in those of his district. He has occupied the position of Reeve of Cowichan, and is one of the most prominent members of the Agricultural Society. In religion he is an Episcopalian, and has been warden of that church for twenty consecutive years.

Dunsmuir, Hon. Robert. born in Hurlford, Ayrshire, Scotland, in 1825, died on April 12th, 1889, at Victoria, British Columbia. His father and grandfather had been coal masters, and he was brought up to their business. He was educated at Kilmarnock Academy. In 1847 he was married in Kilmarnock to Joanna, daughter of Alex. White. He came to Canada in the early fifties, as a coal expert, and was employed by the Vancouver Coal Co., and remained in their employ for a number of years. In his explorations for himself he discovered a rich vein of coal at Wellington,

HON. ROBERT DUNSMUIR.

which, it is needless to state, subsequently amassed him a great fortune. In his early operations he was assisted financially by Admiral Hornby, Capt. Egert, and Lieut. Diggle, of the Royal Navy, the conditions on his part were, that he should own half the mine and have entire control of the operations. The mine was opened successfully and developed with such profit to Mr. Dunsmuir that he was enabled to become sole owner, buying out one partner after another, the last being Lieutenant Diggle, to whom he paid a cheque of $750,000 or $800,000 in full of all claims. His mining property made him very wealthy and consequently very influential, and he died probably the best known man in British Columbia, and certainly the richest in the Province, if not in all the Dominion. Mr. Dunsmuir, while rich, was also very enterprising, and few large enterprises and industrial projects undertaken in the Province, but were largely assisted by him. Besides the mines at Wellington and Comox, of which he was sole proprietor, he was president of and the largest shareholder in the Esquimalt and Nanaimo Railway and its extensive coal, timber and farming belt; he was one of the most extensive owners of quartz claims in the Province; he was one of the large shareholders in the Matsqui Dyking Co., the Albion Iron Works and the Canadian Pacific Navigation Co., and an extensive owner of real estate, besides numerous other investments. He also was one of the promoters of the proposed Canadian Western Railway, to which the Provincial Legislature at its session in 1889, granted a charter and a subsidy of some fourteen million acres of land. In fact, it may be said that there was not an enterprise of any magnitude in the Province in which he was not financially interested. Although politically Hon. Robt. Dunsmuir did not enter the arena until a comparatively late period in his career, his prominence in parliament, was scarcely less than in business circles. He was elected to represent Nanaimo in 1882, and returned again at the general election of 1886, succeeding as President of the Council the late Premier, Hon. William Smythe. He was neither a politician nor a statesman, judged by the usual standard of what constitutes a success as such, but he was a very practical, hard-headed and level-headed legislator, who knew what he wanted and usually took the shortest road to its accomplishment. Personally there were many estimates of his character. He had in life many enemies and many ardent and admiring friends, a fact which denoted strong individuality in his make-up. Brusque and energetic in his manner, he was at the same time genial, kind-hearted and generous, and numerous are the acts of a benevolent character recorded of him in life.

Earle, Thomas, M.P., (Victoria), was born in Landsowne Township, county of Leeds, Ontario, on the 23rd of September, 1837. He is the youngest son of the late William Earle, who emigrated from Ireland during the early part of the present century and who was among the first settlers in Western Ontario. Mr. Earle was educated at his native place, and after gaining a thorough knowledge of mercantile pursuits opened a general store in the town of Brockville, which he continued to conduct till he left Ontario for British Columbia in 1862. In the spring of 1863 he went to the Cariboo District and mined for two seasons on William's Creek without, however, having much success. In the autumn of 1864 he returned to Victoria, and during 1865 and 1866 he held the position of bookkeeper in the grocery establishment of J. Rueffe & Co. In the spring of 1867 he was attracted to the Big Bend region by the excitement there, and he opened a general store at French Creek, which he conducted for two years. When the mines gave out he returned once more to Victoria where he formed a partnership in the wholesale grocery business with his former employer, Mr. James Rueffe. In 1873 Mr. Rueffe died, and Mr. Earle purchased his interest in the business, which he has since conducted. When the charter for the Esquimalt and Nanaimo Railway was given, Mr. Earle, in conjunction with Mr. McLellan, took a contract for the construction of twenty miles of the road, and on this work they expended over a million of dollars. During the past four years Mr. Earle, in conjunction with Mr. J. W. McLeod, has been continuously engaged on railway contract work on Puget Sound, and has assisted in the construction of most of the railway lines in Oregon and Washington, and is now interested in the West Shore road, which will connect with the C. P. R. Mr. Earle is interested in a great many of the important enterprises in the Province: as the Esquimalt Water Works Co., the Vancouver Water Works Co., the Alert Bay Canning Co., and many others. He is also interested in a number of quartz mines in the Selkirk range. He has been a member of the British Columbia Board of Trade for many years and has filled the position of Vice-President of the Board for a number of terms. He has been offered but has declined the presidency. He represented the city in the municipal council in 1885, and was urged to stand for the mayoralty, but refused the nomination. In the byeelection of 1889 he was sent, by acclamation, to represent Victoria in the House of Commons. In January, 1875, he married Miss Lizzie Mason, of Victoria. Mr. Earle is an adherent of the Methodist Church.

Eberts, Duncan William, M. D., C. M., (Wellington), son of Wm. D. Eberts, commission merchant, Chatham, Ontario, where Dr. Eberts was born on the 25th of December, 1856. He was educated at Chatham High School, and after completing his studies there, spent sometime in general business. In 1881 he matriculated in the honor class at McGill University, Montreal, and decided to take a medical course. He graduated with honors in 1885, and the same year entered the competitive examination for a position on the staff of the Montreal General Hospital. He was successful and remained there as house surgeon for a year. In 1886 he received the appointment of superintendent of the Winnipeg General Hospital, which he held till May, 1887, when he was offered and accepted the position of surgeon for the Wellington mines, owned by Mr. Dunsmuir. He took charge at Wellington the day the explosion occurred at the Vancouver Coal Company's shaft No. 1. He placed his services at the disposal of the Vancouver Company during this period of distress. Since that time Dr. Eberts has resided at Wellington. At the meeting of the Canada Medical Association at Banff last year Dr. Eberts was elected vice-president of that association for British Columbia.

Eckstein, Louis Philip, (New Westminster), member of the firm of Armstrong, Eckstein and Gaynor, barristers of New Westminster, was born in Victoria on 15th June, 1866. His father, Mr. Leon Eckstein, came to California in 1849, and afterwards settled in Victoria in 1858, where he engaged in business, at one time gaining considerable wealth, which he afterwards lost in speculation. Mr. L. P. Eckstein was educated principally in New Westminster. His intention being to enter the priesthood he studied theology at St. Louis College in the Royal City; later on, however, he determined to join the legal profession and studied law under the present

Judge Bole, at that time a practising barrister and a Queen's Counsel. Mr. Eckstein became a member of the Law Society of B. C., in February, 1888, and was admitted to practise as a barrister. He then entered into partnership with Mr. Bole until May, 1889, when he became a partner of Mr. R. W. Armstrong. Mr. Eckstein is a member of the New Westminster Club and is, by religion, a Roman Catholic.

Edmonds, Henry Valentine, (New Westminster), born in Dublin on the 14th of Febuary, 1837, is the second son of the late William and Matilda E. Edmonds, nee Humphries, of that city. He is descended on his father's side from an old English family who some four generations previously had settled in Dublin, and on his mother's side from a Huguenot family who had emigrated from France at the time of the massacre of St. Bartholomew. Mr. Edmonds while residing in Dublin attended the Collegiate schools kept by the Rev. Dr. Wall and Rev Mr. Kearney, both on Stephen's Green, but when about 12 years of age his family moved to Liverpool where they have since continued to reside. Mr. Edmond's education was here continued at the Collegiate Institute and High School Mechanics' Institute for several years, after which he was sent to the Moravian Institute, at Neuwied on the Rhine, near Coblentz, and finally finished his education at Dresden, in Saxony. After some time spent at business in Liverpool Mr. Edmonds, in the year 1859, established himself in London, and on the breaking out of the volunteer movement was one of the first to join, connecting himself with the first Surrey volunteers, the first of the new corps established there. Subsequently on the formation of the London Irish Volunteers he joined his national corps and after passing rapidly through the non-commissioned ranks was selected by the colonel commanding, the Marquis of Donegal, as ensign of a new company especially formed for the Marquis' son-in-law, Lord Ashley, subsequently Earl of Shaftsbury. On his appointment on 5th July, 1860, Ensign Edmonds was attached to the 3rd Batt. Grenadier Guards for drill instruction and passed with a first-class certificate of efficiency. On the 13th April, 1861, Ensign Edmonds was promoted to a lieutenancy which he held until he resigned in April, 1862, in order to emigrate to British Columbia at which time he stood second on the list for captaincy. Whilst serving in this corps

THOMAS EARLE.

Lieut. Edmonds took part in the celebrated reviews held in 1860 in High Park, 1861 at Wimbleton and 1862 at Brighton, under the late Lord Clyde. He also, after a parade, was present with part of his company at the great fire at London bridge where they rendered material service in keeping the grounds clear for the firemen. Leaving England in May Mr. Edmonds arrived in San Francisco on the 4th of July, 1862, and whilst there participated in the rejoicing occasioned by the passing by Congress of the Pacific Railway Bill. After a short stop in Victoria Mr. Edmonds settled in New Westminster with whose interests he has ever since been closely connected. For twenty-five years he carried on business as a real estate agent conveyancer, holding the agency of nearly all the principal property owners in the city. Mr. Edmond's ability in his adopted home was speedily recognised by his fellow citizens and his services were always given gratuitously where needed, in such institutions as the Royal Columbian Hospital, Mechanics' Institute and other organizations of a kindred character. His services as president, secretary or treasurer, were always in demand and the duties were ably performed. On the formation of the Board of Trade for New Westminster Mr. Edmonds undertook the duties of secretary for the first year and on his shoulders rested the carrying out of the whole details of the organization of the Board. He subsequently served a term as vice-president but pressure of business prevented him continuing to hold office although he still remained a member of the Board. In connection with any matters affecting the city of New Westminster, whether for its pleasure or advancement, Mr. Edmonds was always found assisting in the front rank. In the former line in nearly all the committees formed for celebrating the Queen's birthday, Dominion Day, or the reception of the different Governors-General his name is to be found and he gave also as freely of his means as of his time towards ensuring their success. Mr. Edmonds claims to have been the originator of the idea of the May Day celebration in the province, the first one being carried out at New Westminster almost entirely by the late Captain Bushby and himself. Mr. Edmonds helped to organize the Howe Sound Silver Mining Company and the Fraser River Beet Sugar Company, both of which failed for want of capital, and he was also connected with other organizations having for their object the promotion of the business interests of New Westminster. In 1873, recognizing the benefits to be derived from railway communication with our southern neighbors, he joined in forming a company for that purpose and became the secretary of the Fraser Valley Railway Company, one of two companies afterwards virtually amalgamated into what is now known as the New Westminster Southern Railway Company, in which he remained interested. Mr. Edmonds has during his residence in New Westminster held several official positions with credit to himself and advantage to the public interests. In December, 1867, he was appointed clerk of the municipal council, which office he held continuously for about seven years and it is evidence of his tact and ability that during the whole of this period he carried on the business of the city without a single law suit and without incurring any law costs or lawyer's bills, drawing up himself all the necessary by-laws required and performing all the work necessitated by the incorporation of the city in December, 1872. On the formation of the Walkem Government Mr. Edmonds was selected as their agent for New Westminster district and was appointed to the Government offices for that district. He continued to perform the duties involved in the discharge of these offices in addition to his own private business with satisfaction to the government until June, 1876, when on the defeat of the Walkem and the assumption of power by the Elliott Government, it was decided to appoint a salaried officer to these positions, Mr. Edmonds retaining only the position of Sheriff. This position he continued to occupy until July, 1880, when he fell a victim to political exigencies and was deprived of office. The same success which attended his administration of municipal affairs was equally apparent in those of the Shrievalty as during the period he held office, over seven years, he had the confidence of the legal profession and had not a single suit brought against him and had himself only to bring one against other parties in which he was successful. In September, 1870, Mr. Edmonds, on the re-organization of the New Westminster Rifle Volunteers under Capt. Bushby was appointed lieutenant and adjutant, which position he held until 1874, when, on the formation of No. 1 Rifle Company of New Westminster militia he was gazetted as captain with the following memo : "Formerly Lieut. London Irish Volunteers, holding A 1 class certificate of efficiency," and remained in command until, May, 1875, when he retired retaining rank as Lieut. Mr. Edmonds has also served as municipal councillor and Mayor of the city of New Westminster and ran for the Provincial Legislature as an independent candidate but was defeated by the government candidate. In 1883 he was appointed a Justice of the Peace for New Westminster city and district. He had great confidence in the future of New Westminster, both city and district, and in the Fraser Valley as the route for the Canadian Pacific Railway with Burrard Inlet as its terminus, in consequence of which he early invested in real estate both in the city and district especially at Port Moody and what is now known as Vancouver and his judgment proving successful he is now one of the largest real estate owners of valuable property in these places. He is also largely interested in saw mills and timber limits in the district of New Westminster and in mines in Illecillewaet and other districts; is a large shareholder in the New Westminster Street Railway, the Vancouver Electric Railway and Light Company and the New Westminster and Vancouver Street Railway. As a philanthropist he stands well to the front, giving liberally in aid of any charitable project. The city of Vancouver owes to him the site for their Mount Pleasant public school and the Episcopal church the sites of the Mount Pleasant church and parsonage. In New Westminster he also presented the site for the Sapperton public school and to his efforts and subscriptions the Episcopal Diocese of New Westminster is also largely indebted as has been repeatedly acknowledged in the *Churchman's Gazette*. In November, 1867, Mr. Edmonds married Jane Fortune Kemp, eldest daughter of the late Thomas P. Kemp, of Cork, Ireland, and granddaughter of James Casey, of Blossom Grove county Cork, and has issue three sons and two daughters.

Elford, John Pitcairns. (Victoria), was born in the city of Adelaide, New South Wales, on March 10th, 1851. His father, Robert Elford, a native of Plymouth, Eng., came to British Columbia in 1859, and settled in Victoria. Mr. Elford received his education at San Francisco and Victoria, and learned the trade of a carpenter in the former city. He worked at his trade about six years in San Francisco, and from 1872 to 1875 in Victoria, when he engaged in the contracting business. In 1886 he took into partnership Mr. W. J. Smith, and in the same year the firm opened up the "Queen City Brick and Tile Works," which since that date they have greatly increased and extended, and fitted up with the latest and most improved machinery. Mr. Elford has constructed some of the finest buildings in the Province, amongst which may be mentioned the Jubilee Hospital. He is a member of the Oddfellows and Masons Orders, and has been twice married,—in 1875 to Hettie, eldest daughter of Capt. John Robertson, of Cleveland, Ohio, who died in 1877, and in 1889 to Agnes Francis, second daughter of H. A. Lilley, Esq., of Maple Bay, British Columbia. Mr. Elford is one of the most successful contractors in the Province and a first-class business man.

Ellison, Price, (Vernon), was born in the town of Dunham, Cheshire, England, in 1853. His father, Mr. James Ellison, married Ellen, youngest daughter of Mr. Fearnaught, a well-known citizen of the town of Lyme, in the same county. Mr. Ellison received his education at St. George's parochial school, Manchester, and after having finished his studies commenced business in the blacksmith and hardware line. Mr. Ellison married in British Columbia in 1876 and settled at Vernon the following year. Not meeting with success at the mines, Mr. Ellison resumed his business as a blacksmith, which, however, he discontinued entirely about three years ago, since which time he has devoted his entire attention to stock-raising and general farming. Ever since his arrival in British Columbia, Mr. Ellison has given the present government his hearty support. He has served as a school trustee since the opening of a school in the district. He married Sophie Christine, third daughter of John Johnson, Esq., of Peoria, Ill. He is a member of the Ancient Order of Foresters, and an adherent of the Church of England. Mr. Ellison started the first blacksmith's shop south of Kamloops, and was the first to grow wheat in the bush land in the interior without irrigation,—his venture proving a wonderful success. At the present time Mr. Ellison holds a four-year contract, with the Dominion Government, to convey the mails from Sicamous to Vernon and Okanagan Mission, a distance of ninety miles.

English, Marshall Martin, (New Westminster), was born at Charlestown, Jefferson county, Virginia, United States, on the 8th of April, 1840, his parents being, John Marshall English and Ann Maria Martin English. He was educated in the Virginia public

HON. THEODORE DAVIE.

schools, and after completing his studies, followed farming, milling and mining pursuits. In April, 1877, he came to British Columbia and settled at New Westminster. Since his arrival in the Province, Mr. English has followed the occupation of salmon-canning, in which he has been very successful. He has not in any way mingled in Provincial politics, and has never held a public office of any kind, but is connected with several workingmen's societies. He was married in 1868 and has several children. In religion, Mr. English is an Episcopalian. He has travelled a good deal, but his life has been unmarked by any remarkable adventures or accidents. He is a very highly esteemed and valuable citizen of New Westminster, and is reckoned one of Westminster's most prosperous and successful business men.

Erb, Louis E., (Victoria), was born in Fulda, Prussia, in January, 1830, and lived there till he was sixteen years old, when he went to Bavaria. While in Munich he studied the theory of brewing at Liebig's College, and afterwards obtained a practical knowledge of the business in breweries, in Bavaria, Austria and Hungary. He then went to Warsaw, where he had charge of a large brewing establishment for several years. From Warsaw he went to Constantinople to take charge of a business there, and from Constantinople he removed to Bucharest, Roumania, where he conducted a brewing establishment for two years. In 1863 he came to America, and for a year had charge of one of the largest breweries in New York. He then came west to San Francisco where, after a few year's residence, he removed to British Columbia. He was in Lillooet when the Big Bend excitement broke out, and he started a brewery in Seymour City, at the head of Shuswap lake. When the Big Bend excitement failed, Mr. Erb went to Cariboo, where he took charge of the principal brewery in Barkerville, where he remained till the Mosquito creek excitement broke out when he started a brewery there and conducted it till the mines were worked out. In the spring of 1870, he went to Victoria and purchased an interest in the Victoria Brewing Co., which he worked up to what it now is, the largest brewing business in British Columbia.

Evans, Thomas, (Donald), was born at Birkenhead, Cheshire, England, on November 29th, 1840. His father, John Evans, Esq., of Liverpool, married Miss Sarah Shepherd, of Sanghall, Cheshire. Mr. Evans was educated at Hawarden Grammar School, and after completing his studies, passed several years as a teacher, until he was appointed clerk to the Chester corporation. Before his arrival in British Columbia, Mr. Evans was connected with the "*Chester Chronicle*," and was afterwards appointed publisher of the "*Liverpool Daily Post and Journal*." On quitting journalism, Mr. Evans acted as chief accountant to Dodd, Ontel & Co., of Liverpool, of which firm he became afterwards manager. During his residence in England, Mr. Evans was a prominent member of many musical societies, amongst others "The Liverpool Musical Society" and the "Chester Choral Society," of which latter he was secretary. He was also secretary to the sanitary committee of Chester city. Mr. Evans came to Canada in 1880, and in the winter of 1882, settled in the North West Territories. In 1883 he had the misfortune to lose everything he had, by fire, when at Qu'Appelle, including a very valuable musical library. Shortly afterwards he took up his residence in Broadview, and was appointed a Justice of the Peace. In 1885 he was solicited to contest Broadview electoral district, as member of the North West Council, but declined. While in Broadview he acted as secretary of the local Liberal-Conservative Association. Early in 1887, Mr. Evans came to British Columbia, and settled at Donald, where he was employed in the Canadian Pacific Railway offices. On the removal of the head office of the store department of the Pacific Division from Donald to Vancouver, he was appointed assistant storekeeper of the Pacific division, with charge of the Donald office of the department. Shortly after his arrival in Donald, he was appointed Justice of the Peace. He is an adherent of the Church of England, and takes great interest in church and school matters. He is sec.-treas. of the Donald School Trustees and chairman of the Library Committee. He is a member of the Order of Free Masons, and married Jessie, second daughter of T. A. Baker, Esq., of Chester, England.

Ewen, Alexander, (New Westminster), eldest son of the late George Ewen and Elizabeth Sheppard Ewen, was born on the 22nd of November, 1832, in Aberdeenshire, Scotland, where his father

H. V. EDMONDS.

was largely interested in the extensive fishing industry carried on on the coast of that shire. He attended school in old Aberdeen til'l he had reached the age of twelve years, when he took to his father's occupation. From that time till he left the old country he was engaged in the salmon fishing on the east coast of Scotland and England. He went through and learned thoroughly every department of the business, and at an early age was placed in the position of foreman of the fishing stations, and later had the direction of affairs of the stations. In 1863, a Mr. Annandale, who had been mining in British Columbia, and had become acquainted with the Fraser's vast wealth in fish, thought to put his knowledge to account, and advertised in the Scotch papers for practical men to take charge of the fishing station which he had decided to erect on that river. Mr. Ewen made enquiries and was induced by Mr. Annandale's representations to come to British Columbia. He landed at Victoria, in January, 1864, having come by way of Panama. Mr. Annandale insisted, against Mr. Ewen's advice, in employing the Scotch system of trap nets, and as this was not adapted to fishing on the rivers in this country, the enterprise fell through. Mr. Ewen then began business himself, salting fish for the Australian and Sandwich Island markets. The trade with Australia became large and remunerative, as the export lumber business increased. Mr. Ewen continued at this business with increasing success, till 1870, when in conjunction with Messrs. Logie & Wise, he established a cannery, where the British Columbia cannery now is. The title of the firm was Alexander Logie & Co. The firm continued to do business for some years, but eventually Mr. Ewen purchased his partner's interest and conducted the establishment himself. In 1884, Mr. Ewen built the present cannery he possesses on Lion Island, which is the largest and most fully equipped establishment on the Fraser river, and has a capacity of two thousand cases per day. He is also interested in a number of other canneries in the Province, and in a fish freezing establishment. He was the first man who made a practical success of the salmon fishing on the Fraser, and of salting and drying fish for the export trade. Mr. Ewen's interests are not confined to the fishing industry. He is one of the largest land owners on the river Fraser, possessing six hundred and forty acres of choice agricultural property in the neighborhood of his cannery, and it is with a view to assist in developing the farming industry of the Province, that he acquired this land. He is also a stock holder in the New Westminster Southern Railway Company, and is one of the provisional directors. He has stock in the Gas Company, and in a number of other enterprises in New Westminster City and District. He has served the city in the Municipal Council for several years, and is a member of the Board of Trade, and on the executive council of that institution. He has been a member of the Oddfellows' society since its inception in New Westminster and has passed through all the chairs in the lodge. In 1876 he married Miss Rogers, daughter of James Rogers, formerly of the township of Dorchester, county of Middlesex, Ontario. Mr. Ewen is an adherent of the Presbyterian Church.

Fell, James. (Victoria, born on October 13th, 1821, at Muncaster Head, county of Cumberland, England. Educated under the Rev. Joseph Taylor, at Raven Glass, and then apprenticed for five years to the grocery business. In 1841 went to London and obtained an appointment through General Minden, brother of the Earl of Egmont, in a large establishment in Piccadilly. Remained there twelve months and was then sent to Liverpool by a tea importing firm to conduct a branch house in that city. After being about one year at this business, Mr. Fell went into partnership with a gentleman named Gee, and opened a business at Liverpool, which they conducted for two years. Mr. Fell then established a wholesale tea business, which he continued to manage till 1858. Shortly after that date he came to British Columbia and settled in Victoria, where he first opened in partnership with John Finlayson, a spice and coffee business. They had no opposition, and their business was not only remunerative, but increased very rapidly in size. In two years they were compelled to lease larger premises, and at this time they branched out into a general grocery trade. After a brief period they had again to remove their business, and they then leased the site on which Mr. Fell's business is now carried on. The firm did business till near 1868, when in consequence of an employee whom they had entrusted with the management of a branch business on the Skeena river, they became pressed for money and a meeting of their creditors was called. Had Mr. Fell's advice been acted upon the business would have paid far more than the amount of indebtedness but hasty measures and careless management made this impossible. Mr. Fell, through the assistance of his friends, was again able to establish himself and has since carried on his business with much success. Ever since his arrival in the country Mr. Fell has taken a strong interest in public matters. He was prominent in the battle for responsible government and confederation with the Dominion. Mr. Fell was not in sympathy with the commercial policy of the Dominion Government, being a strong and uncompromising free trader. In 1882 he stood as a candidate for the House of Commons, but was defeated. In municipal matters Mr Fell has, for a great many years, been very prominent. In 1886 he was elected chief magistrate of the City of Victoria and again in 1887, and during his incumbency of this office he had a number of questions of importance to deal with, which he disposed of to the satisfaction of the citizens. In the following year an attempt was again made to bring him out for the Mayoralty, but he refused to stand. He has always taken a strong interest in educational matters, and was for fourteen years a member of the School Board. He was one of the organizers of the first Mechanics' Institute in Victoria and a trustee of the Institute. Mr. Fell is a trustee of the Jubilee Hospital, a member of the Pioneer society and of St. George's society and President of the British Columbia Benevolent society, of which he was one of the founders.

Finlayson, Roderick. (Victoria), was born in the parish of Lochash, Rossshire, Scotland, in the year 1815. His father was an extensive sheep farmer, and gave his son such advantages in the way of education as the parochial school afforded. When Mr. Finlayson left school he for some time assisted his father in the management of his farm, and at the age of eighteen years he left home for the purpose of seeking his fortune in the new world. He took passage on an emigrant ship for New York, which he reached in the spring of 1837. An uncle who resided here secured him a position in the Hudson's Bay Company's service as an apprenticed clerk, and he was sent to the headquarters at Montreal, where he was employed for some months in the office. In the autumn of the same year he was transferred to Bytown, a post on the Ottawa River, of which, after a short residence, he was placed in charge. In the fall of 1839 he was sent across the Rocky Mountains to Fort Vancouver, where he passed the winter. In this year, 1839, the Hudson's Bay Company took a lease of Russian territory lying along the coast between Cape Spencer and parallel 54° 40', for a period of ten years, and Mr. Finlayson was sent to Fort Taco as assistant at that post. Here he remained for eighteen months, at the expiration of which time he was transferred to Fort Stickeen, where he took command, and where he remained for six months. He was then sent to Fort Simpson as trader. It was while he was in charge of Fort Simpson that John McLoughlin was assassinated at Fort Stickeen, and as soon as the news was brought to Fort Simpson Mr. Finlayson proceeded to the scene of the murder. He found on arriving that Governor Simpson had been there before him and had placed a man in charge. Mr. Finlayson accordingly returned to Fort Simpson, where he remained till the spring of 1843, when he was transferred to Fort Victoria, which post had just been erected, as second in command. During the next spring the officer in charge died and Mr. Finlayson was appointed to his position. During the early period of the posts existence he had a great deal of difficulty in keeping the Indians in order, and one attempt to seize the fort he defeated. It was under his supervision that the first land about the fort was cleared of the forest, and he has ever since, during nearly half a century, watched with interest Victoria's growth from a trading post to a populous and splendid city. In 1845 the Company's ships from England began to call at Victoria with supplies for the northern and interior posts, and the place was recognised as the second depot west of the mountains. In the year 1846 Mr. Finlayson, in his capacity as commander of the fort, was called upon to entertain a number of the officers of Her Majesty's navy, who had been sent to British Columbia to ascertain and report to the Home Government on the value of the country as an Imperial possession. He continued in charge of Fort Vancouver till 1848, when Sir James Douglas, the chief factor, removed the headquarters of the Company from Fort Vancouver to this place and settled here himself. Mr. Finlayson then occupied the position of accountant. In 1850 Governor Blanchard came to Victoria with the intention of taking charge of the Colony of Vancouver Island, but after a year and a half's residence gave up the attempt to govern a wilderness full of barbarians and a handful of whites, and returned to England. Mr. Douglas was then made governor. When Mr. Blanchard left the colony

he appointed a provisional council of three persons, viz.: James
Douglas, James Cooper and John Tod. The following year
Mr. Cooper retired and Mr. Finlayson took his place at the Board.
From this time until 1859 Mr. Finlayson continued to act as chief
accountant at Victoria. Sir James Douglas severed his connection
with the company in 1859, and Mr. Finlayson was made chief
factor. During the greater portion of this time the colony had been
struggling forward, but not making much headway in the direction
of settlement. In 1857 gold was discovered by the agents of the
company on the Thompson River and the following year, news of
this getting abroad the great rush took place from California and
the east. Through all the excitement Mr. Finlayson continued to
act for his company, and by judicious management of its affairs put
considerable money in the pockets of the stockholders. He continued to act on the executive council appointed by the Governor
until the abolition of that body. In 1872, when the organization of
the Hudson's Bay Company was changed, Mr. Finlayson retired
from the service. During that year he paid a visit to the old country and the scenes of his youth. Since that time he has resided at
Victoria, of which place he has occupied the position of mayor.

Fisher, Isaac Birch. (New Westminster), third son of Wm.
Fisher, Esq., J.P., of Esquimalt, was born in Liverpool, England,
December 28, 1847. He was educated at the Liverpool College and
accompanied his parents to British Columbia in May, 1863. He
entered the service of the Bank of British Columbia two months
after his arrival in the colony, and has therefore been nearly 27
years in their employ. He occupied the position of manager of the
Bank's Branch in the gold fields of Cariboo, from 1872 to 1876,
(during the palmy days of Lightning Creek), and for the last eleven
years has had charge of the New Westminster branch.

Fisher, William, (Esquimalt), claims descent from a brother
of John, Bishop of Rochester, who suffered in the reign of Henry
VIII. He is the eldest son of the seventh William Fisher, of
Winscals Dovenby and Workington, in the county of Cumberland,
England, whose father married Jane Younghusband, of Mealing
Abbey Holm Cultrum, by Margaret, only daughter of Isaac Simon,
Yoeman, who married Margaret, daughter of John Fearon, of Dean,

by Sarah Fletcher, of Pardshaw, all in the said county of Cumberland. Born 18th of March, 1811. Educated at the Workington Academy, and at the boarding school of Rev. J. C. Price, Liverpool, where he served an apprenticeship of seven years to Alderman J. N. Wood, and acquired the freedom of that borough, and of Bristol, Waterford and Wexford, in 1832. He married, 17th February, 1844, Harriet Alice, second daughter of John Birch, Esq., of Tees Hall, Werneth, and Manor House, Ardwich, Manchester, cotton spinner. He commenced business in 1832, as junior partner, in the firm of William Fisher & Son, merchants in the African trade, and ship-owners in the East and West Indies, Brazil, River Plate and China trades; and owner of the Quebec and Montreal line of traders, which was superseded by the Allan line of steamers. Elected a member of the Liverpool Town Council, 1848: and a member of the dock committee (now the Mersey Harbor Board), 1848. He was an overseer of the poor for Toxteth Parks, and a Poor Law Guardian for the West Derby Union; a director of the Metropolitan Life Assurance Co.; and of the first Liverpool Marine Assurance Co.; a Commissioner of Pilots; a member of Lloyd's Classification Committee of British and Foreign Shipping; a member of the Ship Building Committee; a member of the committee of the Ship-owners' Association; and of the committee of the Constitutional Association; a vice-president of the Philomathic Society; and of the association for the protection British industry and capital; a member of the town improvement committee; a trustee of the Royal Infirmary; and of the Northern Hospital; and treasurer of the Southern Toxteth Hospital; life member of the Queen's College and Mechanics' Institute; and a member of the Royal Mersey Yacht Club. First came to British Columbia in 1860, and was a delegate to England in 1861, to obtain Imperial aid, and a mail subsidy for improved postal communication. Returned to British Columbia, 1863, and settled in Esquimalt. Was a member of the committee (aided by Governor Kennedy) for exploring Vancouver Island; a road commissioner; chairman of the board of education of Esquimalt and Craigflower. He was an unsuccessful candidate at the general election of 1871. In 1876 he was elected independent member for Esquimalt district. He is a Justice of the Peace for the Province.

ROBERT DICKINSON.

Fortune, Alexander Leslie, (Spallumcheen), was born in 1830 at Godmanchester, P. Q., his father, Dr. Fortune, being one of the leading practitioners of the same place. Mr. Fortune arrived in British Columbia in 1862 and at first made his home in Victoria. From 1862 to 1864 he tried his luck at the Cariboo mines, and since the latter date has been engaged in farming and stock raising in Spallumcheen, where he now possesses one of the best cultivated farms in the Province, and as a rancher is noted for the superiority of his stock. He is a Presbyterian, and married Miss B. M. Ross, eldest daughter of Murdock Ross, Esq., of Lancaster, Ont. Mr. Fortune was the first settler in Spallumcheen, and has an intimate knowledge of the district. While freighting goods for the pioneer settlers in the Okanagan country, in the fall of 1870, he conveyed the first keg of intoxicating liquor ever brought into that valley, and strange to relate when the consignee of the liquor was entertaining his friends therewith in the room of one of the early settlers a frightful and appalling noise was heard, as if large herds of cattle were wildly rushing over a hard pavement. Immediately afterwards the floor of the house rose and fell, the lamp was violently swung to and fro, and a violent trembling of the earth took place. The terrified pioneers all rushed wildly to the door and saw one of the grandest and most awful spectacles ever witnessed by human eyes. The immense mountain literally shook, the valley trembled and the huge trees swayed up and down, whilst a terrible and wierdly mysterious rumbling and crumbling of rocks and earth continued to sound in their ears. This is the first and only earthquake known to have taken place in that region, and it seemed to those early settlers as a message from Heaven, warning them against the introduction of the curse of strong drink.

Fraser, Angus Carmichael, (Vancouver), son of Allen Fraser, Esq., of Crow Harbor, Nova Scotia, was born on 8th of May, 1848. Mr. Fraser was educated in Escuminac, P. Q., and before coming to British Columbia was engaged in farming. In 1868 he arrived in Victoria, and since that date has been engaged in the lumber trade, and is the most extensive lumberman in British Columbia. He has a most intimate knowledge of the forest wealth of the Province, and is of the opinion that more lumber is grown per acre in British Columbia than in any other Province of the Dominion, and has scaled as high as 350,000 feet per acre. In 1875 he came to Burrard Inlet, and during the same year cut out of English Bay 9,470,000 feet of lumber from eighty acres of land,— nearly all of which was shipped to Australian ports. From 1869 to 1874, he logged for the Washington Mill Co., and from 1875 to 1886 for the Hastings Saw Mill Co., Vancouver. From 1886 until the present time, Mr. Fraser has been logging for the Royal City Saw Mill Co. and the Chemainus Saw Mill Co.,—having each year held contracts to deliver several million feet of lumber to those mills. At the present time Mr. Fraser has contracted to deliver 6,000,000 feet of lumber for the Cowichan Milling Co. In 1883 he delivered to the Hastings Saw Mill a log 28 inches x 28 inches and 112 feet in length, clear of knots, which was sent to China. In 1882 he delivered to the Hastings Saw Mill Co., $64,000 worth of lumber. Mr. Fraser served in 1882, as Councillor for Sea Island in the Richmond Council. He is a member of the Masonic Order, of the Order of United Workmen and the Caledonian Society. On September 2nd, 1879, he married Anabella, third daughter of Malcolm Smith, Esq., of Wallace, Nova Scotia. He is an adherent of the Presbyterian Church.

Fry, Henry, M. P. P., (Cowichan), was born at Barnstaple, Devonshire, England, on January 29th, 1826. His father was a merchant at Barnstaple. Mr. Fry was educated at his native place with a view of fitting him for a mercantile life. After completing his studies he entered his father's business, where he obtained a practical acquaintance with commercial pursuits, and subsequently was engaged in business in other parts of England. In 1855, he came to America and settled in Hamilton, Ontario, where he went into business. In 1860 he disposed of his interests in Ontario and returned to England, where he remained till 1862, in which year he came to British Columbia. After a few weeks in Victoria he went to Cariboo, where he mined during that and the following season. In 1864 he returned to Victoria and went into business, at which he continued until 1869, when he purchased the farm in Cowichan on which he now resides and on which he then settled. In 1887 he was elected for Cowichan District to fill the vacancy occasioned by the death of the late Premier, Hon. Wm. Smythe. Mr. Fry is a member of the Episcopal Church.

M. M. ENGLISH.

Good. Rev. John Booth, (Nanaimo), rector of St. Paul's church, was born at Wrawby, Licolnshire, England. Educated at Lincoln College and then at St. Augustine College, Canterbury, in which latter institution he distinguished himself by taking first class in medicine, mathematics, science and theology. After three years attendance at this college he was accepted by the examiners of the Society for the Propagation of the Gospel, and went to Nova Scotia under orders to come to British Columbia when required. He spent three years in Nova Scotia, where he was ordained by Bishop Burney. After spending some months in England where he married Miss Watson, of Fieldhouse, Lincolnshire, he came to British Columbia, reaching Victoria in 1861. For five years he resided at Victoria, working among the natives with great success. He then removed to Comox, where he erected a mission church and parsonage. While here and subsequently throughout his career his knowledge of medicine stood him in good stead. From Comox he went to Yale and from Yale to Lytton. His mission field was now a most extensive one, and he had the care of about 8,000 Indians, distributed in 72 villages. Mr. Good in ministering to this charge had to cover a very large extent of territory, but notwithstanding this fact and innumerable difficulties which hampered him, he performed his labor so successfuly that this mission has gone on ever since, prospering on the foundation he built. He not only interested himself in the spiritual but also in the material prosperity of the natives and was instrumental in settling many on farms which they have since continued to cultivate. In 1874 Mr. Good obtained leave of absence for a year, and this time he employed in lecturing and preaching in Eastern America and Great Britain and in raising money for mission work. Shortly after he returned from England the diocese of New Westminster was formed, and for four years Mr. Good labored under Bishop Sillitoe. In 1882 he sent in his resignation to the society, and on going to Victoria was appointed to the rectorship of St. Paul's church, Nanaimo, where he has since resided. Mr. Good is perhaps better versed than any person in the Province on the native languages of the Pacific coast. He has acquired perfectly all the languages (about 12) spoken from the sea to the Rocky mountains and has written treatises regarding them and translated the litany, prayers and hymns of the English church into most of them.

Goodacre, Lawrence, (Victoria), was born in Nottingham, England, in October, 1848. His father, Samuel Goodacre, was a corn factor and miller of that place. When he left school at the age of sixteen years Mr. Goodacre was apprenticed to a butcher in Nottingham to learn the business. In 1870 he came to British Columbia, and settled in Victoria, where he worked six years as a journeyman and then went into business in partnership with John Stafford, under the firm title Stafford & Goodacre. They opened up their business on the site which Mr. Goodacre now occupies, and continued it together till Mr. Stafford's death in 1882. Mr. Goodacre then formed a partnership with John Dooley, which continued for six years, when Mr. Goodacre purchased Mr. Dooley's interest and has since continued to conduct the business himself. Mr. Goodacre represents Johnston street ward in the City Council, having on every occasion on which he stood for the position been elected by very large majorities. He is a member of the Oddfellows' society and St. George's society, and in religion is an adherent of the Methodist Church.

Gordon, David William, M.P., (Nanaimo), was born at Camden, in the county of Kent, Ont., on February 27th, 1832. He is of United Empire Loyalist stock. His grandfather, John Gordon, who was a citizen of Coventry, Eng., left home at an early age and travelled to India, and afterwards settled in the American colonies. At the close of the revolutionary war he removed to Canada with the Loyalists and made his home in Ontario. His father, Mr. Michael Gordon, married Miss Judith Marsh, of Ridgetown, Ont. His maternal grandfather, Mr. Alexander Montgomery, removed from Connecticut after the revolution to Gagetown, N. B., and later on in 1798 to Little York, (now Toronto), where one member of the family became conspicuous during the rebellion of 1837. Mr. Gordon was educated in the public schools in the county of Kent, and after completing his studies served an apprenticeship with the firm of Fisher and Smith, contractors, Wallaceburg, at the completion of which he followed the trade of a builder and joiner. Mr. Gordon left Ontario early in 1858 and arrived at Victoria in June. Here he at first remained but a short time, going to California in 1859, where he remained four years and passed through many mining and other adventures. On his return to British Columbia he settled at

Nanaimo, where he engaged successfully in business as a contractor and builder. In 1876 he was an unsuccessful candidate for the representation of Nanaimo in the British Columbia Legislature, but in 1877 he was returned at the head of the poll, and represented that city during two sessions. He was again defeated at the general election of 1878. While member for Nanaimo Mr. Gordon was one of the committee who arranged the order of procedure of business which terminated the deadlock in the Provincial Parliament, and he was chiefly instrumental in forcing the Elliott Government to carry through the Assembly the bill known as the "Coal Mines Regulations Act, 1877." At the general election of 1878 Mr. Gordon contested the seat he now holds in the Commons, but lost the election, being first returned to Ottawa on August 4th, 1882, which seat he retained at the last general election. In politics Mr. Gordon is a Liberal Conservative. He is a prominent member of the Free Masons' and Oddfellows' Societies. He has been twice married, first to Emma Elizabeth, eldest daughter of James Robb, Esq., of Comox, who died February 15th, 1882, and again on June 5th, 1886, to Statira Kitty, youngest daughter of Joseph Shepard, Esq., of Lansing, Ont. He is an adherent of the Church of England.

Gordon, Marshall Pollock, (Kamloops), son of Daniel and Eliza Gordon, of Goderich, Ontario, was born in that city on June 22nd, 1862. Mr. Gordon received a good commercial education in the High School at Goderich, and previous to his arrival in British Columbia, on the 17th March, 1883, was engaged in the furniture business. On his arrival in Victoria, he worked one year in the furniture factory of J. Sehl, and on leaving that city settled in Kamloops, where, in partnership with his brother, Mr. James Gordon, he started his present business. In February, 1889, Mr. Gordon bought his brother's interest in the business, and at the present time is carrying on a large and remunerative furniture trade in the interior of the Province. Mr. Gordon is a Methodist, and a member of the Oddfellows' Order.

Grant, John, M. P. P., (Victoria), son of John Grant, of Tochbers, Moreyshire, Scotland, and Margaret Buie, only daughter of John Buie, of Buckie, Scotland, captain in the Coast Guards, was born at Alford, Aberdeenshire, Scotland, on June 1st. 1841.

He was educated at Midmar, under George Mortimer, M. A., with a view to fitting himself for a commercial career. In 1855 he came to Canada with his parents, who settled in Elora, Wellington county, Ontario, where Mr. Grant subsequently engaged in the lumber business. He was attracted by the reported riches of British Columbia, and in 1862 came to the Pacific coast, landing at Victoria, on the 11th of March. During 1862 and 1863 he was engaged as chief commissary and pay master on the trunk road from Lillooet to Alexandria. In 1864 he was chief commissary and paymaster during the building of the wagon road from Quesnelle mouth to Cottonwood river. In 1866 he engaged in mining in Cariboo and continued at this business with success till 1871. In that year he superintended the building of the Seymour portage and wagon road. He subsequently had contracts for building portions of the wagon road from New Westminster to Hope, and also for the road from Spencer's bridge up the Nicola valley. During part of 1871-2 he was engaged in general merchandise on the Peace river. Since 1876 Mr. Grant has been engaged largely in the freighting, mining and steamboat business and has rendered material assistance in developing the quartz mines of the Province, notably in Rock creek, Yale District, where he applied the hydraulic system. Mr. Grant was general superintendent during the building of the wagon road from Cache Creek to Savona's Ferry in 1886. In the general election of 1882 he was elected to the Legislative Assembly of British Columbia as representative for Cassair district, and in the election of 1886 was again returned. At the last general election in June, 1890 Mr. Grant stood for the city of Victoria and was elected at the head of the poll. From 1885 to 1887 he was a member of the municipal council of the city of Victoria, and from 1888 till the present time he has held the position of Mayor of that city. Mr. Grant has never failed of election to any public position in the gift of the people. In Dominion politics he is thoroughly independent, contending that from neither party has this Province received that consideration to which she is justly entitled. In Provincial politics he is opposed to the present government, believing that the course pursued by it is not in the best interests of the Province. Mr. Grant is one of the most enterprising and successful men in British Columbia. He has been in this country almost since the birth of the colony, has been engaged in business in almost every

part of it and knows thoroughly its requirements and resources.
Personally he is greatly esteemed for the generosity of his disposition and his willingness to render assistance wherever needed. He
is a member of the St. Andrew's and Caledonian society, the Pioneer
society, the Oddfellows' Order, the Benevolent society of Victoria
and the Masonic Order. On December 20th, 1878, he married
Miss Laura R., only daughter of Joseph Haywood, Esq., of Victoria.

Gray, Alexander Blair, (Victoria), was born in Edinburgh,
on November 6th, 1841, and attended school in that city till he
was fifteen years of age. During the next five years he resided in
Dublin, Ireland, where he served his apprenticeship to the dry
goods business in the large wholesale and retail establishment of
Todd, Burns & Co. In 1862 he left the old country for British
Columbia, coming by way of Panama. He arrived in Victoria in
June, and occupied several positions in Victoria and New Westminster till 1864, when he was seized with the gold fever and set
out from New Westminster, with a company of fellow prospectors,
for the Cariboo mines. They covered the distance, five hundred
miles, on foot. Mr. Gray held an interest in the John Bull mining
claim during the summer, and in the autumn he started back to
the coast lighter in pocket than when he reached the gold fields and
using the same means of locomotion on his return journey that he
had in getting to that auriferous region. When he got to Victoria
again, he entered the establishment of John Wilkie & Co. and continued in the employ of this firm for three years. He then crossed
to New Westminster, where he opened a business of his own.
When the capital was removed from New Westminster, Mr. Gray
returned to Victoria and bought out the dry goods firm of Fabien
Mitchell, on Government street, and subsequently put up the large
building now know as the Albion House, into which he moved his
business, and which seven years ago he transferred to the present
occupants, Messrs. Brown & White. He then removed to his
present premises on Wharf street, and has since been engaged
exclusively in the wholesale trade. Mr. Gray took an active interest in Provincial politics during the Elliott administration, though
he never stood for any public office. He was one of the strongest
and earliest advocates of confederation with the Dominion. Of

late years, however, he has eschewed politics entirely. He is a member of the St. Andrew's and Caledonian Society, and connected with the Oddfellows' Order. In religion he is a Presbyterian, and is one of the oldest members of St. Andrew's Church. He is a Justice of the Peace for the Province. Mr. Gray is an ardent Imperial Federationist and considers that this scheme which he firmly believes will be accomplished, is simply a step towards a federation of the English speaking races throughout the world.

Guichon, Laurent, (Ladner's Landing), one of the earliest French settlers of British Columbia, was born in 1836 at Chambery, in the province of Savoie, France, where his father M. Jean Guichon, had an extensive farm. Mr. Guichon spent his early life in Savoie where he received his education. In 1857 he went to California where he was engaged in mining enterprises until 1859, when he left the Golden State and came to British Columbia, making Lytton his headquarters. During nine years Mr. Guichon, in partnership with his brother, Mr. Charles Guichon and a friend, Mr. Vincent Girod, carried on a very extensive and remunerative business in mining supplies and general merchandise from Yale to Quesnelle and Cariboo. In 1869 Mr. Charles Guichon left the firm and in 1873 Mr. Guichon sold out all his interests to his partner, Mr. Girod, and settled in Nicola Valley where he resided ten years. In 1883 Mr. Guichon removed to New Westminster where he speculated to a considerable extent. In the fall of the same year he bought the farm he now cultivates at Ladner's Landing and in 1886 built a store on his property, which he afterwards sold, devoting his whole attention to agricultural pursuits. Mr. Guichon married Perome, ninth daughter of Antoine Rae, a landed proprietor of Chambery, by whom he has six children.

Hall, Thomas Sylvester, M. D., (New Westminster), son of Henry Hall, of Toronto, was born at Toronto, July 7th, 1860. He received his primary education at the Model School and after having passed through the various divisions he matriculated at Queen's College, Kingston. From his earliest years he had an inclination for the study of medicine and this leaning had been fostered by his family. Two of his uncles had been professors in Dr. Rolfe's School of Medicine and Mr. Hall had therefore from his youth been surrounded by medical influences. After graduating at Queen's he

ALEXANDER EWEN.

returned to Toronto and studied for two years at Trinity School of Medicine. During the next three years he attended Michigan College of Medicine, which is in affiliation with Michigan University. He graduated here and then went to London, England, where he spent two years walking the hospitals and pursuing his studies there After taking his degrees in London he went to Berlin, Germany, where he studied chemistry under Dr. Hoffman the celebrated chemist. He then returned to Canada and after spending a few months in Ontario he decided to go to Australia. He missed the steamer, however, and changed his route to British Columbia. He began practice in New Westminster in 1885 and has continued there since. He has taken an active interest in politics both Dominion and Provincial during the period of his residence in British Columbia. He is a Liberal Conservative in his principles. He is an ardent believer in the greatness of British Columbia and has shown his faith in a practical manner by investing largely in property in the district. He is a member of the Order of Oddfellows and in the east filled the highest offices in the lodges. In religion Dr. Hall is an adherent of the Methodist church.

Hamilton, Alexander. (New Westminster), was born in June, 1861, in the Parish of Carluke, Lanarkshire, Scotland, and is the son of James Hamilton, Esquire, of the same place and formerly of Strathhaven. Mr. Hamilton was educated in his native town and after completing his studies apprenticed himself to a large firm of workers in marble and monument engravers, and at the completion of his trade studied the higher and more artistic branches of the trade at Edinburgh. Previous to his arrival at Victoria on December 24th, 1884 Mr. Hamilton resided in the States of Missouri, Kansas and Oregon. Since his arrival in British Columbia he has followed his trade with ever-increasing success. Although a strong free-trader and a supporter of temperance legislation he has taken no part in politics, devoting his whole time to his business. In 1887 Mr. Hamilton returned to Scotland in charge of a nephew whose parents had both died in Missouri and soon after his arrival in the "Land o'cakes" married Jeannie Terrance, eldest daughter of John Leiper, Esquire, of Carluke. On his return to British Columbia in 1888, after having visited the most important granite establishments in Scotland, Mr. Hamilton settled in New Westminster. He is a large importer of Scotch and Swedish granite and is now the owner of the largest marble works in the province.

Harrison, Eli, (Victoria), born in September, 1824, in Cheshire, England, son of Samuel Harrison, civil engineer of Staffordshire, England. Educated at his native place and subsequently in business in Crewe. Left England and went to Georgia, United States of America, where he was in business in Macon, during 1850-1. He then removed to San Francisco, where he opened a business and conducted it till 1858, when he came to British Columbia and settled in Victoria. He established his present business at Victoria, a short time after his arrival. In 1860 he joined the Masonic fraternity and passed through the various offices in the subordinate lodge and grand lodge. In 1877 he introduced a scheme to build a Masonic Temple in Victoria, which was accepted by the Order and Mr. Harrison, his son and Mr. Trounce were appointed a board of trustees and two lots placed in their charge on which to begin work. Mr. Harrison held the office of Grand Master Mason of British Columbia for three years and nine months. He laid the corner stone of the Masonic Temple in Victoria, and dedicated the structure in October, 1878, and at the present time he and his fellow trustees hold $30,000 worth of property in trust for the Masonic fraternity. He is a member of the Episcopal Church, and a Conservative in politics.

Haskins, John Wesley Washington, (Revelstoke), was born in Westport, Ontario, on November 5th, 1855, his father being of Welsh and his mother of Dutch descent, and both belonging to Loyalist families. When young, Mr. Haskins mastered the blacksmith trade and was educated at Smith Falls Ontario. Before coming to British Columbia he carried on the business of a blacksmith and carriage builder and later was extensively engaged in lumbering and mining enterprises. In some of his prospecting expeditions Mr. Haskins met with many strange adventures and passed through dangerous and thrilling experiences. At one time when out with a party of forty on the borders of Wyoming and Utah Territories an attack was made on the encampment by Indians and Mr. Haskins and one other were the only survivors. On another occasion, having sold out a mine in Nevada for a considerable sum, Mr.

Haskins travelled from Victoria to Aspinwall and up the Mississippi to St. Louis. At a later period he sailed from Halifax to York Factory on Hudson's Bay and then started in winter time overland from Moose Factory to Pembroke, Ont. Before the completion of the Canadian Pacific Railway through British Columbia he travelled in the Rockies and Selkirks propecting for timber and mineral, arriving in British Columbia on May 1st, 1884, and finally settling at Revelstoke. Mr. Haskins discovered the "Monarch" mine at Field, and also located and recorded several quartz prospects in the Big Bend, Arrow Lakes and Toad Mountain districts. He has also been chiefly instrumental in establishing smelting works at Revelstoke, he having used his efforts and energies to circulate information respecting the mineral riches of the interior. He is a Methodist and an Orangeman.

Haslam, Andrew, M. P. P., (Nanaimo), was born at Woodhill, in the north of Ireland, on the 23rd of June, 1846. His father, John Haslam, was attached to the excise department at that place. Mr. Haslam was educated at his native place, and in 1861 emigrated from Ireland with his parents who settled in Albert county, New Brunswick. In 1870, Mr. Haslam left home and went to Winnipeg, where he was engaged with McArthur & Co. in the lumber business. A year later he went to Texas where he remained for two years, being engaged during that time in erecting bridges and in saw-milling. In 1876 he came to British Columbia, and seeing the immense wealth of timber in the Province, he engaged in the lumber business. He was one of the proprietors of the Royal City Planing Mills Co., and was a director and large owner in the company till 1885, when he established the Nanaimo Saw Mill Co. which business he now conducts. Mr. Haslam is one of the men who by their enterprise and energy are doing so much to develope the resources of the country. While living in New Westminster he was thrice elected to the City Council, and in 1889 was just elected to parliament to fill the vacancy caused by the death of Hon. Robt. Dunsmuir. He is a member of the Masonic fraternity, and a Presbyterian.

Hastings, Oregon Columbus, (Victoria), born at Pontonsick, Hancock county, Illinois, U. S. A., on the 26th of April, 1846, is the son of Loven Brown and Lucinda Bingham, Hastings. His father, who was engaged in the manufacture of woolen goods in Illinois, brought his family west to Oregon Territory in 1847, and settled in Portland, where the family remained till 1852, when they removed to Port Townsend. From 1848 to 1851 Mr. Hastings' father had been engaged in mercantile business at the California gold mines, but when he removed his family to Port Townsend, he established himself there, having disposed of his interests at the mines. Mr. Hastings attended school at Port Townsend till he was sixteen years of age, when he purchased a farm near Port Townsend and conducted it till he was twenty-five years old. His health was giving way, owing to hard work, and he left the farm and removed to Port Townsend, where he purchased his father's business. He continued at this business for three years and then sold out and came to British Columbia. He settled in Victoria and took the position of manager of Spencer's photographic business on Front street. Mr. Hastings had not previously been engaged at this business, but he had studied it as a pastime, and now concluded to put his knowledge to account. He remained as manager for Mr. Spencer for six years, when in consequence of the illness of his wife he moved away from Victoria. His wife died, however, and he returned in the following year and went into partnership with Spencer. A year later he bought Spencer's interest in the business and continued to conduct it from that time till January, 1889, when he sold out. During all these years he had been doing a very prosperous trade having virtually all the patronage of the city. In May, 1867, he married Miss Matilda Caroline Birch, of Dungeness, who died in 1881, and again on October 2nd, 1884, he maried Mrs. Phillips Smith. Mr. Hastings has made a close study of astronomy and geology and in these sciences is one of the best versed men on the Coast. His father, Hon. Loven Hastings, was for many years a prominent member of the Washington legislature.

Haughton, Thomas, (Victoria), was born on the 19th of June, 1842, at Duckingfield, Cheshire, England. His father was engaged in the grocery business in Ashton-under-Lyne, Lancashire. Mr. Haughton was educated at his native place and after learning the drygoods business opened an establishment in Duckingfield. His business prospered till he became prominently connected with the Radical wing of the Liberal party and placed himself on record in regard to the question of the disestablishment of the Irish church. He was chairman of the Liberal election committee of his riding in 1868 and gave such an unqualified and ardent support to the Liberal candidate that a great deal of his custom forsook his business. In 1870 he left England, and during the following six years he resided in New Hampshire and Massachussets, after which time he came to British Columbia. He rented a farm in the neighborhood of Victoria and lived on it for a year, when he gave it up and engaged for two years in gardening at Esquimalt. He then leased another farm and sank in it what money he had previously made. For the next five years he followed various occupations, and finally with a small capital opened a modest shop where his present handsome store is situated. His business prospered and enlarged so rapidly that he was very soon able to purchase the property and erect a large building. In time he took a partner into his business in the person of Mr. Wescott, his son-in-law. Mr. Haughton has not taken a very active part in politics in British Columbia except during the general election of 1876, when he acted as financial agent for Mr. J. M. Duval, who then contested Victoria in the interest of the workingmen. Mr. Haughton then held that the laboring classes should have a representative in the house, especially in view of the anti-Chinese agitation. He has been pressed to stand for the Legislature, but has persistently refused, owing to the demand his business makes on his time. Mr. Haughton has not taken much interest in civic politics. He is a member of the Ancient Order of United Workmen and of the Legion of Honor. He is also one of the most prominent members of the Baptist denomination, and took an active part in developing the scheme and raising the money for the erection of the present Baptist church.

Haynes, George W., (Victoria), was born near Bangor, Maine, U. S., on August 7th, 1833. His father, Peeley Haynes, was engaged in the lumber business, and after leaving school Mr. Haynes was employed by him till 1852. He then removed to California and settled at Downieville, where he continued in the lumber trade till he came to British Columbia in 1861. He had intended going to the Cariboo mines, but it was late in the autumn when he arrived so he changed his mind. During the following winter he was engaged in J. R. Homer's lumber mill, and in the summer went to Pt.

Douglas, where he took charge of the milling business of P. Smith. During 1863 and 1864 he was engaged at New Westminster, constructing a new mill for Webster and Millard, and as soon as he had completed this work he went to Moodyville where he took charge of the milling business there and where he remained till 1876. During that period he erected two mills at Moodyville, one of which is now standing. He abandoned the milling business to take charge of the Baynes coal mines, and since 1882 he has resided in Victoria. In 1884 he joined Mr. H. F. Heisterman in the real estate business. He is a member of the British Columbia Board of Trade. In 1869 he married Miss S. Adelaide Hart, of Bangor, Maine, U. S. A. Mr. Haynes is a member of the Masonic Order.

Hayward, Charles, (Victoria), was born in Stratford, Essex, England, in 1839, and educated at Salem College. Came to British Columbia in 1862 and settled at Victoria, where he has since continued to reside. During that time he has been prominently identified with the mining, building and manufacturing interests of the Province, and has taken an active part in the municipal matters tending to the material advancement of the City of Victoria. He is owner of large tracts of land in various parts of the Province, and many valuable buildings in Victoria city. He is a Justice of the Peace, an ex-councillor of the British Columbia Board of Trade and chairman for several years of the local school board. He married Sarah, second daughter of John McChesney of Middlesex, England.

Heathorn, William. (Victoria), was born on July 30th, 1828, in England and in 1842 went to New York, U. S. A., where he remained till 1853 when he removed to Australia. In 1858 he returned to New York and resided there till 1862, when he came to British Columbia. He settled in Victoria and has lived there since that date. He followed the occupation of boot and shoe-maker, and in 1872 established the Victor Manufactory, which on a small scale at first, gradually assumed large proportions till the output was raised to $100,000 per annum. Shortly after he began the boot and shoe manufactory he bought out the Rock Bay Tannery and added the business of tanning leather. He continued this business till February, 1889, when he sold out the shoe manufactory to the

J. B. FISHER.

Ames, Holden Company, retaining however, the tanning and hide business. When the Bay tannery suspended operations owing to the death of the principal partner, and the property was offered for sale in 1888, it was purchased by Mr. Heathorn and the building used as a warehouse. Mr. Heathorn, while he did not take any very active interest in politics, was a Liberal in his leanings. He served the city during one year at the City Council Board.

Heisterman, Henry Frederick. (Victoria), the younger of two sons of William Segismund Heisterman, was born in Bremen, one of the free cities of Germany, on the 22nd of July, 1832. He was educated in his native city and after completing his studies entered on mercantile pursuits. At the age of eighteen he removed to Dantzig, where for three years he was engaged in a commercial house. In 1853 he went to England and settled in the seaport town of Liverpool, where he established a commission business which he conducted until 1862, and where he became a naturalized British subject in 1861. The fame of the British Columbia gold mines attracted him to North America in 1862, and he landed at Victoria in August. His first essay in the new country was towards mining. He set out shortly after his arrival for Stikeen with a number of others. The journey was, however, unsuccessful. They lost their canoe and all it contained in the nature of provisions and outfit, and in September Mr. Heisterman found himself back in Victoria. Matters were not of a rose-colored hue at this time. He had very little money and no friends in a strange country. After casting about for some opening and finding little promise, he opened a reading room in the St. Nicholas building, and shortly afterwards formed a chamber of commerce. His reading room paid him very well and after continuing it for six months he sold out, and, having formed a partnership with John Banks, engaged in a wholesale business in paints and glass. At the expiration of eight months the partnership was dissolved, and Mr. Heisterman, in 1864, established the real estate business which he still continues to conduct. This business has since that time steadily continued to increase, and is now the largest and best known in the Pacific Province. During the period of its existence the greater portion of the valuable business property of Victoria, has passed through Mr. Heisterman's hands. Mr. Heisterman has the agencies for most of the large companies in the east, doing business in Victoria, as the Montreal Life Insurance Co., the Phœnix and Western Fire Assurance Co's., and many others. In 1884 he took his present partner, Mr. J. W. Haynes, into his business. Mr. Heisterman has been an active member of the Board of Trade since its inception, and a member of the council of that organization. He has been for seven consecutive years a member of the Board of School Trustees. He is a member of the Pioneer Society and one of the most prominent members of the Masonic fraternity. In 1873 he married Miss Haynes, of Victoria.

Helmcken, James Douglas, M. D., (Victoria), was born February 8th, 1858, in Victoria, British Columbia. In 1870 he was sent to Jedburgh Academy, Scotland; thence to Edinburgh University where he studied medicine. After obtaining his degree at Edinburgh he proceeded to Bellevue Hospital College, New York city, where he studied under the best professors in America, and returned to his native city in 1884. Shortly afterwards he married Mary Jane, daughter of James Halliday, Esq., of Dumfries, Scotland. By this union he had one daughter, and his wife died in 1887. Dr. Helmcken married again in 1888, Ethel Margaret, daughter of the late Captain White of Victoria. Dr. Helmcken is a grandson of the late Sir James Douglass, K. C. B., after whom he is named. He is surgeon of St. Joseph's Hospital, Victoria, and has been a very successful physician. Ophthalmology and gynaecology are his favorite branches of medical practice, although he has effectually demonstrated his skill and knowledge in all other departments of Medicine. He has no particular political leanings. He is the first British Columbian who ever took a medical degree. His practice is one of the most extensive and valuable in the Province, and the great success which has attended many critical cases reposed in his care have given him a most enviable reputation among the medicos of the Pacific slope.

Helmcken, Hon. John Sebastian, M. R. C. S., (Victoria), born June 5th, 1823, in London within sound of "Bow Bells." His parents were German—his grandfather from Misskirch, his father from Bruneslai, the latter an emigrant during the Napoleonic wars. The former had been a soldier in the Swiss guards. When old enough Mr. Helmcken was sent to St. George's school, and as he was regarded as fragile it was the intention that he should be made a teacher. When fourteen years of age Dr. Graves, while attending his mother, took a fancy to him and asked for him as an office boy, promising to make him a druggist. His mother consented and Mr. Helmcken entered the doctor's office, in which he made himself useful and obtained a knowledge of the secrets of making pills and potions. There were two medical apprentices in the office who petted him and made him useful to themselves. In those days every practitioner had to do his own dispensing and Mr. Helmcken got plenty of practice therefore. He picked up a knowledge of Latin, and after a couple of years of work was able to dispense medicines with the best practised hands. It chanced that when he had been for two years an office boy, that Dr. Graves fell ill, and as the senior apprentice had by this time become a full-fledged practitioner it fell to Mr. Helmcken's lot to dispense medicine for all the patients. When Dr. Graves recovered after a long illness, he was so pleased with his office boy's conduct that he offered to take him as an apprentice for five years and make him an allowance during that time. Mr. Helmcken's parents accepted this liberal offer, and accordingly he was apprenticed to Dr. Graves. Shortly afterwards his father died and while his mother was not left in the most comfortable circumstances she refused to permit her son to miss his opportunity for her sake, and declared that she herself could, would and was not afraid of work. During this period Mr. Helmcken had all the drudgery of an apprentice to do and saw a great deal of the poor in some of the worst of slums in his visits to cup, bleed or otherwise physic them. In due course his five years expired, but during a considerable portion of that time he had been going to a private teacher, a Lutheran clergyman, to learn Latin and finish his education generally. Before the expiration of his apprenticeship he became a student at Guy's hospital and attended there for five years. Having passed the apothecary's examination and been pretty well used up by hard work, Mr. Harrison, the treasurer of the hospital, offered him an appointment, as a reward of merit, to the Hudson's Bay Company's ship Prince Rupert, to go to York Factory on Hudson's Bay and back again, a journey of some five months. It so happened that on the same vessel, Chief Factor Hargraves and his wife were passengers and also a number of men belonging to an expedition in search of Sir John Franklin. He returned to the hospital in rugged health, spent another year, graduated at the college of physicians and surgeons, and then determined to enter the navy. Just when he was about to receive an appointment, he met Mr. Barclay, secretary of the Hudson's Bay Company, who advised him not to go into the navy where he must necessarily become a fixture, and who gave him a letter to Mr. Green, the large ship owner. Mr. Green appointed him surgeon on the ship Malacca, Captain Consett, en route to Bombay. After eighteen months of sojourning in the Indian seas, Dr. Helmcken returned to London and was offered an appointment on the Hudson's Bay Company's service on Vancouver Island. After finding where Vancouver Island was, the kind of climate it possessed and obtaining other information, he accepted the appointment. The ship Norman Morrison, Captain Wishart, was being sent with emigrants to Vancouver Island and Dr. Helmcken came out as physician in charge, intending to remain only five years. On the voyage smallpox broke out among the emigrants, but owing to the prompt action and skill of the surgeon only one death occurred. They reached Victoria in March, 1850, and were ordered into quarantine for a time. Dr. Helmcken was almost immediately transferred to Fort Rupert where the coal mines were being opened. It was during the first few months of his residence there that the trouble among the miners which is described in the introduction took place. The men wanted to get away to California to the gold mines and desired to break their agreement with the company. After six months at Fort Rupert Dr. Helmcken was called to Victoria to attend Governor Blanchard, who was ill. He continued from that time forth to reside at Victoria. In 1852 he married the daughter of Governor Douglas and in 1855 he was elected to the first legislative assembly of Vancouver Island to represent Esquimalt. He was appointed speaker of the assembly, and continued to occupy this position till confederation with the Dominion in 1871 when he abandoned politics. From 1864 till 1871 he was a member of the executive council of British Columbia. At that time a seat in the house did not bring any remuneration with it, and Dr. Helmcken labored during the best years of his life in the interests of the colony without desiring or obtaining any reward for it. During the agitation for confederation he was strongly opposed to the movement and was regarded as the fore front of the opposition. When terms most favorable to British Columbia, which he.

together with Mr. Trutch and Dr. Carroll, were sent to Ottawa to negotiate, were agreed upon, only then did he change his attitude, and it was in a great measure owing to him that the transcontinental railway was made a condition of union. Immediately after confederation Dr. Helmcken was offered a senatorship, but declined the honor, chiefly because he deemed it his paramount duty to educate his family. He accordingly agreed to the appointment of Mr. W. J. McDonald, it being an understood thing that he should retire in case Dr. Helmcken should change his mind in the future. Since confederation Dr. Helmcken has devoted himself to his private practice. He has large interests in Victoria and Vancouver Island.

Hendry, John, (New Westminster), born in the district of Belle Dune, county of Gloster, New Brunswick, on the 20th of January, 1854, is the second son of the late James Hendry, who left West Kilbride, Ayrshire, Scotland, in 1840, and settled at Belle Dune, where he engaged extensively in milling enterprises, establishing both flour and lumber mills. Mr. Hendry was educated at the public school in his native county, and at an early age entered the same occupation as his father. In conjunction with his elder brother he established a mill in the distant part of the county and continued to conduct it till his father's death, when he took charge of his business and carried it on till his younger brother became old enough to take control of it. His father had towards the close of his life, gradually centred his interest in flour milling, and this business not being congenial to Mr. Hendry's tastes, he withdrew himself from connection with it at as early a date as possible. In 1870, before going into any other enterprise, he took a trip through a portion of the Western States and was greatly inclined to begin a business in Duluth, which was then just springing into existence, and whose excellent situation as a lake port Mr. Hendry clearly saw. He returned to New Brunswick, however, and again established a lumber mill. For two years he continued at this, doing a large export business, one of his chief markets being the West India Islands. He was restless, however, in New Brunswick, and like most young men of enterprise, desired to enlarge his knowledge of the world. He had determined to go to the Argentine Republic, and would have done so had it not been that the

yellow fever broke out there and continued to rage. He then
turned his attention to British Columbia, which had just entered
the Canadian Confederation, and about which there was a great
deal of talk. Early in the summer of 1872 he made preparations
for leaving Eastern Canada, and in August he came by way of
Duluth, which he desired again to visit, and over the United
States system of railways. He reached Victoria in the latter part
of September. He found the lumber business very dull in British
Columbia at that time, this industry on the Pacific coast being
chiefly confined to Puget Sound. He accordingly did not remain in
the Province, but returned to Washington Territory. As he was
anxious to obtain a knowledge of any details of the business peculiar to this Coast, before investing capital in an enterprise, he spent
the winter at Seabeck, in the employ of the Washington Saw Mill
Company, engaged in surveying logs and mill-wrighting. He
remained there till April, 1873, when he decided to return to
British Columbia. He stopped on his way at Port Gamble, where
he was induced to enter the employ of the Puget Sound Saw Mill
Company, of which Mr. Cyrus Walker was then the local manager.
Here he was engaged at the same work as at Seabeck, and he had
thus every facility to obtain an insight not only into the manner
in which the milling business was conducted on the Pacific coast,
but also of thoroughly learning the quality of the timber, and
especially that employed in the export trade. In January of 1874,
he left Port Gamble. The Moodyville Saw Mill on Burrard Inlet,
had been destroyed and the manager, Mr. Moody, had gone
over to Puget Sound to engage millwrights for its reconstruction.
Mr. Hendry determined to see how matters stood and accordingly
came to British Columbia. He went to Moodyville where he
obtained the position of foreman of the millwrights engaged in
putting in the machinery. When the mill was completed it ran
day and night to make up for lost time, and Mr. Hendry had
charge during the night. He remained at Moodyville until June,
1875, using his opportunities during all this time to study the
business. It seemed to him then, however, that it would be many
years before the timber in this country would be very valuable,
owing to its abundance and the sparse population. The Red river
country was then coming into prominence and he observed the
large prices that were being given for lumber in Winnipeg. He

JOHN GRANT,

thought, therefore, that that would be a better country than British Columbia to engage in the industry. He accordingly went to Winnipeg where he remained for a very short time indeed. He was disgusted with the stunted and sickly growth of the forests of the plains, after the magnificient woods of British Columbia, and he could hardly bring himself to regard as timber the article so termed. At this time too, business was very dull in Winnipeg, owing to the grasshopper visitation. From there he returned to the Coast and determined to settle in California. When he arrived at San Francisco he deposited his money in the bank and looked about the country for some time. He finally decided to go to the Red Wood country, and was on the eve of starting when the bank in which all his money was deposited went into liquidation, and all he could get at that time was $50.00. He saw it was useless to remain longer in California and he accordingly came to British Columbia, where he was known. He went to Nanaimo first where he spent the winter building a saw mill for Mr. Carpenter. He then went to New Westminster, where during the summer of 1876, he put up a mill for Mr. W. J. Armstrong. In the autumn he returned to Nanaimo and formed a partnership with Mr. David McNair, to build and operate a sash and door factory. Early in 1877 he went to San Francisco and purchased the machinery, and at the same time he drew the money which he had deposited in the bank there, that institution having turned out to have considerably more assets than liabilities. During 1877 he lived in Nanaimo, conducting this sash and door factory, and in the spring of 1878, a partnership company composed of Mr. Hendry, Mr. McNair and Messrs. Andrew Haslam and R. B. Kelly, was formed under the firm title of Hendry, McNair & Co., and a small saw mill, sash and door factory, and box factory were established at New Westminster. The fishing business on the Fraser river which was yearly becoming more important, made the need of a box factory apparent. The business at Nanaimo was still carried on by Messrs. Hendry & McNair. In both places the business increased rapidly. In 1880 the Westminster company found it necessary to become incorporated in order to hold real estate, and accordingly the Royal City Planing Mills Company composed of the same persons as the partnership company, was organized and incorporated. Shortly after this Mr. A. E. Lees joined the company. Of this company

Mr. Hendry became president and general manager and has since continued to hold these positions. In 1885 the Royal City Planing Mills Company purchased the Mill at Nanaimo and continued to conduct it for a year, when Messrs. Haslam & Lees bought it giving their share of stock in the company for it. These gentlemen having gone out the company was now composed of Messrs. Hendry, McNair, Kelly and Beecher, the latter having purchased an interest in the industry. During the period of the boom in Port Moody real estate, Mr. Kelly sold out, leaving three interested in the concern. The business had greatly increased and continued to increase so rapidly that when Vancouver came into existence the company established a branch there in 1887. During the great fire their mill was in course of construction and was one of the few buildings left standing. During this time the company had been acquiring timber limits, and had secured some of the best in the Province. They had hitherto done a purely local business but they now determined to begin an export trade. Owing to the difficulties at the mouth of the Fraser river and the want of a proper chart, lumber ships were chary about going up the river. The company however, in conjunction with the Board of Trade, of which Mr. Hendry was president, succeeded finally in inducing the government to survey and improve the mouth of the river, and in 1888 Mr. Hendry had the satisfaction of seeing foreign ships loading at his mill for all parts of the world. During the autumn of 1888 he conceived the idea of purchasing Hastings Saw Mill for the purpose of increasing the company's export trade, and negotiations with this object in view were closed in October, 1889, when Hastings mill became the property of the Royal City Planing Mills Co., with Mr. Hendry as president and general manager. During the last session of the Provincial Legislature a bill was passed through the house consolidating the two companies under the title of the British Columbia Mills, Timber and Trading Co. The success and prosperity of the company has been very marked and has been due almost entirely to the untiring efforts and foresight of the original founder, From its establishment in 1878, the business has increased from a local trade of 7000 feet per day, to a foreign and local trade of 250,000 feet per day. The other portion of the company's business has also increased in size and importance. The factories are successful in the extreme and the importations of glass are the largest in the Province. Mr. Hendry settled in New Westminster in 1878 and was elected to the City Council in 1888 and was chairman of the committee which had in hand the work of re-surveying the city. He was one of the charter members of the New Westminster Board of Trade, and has been on the council board of the organization ever since, having for several terms been vice-president and during the last three years president of the board. He had a good deal to do with obtaining the charter for the New Westminster Southern Railway Company, and is interested in the company. He has also been largely instrumental in pushing forward the improvements on the Fraser river. He was urged to accept the mayoralty of the city in 1889, as the new charter was being introduced and a resolute hand was required at the helm. He accepted and continued to act for six months, when he resigned in consequence of his position as chief magistrate clashing with his position as a member of the New Westminster Southern Railway Company. He is largely interested in many enterprises, both in New Westminster and Vancouver, and is one of the most prominent men of the Province. He is a member of the Masonic fraternity and was treasurer of the lodge for four years. He is also a member of the Ancient Order of United Workmen and an adherent of the Presbyterian church. In February, 1882, he married Adeline, daughter of the late Donald McMillan, of Picton, Nova Scotia.

Hibben, Thomas Napier, born 1828 at Charleston, North Carolina, died January 10th, 1890, at Victoria, B. C. Mr. Hibben had been a familiar figure in the city of Victoria since 1858, having in that year arrived there from San Francisco. He was educated at his native place, and when twenty-one years of age went to California during the great mining excitement in 1849. He made a good deal of money at the mines and then established a stationery business in San Francisco, which he sold to Bancroft in 1858 when he came to British Columbia. Shortly after his arrival in Victoria he formed a partnership with Mr. Carswell and purchased Kierski's bookstore, which they continued to conduct till 1866 when Mr. Hibben bought his partner's interest and thereafter managed the business himself. At no time did he take an active interest in politics, but was a thorough business man and by his unassuming virtues he gained the highest respect of his fellow-citizens. He was a member of the Pioneer society, and of the Board of Trade and an adherent of the Reformed Episcopal church.

Higgins, Hon. David Williams, (Victoria), was born in Halifax, Nova Scotia, on November 30th, 1834. His father was a native of Manchester, England, and in 1814 emigrated to Canada and settled in Nova Scotia. In 1836 Mr. Higgins' parents removed to Brooklyn, New Jersey, and here Mr. Higgins was educated. He went to California in 1852, and in 1856 he founded the *Morning Call* newspaper, which he sold in 1858, when he removed to British Columbia. He settled in Victoria and for many years subsequently he was connected with the newspaper business. For a number of years he was editor and proprietor of the *Colonist*. He organized and was first president of the Victoria fire department and was a member of the Board of Education from 1866 to 1869. He has been a member of the city council and was returned to the Local Legislature as member of Victoria district at the general election of 1886. In 1869 he was elected speaker of the house and at the recent elections was returned by his constituents. In politics he is a Liberal-Conservative. Mr. Higgins is interested in many important enterprises in the Province. He was the promoter and is president of the electric street railway of Victoria.

Hilbert, John, (Nanaimo), son of the late John Hilbert, was born on the 29th of July, 1845, at Isle Haxey, Lincolnshire, England. He was educated at his native place under Rev. Charles J. Hawkins, and at the age of 15 years left school and went to the town of Leeds, Yorkshire, where he apprenticed himself to the pattern-making business in the establishment of Tannet, Walker & Co., who employed eleven hundred men. After finishing his apprenticeship he went to Sheffield where he followed his trade for a time and afterwards returned to Leeds where he continued to reside till 1874. In 1866 he married Miss Mary Jane Gilligan. In 1874 he determined to try his fortune in the new world, and selected Nanaimo as the place at which he should settle. He accordingly sailed for New York, and from there came by way of the Central Pacific to British Columbia and located without delay in the Diamond City. During his first year's residence in Nanaimo he followed the contracting business and put up several fine buildings.

The Methodist church at Wellington and the school building in Nanaimo are both his workmanship. In 1875, about twelve months after his arrival, he established the furniture business which he has now, renting the premises which he now occupies. His business flourished under his judicious management and he was soon in a position to purchase the place he had leased. Mr. Hilbert has taken a prominent part in politics since his arrival in the Province and especially in municipal affairs since the incorporation of the city. He has been repeatedly urged to stand for the Local Legislature, but has firmly declined to do so. He represented the city for six years at the council board, and during five of these terms he filled the positions of chairman of the Street committee and of the Police Committee. In 1879 he stood for the position of Mayor of the city, and was defeated by only seven votes. Last year he was elected to the position of chief magistrate. Outside of his furniture business Mr. Hilbert has large interests in Nanaimo, and is a stock holder in many important enterprises, notably the gas and water works and the tannery. In Dominion politics he is a Liberal-Conservative and a supporter of the Macdonald administration. Mr. Hilbert is the founder of the Order of Foresters in Nanaimo and passed through all the chairs in the lodge. He is a member of the Order of Oddfellows and has occupied all the offices in the gift of the lodges in British Columbia. He is District Deputy Grand Commander of the American Legion of Honor and treasurer of the Order of Druids. He is a charter member of the Knights of Pythias and treasurer of the Uniform rank. Mr. Hilbert was also the founder of the Ancient Order of United Workmen in Nanaimo and has twice been a delegate to the grand lodge.

Herring, A. M., (New Westminster), was born in the Ionian Islands, on May 2nd, 1852. Some few years later the family removed to England, where Mr. Herring received his primary education, from which place they emigrated to British Columbia in 1859, during the great Fraser river gold mining excitement. Mr. Herring's education was continued as far as the then educational facilities of the colony would allow and finally completed by a four year's collegiate course in California where he grduated with great honor in chemistry and the science of electricity. Mr. Herring pursued his calling as chemist and druggist for several years with much success. Some years later the science of electricity began to attract great attention and owing to the rapid development of California and the extension of the electric telegraph the demand for telegraph operators became so great that Mr. Herring and several others opened what was known as the San Francisco Electrical College, where pupils were fitted in a few month to assume the duties of telegraph operator and were immediately placed in positions on the Western Union Lines. He finally disposed of his interest to his partners, and removed to New Westminster, and for several years after, he engaged in mining in Cassiar, Peace river and Cariboo, finally resuming his profession of chemist and druggist, and opening a business in Barkerville, Cariboo, which proved very successful. On the decline of Cariboo Mr. Herring removed to New Westminster where he opened a wholesale and retail drug business, which finally developed into one of the largest and most extended businesses of its kind in British Columbia, from the proceeds of which and their successful reinvestment in real estate he has secured a large fortune. Mr. Herring possesses the rare quality of being a good financier. He is an ex-alderman and was chairman of the finance committee of the City of New Westminster for some time, which position he filled with honor and integrity and to the advantage of the city. He is president and financier of the New Westminster Electric Light and Motor Power Company, and a prominent member of the Board of Trade, the Agricultural Society, the Independent Order of Oddfellows, Knights of Pythias and other societies, and is a public spirited man always assisting any worthy object. Mr. Herring's energy, perseverence and push have assisted in the rapid advancement of the city of New Westminster. In 1887 Mr. Herring erected "Herring's Opera House," a building 50 x 130 feet, seating 1,200 persons, which is a great boon to the city, Mr. Herring always securing the very best talent he can to occupy the same, often at his own loss. He is one of the pioneers of British Columbia and has witnessed all the vicissitudes and experienced all the hardships of a pioneer's life, the incidents of which if recorded would make a very interesting book. He is one of the many self-made men of the province, who owe all their success to their indomitable will and perseverence. Mr. Herring has been married to a most estimable lady for the past fifteen years and has four children.

HON. J. S HELMCKEN.

Hill, Albert James, (New Westminster), born at Sydney, Cape Breton, Nova Scotia, April 7th, 1836, the third son of John Lewis Hill, Esq., and Margaret, daughter of Joseph Whyte, Esq., M. D., R. N., of Banff, Scotland. On the paternal side Mr. Hill is of good old United Empire Loyalist stock, his great grandfather William Hill, in his devotion to the King's cause having forfeited a very considerable property in New England, and accepted exile in the then infant colony of Nova Setia with his household of sixteen persons, rather than yield his faith in the divine right of his sovereign. He received the appointment of Comptroller of His Majesty's Customs in the then crown colony of the Island of Cape Breton, and died at Sydney in 1802. On the maternal side the familiar names of Baris, Stroud and Whyte-Melville are among his near kin in Scotland. Mr. Hill received his earlier education at home, the excellent system of public schools of Nova Scotia not being then established. He spent several years in ship building and in conjunction with his brothers added two trim schooners to the fleet of Cape Breton county. Went to Boston as supercargo of the schooner "Marian" with the first cargo of coal from the Island after the purchase of the rights of the Duke of York in 1860. Entered Harbor Collegiate Academy, August, 1861, and matriculated into Acadia College September, 1862, taking the full curriculum and graduating in the first class A. B., 1866. Married, July, 1866, Agnes, daughter of Alexander Lawrence, Esq., of St. John, New Brunswick, and sister of W. Lawrence, Esq., for many years prominent in the political history of the province, a union blessed with two sons and two daughters. Spent the first two years after graduating on the teaching staff of Harbor Academy and immediately afterwards, May, 1868, accepted an appointment on the E. & N. A. Ry. and assisted in locating that line to Winn on the Penobscot river. In May, 1869, received an appointment on the Government staff of the Intercolonial Railway in Miramichi, N. B., on the surveys and location of sections 20, 21, and 22, in New Brunswick. Was transferred, January 1st, 1870, to construction of section 12, Truro, N. S., and continued on sections 12 and 7 till January 1st., 1872, meanwhile locating the Acadia mines branch and the present Springhill branch lines. In February, 1872, accepted a position on the staff of the Louisburg Mineral Railway and carried out the exploratory work of that line continuing through its location, and as chief engineer for the London contractors to the close of construction in 1874. Appointed manager of the Lorway and Emory collieries and opened and operated the latter in 1872 and 1873, and carried out a geological survey of the eastern Cape Breton coal fields, afterwards embodied with the plans of the Dominion geological survey and published by order of the Government. Prepared and published a map of the Island of Cape Breton, 1875, in the employ of the local government of Nova Scotia and conducted the surveys of the Thompson and Pugwash, and Springhill and Pugwash railway lines. In 1876 appointed manager of the Cumberland colliery and continued this work till its amalgamation with the Coal Mining Association in 1877. Made surveys for the Maccon and Joggins branch railway. Engaged in 1877 on the geological survey staff in examination of the southern portion of Cumberland county, N. S. Surveyed Oxford and Pugwash Railway for the Dominion Government. In 1878 commissioned as provincial crown land surveyor for Cumberland and executed topographical surveys for the local government. In 1869 sent to Algoma by the Dominion Government in connection with the contracts from Southern creek to English river. Prepared an interesting list of geological specimens which were presented to McGill University. On January 1st, 1880, ordered to British Columbia on construction of C. P. R. contract from Yale to Sumas and continued in this work till October, 1882, when he was removed to Port Moody and closed his connection with the Government service in December, 1884. Since that date he has been in private practice in New Westminster. He is engineer for the Municipality of Surrey and conducts an extensive general practice in all parts of the Dominion. Is a charter member of the Canadian Society of Civil Engineers, a corporator of the C. W. W. Co., a member of the New Westminster Club and a corresponding member of the Ottawa Field Batonists Club. Was chief engineer of the New Westminster Southern Railway from its inception to August 1st, 1889 and carried out the location surveys for the line. Resigned his position at the latter date in order to devote his whole attention to his increasing private practice. Mr. Hill has rendered efficient service both in public and private capacities to geological research in his native province and in British Columbia. In politics he has been a steady and consistent Conservative but sets principle above party.

Hoffar, Noble Stonestreet, (Vancouver), son of Dr. A. M. Hoffar, of Washington, D. C., and Mary Ellen Stonestreet Hoffar, was born at Washington, D. C., December 12th, 1843. Educated at Georgetown College, where he graduated as B. A. at the age of twenty years. He took a post graduate course and left with the degree of M. A. In 1866 he came to the Pacific coast, and during the next seven years engaged in mining in Nevada, Utah and Arizona. Tired of the wild life which had become so familiar to him he decided to get back into civilization. In 1872 he settled in Los Angeles, where he began his present business as an architect and builder. In 1878 he removed to Oregon, and settled in Baker's City, where he remained till 1883 when he came to Victoria. While in Victoria he was ill, and after recovering he went to Nanaimo where he built the hospital and other large structures. He was subsequently engaged on several large structures at New Westminster, and the day before the great fire which destroyed Vancouver he arrived in that city where he has since resided. He has designed many of the splendid structures for which the terminal city is celebrated, and has been identified with a number of enterprises which have had their origin there. He married Miss Annie Odon, of St. Louis, Missouri.

Horne, James Welton, M. P. P., (Vancouver), eldest son of the late Christopher and Elizabeth Harriet Orr Horne, was born 3rd November, 1853, at Toronto, Ontario. His father, a native of Saxe-Cobourg, came to America when a young man, and after a brief residence in the United States, removed to Canada and first settled in Dundas where he established a cloth manufactory. At Toronto he became a partner in the Clarke woollen mills. While this enterprise was still in its infancy he died leaving a widow and five children, of whom the subject of the present sketch was the eldest; when the estate was wound up it was found that only a few hundred dollars remained for the maintenance of the family. At this time Mr. Horne was a lad of nine years of age, attending school, but with the discernment and fortitude of one of maturer years he saw and decided that it was his duty to get out into life, and if possible aid his mother in providing for the family. He was willing to take any employment which offered, and the first thing at which he engaged was doing the lighter work on a farm situated near Toronto. He continued at this place for two years, and after his hours of labor were over he worked hard at his books, being fully convinced of the value of an education. He left his first employer to engage with a farmer in Pickering township, who had agreed to allow him every alternate day to attend school. On these terms he remained in Pickering for about a year and a half, when he removed to Scarboro, where he entered the employ of a minister of the Church of England. In this last position he had many advantages; light work, time to attend school and assistance in his studies from the clergyman, who took an interest in his progress. He remained here till he reached the age of 15 years. Always looking to the future Mr. Horne decided that it was time for him to learn some useful trade or profession. After mature consideration he concluded that circumstances were too much against him to admit of his entering on the study of a profession. Without money or friends to give him his first start it was impossible for him to accomplish much. He accordingly looked about him for some trade, and having a strong bent toward mechanical studies he decided to apprentice himself to a large machine manufactory at Whitby. He did so and for the next five years he remained in this establishment sedulously devoting his attention to the acquisition of a knowledge of all the branches of the business. Not only did he bend all his energies during his hours of labor to the accomplishment of this task, but his evenings and all his leisure time were devoted to study. The result was that he became a first-class mechanical draughtsman, pattern-maker and wood-carver, while at the same he acquired a thorough knowledge of the higher branches of mechanics. During the five years of his apprenticeship Mr. Horne denied himself, in his anxiety to fit himself in every manner for the future struggle in life, of all luxuries and pleasures and allowed his salary to accumulate in the business. At the end of that time there was about £5,000 to his credit. This he invested in the business, and was almost immediately after elected a director of the company, and also on account of his thorough knowledge of the whole business, his sound practical judgment and skill as a workman he was appointed assistant-superintendent of the whole establishment. He continued to conduct this immense establishment for two years when, owing to the failure of his health, he was obliged to resign this position. He accordingly sold out his interest and took a much-needed rest. He subsequently began business as an insurance agent with headquarters at Whitby and latterly at Belleville, and he succeeded so well that before long he held the agencies for eleven companies. When he had been two years engaged in this business he obtained the inspectorship between Kingston and Toronto for two large companies. His salary for this work was a handsome one, but Mr. Horne was not content to work for salary, however large. His mind was filled with the possibilities of Western America and he felt confident that fortune awaited him there. His energy and enterprise, and his business ability and knowledge, he felt, would find a readier sphere in the new world than in the conservative cities of the east. Accordingly in the spring of 1878 he threw up his position as inspector and went to Southern California. His health at this time was not very good, and he thought that that climate would benefit him. He found everything so dull and flat from a business point of view that he remained only a few months. Manitoba then known as the Red River Country was at this time coming prominently into notice as one having a great future before it. There was rumor of the Dominion Government building a branch railroad (afterwards when built known as the Pembina branch) on the east side of the Red river from St. Boniface to St. Vincent to connect with the Manitoba, St. Paul and Minneapolis road. Mr. Horne in looking at the matter from a business point of view saw that this territory must become an important province, and that it must have a commercial centre, and he decided that a splendid opportunity was afforded him of establishing himself. He accordingly went to Winnipeg, which was then a struggling collection of wooden cabins with a population of about 3,000 persons. He opened an insurance and shipping office and in a short time succeeded in building up a good business. Not long after his arrival in Winnipeg he was appointed by the Northwest Navigation Company agent for the Red river steamers plying between Winnipeg and Grand Forks, the terminus of the St. Paul R. R. The Red river at that time was the only highway to Manitoba, and it was found necessary to establish a bonded warehouse at Emerson, the point where the river crossed the international boundary line. Mr. Horne opened an office here which he placed in charge of an agent. At this time he secured the appointment of valuator and inspector for the Northwest Loan Co., which did a large business in Manitoba.

In the spring of 1881 after the charter for the C. P. R. west from Winnipeg to the Rocky mountains had been granted there were hundreds of people in Winnipeg on the *qui vive* to be the first on the site of the large town which was expected to spring up on the line of railway in the centre of the fine agricultural country west of Winnipeg. Mr. Horne concluded that he would be first on the site and be one of the chief founders of this proposed city, and when General Rosser laid out the route of the railway Mr. Horne followed him on horseback. When he reached the Assiniboine river he decided that he had found the site of the future metropolis, and three reasons confirmed him in this opinion. It was at the head of navigation on the Assiniboine; it was in the centre of a magnificent agricultural district and it was sufficiently far away from Winnipeg, and would, if it once got fairly under way attract the crowd leaving that city. The site of the future town was at this time indistinguishable from the prairie which stretched on every side except by the grade stakes of the Canadian Pacific Railway. Mr. Horne entered into an agreement with the railway company by which he was given a certain quantity of land at a fixed price, and on his erecting business buildings he was to have a rebate. He at once opened an office, or rather erected a tent on the prairie, divided his land into lots, opened and graded streets and when this preliminary work was accomplished began the erection of buildings. His desire was to attract attention and residents to the new place, and in order to do this he went to Winnipeg and got business men on condition of their obtaining their stores free of rent for the first six months to cast in their fortunes with the young town. The plan worked admirably. Every new citizen attracted others, the town became advertised, people talked about it and then came to it. The Government land agent was induced by Mr. Horne to make this his headquarters, and thus the first official building was located here. Mr. Horne then went to Winnipeg and after strenuous efforts succeeded in getting the Gevernment to establish a postoffice at the place. The newspapers began finally to talk of the new town and its growth and it thus became better known. The result of all this energy was that in the autumn of the first year between two and three hundred persons had taken up their abode in Brandon. During all this time Mr. Horne continued erecting buildings on his own property, and Rosser avenue, the street on which these were put up, became the principal thoroughfare of the place. In November the railway came through and with it a large number of people poured in. In the spring of 1882 there were over two thousand residents in the place and a public meeting was accordingly held, and a charter of incorporation as a city was applied for and granted. Mr. Horne declined to accept the mayoralty, but allowed himself to be placed on the council board. At the first meeting of the aldermanic board Mr. Horne was appointed chairman of the board of pub works. In this capacity he brought in a report recommending the opening up of streets, laying of sidewalks and similar improvements to the extent of $150,000. The recommendation was adopted and the work of carrying it out in detail was left to Mr. Horne. He at once advertised for tenders in the principal papers of the east, and the attention of contractors and workingmen was thus drawn to the place. The result was that a large number of people were attracted thither and by the end of the year Brandon had a population of 4,000 persons. It was through Mr. Horne's influence and energy that Brandon was appointed the western judicial seat, and a jail and courthouse were built. A registry office was also established there, and the position of registrar was offered to and declined by Mr. Horne. Mr. Horne's property increased with that of the town and he was regarded as not only the most enterprising and successful, but as the wealthiest citizen of Brandon. Mr. Horne had always kept a watchful eye on the Pacific Province, and was especially re-regardful of the terminus of the railway. In the spring of 1883 he took a trip to Southern California, and on his return visited Burrard Inlet and the Fraser. He perceived, however, that he was too soon, and he accordingly returned to Brandon. In the spring of 1884 he again visited Burrard Inlet, but found he was too soon yet and the only investment he made was some farming land which is now very valuable. In March, 1886, he he finally came through to Vancouver, one year and a half before the railway had been extended to it. He took up his residence there, however, and invested largely in real estate. He had intended going into the banking and loan business, but his health was so poor that he felt the close attention necessary in those pursuits would have injured him. In 1888 he was elected a member of the city council of Vancouver and again in 1889 on both occasions heading the poll and in 1890 he stood successfully as a candidate for the Local Legislature. Since coming to British Columbia Mr. Horne has been identified with almost every enterprise which has for its object the development of the country and the building up of Vancouver. He has centered the most of his interests here and these now amount to over a million and a half of dollars. He is president of the Vancouver Foundry, chairman of the Board of Public Works, chairman of the Board of Park Commissioners, director on Electric Railway and Light Company, president on the Pacific Coast Fire Insurance Company, president of Colonization and Trading Company, director Northwest Loan Company, and director on the Northwest Insurance Company, and is on the boards of a large number of other important companies. He is one of the most public-spirited men of Vancouver and has the full confidence of the citizens, as has been shown repeatedly at the polls. He is a prominent member of the Masonic fraternity and a member of the Presbyterian church. Mr. Horne's career is one which young Canadians would do well to consider with attention. His marvellous success is the result of unswerving fidelity to the motto so often preached, so little practiced: "Industry, intelligence, integrity."

Hume, Fred. J., (Revelstoke), is a Canadian, of Irish descent, and was born in Jacksontown, New Brunswick, on August 8th, 1860. In his early life Mr. Hume received a thorough business education and training at Fredericton, N. B. In the spring of 1883 he travelled to British Columbia and chose Revelstoke for his home, engaging in the dry goods business, and also carrying on a general trade between Nelson, on the Kootenay Lake, and Revelstoke. Mr. Hume is largely interested in the mineral development of the Kootenay District, and also in the Columbia and Kootenay River and Lake Steam Navigation Company, of which he is a managing director, besides having considerable interest in the townsite of Nelson, British Columbia, apart from his mining and other occupations. Mr. Hume is a Justice of the Peace for the District of Kootenay, B. C., and a Notary Public. He has suffered large losses from fire, having twice had his warehouses, together with their contents, destroyed. In spite of these misfortunes Mr. Hume is doing a flourishing business and is one of the most prosperous men in the Rockies.

JOHN HENDRY.

Humphreys, Hon. Thos. Basil, (Victoria), born at Liverpool, England, in 1840. Educated at Walton and came to British Columbia in 1863. Was first returned to the Legislative Council as representative of Lillooet in 1867, and continued to occupy this seat till confederation. He was returned to the first Provincial parliament as representative of the same constituency, and at the general election of 1875 stood successfully for Victoria district. Mr. Humphreys continued to hold his seat till the session of 1890, when ill health forced him to seek a change of climate. He was one of the most active politicians in the early days of the colony and after confederation was Provincial secretary in the Walkem government. In November, 1873, he married Miss Carrie Watkins.

Innes, James Henry, (Esquimalt), was born in London, England, on May 31st, 1834, his parents being of Scotch descent. Mr. Innes was educated for Her Majesty's Civil Service in London, and previous to his arrival in British Columbia served in the civil department of the Royal Navy from October 8th, 1848, his first appointment being at Malta, and later on he was stationed at Constantinople throughout the Crimean War. He was afterwards sent to Bermuda and thence removed to London, England, and on May 24th, 1873, was given his present appointment at Esquimalt, where he is naval and victualling storekeeper and accountant in charge of the Royal Naval Yard. Mr. Innes is a member of the Masonic Order, and an adherent of the Church of England. He has been in Her Majesty's service for over forty-two years.

Irving, Captain William, born 1816 in Annan, Dumfrieshire, Scotland, died August 28th, 1872, at New Westminster, British Columbia. Captain Irving was the first citizen of British Columbia who placed the steamboat and shipping industry on the Mainland on a regular and systematic basis and his energy and enterprise, sustained by a belief in the future of the country, gave him during the latter part of his life a practical monopoly in this business on the Fraser river. He was reared to a seafaring life, and in 1849 he arrived at Oregon as master and part owner of the bark "Success" with which he engaged in the lumber trade in Oregon and California. He continued at this business with great success for a number of years, and during that time purchased considerable property in what is now the city of Portland, and which has since turned out extremely valuable. He subsequently purchased an iron steamer the "Eagle," the first vessel of this kind that ever plied in Oregon waters. In 1859, during the mining excitement he turned his attention to British Columbia, and became interested in the Fraser river steamers, the "Moody" and the "Douglas," the construction of which vessels he personally superintended. In 1861 he made the first successful trip from New Westminster to Yale in the "Moody." In the following year he sold out his interest in the "Moody" and "Douglas" and built the "Reliance" which was for years the finest steamer on those waters. In 1866 he added the steamer "Onward" and continued to increase his fleet as business justified. In 1862 he brought his family from Portland and established himself in New Westminster. He took considerable interest in municipal matters and served several years on the Council Board, acting during one year, 1868, as president of the Council. Captain Irving was associated with many enterprises which had for their object the opening up of the Province, and his shrewdness, business ability and unassailable rectitude, gave character to and insured the success of any venture which he might invest in. He was a man of large endowments, and of a singularly frank and generous disposition. He was ever ready to assist a friend or for that matter an enemy who might be in deep water. He was a member of the Masonic fraternity, and an honorary member of the Hyack Fire Company of New Westminster.

Irving. John, (Victoria), born at Portland, Oregon, on November 24th, 1854. Son of the late Captain William Irving, so well known in the early history of the Province, as the largest and most enterprising steamboat owner in British Columbia. Educated at New Westminster and Victoria with a view to ultimately taking charge of his father's extensive business and, with a natural instinct for navigation, studied this science and at an early age got a practical acquaintance with steamboating. After his father's death he continued the business, personally superintending its management and became thoroughly acquainted with the waters of British Columbia. Under his supervision the business continued to increase and run so smoothly that accidents were unknown. In 1882 the various steamboat companies at Victoria amalgamated and the consolidated company was called the Canadian Pacific Navigation Company. Captain Irving was appointed manager of the new company and has since continued to hold that position. During the last six years the company has expanded and has now a service equal to any in America. Captain Irving has large interests outside of the Canadian Pacific Navigation Company, and is deeply concerned in the rapid development of the latent resources of the Province. He is president of the Vancouver Water Works Company, and a director in a large number of important enterprises. In 1882 he married Miss Munro, youngest daughter of Mr. Alexander Munro, chief factor of the Hudson Bay Co., at Victoria.

Jackson, Robert Edwin, Q.C., a member of the bar of British Columbia, and member of the law firm of Drake, Jackson & Helmcken. Third son of the late John Robert Henry and Jane Scarlett Jackson, of Swallowfield, Wellington, Somersetshire. Claims descent from the Jacksons of Bedale, Yorkshire, and is great grandson of James Jackson, Vicar of Farnham, Surrey. On the paternal side Mr. Jackson is descended from the Earls of Carnwarth, through his father's mother, Henrietta Teresa Carolina Dalzelle, grand daughter of John Dodd, of Swallowfield Place, Berkshire, the father of Captain Dodd, of the Guards, referred to in Junius' letters. On his mother's side he is descended from the Scarletts of Jamaica, ancestors of the Lords Abinger. Born December 15th, 1826. Educated at Blundell's school, Tiverton, Devonshire, and Elizabeth College, Guernsey. Admitted an attorney in England in 1849. then became a pupil of John Patch, Pump Court, Temple, and by purchase, the junior member of the firm of Maltby, Robinson & Jackson, which was not a profitable investment. Emigrated to London, Ontario, (then Canada West), 1858, where he entered the office of the late Mr. Justice Wilson, then John Wilson, Q.C. Became student at Osgoode Hall, 1859, and the following year was admitted an attorney of the Courts of Canada. Practised his profession in London, Ontario, until the autumn of 1864, when he left Canada to enter into partnership in Victoria, V. I., with an old friend, his late partner, now Mr. Justice M. W. Trywhitt Drake. Called to the Bar of British Columbia in 1877, appointed a Q.C., in 1889, and is a Bencher of the British Columbia Law Society.

Was mainly instrumental in the formation of the British Columbia Benevolent Society, of which he was Vice-President for several years, and in 1871, during the McCreight administration, he declined the office of Registrar-General, vacated by the Hon. E. G. Alrton, on the latter becoming Attorney General immediately before the confederation of the Colony of British Columbia with Canada. Married 1867 Eleanor Fanny, second daughter of the late George Leggatt and step daughter of the Hon. T. L. Wood, then Solicitor-General of British Columbia. A member of the Primrose and Imperial Federation Leagues; Conservative, Swallowfield Cottage, Victoria, B.C.; Conservative Club, (1852), St. James street, Eng.; Union Club, Victoria, B.C.

Jessop, John, (Victoria), is a thirty years resident of British Columbia and is the only known survivor of a party of eight who walked across the continent from Fort Garry in 1859. The hardships, adventures and dangers of such a trip with meagre supplies, without a guide or semblance of a trail, and hostile Indian tribes just on the boundary of Minnesota and Dakota, were many and various. In those days the plains of the South Saskatchewan, Bow and Belly Rivers were swarming with buffalo, now, unhappily, extinct, and Mr. Jessop's party subsisted on buffalo and antelope meat exclusively for nearly two months, during which time more than 750 miles of prairie travelling were accomplished in an air line, increased by zigzaging here and there to pass deep ravines, etc. While searching for an entrance to what was then called the Boundary Pass, they fortunately fell in with a band of Blackfeet Indians, among whom was a Kootenay, who was crossing over to his camp on Tobacco Plains, South Kootenay. For all the ammunition, tobacco, clothing and blankets that could be spared, together with a rifle, this Indian acted as guide through the Rockies. By his so doing the lives of this small company of foolhardy adventurers were undoubtedly saved. On the Pend d'Orielle River Mr. Jessop and three of the party crossed and went by way of Coeur d'Alane and Spokane valleys to Colville. In those days the Roman Catholic missionary in Coeur d'Alane valley was the only white man from Kootenay to Colville. From the latter place to Vancouver, Wash., over the Cascade Mountains, with navigation entirely closed on the Columbia, in zero weather, and camping out night after night in more or less snow, was an experience anything but agreeable. When the subject of this sketch arrived in Victoria there was nothing for him to do in his profession of school teacher, for the simple and sufficient reason that there were no children to be taught, outside of the few attending the old Colonial school in the reserve. The early spring of '60, therefore, found him tramping it to Cariboo, or all that was then known of this far-famed gold region, namely, the Forks of the Quesnelle, over the unfinished roads on the old Douglas route, via. Lillooet, with a heavy pack and continuously weary muscles. Part of the summer was spent in hard work—returns *nil* —on Harvey Creek, and afterwards on another claim on Keithley's Creek, with no better results. Mr. Jessop left the mines and returned to New Westminster. Knowing something of type-setting and newspaper work he spent the winter with his friend Leonard McClure, long since deceased, on the *Times*. In the spring of '61 the *Times* was purchased by Hon. John Robson, and its title changed to *The British Columbian*. McClure, Jessop and two compositors then formed a co-partnership and started the Victoria *Daily Press*. The editor set up his leading articles out of the case himself; the "local items" did likewise, and at 3, 4 or 5 o'clock, a.m., the paper would get to press, sometimes on colored wrapping paper, on account of lack of funds to purchase white. In August of that year, the newspaper business not being a success financially, Mr. Jessop start a private, non-sectarian school on the system then carried out in Canada west, now Ontario, in the old Assembly Hall, at the foot of View street. This rickety place being neither wind nor water-tight, a new building, that for many years afterwards did duty as the Central School, was erected on the site of Philharmonic Hall, Fort street at the cost of over $3,000. As soon as the old Vancouver Island colony school system was inaugurated in the following year, the Central School building was rented by the Colonial Government and the owner appointed principal of the first free, non-sectarian school north of the 49th parallel on the Pacific coast. Matters and things educational went on satisfactorily till the union of the colonies of Vancouver Island and British Columbia in '66, when a systematic "freezing out" process was commenced by Governor Frederick Seymour and a majority of his council. Mr. Jessop and two or three other teachers continued at their posts meanwhile, with little or no salary, when Christmas, '68, found them in almost a starving condition. At this juncture a circus company wintering in Victoria, aided by several amateur performers, offered them a benefit. The old Theatre Royal was packed from "floor to ceiling" on that occasion, and about $400 proceeds was divided *pro rata* among the destitute teachers. A little more than a year after this the Governor succeeded in closing all the Vancouver Island schools, and over four hundred children, or very many of them, were then left without instruction. Confederation, in '71, brought about a new order of things educational. The late lamented Mr. Justice Robertson, as Provincial Secretary of the first responsible government of the Province, aided by Mr. Jessop, introduced and passed a School Act, similar in most of its provisions to that then in force in Ontario; and which still forms the groundwork of the present system. Under this Act Mr. Jessop received the appointment of Superintendent of Education for British Columbia; and, with the assistance of an efficient Board of Education, laid broadly and deeply the principles of free, non-sectarian schools. In '78 the government of the day made some radical changes in the School Act that the Superintendent and the Board of Education did not approve of, when their resignations were all sent in at the same time. For several years past Mr. Jessop has been Dominion Immigration Agent in this city, a position for which his personal knowledge of almost every district in the Province, admirably qualifies him. This old pioneer of British Columbia spent the first 17 years of his life near Norwich, England, where he was born in 1829. An adventurous disposition in his younger days induced him to try his fortunes in the new world. On the voyage out to Boston the ship met with such hard usage that all on board felt thankful when she made Halfax Harbor in a sinking condition, minus cargo (mostly jettisoned) spars, one mast, bulwarks and deck houses. Thence he proceeded via New York and Watertown to Kingston, Ont., and thence to Toronto, where he qualified for school teaching at the Toronto Normal School, where a first class A certificate was obtained by him in '55. Two years' teaching in the county of Elgin, and two more near Oshawa county, Ontario, brought him to the spring of '59, when with knapsack, pistol and bowie knife, he started for Fort William, and thence over the old Hudson's Bay Company's canoe route to Red River. Mr. Jessop was married in Victoria more than 21 years ago to Miss Faussette, also a pioneer

J. W. HORNE.

teacher, who arrived in '62 from the old country. His father is still living in Ontario, hearty and strong, notwithstanding his burden of 90 years; his mother died a few years ago at the advanced age of 86.

Jewell, Henry, (Victoria), is of United Empire Loyalist stock and was born in Toronto, Ontario. During his childhood the rebellion under Wm. Lyon McKenzie broke out and his uncle and father were both in arms for the crown. His uncle carried the mail on horseback between Kingston and Toronto, and on many occasions had close calls for his life at the hands of rebels whose object was rifling the mail bags of Government dispatches. When Mr. Jewell was nine years of age his father died and he removed to Oshawa, where he resided with an uncle and worked as a carpenter till he was twenty-two years old. He then came to British Columbia. He resided in Victoria for two years, and then went to Cariboo, where he mined for seven years but without much success. When he left the mines he settled in Victoria and established his present business.

Jirouard, Sue, (Vernon), was born on July 4th, 1835, at Quebec, and was educated in the public schools of that city. On leaving school he went to sea for a number of years, but not finding a sea-faring life to his taste he returned to Canada and resided in Ontario till 1852. When Governor Stephenson formed an expedition to explore a route for the Northern Pacific Railway, he was accompanied by Mr. Jirouard who remained with him for two years, during which time he crossed the continent to Vancouver, Washington. At the completion of this expedition in 1854, Mr. Jirouard went to the gold fields of California, where he mined for seven years with varying success. In 1861 he visited the mines in Idaho, and at the close of the same year came to British Columbia and settled at Cherry Creek where he mined three years. In 1864 he pre-empted his present farm at Vernon, of which place he is now postmaster, and where he has been largely engaged in stock-raising. Mr. Jirouard is a Conservative but has taken no part in politics. He is one of the best agriculturists in the Okanagon district, and as a stock-raiser stands in the first rank.

Johnston, Angus R., (Nanaimo), was born in Ayrshire, Scotland, on August 12th, 1842. He was educated partly at Inverness and partly at Glasgow and Edinburgh, for the profession of railway engineer, and shortly after completing his studies he left Scotland with a party of engineers going to Chili, South America, to survey a line of railway between Valparaiso and Santiago. He continued with this survey for some time, and then joined a scientific exploring party, making explorations in Chili, Peru, and Ecuador, and in the course of his connection with this party he became familiar with a considerable portion of South America. He subsequently drifted into Central America in connection with a similar party. He was in Nicaragua during the time Walker made his celebrated filibustering expedition into that state. Mr. Johnston offered his services to the government of Nicaragua and received a Lieutenant's commission. While acting in this position he was severely wounded and for eight months was laid up with illness which followed from this cause. He then returned to Chili and took shipping in the "Florence Hamilton" of Boston for California. On the voyage the vessel was wrecked and all on board but Mr. Johnston and two others were lost. Their fate seemed almost as bad, as they were captured by Indians and treated as prisoners. After two months they succeeded in escaping and getting back to Valparaiso. Here Mr. Johnston again took shipping for San Francisco which he safely reached. After some weeks in that city he joined an exploring expedition, to which was attached a party of scientists, just then setting out to make explorations in Southern California, Arizona and Utah. He remained for a year with this party, and after wintering in Salt Lake City he returned in 1857 to San Francisco. During that year he prospected in California and Southern Oregon, and in February of the following year he came to British Columbia with the American Boundary Commission composed of Captain Campbell and Lieut. Parkes. It was Mr. Johnston's intention to accept a position which had been offered to him on this commission but when he reached Victoria he changed his mind and went up the Fraser with a party of miners to prospect for gold. They were on the river considerably before the arrival of the crowds which poured in during that year, and in their search they were given considerable assistance by the agents of the Hudson's Bay Company. When they reached Fort Hope they were given Indian guides and went by way of the Harrison-Lillooet portages to the point where Lillooet now stands. When they reached the Fraser they descended the river examining the bars, and at length located on Mormon bar a few miles above the mouth of the Thompson river. Here they remained working with great success till they were forced out by lack of provisions. Leaving one man behind, the others made their way down the river. At Yale they encountered a large throng of incoming California miners. They journeyed to Victoria and after purchasing supplies returned to the river. They were unable, however, to proceed owing to the high water and the hostility of the Indians above Chapman bar, and when these obstacles had been removed they found that the man they had left to guard their claims had been starved out. Mr. Johnston remained on Chapman's bar during 1858 and 1859, and had very fair success. In the autumn of 1859 he returned to Victoria, and after sojourning there awhile went over to the American side and purchased land on what is now the site of Port Angeles. Until 1862 he remained on his land and then in consequence of the reports of Cariboo's marvellous wealth he tried that region. For the next eleven years he remained in Cariboo, experiencing all the varying fortunes, the hardships and dangers incident to a miners life. During this period he was interested in claims on Williams, Lightning, Antler, and other famous creeks, and on the whole was remarkably successful. He finally left Cariboo in 1873 and went to Burrard Inlet and from there to Seattle where he remained for two years. He then returned to Victoria and from there he went to Nanaimo, where in 1877 he established his present wholesale and retail business. Mr. Johnston is also interested in a large number of enterprises throughout the Province. He is president of the North Pacific Canning Company, and a director of the Nanaimo Gas Works. He is agent for the Pacific Coast Steamship Company, the Union Pacific Railway Company, and the East Coast Steamship Company. He has been urged repeatedly to stand for the position of Mayor of Nanaimo, and for the local and Dominion Parliament, but has steadily refused. He is a member of the Ancient Order of United Workmen, of the Oddfellows' Order, the St. Andrew's Society and the Pioneer Society. In September, 1880, he married Miss Ella Cook, of Nanaimo.

Ker, David R., (Victoria), born October 2nd, 1862, at Victoria, British Columbia, and educated there. His parents were both of

Scotch birth and arrived in British Columbia in 1859. His father, Hon. Robert Kerr, who acted as Colonial Treasurer during 1868, occupied the position of government auditor both before and after confederation with the Dominion, and died in 1879. After leaving school Mr. Ker, who had prepared himself for a mercantile career, decided to engage in the milling business and with that intention learned the business thoroughly, spending several years in establishments at Victoria and San Francisco. In the latter city he spent some time in the employ of the Golden Age and Caledonian Milling Companies. He returned to Victoria in 1882, and shortly afterwards formed the partnership with his present associate, Mr. Brakeman, and established the mills at Saanich. Their business prospered even beyond their expectations, and in 1886 they opened their office and warehouse at Victoria, Mr. Ker taking charge there. Mr. Ker is a Conservative in politics, but is not a servile follower of the party. He has many objections to the manner in which the Government conducts the affairs of the Dominion, and thinks that greater efforts should be made to develope this Province. He takes great interest in municipal matters and is a supporter of any measure for the betterment of the city. Mr. Ker is one of Victoria's most prosperous and energetic business men. In religion he is a member of the Episcopal Church.

King, William R., (New Westminster), was born in the beautiful and historical Cathedral city of Canterbury, England, in July, 1846. While Mr. King was still a boy his father's duties as railway engineer necessitated the removal of the family to the town of Ashford, in the county of Kent, some fifteen miles distant, and it was there that he received his education at one of the public schools, under an eminent teacher who had spent many years in eastern Canada. It was owing to the tuition therein received that Mr. King was inspired with a desire to visit the distant yet promising colony of British Columbia. After the completion of his studies Mr. King apprenticed himself to an architect, and learnt not only the theoretical but also the practical part of the profession. During all his early life he kept up an intimate knowledge of the progress of the Canadian Pacific Railway, and the opening up of this Province by its construction through the Rockies. At the age of twenty-one he commenced the practice of architecture, in partnership with his father, and soon after commencing business married the daughter of John Fowler, Esq., one of the leading builders and contractors in the town. Whilst carrying on a busy professional practice in his native place, Mr. King was for a period of fourteen years, manager of the Local Water Works Company, surveyor for Building and Insurance Societies, manager of a House and Land Company, and also filled many other important and responsible offices. When his boys became old enough to start in life for themselves, the over-crowded condition of the mother country caused him to direct his attention to British Columbia. Early in the spring of 1888, Mr. King and family set sail from England, arriving in New Westminster a few weeks later with letters of introduction to the most prominent men of the Province. Commencing at once, Mr. King has carried on the the practice of his profession in the Royal city and has lately added to it the business of an accountant, auditor and real estate agent.

Kipp, Isaac, (Chilliwhack), a descendent of a family of United Empire Loyalists, who moved from New York in 1776; was born on November 10th, 1839, in Burford, county of Brant, Ont. He was educated in the public schools, and commenced farming early in life. In 1858 Mr. Kipp settled in California, where he resided four years and engaged in mining and agriculture with varying success. In the spring of 1862 he removed to Cariboo, where he both lost and made money in mining speculations, and in the fall of the same year took up the farm in Chilliwhack, which he now possesses, and which is one of the best in the district and especially noted for the excellency of its stock. Mr. Kipp has been for several years a membes of the Municipal Council of Chilliwhack. He has encountered all the hardships which befall a pioneer in an unsettled province, which have been shared by his wife, *nee* Mary A. Nelmer, of Oxford County, Ont., whom he married in March, 1865. In religion he is an adherent of the Methodist Church.

Kurtz, John. (Victoria), one of the most enterprising of the early pioneers of British Columbia, was born in Pennsylvania, United States of America in 1831, and educated there. In 1850 he came to the Pacific coast and engaged in mining in California. During the early days of the gold excitement in 1858 he came to British Columbia and engaged in steamboating and mining. He was chairman of the Yale Steam Navigation Company and was interested in other enterprises. In 1860 and the two following years he owned and operated mines in Cariboo, and was again engaged in that industry in 1870. In 1878 he established the Pioneer White Labor Cigar Factory which he still conducts.

Ladner, Thomas Ellis, (Ladner's Landing), was born at Trenant Park, in the Duchy of Cornwall, England, on September 8th, 1837, where his father, Edward Ladner, Esq., resided. Mr. Ladner received his education at Falmouth high school. In 1852 he travelled to California, where he was engaged in mining and trading during six years. On leaving California he came to this Province, where he arrived on September 20th, 1858. After having tried his luck at the mines Mr. Ladner, in company with his brother, Mr. W. H. Ladner, J. P., settled at Ladner's Landing, which place was named after them, they being the two first settlers south of the Fraser river below New Westminster. Since that time Mr. Ladner has been very extensively engaged in the farming industry and fish-canning trade. He owns 1,200 acres of improved prairie land, on which he keeps a large quantity of thoroughbred stock, which he has imported. In 1887 together with Mr. J. A. Laidlaw and other gentlemen he built the Delta salmon cannery at Ladner's Landing, which was the first cannery of importance ever erected below New Westminster, and which has a capacity of 30,000 cases per season. Mr. Ladner also owns, in partnership with Mr. F. Page, the Wellington Packing Co.'s cannery at Canoe Pass on the Fraser river, of which he is manager. This cannery has a capacity of over 25,000 cases. Mr. Ladner is interested in almost every industry existing throughout the Province. He is an adherent of the Church of England, a Free Mason, and a member of the United Workmen and Pioneer societies. In 1865, Mr. Ladner married Edna, daughter of Wm. Booth, Esq., of Victoria, who died in January, 1882. In February, 1884, he married Minnie, daughter of Wm. Johnston-Parr, Esq., of Los Gatos, Santa Clara Co., California.

Ladner, William Henry, (Ladner's Landing), elder of two sons of Edward Ladner, of Cornwall, who came to America in 1848 and settled on a farm in the State of Wisconsin, where he died in 1851. Mr. Ladner was born in Cornwall, England, in 1826 and

J. H. INNES.

was educated there, and after leaving school worked on the farm till the autumn of 1848, when he came to America to join his father. In the autumn of 1850 he returned to England on business, and when he had completed this work he came back to America bringing his brother with him. Upon reaching Wisconsin they found that their father had died. The brothers remained in Wisconsin till the following spring and then joined a caravan crossing the plains to California. They travelled by way of Omaha, then an Indian mission, and from there straight across the plains and over the mountains to Salt Lake City where they stopped to recruit their stock. Their journey was one of great hardship and suffering from disease and danger from Indians. When they left Salt Lake City they journeyed on to Sacramento which they reached after five months' travel from Omaha. From Sacramento Mr. Ladner and his brother went to Grass Valley where they settled and remained engaged in mining with very fair success till 1858 when they were among the first to come to British Columbia during the great rush. They reached Victoria in May and remained there several days constructing a boat, in which they were towed across the gulf to Point Robert by the steamer Plunger. From here they went up the Fraser, avoiding H. M. S. Satellite, which was stationed at the mouth to collect tolls, and after some days' hard work pulling against the tide they reached Hope. Here Mr. Ladner remained till 1859 when he purchased a pack train, and began packing goods from Hope to Lytton. From 1862 to 1865 he conveyed goods from Yale to Lytton. In the latter year he purchased a cargo of goods which he shipped to Kamloops and from there by boat to the head of Shuswap Lake. From this point he cut out an old Indian trail to the Columbia river at the mouth of Gold Creek. During the summer and fall of that year he did a splendid business packing to the Columbia mines, but in the spring of the following year the diggings did not pan out so well, and he returned to his old route. At the meeting of the Local Legislature he applied for compensation for cutting the trail to the Columbia, which had come in to general use, but this was denied him on the ground that the work had been done as a commercial speculation. In 1868 he took up land at the mouth of the Fraser, where his magnificent farm is situated, and he has continued to reside there since that time. He was reeve of Delta municipality from 1880 to 1886 inclusive and in 1882 stood for the Local

Legislature, but was defeated. He was a candidate again in 1886, and was elected as an opponent of the present government. In Dominion politics Mr. Ladner is a Liberal-Conservative. He is a justice of the peace for the Province, and an adherent of the Episcopal church. In 1866 he married Miss Mary Ann Booth, of Esquimalt.

Laidlaw, James Anderson, (New Westminster), was born on the 12th of August, 1836, in Rossshire, Scotland, where his father, Andrew Laidlaw followed the occupation of a land surveyor. In 1848 his parents removed to Canada, bringing him with them, and settled on a farm in Oxford county, Ontario. Mr. Laidlaw attended school in Rossshire and afterwards in Ontario, and then worked with his father on the farm till 1858, when he was attracted by the gold discoveries on the Fraser river and set out for British Columbia. When he reached California the Fraser excitement had calmed down, and Mr. Laidlaw remained in that state for two years engaged in mining. He then went to Virginia City, Nevada, where he worked for two years at quartz mining, with indifferent success however. In 1882 he came to British Columbia and went direct to Cariboo. At that time the road to the mines had not been opened up, and Mr. Laidlaw made the journey from Lillooet on foot with one hundred pounds of provisions on his back. He remained in Cariboo till 1873, and during that period he was interested at different times in almost every creek in the upper country, and prospected on them all. He had varied success, at times making money rapidly and in large amounts and again spending it as rapidly in opening up and working unprofitable claims. He had good success on Williams, Grouse and Harvey Creeks, but when he left the mines in 1873 had only six dollars to represent his eleven years of labor and hardship. He came down to New Westminster and for the next year and a half was engaged in various employments, but chiefly in hand logging at Jarvis Inlet. During this time he had been on the Fraser river, and had observed with considerable interest the salmon fishing and had concluded that this business, if he once acquired a knowledge of it, would turn out profitably. In 1874 he accordingly went to the Columbia river to learn the business. He obtained a position in Booth & Co.'s cannery and remained there for three seasons. He then returned to the Fraser and engaged for one season with English & Co. In the autumn of 1878 he organized a company and established the Delta Canning Company with an establishment at Ladner's Landing. He conducted this business for three years and then purchased the Holbrook cannery, above New Westminster. He did not operate this establishment however till a good year came, when he added to its capacity and had a most successful season. Next year he built the new cannery which he at present owns. He had now two canneries of his own which were both doing a profitable business, and during that season he put up twenty-nine thousand cases, besides doing a large salting business. In the following year one of the canneries was destroyed by fire before all his shipments had been made, and he lost four thousand cases in the flames. He conducted one cannery next year, and the year after he took control of the Delta cannery and has since been personally conducting these two establishments. He is also interested in two canneries on Smith's Inlet and one on Naas river, and he is erecting a large one, which he will name the Standard on the Skeena river. Besides his interests in the fishing industry Mr. Laidlaw has done a great deal of business in buying and selling land both here and in the territories, but his large interests are chiefly centered in New Westminster and Victoria districts. Mr. Laidlaw is a member of the Masonic fraternity, of St. Andrew's society and of the Ancient Order of United Workmen and in religion is an adherent of the Presbyterian church. In 1882 he married Miss Anderson, daughter of Robert Anderson, of Rossshire, Scotland.

Leahy, John, (Victoria), son of John Leahy, a farmer of Tipperary, Ireland, where Mr. Leahy was born in September, 1846. He attended school in his native place till he was seventeen years of age when he went to Dublin and apprenticed himself to the grocery business. He remained in Dublin till 1864 when he came to America and for six months lived in the city of New York. The climate, however, injured his health and he moved west to Colorado and from there after some time to British Columbia. He went direct to Cariboo where he engaged in mining. Subsequently he joined a Canadian Pacific Railway survey party with whom he explored for a route along the Thompson river. In 1874 he went to the Cassiar mines where he remained for a year. In 1875 he returned to Victoria and went into the brewery business with Arthur Bunster. In 1882 Mr. Bunster sold out his interest, and Mr. Leahy has continued it himself since that time. He devotes all his time to his business and the result of this is that his brands have taken prizes at all the Provincial exhibitions for years.

Leask, James Charles, (Victoria), was born at the Orkney Islands, on May 10th, 1830. He attended school at his native place and was then apprenticed to a tailor to learn the business. In 1851 he came to British Columbia in the employ of the Hudson's Bay Company, having signed a contract to give five years service. He came by way of Cape Horn in the sailing ship Norman Morrison of which Captain Wishart was skipper. When he landed at Victoria there were no habitations of white men save those of the Hudson's Bay Company's agents. Mr. Leask fulfilled the terms of his five years' contract and engaged for two years more. At the expiration of this time he left the company's service and went to the gold mines on the Fraser river, where he remained for eighteen months with very good success. During this time he sent to Scotland for his affianced wife, who came out in the Sea Nymph accompanied by her two brothers and sister-in-law. They had a very stormy passage being thirteen months on the ocean. After his marriage Mr. Leask resided for a time in Yale where he held the position of chief constable. He resigned this post however, and went to Cedar Hill, Victoria district, where he took up a farm. He remained only a short time on this place and abandoned it, and leased a farm for three years from Mr. R. Harris. At the end of that time he engaged in the carpentering and building trade at which he continued for two years and then went to Cowichan district where he took up a farm on which he resided for eleven years. He cleared this farm of timber and sold it in 1874. He then returned to Victoria where he went into business as a teamster and transfer agent, at which he continued for seven years. At the end of this time, in 1883, he purchased an interest in a tailoring business in Victoria and in a few months bought his partner out, and took in another partner, Mr. Kurtz. At the end of two years Mr. Kurtz died and Mr. Morrison then entered the firm. At the end of three and a half years the firm opened a branch business in Vancouver. In September of 1888, the firm dissolved and Mr.

Leask alone conducts his business in Victoria, which has grown to be the largest in the Province in this line. Mr. Leask is interested in a number of enterprises in Victoria. In Dominion politics he is a Conservative and in local an Independent. He is a member of the St. Andrew's and Caledonian Societies, and of the Ancient Order of United Workmen. In religion he is a Presbyterian.

Lewis, Captain Herbert George, (Victoria), was born at Aspenden, Hertfordshire, England, in 1828, where his father Edward Lewis, Esq., a gentleman farmer, resided. Captain Lewis was educated at Cheltenham College,—the great public school of the West of England. Having an intense love for the sea and being of an adventurous disposition he, early in life, made several voyages from England to India and China. In 1847 he entered the Hudson Bay Company's service, in which he remained till 1883. Captain Lewis arrived in Victoria, in 1847, on board the Hudson's Bay Company's barque "Cowlitz," and soon after his arrival in British Columbia was stationed by Sir James Douglas at Fort Simpson. During the sixteen years in which he worked for the Hudson's Bay Company, he, at various times, had command of the "Otter," "Beaver," "Labouchere," "Enterprise," and "Princess Louise." He had charge of the whole of the fur trade in the Russian territory while commanding the "Labouchere" and "Otter" from 1864 till the acquisition of Alaska by the United States. In 1869 he returned to the old country, and on his arrival back in British Columbia in the following year he settled in Victoria. On leaving the service of the Hudson's Bay Company in 1883, he entered that of the Marine Department of Canada. Captain Lewis is a thorough sailor and has a very intimate knowledge of the Pacific coast. He is a Protestant and a member of the Independent Order of Oddfellows. In 1870 he married Mary, daughter of Edward Langford, Esq., who came to this Province in 1852, and was a well-known official of the colonial government and also of the Puget Sound Company.

Lewis, Lewis, (Victoria), was born in Poland, in 1828, and when nine years of age was taken to England by an uncle. He remained in England for over eight years during which time he attended school. He then came to America and obtained a position in a large wholesale jewellery establishment in New York, where he remained for two years. At the end of that time he went to Brazil and from Brazil to Peru. In 1849 he removed to California where he spent the next nine years. For a portion of this time he was interested in mining, then in general business in San Francisco, and towards the latter part of the time he conducted a dry goods store in Sacramento. While in Sacramento he married Miss Rachael Nathan. He came to British Columbia in June, 1858, and first visited Fort Yale. In the following year he opened a grocery business in Victoria. He continued at this for eighteen months and then started the dry goods business he now conducts. Mr. Lewis has been a member of the Masonic fraternity since 1850, and of the Oddfellows' Society for twenty-two years. He is a member of the Hebrew Society and an adherent of that religion.

Lilley, Herbert A., (Victoria), born February 9th, 1859 in Greatbridge, Staffordshire, England, where his father George A. Lilley, was engaged as a conductor on the railway. Received his elementary education at a private school in his native place, and in 1868 came to Canada with his parents, who settled first at Pt. Edward and then at Petrolia, Ontario. At both places Mr. Lilley attended school and after completing his studies was apprenticed for four years to the confectionery business. In 1874 he came with his parents to British Columbia and remained in Victoria while they went to Maple Ridge where he had purchased a farm. In 1879, Mr. Lilley began business for himself, opening a modest store on the site of his present handsome premises. He is a man of great energy and business ability. He is a member of the Reformed Episcopal Church.

Lombard, Charles A., (Victoria), was born in Paris, France, on October, 27th, 1846. His father died while Mr. Lombard was yet young. His mother, Madam Ballagni, was the celebrated singer to whose powers the crowned heads of Europe paid homage. Mr. Lombard attended school in France for five years, and in 1857 went to Chili with his mother who had a large engagement there. While in Chili his mother, who had now been a widow for eight years, married a wealthy French gentleman, M. L'Hotelier and abandoned the stage. Shortly afterwards M. L'Hotelier lost all he had in

CAPT. JOHN IRVING.

commercial speculations in Peru, and came to British Columbia with his wife and son-in-law, settled in Victoria and began a commission business on Wharf street. Mr. Lombard was sent to Santa Clara College, California, in 1862, and remained there for two years when he returned and entered his father-in-law's business as a clerk. In 1866 M. L'Hotelier returned to Peru with his wife and Mr. Lombard secured employment with Jungerman & Co., wholesale jewelers, with whom he remained for two years when he entered the office of Caire and Grancini, hardware merchants, as confidential clerk. He held this position for twelve years, when in 1879 Mr. Grancini died. Mr. Lombard then took a position as purser on the steamer North Pacific. In the following year he went to Portland, Oregon, where he held several positions and where he was prostrated for six months with a dangerous illness. He was forced to return to Victoria owing to ill health and took the managership of the music business of Bognall & Co. Mr. Bognall died very shortly after and the business ceased. Mr. Lombard then established the prosperous business he now has. Mr. Lombard is a member of the British Columbia Pioneer society and of the Victoria club. In religion he is a Roman Catholic and has been conductor of the choir for three years, always giving his services to the church and charitable institutions gratuitously. Mr. Lombard has been twice married. His first wife whom he married in 1875 died two and a half years later, and in 1880 married the daughter of T. I. Wilson, Esq., of Victoria.

Lord, John E., (New Westminster), was born in Lunenburg, Nova Scotia, both his parents being descendants of United Empire Loyalists. Mr. Lord has had a most adventurous career, having travelled far and wide in new and comparatively unknown countries. During the gold excitement in California Mr. Lord left home, and after spending some time in the gold fields of the Pacific slope sailed for New Zealand, where he stayed but a short time, proceeding from there to Australia. After remaining seven years in the mining districts he sailed to San Francisco and finally arrived in British Columbia in 1861. Since his arrival in the Province Mr. Lord has been principally connected with the agricultural, shipping and mining industries. During three years he resided in Tenas Portage, where he engaged in farming, and two years were passed by him as a teacher at Lillooet. It is seventeen years since Mr Lord decided to make New Westminster his home.

Lowen, Joseph, (Victoria), was born in Prussia, in June, 1832, and came to America in 1850. Settled first in New York, and in 1856 removed to California where he was engaged for two years in mining. Came to British Columbia on July 4th, 1858 and from that time till 1870 followed various occupations. In 1870 he became a partner in the Victoria brewery in which business he has since continued.

Lumby, Moses. (Okanagan), was born in Lincolnshire, England, in 1842. He received his education at Gien, France, and at Stampford Grammar School, England. In 1862 he came to British Columbia and for a few years mined with varying success at Stikeen and later on at Cariboo. On leaving the mines he commenced farming on the South Thompson river, and until 1870 held a contract to carry the mails to the Big Bend of the Columbia river. In 1870 he left his farm on the South Thompson, and was one of the first settlers in the Osoyoos division of the Yale district, where he now possesses the largest and best cultivated farm in the interior. He has introduced all the latest agricultural machines and improvements, and has at present over six hundred acres of rich agricultural land under cultivation. In 1884 he was chief commissioner of the Yale district and in 1886 received a requisition to represent that district in the Provincial Legislature but withdrew in favor of the Hon. F. G. Vernon. Ever since 1884, he has been unremitting in his efforts to have a railroad constructed, which would open up the rich farming lands of the district, and is now on the eve of seeing his labors in that direction crowned with success. He is a Justice of the Peace and a supporter of the Robson administration. He is a member of the Pioneer Society, and of the British Columbia Board of Trade.

Macaulay, William James, (Victoria), was born on the shores of the Bay of Quinte, in the township of Sidney, county of Hasting, Ontario, on October 20th, 1828. His father, D. Macaulay, Esq., of Belfast, (a gentleman of Scotch descent) married Eleanor, daughter of John Macaulay, Esq., of Belfast, Ireland, in Kingston,

Ontario, in 1818, whence he had emigrated in 1812. Mr. Macaulay, was educated at a private school in Trenton, Ontario, where he received a mercantile training, after which he associated himself with his father, and uncle who carried on a large lumber business in the county of Hastings. In 1848 he succeeded his father, and in 1856 went to South Bend, Minnesota, where he engaged in the real estate business. At the close of the Indian war of 1862 he went to Pennsylvania and embarked in the lumber trade there until 1865, when together with Mr. Anson Dodge, he established lumber mills on Georgian Bay, Ontario. He acted as vice-president, general manager and treasurer for the company until 1872, when he resigned and moved to Winnipeg—then called Fort Garry—and established a saw mill, planing mill and sash and door factory at that place. In 1878 he sold out to the Winnipeg Lumber Company and built a mill on the Lake of the Woods, (where he owned extensive timber limits) which he sold to the firm of Dick & Banning in 1881. He then removed to St. Paul and opened up the "People's Bank," of which he was president for four years and which is still in a flourishing condition. While at St. Paul he entered into a large timber deal in Minnesota, and later on built another mill on the Lake of the Woods, which had a capacity of 125,000 feet per day. In 1888 he sold out to Messrs Dennis & Ryan and moved to Victoria. Soon after his arrival in British Columbia, Mr. Macaulay, together with Mr. Charles Peabody, negotiated a deal with the late Hon. Robert Dunsmuir, for the Chemainus Mills and one hundred thousand acres of timber lands. He afterwards formed a syndicate, for the operation of the mills, of the following gentlemen: John A. Humbird, John E. Glover and W. H. Phipps, the former of whom is now president of the company, and Mr. Macaulay is vice-president. On April 29th, 1868, he was married to Miss Harriet Freeman, at Niles, Michigan. In 1862 the Indian war broke out in Minnesota, and Mr. Macaulay shut down his mills and together with Mr. D. Buck, of Mankato, Minnesota, formed a military company, of which Mr. Buck was Captain and Mr. Macaulay, Lieutenant. Mr. Macaulay is an adherent of the Roman Catholic Church.

Macdonald, Hon. William John, Senator. (Victoria), was born in the Isle of Skye, Invernesshire, Scotland, and is the third son of Alexander Macdonald, Esq., of Valley, North Uist, by his wife Flora, daughter of Captain McRae of Inverinett, Kintail. He was educated in his native county and remained in Scotland till 1851. After his arrival at Victoria in the same year, he travelled over the greater part of British Columbia and the great North West and met with many interesting adventures, such as troubles with the Indians and expeditions for their punishment. In those early days the arrival of the Hudson's Bay Company's annual ship from London with the yearly mail was the occasion of much festivity, especially when a few passengers arrived. Epochs were sometimes marked by the arrival of distinguished visitors across the great unknown continent, as when Captain Palisser, Hector, Lord Milton and others accomplished that feat; and a British man-of-war was always welcomed. In 1859, Mr. Macdonald was elected to the Assembly of Vancouver Colony, and on its union with the Mainland in 1866, was called to the Council by Governor Seymour. Mr. Macdonald was twice elected Mayor of Victoria, and has acted in many honorary capacities, such as Collector of Customs, Captain of Militia, member of the first Board of Education, commissioner of Saving Banks, road commissioner, etc., always giving his services gratuitously. On the union of British Columbia with Canada in 1871, Mr. Macdonald was called to the Senate, of which body he has been a member over seventeen years, and has during that period had to do with the administrations of five Governors-General, Lords Lisgar, Dufferin, Lorne, Lansdowne and Stanley. He has always taken an active part in the work of the Senate, is an important member of various committees and has acted with acceptance as chairman of the most important parliamentary committee,—that of Standing Orders and Private Bills. He is married to Catherine Balfour, daughter of James Murray Reid, Esq., by whom he has three sons and three daughters, his eldest son being an officer in the Royal Artillery, and his second son a naval officer. He is a Protestant and a member of the British Columbia Benevolent Society.

Mahrer, John. (Nanaimo), was born at Prague, Austria, on the 14th of September, 1847. His father, Joseph Prague, was a distiller at that city. Mr. Mahrer, first followed the business of a confectioner in his native place and then went to England where he remained for about a year. In 1867 he came to America from England, and first settled in New Jersey where he at once indentified himself with the Republican party. A year later he came west to California. While in San Francisco he one day saw some specimens of rich quartz rock taken from the Juliana mines and he was at once attacked with the gold fever. He made immediate preparations and left the next day for the mines. For two years he remained at the gold fields in California and Arizona, and lost money continously. During this time he with others worked with out success on claims which were subsequently developed and yielded immense returns. He and five companions prospected the Cosmopolitan and Stonewall Jackson claims and sunk shafts. As they did this work imperfectly however, they abandoned both claims under the impression that they did not contain the metal in paying quantities. When he returned to San Francisco he made arrangements with a friend to go to Chili, and had taken his passage in the vessel "Shillahoff". He met with an accident and was unable to go, and he had reason to congratulate himself afterwards, as the vessel was wrecked and all on board, save the captain, were lost. Mr. Mahrer then, in the fall of 1870, came to British Columbia and went to Nanaimo, where he remained for a year. The year following he went to Cariboo where he opened a bakery and restaurant and where he remained till 1876. He then returned to Nanaimo, where he has since resided and done business with ever increasing success. In 1876 he started a bakery business, in 1877 a soda water factory and a soap factory, and in 1879 a brewery. The brewery was an especially successful venture and is now one of the principal brewing establishments in the Province. For eight years continuously, Mr. Mahrer has served in the city council. He is interested in a great many of the enterprises which have for their object the development of the Province, and particularly the benefit of the city of Nanaimo. He is interested in the North Pacific Canning Company, and in a number of gold mines in the upper country. He is president of the Water Works Company and a director of the Gas Company. Mr. Mahrer is a member of the Masonic fraternity, of the Oddfellows' and the encampment, of the Ancient Order of United Workmen, the Foresters, the Knights of Pythias, of the Legion of Honor, and of the city band. He was married on September 7th, 1879, to Miss Sarah Jane Woods, of Nanaimo.

(16)

Mallette, Charles Edwin, (Victoria), was born in Rock county, Illinois, U. S. A., in 1861, his father, Henry Mallette, Esq., being of English descent. He received his education in the town of Santa Clara, California, and previous to his arrival in British Columbia was principally engaged in agricultural pursuits. In March, 1885, he came to this Province and settled at Victoria, where he was engaged in the lumber trade till December, 1889, and was manager of the Victoria Coal, Wood and Lumber Yard. Since that time he has been engaged in the real estate business, in connection with the firm of Bouchier, Croft and Mallette. He is a member of the Oddfellows' and Masonic Orders, and on April 12th, 1882, he married Mary, eldest daughter of J. W. Johnson, Esq., of Santa Clara, California.

Manson, Lawrence. (Nanaimo), was born on Shetland Island, to the north of Scotland, where his father, John Manson, was engaged in farming, on November 12th, 1854. He attended the parish school till he was fifteen years of age, when he was apprenticed to the grocery business in Edinburgh. He lost his health while there and returned home where he remained recuperating for some months, and then obtained a position on the Ordinance survey operating on Shetland Island. He remained in this service for a year and then resigned to come to America. He had made up his mind to come to British Columbia and he accordingly did not delay on the journey hither. He crossed the Atlantic to Quebec in the steamship Manitoban and went by way of the Central Pacific to San Francisco. From San Francisco he went direct to Nanaimo which he reached on the 14th of June, 1877. He obtained a position with the Vancouver Coal Company as weighman which he continued to hold for ten years. He was on duty when both of the disastrous explosions occurred in the mines and narrowly escaped with his life on each occasion. On the 27th of November, 1880, he married Catherine J. B. Duncan, daughter of Sinclair T. Duncan, formerly a wholesale merchant of Leith, Scotland. In the same year Mr. Manson established his present business which he employed a clerk to manage until 1888, when on the 30th of November he severed his connection with the coal company. Mr. Manson has taken considerable interest in the public affairs of the Province, and especially in those of Nanaimo, although he has not stood for any position. He has by careful attention to business built up a large and increasing trade. He is a member of the Ancient Order of Foresters, and an adherent of the Methodist church, being a class leader and superintendent of the Sunday school.

Manuel, George Evan, J. P., (Donald), was born in Leeds county, Ontario, on October 3rd, 1854, his parents being of Welsh origin. Mr. Manuel was educated in his native county and received a thorough mercantile training. Previous to his arrival in this Province he was engaged in contracting and general mercantile pursuits. In 1883 he settled at Donald and since that date has carried on business as an insurance and general agent besides cultivating a farm of five hundred acres at Golden City, at which latter place he has a large herd of milch cows. As a boy Mr. Manual was obliged to start in life for himself, and after serving a three year apprenticeship in a general store, at the village of Morton, on the Rideau Canal, removed to Toronto where he resided one year. On leaving the Queen city he proceeded to the town of Walkerton, Bruce county, where he remained five years. During his stay at Walkerton he was engaged in the stationery business and in the fall of 1879 removed to Winnipeg, where he secured the position of purchasing agent for the Manitoba Southwestern and Colonization Railway, the first chartered railroad in Manitoba, and now owned and controlled by the Canadian Pacific Railway Company. After acting some time in that capacity, he was advanced by the company to the position of paymaster, which he retained for over two years. In Winnipeg, Mr. Manuel made a large fortune which he afterwards lost when the boom-bubble burst, but since his arrival in British Columbia he has met with success in every enterprise which he has entered into. In 1881 he married Miss S. M. Mordin, in Walkerton, Ontario. He is a member of the Masonic and Oddfellows Orders, and is a Justice of the Peace, Notary Public and Coroner for the Province. Mr. Manuel has the finest store at Donald, and is looked upon as one of the rising men of the district in which he resides.

Mara, Hon. John Andrew, M. P., (Kamloops), eldest son of the late John Mara, of Toronto, was born at Toronto and educated there. Removed to this Province in 1862 and first settled at Yale where he engaged in business. He was one of the strongest advocates of confederation and on the consummation of this movement was elected a member of the first Provincial Parliament for Kootenay. He occupied this seat till 1875 when he stood successfully for Yale district and occupied this seat till 1886, when he was elected to represent the same constituency in the House of Commons. In 1883 Mr. Mara was elected Speaker of the Provincial Legislature and occupied that position till he gave up his seat. In politics Mr. Mara is a Conservative. He is one of the most enterprising business men of British Columbia, and has unbounded faith in the future of the country. He married Alice, daughter of the late F. J. Barnard, Esq., and sister of Mr. F. H. Barnard, M. P. He is a member of the Union Club, Victoria.

Martin, George Bohun, M. P. P., (South Thompson), son of the late Captain G. B. Martin, C. B., Royal navy, was born at Cheltenham, England, on December 25th, 1842, and educated there. Came to British Columbia in 1865 and settled on the South Thompson river, where he has one of the finest cattle ranches in the Province. He is engaged exclusively in ranching and cattle raising. He was elected to the local Legislature in 1882 to fill the seat left vacant by the death of Mr. Preston Bennett, who had been elected at the general election of that year. Mr. Martin has since continued to represent this constituency. In politics Mr. Martin is a Conservative. He is a member of the Union Club, Victoria.

Marvin, E. B., (Victoria), was born in the city of Halifax, province of Nova Scotia, in the year 1830, and left his native place in 1852 to seek his fortune in California at which place he arrived on November 30th of the same year, after a passage of one hundred and sixty-two days via Cape Horn. When he arrived in San Francisco it was a very small place of about 25,000 inhabitants, the population being composed of all nationalities, Mr. Marvin remained in San Francisco until the year 1857 and passed through all the excitement of the Vigilance Committee of 1855 and 1856 when so many men were hung. In the year 1857 he left San Francisco for Australia to seek his fortune in the mines and remained there until September, 1868, when hearing of the rush to Fraser river he left Melbourne bound for Victoria. On the passage

J. A. LAIDLAW.

up the vessel put into Honolulu and remained six weeks, leaving Honolulu on December 26th, 1858 and arrived at Esquimalt Harbor on January 13th, 1859. Mr. Marvin remained in Victoria until June of the same year, when he returned to San Francisco at which place he remained until February, 1860, when he came once more to Victoria and proceeded to the Fraser river mines. He went by canoe as far up as the mouth of the Quesnelle a very hazardous trip indeed. Not being successful in mining, Mr. Marvin returned to Victoria and commenced business in July, 1860 and is now carrying on the largest ship chandlery business in Victoria. He has been a member of the city council for three years from 1876 to 1878, is also a Justice of the Peace of the Province and is extensively interested in mining. He is owner of several sailing vessels and is largely interested in that business. Mr. Marvin is a self-made man having started business with very small means. The firm is now E. B. Marvin & Co.

Mason, Joseph, M. P. P., (Barkerville), born at Nottingham, England, 1839, educated in the Nottingham common schools. Came to British Columbia in 1862, by way of Cape Horn in a sailing vessel. Landed in Victoria and remained there in business four years. Left Victoria for Big Bend during the gold excitement at the latter place in 1866, and after great hardships and vicissitudes went with the rush to the Hixson creek gold excitement. From thence to Barkerville, Cariboo, where he has lived ever since. Is extensively interested in mining and the business of a general merchant. Married Miss Skinner of Barkerville, in 1882, and has five children. After repeated refusals he consented to stand for parliament on no less than three requisitions in 1886. He was elected at the head of the poll and has represented the district in the Legislative Assembly since that time. He is a Conservative in politics, and in religion a member of the Church of England.

Maynard, Richard, (Victoria), was born at Stratton, Cornwall, England. When he was two years of age his parents removed to Buda and there Mr. Maynard at an early age was apprenticed to the shoemaking business. He had always a strong inclination for a sea-faring life, and at the age of eleven years he left home and went to sea. He returned to Buda the following year and after that put in the summer at sea and the winter on land. He married, while not yet twenty years of age, and in 1852 with his wife came to Canada, and settled in Bowmanville, Ontario, where he remained till 1859 when he removed to British Columbia. He went to the mines on the Fraser river and made considerable money during that season on Hudson Bar. In the winter he returned to Bowmanville for his wife and family whom he brought to Victoria in 1862. His wife while in the east had learned the photographic business and when they arrived at Victoria she established a business there, while Mr. Maynard went to Stikeen where he made considerable money mining. When he returned he began his present business. Mr. Maynard has been a life-long temperance man though he has never joined any society.

Miller, Jonathan, (Vancouver), was born in Delaware, county of Middlesex, Ontario, Sept. 5th, 1834. He is descended from United Empire Loyalists on both sides of his house, his grandfathers, paternal and maternal, having taken up arms for the King's cause during the Revolutionary war of 1775 and having after the Declaration of Independance by the United States, removed to Canada rather than live without the pale of British influence. His grandfather Miller, settled in Middlesex county and his grandfather Lockwood, in Wellington county, where he became possessed of a considerable portion of the land on which the city of Hamilton now stands. Mr. Miller received his education at Caradoc Academy, and after leaving school engaged in mercantile business at which he continued, within nine miles of his native place, until 1861. In 1856 he married Margaret, daughter of Colonel Benjamin Springer. He was appointed a Justice of the Peace for the county of Middlesex in his 22nd year. In 1862, during the excitement over the discovery of large deposits of gold in Cariboo, Mr. Miller left Ontario and came to British Columbia. He established himself without delay in New Westminster district where he has since continued to live. On his arrival he engaged in business in New Westminster and in 1864 he brought his family from Ontario. In the following year he turned his attention to the lumber business and disposing of his commercial interest in New Westminster city, took a number of large contracts to get lumber out of the forests for the mills. In his connection with this business he came to Burrard Inlet where he has resided continuously since. Mr. Miller remained in the lumber business till 1871. In that year he received an appointment from the Provincial Government and was stationed at the old town of Granville, where the city of Vancouver now stands. He brought his family from New Westminster to Granville and continued to reside there in the capacity of government agent till 1886, when he received the appointment of postmaster for the new city of Vancouver and has since filled that position. In 1864 he was elected a member of the New Westminster City Council, the present Premier of the Province, Hon. John Robson, serving on the board during the same year. While in Ontario, Mr. Miller took a personal part in politics and was associated with the Conservative party, but since his arrival in the Province of British Columbia he has not actively interested himself in public affairs. He has large interests in Westminster District and the city of Vancouver, where he, more than any other man in the Province, has marked the transformation that has taken place during the past twenty years, having resided on the shores of Burrard Inlet longer than any other white man. Mr. Miller is a member of the Ancient Order of United Workmen and a Protestant. His mother is still living at the age of 78 years in Middlesex county, Ontario, where she and her husband first settled after their marriage.

Milligan, David Shibley, (New Westminster), is a native of Ontario, having first seen the light in the town of New Burgh in that Province on February 27th, 1837, where his parents, both of whom were of Irish origin, resided. Mr. Milligan received a first-class business education in the academy of his native town which proved to be of great use to him in after years. On his arrival in British Columbia in May, 1862, Mr Milligan settled at Victoria. He remained there however but a short time and went to the mines "with the great rush" a few months after his arrival. Fortune not favoring his eager search for "the root of all evil" in its natural condition, Mr. Milligan returned during the same season to Victoria where he engaged in business. Since that time Mr. Milligan has been engaged in various enterprises, and, although he has not always been successful, he has gained the reputation of being a man of sterling business qualities and knowledge. For several years

Mr. Milligan served the Dominion Government in the capacity of postmaster at Moodyville, where he was much liked and respected. Mr. Milligan is a Methodist and a member of the Oddfellows' society.

Milne, Alexander Roland, (Victoria), son of Alexander Milne, of Toronto, Ontario, was born in Morayshire, Scotland, on December 20th, 1839, and educated at Marshal College, Aberdeen, with a view of fitting him for a mercantile career. During his boyhood his parents emigrated to Canada and in 1855 he entered the employ of Gage, Hagaman & Co., who did a large business in Oakville and Toronto as dealers in grain. Mr. Milne was engaged in mercantile pursuits in Ontario till 1864, when he came to the Pacific coast. He remained for a period in Victoria and then went to Cariboo, at that time attracting much attention, where he was engaged in the general mercantile business of Buie Bros. While in Cariboo he saw and experienced the life of adventure and hardship peculiar to that region and that time. He returned to Victoria in 1874, and in 1875 entered the service of the Custom's Department. At that time Ex-collector Hamley, the late Mr. George Fry and Mr. Charles S. Finlayson, were the only inside officers. Mr. Milne by attention to business, intelligence and knowledge of the requirements of the commercial community, worked himself upwards in the service till in 1890 he was appointed, on the resignation of Mr. Hamley, Collector of the Port of Victoria. In referring to his appointment as collector, the leading paper of Victoria, says:—
" Collector Milne's appointment meets with universal approval. He is long and favorably known to the business public of British Columbia. He has been for many years in the Custom House and has won the good will of all by the efficiency with which he performed his duties, by his courtesy and his readiness to oblige all those with whom he had occasion to do business. Collector Milne has been a model civil servant, and all are pleased to see that he has obtained the promotion he has deserved so well. We are quite sure that he will perform his duties as acceptably to the Government and to the public in his present position as he did in those he formerly occupied. We are glad that the appointment has been a service appointment. It is an encouragement to deserving civil servants who are doing their best to discharge their duties to the satisfaction of

the Government and the public, to see deserving men promoted to the highest and best paid positions. Such promotions afford the very strongest incentive to diligence and efficiency in the service. They are not only just to the meritorious civil servants by giving them the reward to which their industry, efficiency and general good conduct give them a right, but they are besides the very best means of improving the morale and increasing the efficiency of the service. Mr. Milne's appointment, therefore, from every point of view, is an admirable one." Mr. Milne has always been a staunch Conservative but has never taken an active part in public affairs. He is a member of the Masonic fraternity, and during 1887 and 1888, (the Lodge's most prosperous years), he was Grand Master for British Columbia. He is a member of the Royal Arch, and a charter member of the higher Scottish rite degrees. He is also a member of the Oddfellows' Order, the Knights of Pythias, the Ancient Order of United Workmen and other benevolent societies.

Milne, George L., M. D., M. P. P., (Victoria), is of Scotch birth, having been born in the town of Garmouth, Morayshire, Scotland, in the year 1850. When only seven years of age his parents with their family emigrated to Canada, and lived for many years at Meaford, Grey county, Ontario. The Doctor received his medical education at Toronto School of Medicine, Toronto, and graduated in May, 1880, receiving the degree of M. D. C. M., from Victoria University. It is now nearly ten years since his arrival in British Columbia, and during that time has been in active practice of his profession, he has also identified himself with many public acts and institutions of the Province. He has taken a lively interest in educational matters, having for some time been on the Victoria School Board. He was one of the first to institute steps for the providing of a new medical act for this Province, and since the organization of the Medical Council, has continuously held the position of registrar and secretary as well as being an elected member and examiner for that body. There are many public institutions which the Doctor has identified himself with, and in which he takes a lively interest. He is president of the Vancouver Gas Company. As well as a director in the New Westminster and Nanaimo Gas Company ; vice-president of the Victoria National Electric Tramway Company ; director in the B. C. Fire Insurance

Company, as well as being interested in many other enterprises of great advantage to the inhabitants of this Province. Dr. Milne is a Liberal in politics having been president of the British Columbia Liberal Association for some years. Last summer he contested the by-election in Victoria, in the Opposition interest, against Attorney General Davie, and was defeated by a small majority. At that time he strongly condemned the amendments recently made to the public school act, as well as deprecating any idea of allowing separate schools to become a matter for consideration in British Columbia. He was a successful candidate for the city of Victoria at the last general elections.

Moffatt, Hamilton, (Victoria), was born in Shanklin, Isle of Wight, on June 12th, 1832. He is the fourth son of Lieutenant Moffatt of the Royal Navy, who was born at Ovington, near Hexham, Northumberland, England. Mr. Moffatt was educated in Kingston College, in the town of Kingston-upon-Hull, Yorkshire. Before coming to British Columbia he was in the Imperial Government service. He arrived in British Columbia on February 22nd, 1850, in the service of the Hudson's Bay Company, and was stationed at Victoria, where he continued until the spring of 1872, when he retired. In March, 1873, he joined the Indian Department of the Dominion of Canada at Victoria and is still attached to that service. He married Lucy, second daughter of Captain Wm. Henry McNeill, formerly of the Hudson's Bay service at Victoria. He is an adherent of the Episcopal Church.

Morley, Christopher, (Victoria), was born at Luffborough, Leicestershire, England, on the 7th of March, 1841, educated there and lived in England till 1862, when he came to British Columbia. In 1863 he went to Cariboo, and visited William's, Lightning and other famous creeks, but did not mine. He returned to Victoria during the same summer and remained till the following spring, when he went to the Leach river mines and became interested in several claims. After two years' work he got back to Victoria penniless. Next year he started for the Big Bend, the excitement over the discoveries there having just broken out. He only got as far as Shuswap lake, however. He spent the summer in prospecting in this neighborhood, and returned in the autumn to Victoria.

In the following year he went to Comox prospecting. Subsequently he spent several years at ranching, first at Saanich and then at Sydney Island. In 1872 he established his present business, opening his store first on Yates street. Later he removed to Wharf street and formed a partnership with J. K. Greenwood. This partnership continued till 1881, after which date Mr. Morley took sole control and has conducted the business since. In 1883 he removed to the premises he now occupies. He is a member of St. George's society and the French Benevolent society.

Moss, Morris, (Victoria), was born in London, England, May 31st, 1842, and educated at University college, Gower street, London. He arrived in Victoria in April, 1862, coming by way of Panama. During the early Cariboo excitement he became infected with the fever and started for William's creek by way of Bentinck Arm route, being one of the first to go over that road. After surmounting many difficulties he got through safely. He returned to Victoria, purchased a large stock of goods and started again for the mines. At the forks of the Quesnelle he was overtaken by the great snow storm of that season, and finding it impossible to proceed sold his cargo for what it would fetch and returned to Victoria. In the early part of the following year he took up a stock of goods on the Hudson's Bay company's steam Labouchere and started a trading station in Bella Coulla at the head of Bentinck arm. He found only about one-tenth of the native population which had inhabited the locality during the preceding year, smallpox having killed off the remainder. During that season he loaded three or four pack trains for William's creek and in the fall went there himself. He found quite an excitement among the miners about the new route and several hundreds agreed to winter in Bella Coulla on his guaranteeing to have sufficient supplies there. He then proceeded to Victoria, chartered the schooner Rose Newman, belonging to William Spring and Captain McKay, loaded her with a general cargo and was about to start when Mr. Robertson Stewart, then agent for the Koskuma Coal Mining company, called on him and asked as a favor to allow the schooner to call at Koskuma to take winter supplies to the men there. Mr. Moss at first refused, not wishing to take the chances of a trip on the west coast, but upon the representation of Mr. Stewart that there was no other means of sending up provision to the men, he consented. Before leaving Victoria he was interviewed by Governor Douglas several times, and was appointed government agent for the northwest coast. He was also gazetted justice of the peace, but was never sworn in for the latter office. After a rough trip he arrived at Koskuma about the end of November and found the men greatly excited over the accidental shooting of Mr. Munro, which had occurred two days previously. He landed the provisions he had brought for this place and then sailed to Quatseena, at which place he was detained about seven days by a heavy gale. The crew of the schooner consisted of Capt. Walters, formerly of the Hudson Bay company; Ben Spain, the mate, and three Indians. The Indians finding that he was determined to proceed deserted from the boat. On the eighth day he started out, the gale still blowing. He had not proceed far when the mainsail and jib were blown away and the water casks were washed overboard. A thick fog then set in. They drifted about at the mercy of the waves for three days, the fog continuing during the whole time, and on the the third night, the 8th of December, they struck a rock. The waves dashed over the vessel and they clung to the rigging. They could see nothing but breakers around them. The captain sang out : " Every man for himself, I'm going to make for those breakers," pointing ahead. All hands jumped overboard and by chance all got ashore. They got on some rocks, climbed up and found a level place of about thirty feet above water and lay down awaiting daylight. It snowed that night, the first of the season. When daylight came they found they were on a small rocky island, which at low water was connected with a large island by a narrow neck of land. As soon as the water receded they made for the large island, which afterwards they found to be the island of Lochaboo, to the westward of Safety Cove. They were without food, matches or fresh water, but during the day managed to haul in two or three sacks of flour which had drifted out of the schooner. The following day there was luckily a very low tide. They picked up many articles of use as well as food along the beach. Among others was a keg of gunpowder, into which the water had only penetrated about a quarter of an inch, also they found a flint-lock gun. With these and the aid of some linen they managed to get a little fire by shooting into dry moss and blowing the sparks into flame. This they kept burning continuously for the three months which they remained on the island. The next few days they occupied in gathering what they could from the wreck, the gale having subsided. They collected some thirty or forty sacks of flour, some canned meats, drygoods, molasses and two kegs of liquor. These latter they found jammed in rocks, and they could not pack them to camp. After securing all they could from the wreck they turned their attention to building some habitation. They rolled a few logs up for walls, and took the foresail of the boat for a roof. They remained there three months, from December to the end of February, during which time they explored the island and found that the former inhabitants had all died from smallpox, skeletons being discovered in various parts. They also found several clam beds, which added greatly to their larder. They erected signal poles on every part of the island. One morning while eating their frugal breakfast they were delighted to hear shouts from Indians. Upon proceeding to the beach they saw a canoe about 100 yards from shore, in which were three Indians who had been attracted by the signals. They at first appeared very loath to come ashore, but Mr. Moss soon recognized one of them as a half-breed named Yellowbelly Charley who is still alive. He came ashore and agreed to take them to the camp, which they said was about forty miles distant. They found that the canoe would not hold the crowd and it was agreed that Mr. Moss should proceed with Yellowbelly and return with a larger canoe for the other men, which after many difficulties was accomplished. After their arrival at Bella Bella, a small sloop owned by one Sabastopol, an old prospector, came in. Walters and Spain accepted of his offer to go up to Fort Simpson, but Mr. Moss was anxious to return to Bella Coulla, which lay in a contrary direction and therefore he remained with the Indians, they promising to take him over in a canoe. He soon found, however, that he was a prisoner. The island in which the Indians lived was merely a large rock on which was neither wood nor water, the reason for living here being their fear of being attacked by the Hydah Indians, and as there were many hundred Indian dogs roaming around the rock it was impossible for them to be surprised in the night. He remained a prisoner for over a month, parting day by day with what little property he possessed, having to pay for wood and water which were fetched from a neighboring island. One day he discovered some Kemoquit Indians who were about to proceed to Bella Coulla and by big promises induced them to take a letter to the white men there, informing them of his position. In a week from date an answer came in the shape of forty canoes filled with friendly Bella Coulla Indians and seven or eight white men, who came down with the intention of fighting should the Bella Bellas refuse to give him up. The latter, however, were scared and begged of him to make peace for them with the new comers. He then returned to Bella Coulla where he found the clerk he had left in charge, sick in bed unable to move and unable to account for about one-half of the stock he had left with him. This, added to the loss of the schooner and cargo which alone amounted to $10,000, made him desirous of giving up frontier life. The schooner Amelia arrived a few days afterwards and he took passage to Victoria. Before doing so he arranged with one Barney Johnston to freight into the mines by Alex. Macdonald's pack train the remainder of his stock. His friends in Victoria were very much surprised to see him alive, the stern board of the schooner Rose Newman having been picked up, and not hearing of him for four months they naturally supposed that he was lost. Shortly after arriving in Victoria news was brought down of the Bute Inlet massacre. An indignation meeting was held in the old theatre and after many fiery speeches it was determined to send up an expedition to revenge the murder of the whites. In a short space of time one hundred men volunteered, Mr. Moss among the number. At that time Vancouver Island was a separate colony from the mainland. A letter was sent to Gov. Seymour at Westminster, telling him of what had taken place and offering their services as volunteers. A reply came thanking them for their offer, but saying the mainland would supply her own volunteers for the occasion. At the same time Mr. Moss received a communication from Governor Seymour, asking him to report there and assist. He was invited and attended several meetings of the legislative council at New Westminster. It was finally determined to send fifty men from New Westminster and fifty from Cariboo, the former under Judge Brew and the latter under Judge Cox. Mr. Moss was attached to Mr. Brew's corps, and proceeded with them to Bella Coulla. When about fifty miles from Bella Coulla they met a canoe coming down. Among its occupants was recognized Barney Johnston, who had been left in charge of Mr. Moss' goods at Bella Coulla, and several other whites. The war vessel was stopped and they came aboard.

They informed the volunteers that some little time previous to this they had started out with three pack trains bound for Cariboo and on the third day while in camp at Sutledge a number of Indians told them of the Bute Inlet massacre and advised them to return, otherwise they would share a similar fate. A discussion ensued. Most of them believed the Indians, knowing them, and wished to follow their advice. But Alexander Macdonald, who was packing his own cargo and whose partner, Manning, was out at their station some eighty miles from where they were, refused to turn back. During the night the number of the Indians was greatly increased by strangers coming in, and next morning the Indians would not allow them to depart. Finally the Indians showed that they meant mischief. The whites built stockades with their packsaddles and cargoes and also dug rifle pits. They kept the Indians at bay for about two days, and then determined to abandon their cargoes and return to Bella Coulla river with their horses only. Accordingly they made an early start next morning, but soon found out that retreat was cut off by the Indians, who commenced firing at them from the bush. Alex. Macdonald, Clifford Higgins and Peter McDougall were shot dead, but the others managed to escape, all carrying lead in their bodies. Not knowing that the whites in Victoria were aware of the Butte Inlet massacre they started down to bring the news, when they met the man-of-war. They turned back with the vessel; when they reached Bella Coulla Mr. Moss took charge of landing the men, horses and provisions, and then of freighting the provisions by canoes and Indians up the river. He also formed an Indian detachment to assist the whites. Upon arriving at the head of navigation a consultation was held and it was discovered that provisions would run short before the expedition could accomplish it purpose. Mr. Moss volunteered to return to the war ships, bring up a fresh supply to the head of navigation, and there await the return of the pack train. He was given all necessary papers and told to enroll any volunteers he thought necessary for the safety of the cargo. After securing provisions he engaged four white men and returned again to the head of navigation. When within a few miles of a place called Stewy, at the head of navigation, the whites left their canoes and took to the trail. They made for a log house, built by Mr. Moss a year previous. Here to their surprise they found an interior Indian whom Johnston and McCraney recognized as one of those who had done the shooting at Sutlidge He immediately made for his gun which was in a corner of the house. The whites, however, took it from him, and found it to be loaded with a double charge of buckshot and two trade balls. He said he had heard that the volunteers were coming to avenge the Bute Inlet murder and also understood that Mr. Moss, with whom he was acquainted, was coming up with provisions and he had come to help him. No one, however, believed him and it was with the greatest difficulty that Johnston and McCraney could be dissuaded from shooting him on the spot. Next day Mr. Moss took charge of the Indian and conveyed him to the war ship where he handed him over bound as a prisoner. He then returned to Stewy, and a few days later the pack train arrived. He loaded it up with provisions and took it to Punchin Lake, where he arrived the day after McLean was killed. Negotiations were going on regarding the surrender of the chief murderers. It was ascertained, however, that two of them were off in the mountains in a different direction and Mr. Moss was sent with five men to try and effect their capture. They got on the trail of the fugitives and would have succeeded in bringing them in had their provisions not given out. Mr. Moss then returned to Stewy where he secured a letter from Mr. Brew, stating that the main body having accomplished their object, namely the capture of the chief murderers would return in about a week, and ordering Mr. Moss to proceed to Bella Bella and arrest an Indian there who was wanted as a witness of a murder which had taken place two years previously. This was easily accomplished. The expedition then returned and were paid off. Mr. Moss in addition to his pay received the thanks of Governor Seymour and Judge Brew for his efficient services. The following spring Mr. Moss was induced to go north again on a prospecting tour and while at Bella Coulla succeeded in capturing the two Indian murderers he had searched for the previous year. These he took to New Westminster, where one of them was hung and the other pardoned. Mr. Moss was then appointed by Governor Seymour Indian agent and deputy collector of customs for the Northwest coast, which position he held for nearly three years. In his official capacity he visited almost every place in British Columbia from Naas river down. In 1867 he left the Government employ and started as a fur trader at Bella Bella where he built a residence and store on the site of the

E. B. MARVIN.

Hudson's Bay company's fort. While here he discovered what has since been known as the Hebrew mine, on which he devoted much time and considerable money, and although he was at one time offered $25,000 for a half interest, which he refused, he has never yet made a cent out of it. In 1870 during the Omineca excitement Mr. Moss went up the Skeena river in a boat to the head of canoe navigation. During the summer he remained at the forks of the Skeena. During the early part of the fall he fitted out and accompanied a party to search for rich claims near the boundary of Alaska, of which a man named Strachan professed to have knowledge. The party, however, broke up at Fort Wrangle and Mr. Moss came to Victoria where he has since resided. He has the largest fur business in British Columbia and several boats running to the sealing waters. He is largely interested in mining in the interior especially in Yale district. Mr. Moss is a member of the Pioneer society and of the Hebrew congregation, being a trustee of that body.

Mowat, Thomas, (New Westminster), was born on 15th May, 1859, at Dee Side, Bonaventure county, P. Q. His father who was of Scotch descent, was largely interested in the lumber trade and for many years filled high positions in the government service. Mr Mowat received his primary education from private tutors and afterwards attended the public school at Campbelltown, N. B., where he received a thorough business training. On leaving school he engaged in the lumber trade and before his arrival in British Columbia was largely interested in the shipping business. While in the east he also acquired a thoroughly practical knowledge of fish-hatching and the various methods of artificial fish-culture. In 1883 he came to British Columbia and settled at New Westminster, and since that time has been connected with artificial fish-hatching. Mr. Mowat built the hatchery at New Westminster for the Dominion Government, was placed in charge of it and has since filled the position. Apart from the latter appointment Mr. Mowat was made Inspector of Fisheries for the Province, and has by unceasing efforts in that behalf, largely contributed to develope the piscatorial wealth of Canada. Besides being, ex-officio, a justice of the peace Mr. Mowat was appointed a justice of the peace for the Province by the government of British Columbia. He is a member of the Masonic and Caledonian societies and was formerly a lieutenant in No. 1

battery of the British Columbia garrison artillery, but was obliged to give up his commission on account of the press of his official business. In October, 1888, Mr. Mowat married Miss B. C. Herratt, Esq., J. P. of Pedicodiac, N. B. In 1879 Mr Mowat crossed the Atlantic in charge of the first large cargo of frozen salmon for the London market, which turned out a great success. He not only initiated the trade but also built the freezers employed in conveying the salmon across the Atlantic. He was requested by the Minister of Fisheries to take charge of the Canadian exhibit to the London exhibition but declined as he had made up his mind to come to British Columbia. In 1886 Mr. Mowat sailed round Vancouver Island and located all the deep sea fishing banks. He is a Presbyterian and one of the rising men of the Province.

Muirhead, James, (Victoria), son of the late John Muirhead, contractor and builder, of Glasgow, Scotland, was born at Castle Carey, Stirlingshire, Scotland, on November 20th, 1837. When he was twelve years of age his parents removed to Glasgow and Mr. Muirhead was educated in that city, attending the Normal school on Renfield street. After leaving school he was apprenticed to a joiner and after serving his time at this trade he left the old country in 1857 and came to Canada. He went first to Stratford, county Perth, then to Paris, and finally settled in Galt, where he remained for two years working at his trade. At the end of this time he went to New York, and during his stay there worked on the Fifth Avenue hotel which was then in course of construction. From New York he removed to New Orleans where he spent the winter and part of the summer and then visited South America. He remained for two years in Lima, Peru, and during that time was employed by the English Waterworks Company. In 1862 he was attracted to British Columbia by the reports of the wonderful discoveries of gold in Cariboo. When he reached Victoria, however, the excitement to a large extent had calmed down, and Mr. Muirhead instead of going to the mines concluded to follow his trade. In 1863 he began a contracting business and among other large buildings for which he obtained the contract was the Oddfellows' hall. In 1870 his present partner Mr. Mann joined him in the business, and in 1875 they began the manufacturing business which they now conduct. Mr. Muirhead does not take any active part in politics and has not stood for any public position. He is a member of the Masonic fraternity, the Oddfellows' order and the Pioneer society and an adherent of the Presbyterian church. In November, 1868, he married Rebecca Fleming, of Victoria.

Munro, Alexander. (Victoria), chief factor of the Hudson's Bay Company, was born in the town of Tain, Rossshire, Scotland, in 1824. In early life he was engaged in different pursuits – law, banking, etc.—first in Scotland and afterwards in England. He arrived on Vancouver Island in 1857 in the Hudson's Bay Company's service, and has since remained in and near Victoria. He witnessed the great gold rush of 1858. For many years past he has been factor of the Hudson's Bay Company and accountant of their western department, comprising the whole of British Columbia, and has also had charge of their lands and those of the Puget's Sound Agricultural Company in this Province. After the many changes which have taken place under his observation during the third part of a century he is now, on the eve of his retirement, the senior chief factor in the company's service. His life has been a busy and industrious one, but not eventful in comparison with the lives and stirring experiences of many of his predecessors— those adventurous, manly pioneers and veterans who smoothed the way, to a great extent for their successors by themselves undergoing the privations, the arduous labors and "perils by flood and field" incident to establishing not merely the company's trading posts but British authority also, and therewith happily introducing the dawn of civilization among savage tribes scattered over the wide continent from Canada to Alaska and the Arctic regions.

Munsie, William. (Victoria), was born in Pictou county, Nova Scotia, on January 4th, 1849, and educated at Pictou. After leaving school he served his apprenticeship to the foundry business in Truro, and remained their for four years. In 1874 he went to San Francisco, where for four years he was employed at this business. In 1878 he came to British Columbia and settled in Victoria, where he established a stove business for Mr. Joseph Spratt, of the Albion Iron Works, and designed and manufactured the first stoves ever made in British Columbia He remained with Mr. Spratt for over six years. In 1885 he formed a partnership with his present associate, Mr. F. Carne, and established the grocery business the firm now conducts. In the same year in conjunction with Mr. A. J. Bechtel he purchased the schooner Caroline and engaged in the sealing industry. The following year they purchased another vessel, and have since been adding to their fleet.

Mills, Daniel, (Vancouver), fourth son of the late Joseph Mills, farmer of Antigonish, N. S., who in the early part of the century emigrated from Hampshire, England, and settled in Nova Scotia. Mr. Mills was born at Antigonish on July 17th, 1830, and received his elementary education in his native county. At the age of fifteen years he was apprenticed to the stone-cutting and building trade, to which he served four years. At the age of nineteen years he began business as a contractor and his thorough knowledge of the trade combined with his mechanical skill soon obtained for him an extensive reputation. The result was that during the two years he remained in business in his native county he had as much as he could attend to, and in that time erected twenty-one grist mills. In 1851 Mr. Mills, then a man of twenty-one years, left Canada and settled in the state of Maine, U. S., where he remained for two years, following his profession with remarkable success. Returning to Nova Scotia he invested the result of his labor in real estate. He continued his business in Canada from this time till 1858 when, attracted west by the excitement over the discovery of gold in British Columbia he took shipping for San Francisco. He remained in Victoria where he superintended the cutting and placing of the stone of the Bank of British North America then and until long afterwards the only building of this kind in the city. When this work had been completed he undertook the contract to cut the stone for Race Rock lighthouse, which he finished in 1860. In the autumn of the same year he superintended the construction of a wharf for the Hudson's Bay Company, and in the spring of 1861 he purchased a half interest in a brewery business in Victoria. He sold out his share in the brewery in 1862 and went to Cariboo by the Yale route where he mined on Antler Creek. During 1862 he was interested in five claims on this creek and lost about fifteen hundred dollars. He then located a claim on William's creek and purchased one on Lightning and another on Sugar creek. On the latter two he engaged men to work for him. During 1862 and 1863

A. H. McBRIDE.

he lost heavily, and was forced to sell some of his property in the east in order to obtain the money to develop his claims. He abandoned his claims on Lightning and Sugar creeks and sold that on Antler creek, never however getting the purchase money. He clung to his claims on William's creek and spent considerable money in the work of development and during 1864-5-6 succeeded in making the first of these which he had taken up pay very well. In 1867 he again went prospecting and located a claim on Keithley creek, which was very promising, but he abandoned it, owing to its distance from any point where provisions could be obtained. He then went to Red Gulch where he purchased an interest in the Discovery claim, the development of which he superintended during 1867-8. This claim which took eleven months to work "panned out" well. In 1868 he also purchased an interest in claims on Lowhee creek and here he remained till 1875, managing the work of development. The severe labor exposure and anxiety which he underwent during this period wrecked his constitution and he was forced to leave the mines owing to the condition of his health. He accordingly disposed of his interest and went to Victoria, where he remained for about nine months. He then in conjunction with Mr. Donald Chisholm purchased two farms on Salt Spring island and also opened a wholesale and retail flour and liquor store in New Westminster and built the brewery at Sapperton. This business he personally conducted till 1883, when he disposed of all his interests in New Westminster district, except a portion of that in the brewery. These interests were purchased by Mr. Chisholm. Since that time Mr. Mills has not been engaged in active business. He has always been an active politician, taking a deep interest both in Dominion and Provincial affairs. His principles are Liberal-Conservative. In religion Mr. Mills is a Roman Catholic.

McBride, Arthur H., (New Westminster), son of the late Thomas McBride, of county Down, Ireland, was born on June 26th 1835, at Down and educated at his native place. In 1854 he joined the Royal South Down Militia in which he at once took the position of color sergeant and pay sergeant. He remained with his regiment for five years when he decided in 1859, in consequence of the excitement over the discovery of gold on the Fraser river, to come to British Columbia. He first visited Eastern Canada and from there he went to California where he remained for two years and a half and finally reached British Columbia in the spring of 1863. He went direct to the Cariboo region and during the summer he mined on Williams and Lightning creeks. On the latter of these he purchased, in conjunction with others, a large claim but owing to the difficulty of working it, although the prospects were excellent, they abandoned it. At the end of the season Mr. McBride returned to Victoria, without however, having been successful at the mines, and he accepted a position as sergeant of police. He rose quickly in the service and very soon had control of the force, and in 1870 on the death of Captain Pritchard, was appointed to the vacant position. Mr. McBride remained in this position till 1878 when the Provincial penitentiary at New Wesminster having been completed, he was appointed to the office of Warden which position he still retains. He was at the same time given a commission of Justice of the Peace within the jurisdiction of the Sheriff of New Westminster. Mr. McBride possesses in a marked degree the instinct and disposition of a soldier. He is an ardent disciplinarian and it was largely to his efforts that the militia regiments of both Victoria and New Westminster came into existence and for years he gave his services gratuitously as drill instructor and brought both regiments to a good state of efficiency. He is a member of the Masonic Order and also of the Ancient Order of United Workmen. On the 8th of November, 1865, he married Miss Mary D'Arcy of Victoria. Mr. McBride is an adherent of the Presbyterian Church.

McDowell, Henry. (Vancouver), third son of Robert and Mary A. McDowell, was born at Milton, Halton county, Ontario, on March 3rd, 1862. He was educated at Milton public school and for a time followed the occupation of school teaching; but abandoned it to study the business he is at present engaged in, that of chemist and druggist. He came to British Columbia in 1886 and settled at Vancouver in June of that year, establishing the business which he now owns and which has increased with the growth of the city. Mr. McDowell is a strong Conservative in Dominion matters but so far has taken no active interest in Provincial politics, his large and increasing business demanding his entire attention. He is one of Vancouver's most prosperous and loyal citizens, and has centered all his interests in the terminal city. He is connected with the Vancouver Street Railway and Electric Light Co., the Union Steamship Co., the Vancouver City Foundry Co, and is a prominent member of the Board of Trade. Mr. McDowell is a member of the Episcopal Church.

McElman, Albert Theosopholus DesBrisay, (Nanaimo), son of the late James McElman, captain of marine, was born in King's county, New Brunswick. When he was four years of age his parents removed to Westmorland county, and there Mr. McElman received his primary education. After finishing his collegiate course he studied law at Dorchester in the office of Thomas S. Sayers where he remained the full five years required by the articles. He was then called to the bar of New Brunswick and practiced first in Albert county and subsequently in King's county. In 1874 he came to British Columbia and settled at Victoria. In October of the same year he was admitted a solicitor and barrister of British Columbia. For ten years he resided in Victoria and practiced his profession, and then he removed to New Westminster in which city he was, till he removed to Nanaimo, solicitor to the corporation. In 1887 he settled in Nanaimo where he has since resided. Mr. McElman although not an active politician takes an interest both in Provincial and Dominion affairs. His legal practice is principally in criminal law and he has had important cases in this Province.

McFeely, Edward John, (Vancouver), son of Edward and Sarah McFeely, both Canadians of Irish descent, was born at Lindsay, Ontario, on November 3rd, 1863. Educated at his native place and in 1882 went to Winnipeg where he continued during the boom. From Winnipeg he went to Minneapolis and in 1885 came to British Columbia, settling in Victoria and going into business in partnership with Mr. R. P. McLennan. In 1886 the firm established a branch business at Vancouver, and of this Mr. McFeely took the management, Mr. McLennan remaining in Victoria. Mr. McFeely has since resided in Vancouver and is regarded as one of the most energetic and prosperous merchants of that rising city. He is a member of the Board of Trade, and an adherent of the Roman Catholic Church. He married Miss Gracie Cameron of Victoria.

McGregor, William, (Nanaimo), was born at Victoria, April 7th, 1855. He is the son of the late John McGregor, one of the mining experts who came to this country from Ayrshire, Scotland, in 1849, to open up the coal mines at Fort Rupert and who after testing seams at that place and finding them worthless removed to Nanaimo and opened up a number of mines there. Mr. McGregor was educated at Victoria and Nanaimo, and when he left school he went to work in the mines and has filled every position from workman to manager, which office he now holds. During the year 1880 he was engaged for a time contracting on New Castle Island but again returned to Nanaimo and took the position of overman of the Vancouver Company's mines. In 1884 he was offered and accepted the position of manager. Since that time the work of development has largely increased and the business of the company has become very profitable. When the terrible colliery explosion occurred in 1887, Mr. McGregor was the leader of the exploring and rescuing parties and worked night and day untiringly. Mr. McGregor is wrapped up in his business, takes no interest in politics and has been solicited but has refused to stand for the city Council. He is a member of the Presbyterian Church, and in 1875 was married to an English lady, Miss Amanda Meakin.

McGuigan, William Joseph, M. D., C. M., (Vancouver), was born in Stratford, county of Perth, Ontario, on July 28th, 1853. He is the eldest son of Michael McGuigan, who at the age of twenty-five came to America from Castle Dawson, county of Derry Ireland, and after residing two years in New York settled at North East Hope, Ontario, where he married Bridget Quinliven. Dr. McGuigan received his elementary education at the public school in North East Hope, and subsequently at the Stratford High School. He then attended the Galt Collegiate Institute, at that time a noted educational establishment, for a term, and afterwards studied medicine at McGill University, Montreal, where he matriculated at the age of twenty. When a boy he intended studying for the priesthood, but later on changed his mind and took a medical course, graduating with honors in 1879. Shortly after leaving the university he went into practice, and received the appointment of first Grand Trunk Railroad surgeon at Sarnia. After residing one year at Sarnia he was obliged to leave that city owing to ill-health and removed to

London, Ontario. Here he was appointed registrar and lecturer on therapeutics and botany at the Western University. He remained in London five years and in 1885 left for the North West to recover his health which had become impaired through overwork. While at London he was one of the physicians of the city hospital. He did not then resign his position in the university but he had an understanding with the faculty that he might not return and that they should be prepared to fill the vacancy caused by his withdrawal. After visiting all places of interest in Manitoba and the Territories, he came on to British Columbia, meeting at Donald, his brother Thomas F. McGuigan, now city clerk of Vancouver. While there, Dr. Brett chief medical superintendent of the Mountain Division of the Canadian Pacific Railroad, who was desirous of taking a trip east, asked Dr. McGuigan to take his place during his absence. He complied and remained in the mountains till the railway was completed and when the Onderdonk division met the Ross division at Eagle Pass he travelled down to the Coast. Dr. McGuigan was so impressed with the situation and natural advantages of Granville (now Vancouver), that he decided to make his home there and ever since has taken great interest in its extraordinary growth and prosperity. He acted for nearly two years as secretary of the school board of Vancouver city and is a member of the medical council of the Province, of which during one year he was president. He is president of the Vancouver City Medical Association, and a member of the local St. Patrick's Society. In 1889 he was an unsuccessful candidate for aldermanic honors. Dr. McGuigan has a decided taste for literature and is a frequent contributor to the press on questions of the day. He is a vigorous writer and a good speaker. While at the University he was editor-in-chief of the McGill University *Gazette*, and in 1879 wrote the farewell poem of the year. In religion Dr. McGuigan is an adherent of the Roman Catholic Church.

McInnes, Hon. Thomas Robert, M. D., C. M., (New Westminster), is the fourth son of the late John McInnes, Esq., formerly of Inverness, Scotland, and subsequently of Lake Ainslie, N. S. Mr. McInnes was born at Lake Ainslie, N. S., on November 5th, 1840. He received his education first at the Normal School, Truro, N. S., and then at Harvard University. He first settled in

Dresden, Ontario, and in 1874 was elected Reeve of Dresden. He removed to British Columbia and settled in New Westminster, and in 1876 was elected Mayor of that City. This position he held till 1878, when he was elected to represent New Westminster district in the House of Commons. He continued as member for that constituency till 1881, when he was appointed to the Senate of which body he is now a member. He is connected with a large number of important enterprises in the district. He is physician and surgeon to the Royal Columbia Hospital, and medical superintendent of the British Columbia Lunatic Asylum. On October 5th, 1865, he married Mrs. Webster, relict of the late George Webster, Esq., of Dresden, Ontario.

McLean, Malcolm Alexander, (Vancouver), born August 14th, 1842, in Argyleshire, Scotland, is the second son of the late Allan McLean, an extensive Argyleshire farmer who came to Canada from Scotland in 1846 and settled in the county of Victoria, Ontario. Here Mr. McLean received his education and subsequently engaged in merchandise, at which he continued in his native county till 1881, when he removed to Winnipeg, at that time experiencing the famous boom. Mr. McLean engaged in business there and invested largely in property in the city of Winnipeg, and also in the agricultural district, and at present owns one of the finest farms in Manitoba. In 1885 he came to Vancouver where he settled and where he has since continued to reside. He was elected first Mayor of Vancouver after the city was incorporated, and was again placed in that position in the following year. While in the occupancy of this office the city made vast strides in growth and improvement, and to his excellent administration of its affairs it is that the city largely owes its present prosperity. For a year Mr. McLean occupied the position of Police Magistrate of the city. He is largely interested in the advancement of the city of Vancouver, where all his interests are centered.

McLeese, Robert. (Soda Creek) descended from a branch of the MacCallum Mores, of Cantire, Scotland, which settled in the county of Antrim, Ireland, in the time of the Young Pretender. Mr. McLeese, the younger of two children of John McLeese and Jennie McArthur McLeese, was born near Coleraine, Antrim, Ireland, June 28, 1828. He was educated at one of the Kildare

SENATOR McINNES.

street, Dublin, educational colleges. After completing his education he came to America and settled in Philadelphia, Penn., where some of his relatives resided. Here he remained for seven years, and at the expiration of that time, removed to California via Panama. During his progress over the Isthmus the party with which he travelled was attacked by the natives, who had been outraged by the filibustering expedition of General Walker a short time previous. Mr. McLeese remained in California, engaged in mining, till 1858, when he came to British Columbia. He settled first in New Westminster, where he engaged in business, and where he filled several important civic offices. In 1863 he left New Westminster for Cariboo, but remained at Soda Creek, and opened a general business. He has since resided there. In 1882 he was returned as junior member in the Legislative Assembly for Cariboo, and in 1882 was re-elected as middle member. In the Autumn of 1888 he resigned and contested the same constituency for the House of Commons, but was unsuccessful. He has very large interests in the Province, and has been most successful in his commercial ventures. In 1873, in Renfrew, Ontario, he married Mary Sinclair, granddaughter of Col. McLaren, of Renfrew, Scotland.

McLennan, Robert Purvis. (Victoria), the seventh son of J. P. McLennan, J. P., of Pictou, Nova Scotia, was born at Pictou. on December 7th, 1861. He was educated at that famous academy in Pictou where so many leading men in Canada received their early training, such men as Rev. Principal Grant of Queen's University, Kingston; Sir Wm. Dawson, and Chief Justice Macdonald, Mr. McLennan passed through all the divisions of the school and then at the age of fifteen years entered a hardware business, having chosen this as his future vocation. He remained for three years in Pictou during which time he got a thorough knowledge of every department of the business, and he then removed to River John, a shipbuilding town of Nova Scotia, where for two years he conducted his brother's business. During all this time, and indeed before leaving school, he had been dreaming of the possibilities of the western world and had convinced himself that fortune awaited him on the shores of the Pacific. He was unable to obtain much information respecting British Columbia, but the desire to get there grew stronger with the passing years. In 1882 the excitement over

Winnipeg was at its height in the eastern provinces and Mr. McLennan was smitten with the fever. He accordingly went there where he remained following his business till the spring of 1884, when the depression ensued. He returned to Nova Scotia on a visit and six weeks later left for the Pacific coast coming over the Northern Pacific Railroad. He remained till the autumn and then came to British Columbia, landing at Victoria on Septembe 21st, 1884. At that time Victoria was much smaller than it is now, but it had a substantial appearance and there was a great deal of building operation in progress. Mr. McLennan was much pleased with the outlook of the city. The Canadian Pacific Railway was being completed to the mountains, settlers were crowding in from the east and everything gave promise of future prosperity. He at once established his present business of manufacturing ornamental iron work for building, tin roofing material, cornice work and other work of a like nature, and he invested all his money in his venture. When the spring opened building operations began with activity and Mr. McLennan found that he would not be able to cope single handed with his greatly increasing business. He accordingly communicated with his present partner, Mr. E. J. McFeely, with whom he had worked in Winnipeg and who was then in Minneapolis. Mr. McFeely came to Victoria without delay and the existing partnership was formed. During that summer and autumn their business increased as they had expected and they were forced to enlarge their premises. During that winter Vancouver began to come into existence and in the spring the firm decided to establish a branch business there. In May, Mr. McLennan visited the new town and purchased a lot on Powell street and let a contract for putting up a building. The frame work alone was erected when the big fire which destroyed the town occurred. This building, however, was uninjured and was rapidly completed under the supervision of Mr. McFeely who had come up to put a roof on it, and a stock of goods was placed in it. Building on an extensive scale then began in Vancouver and this compared with their large Victoria business taxed the energies of the firm to their utmost to supply the demand. In the autumn of 1886 they purchased the lot on Cordova street, Vancouver, on which their handsome warehouse, which they at once erected, now stands. To this building they at once transferred their Vancouver business, which had attained large proportions. In the spring of 1889 the firm in addition to their manufacturing business in Victoria, opened up retail warerooms on Yates street. In the autumn of 1887, Mr. McLennan revisited his former home in the east, and on the 23rd of November, at River John, married Miss Bessie McKenzie, daughter of John McKenzie, Esq., one of the leading merchants of that place.

McMicking, Robert Burns. (Victoria), the subject of this sketch, first saw the light of day July 7th, 1843, on the right bank of the majestic, and somewhat turbulent Niagara, and almost under the shadow of the nation's monument, erected upon the battle ground of Queenston Heights, to commemorate the heroic valor of General Brock, who fell so nobly defending his country in the ever memorable struggle of 1812. Mr. McMicking was born on the farm forming the north-eastern corner of Welland county, Ontario, in the township of Stamford, where his father, Wm. McMicking, J. P., born 1805, lived and died, and upon which his grandfather, McMicking, located while yet a young man, on arriving from Scotland about the year 1780, while that picturesque, and now productive Eden of our Dominion, as yet the haunts of red men resting in primeval silence, echoed the footfalls of impending Saxon civilization. So that he may be recognized as a Canadian *par excellence*, ingrained, and to the manor born, and to his credit be it recorded, that through all the changing scenes peculiar to rollicking, roving western life, where national sentiment is oftimes deemed dull drudgery---in the early days of our history, when to be loyal was to become the object often of strife and ridicule, his fealty to the land that gave him birth was ever firm and unshaken. Mr. McMicking belongs to one of the largest, as well as one of the oldest, families of the Dominion, being one of twelve children—six boys and a like number of girls—all of whom married. The eldest brother, the late lamented Thomas McMicking, of New Westminster, who was drowned in the Fraser river in 1866 (and who will be referred to later on) having, in company with R. B. McMicking, emigrated to British Columbia overland via Selkirk (now Winnipeg), Edmonton and Fraser river pass in the summer of 1862. At the age of thirteen, on the death of his father, Mr. McMicking engaged in the study of electricity—a science then quite as much in its youth as the student himself, so far as being of practical value to mankind— for it will be within the recollection of many that the introduction of telegraphy—the only important manner in which this wonderful and still unknown force was employed, was practically concurrent with the founding of the Morse system, established about the year 1844, and in the sense therefore of being useful, telegraphy may be said to have been born then. Shortly after this date he was engaged in the operating department of the Queenston office of the Montreal Telegraph Co., the respected and now almost venerable H. P. Dwight, superintendent. Here under the exhilarating and moulding influences of charming scenic environment, clear skies, and loving kin companionship, our subject passed his early boyhood days. And here it was that the British Pacific gold fever, which took such firm hold of eastern Canada, found him in the autumn of 1861. Dwellers in the ancient, and abnormally quiet village of Queenston caught the epidemic, and in company with 23 others from that neighborhood Mr. McMicking set out on the 23rd of April, 1862, overland, through the British Northwest, for the gold fields of Cariboo, and it is doubtless owing in great measure to the westward movement over our fertile plains and the explorations of this band of weary pioneers that our vast and valuable interoceanic possessions came speedily into prominence, destined, in our own day to accomplish so much in the development of our young and vigorous nation. An affectionate farewell with regrets, God-speed and good wishes being over—for the enterprise was regarded as hazardous, and the result somewhat uncertain—the party moved forward, intent upon reaching Selkirk (now Winnipeg) settlement, and from there mark out a course across the prairies. Every preparation had been made and every precaution taken by the party for accomplishing the entire journey alone. It became evident, however, before Selkirk was reached that the inhabitants of other sections of Ontario and Quebec had been led to interest themselves in the Pacific Eldorado, and in consequence small parties were frequently met en route, having their faces set westerly, and their steps turned toward the setting sun. Rendezvousing at Selkirk, preparatory to crossing the great plains, the augmented party numbered one hundred and fifty souls, all intent on a common errand, being impelled westward by a desire primarily to share in the golden harvest of Cariboo. The subject of this sketch was a hero, to the extent of being the most juvenile member of the roving band. Fort Edmonton next became the objective point, and before undertaking the journey through this comparatively unknown region, it was deemed prudent in the interests of good government within, and for mutual protection against all forms and conditions of uncatalogued adversaries from without, that the whole party be organized under a captain and executive board, composed of one member from each original party. The country to be traversed was as yet almost wholly inhabited by the various tribes of native red men, of whose friendship the weary wanderers had no reason to be assured, whose hostility they somewhat feared; but whose passiveness they came to admire. Thomas McMicking at once a favorite wherever known was unanimously chosen captain, and under him the large party accomplished a most remarkable march Pacific coast-ward, passing through many charming, and even enchanting scenes; surmounting innumerable difficulties with meagre appliances, and with all averaging a daily march of twenty-five miles. The first day of the week was religiously observed as a day of rest, and the marvelous results, in a physical sense at least, were a further evidence, if, indeed, evidence be wanting, of the depth of wisdom displayed by the great Creator in so forcibly enjoining upon his creatures the necessity of one day's rest in seven : and as they pursued their journey, which ran into months of travel, they were enabled to realize afresh something of the meaning of the command "Remember the Sabbath day to keep it holy" by the absence of sickness from their ranks, not one, we are informed, having as much as an ordinary headache during the entire journey. Under the guidance of Andre Cardinal, a Hudson bay freeman of St. Alberts, and native of Jasper House, the party left Edmonton, July 29, 1862, for the head waters of the Fraser river via Leather Pass, arriving at Fete Jeune-Cache, on the Fraser, August 27th, a distance of 459 miles from Edmonton; thence down the Fraser by raft to the mouth of Quesnelle river, a further distance of 520 miles, which was reached on the 11th September, completing an exciting and perilous trip by land and water, through the rugged Rockies. The route travelled from Fort Garry to Tete-Jeune-Cache was about the same as was subsequently, eighteen years later, selected by the McKenzie administration for the great national highway, and the same that the Grand Trunk and Northern Pacific now contemplate adopting to link the immense and productive plains of the great British Northwest and Peace river districts with the tide waters of the Pacific at Victoria via Bute Inlet. The scenery contiguous to this route cannot be surpassed, while the marvelous fertility of the soil far exceeds that along any of the more southern lines. At Quesnelle mouth the party disbanded, and after a brief experience in the famous Cariboo mines, with flour, bacon, sugar, etc., at a dollar a pound, Mr. McMicking turned his steps toward the coast, and domiciled at New Westminster during the winter of '62-3. In the early summer of '63 he entered the employ of W. J. —now Sheriff Armstrong, the then leading grocer of that ancient colonial capital. Remaining there until November, '65, Mr. McMicking again entered the telegraph service on the lines of the Collins Overland Telegraph Company, then constructing a line northward through British Columbia with the object of reaching Europe via Behring straits. It will be remembered that this scheme was brought into existence through the failure of the first Atlantic cable laid in 1858, and Mr. McMicking joined in celebrating the event, while working in the Queenston office under the impression, as had been reported, that the cable was intact and working. Upwards of three million dollars had been spent in prosecuting the work in British Columbia in 1864-5-6, and the construction party numbering 250 men had reached a point 300 miles north of Quesnelle mouth, upon the successful completion of the second Atlantic cable, June 26th, 1866. At this date Mr. McMicking was in charge of the Quesnelle mouth office and in communication with the working party north, while the line south to Victoria was open and transmitting commercial business. He was therefore the medium through which the information, fatal to the overland telegraph enterprise, reached the working party at Fort Stager, on Skeena river. The work at once ceased, and after the lapse of a few months the whole line, with material and supplies, north of Quesnelle was abandoned. During the following August, Mr. McMicking was called to mourn the loss of his brother Thomas (previously referred to as captain of the overland party of 1862), who was drowned in the Fraser river, seven miles below New Westminster, while attempting to rescue his son, who had fallen into the treacherous waters, but unfortunately without avail, and father and son sank together in the cold and merciless deep. At the time of his death Thomas McMicking was deputy-sheriff at New Westminster. A graduate of Knox college, Toronto, a ready speaker and writer, a genial companion and withal a man of sterling character; he was destined had he been spared to act an important and foremost part in the upbuilding of the social and political fabric of the country of his adoption—and we may well be pardoned for turning aside here to record our regrets concerning the loss of a life, while yet in the bloom and strength of manhood, and which must have proved so valuable an acquisition in moulding aright the destinies of our young Province. Contemplating this calamity we recall the almost universally yet seldom heeded truism: "There is a Divinity that shapes our ends, rough hew them how we will." This sad circumstance brought Mr. McMicking to New Westminster, and subsequently, after the lapse of a few weeks, to the charge of the Yale telegraph office, where he labored uneventfully until the summer of 1869, at which time he married Maggie B., daughter of David Leighton of Germouth, Scotland, and niece of Thomas R. Buie, J. P., of Lytton, B. C., where she had been for some time residing, the ceremony being performed at Lytton, June 28th, by the Rev. J. B. Good of the Episcopal Church. In the following year Mr. McMicking was transferred to Victoria where he assumed charge of the Western Union Telegraph office, and Barnard's British Columbia Express, May 1st, 1870. On the Provincial Government by covenant with the Western Union Telegraph Co., assuming charge of the telegraph lines, and cables of the Province in 1871, Mr. McMicking was appointed to the superintendency, with headquarters at Yale, B. C., whither he proceeded in December of the same year. The six submarine cables, connecting Vancouver's island with the mainland in Washington territory, forming part of the telegraphic system, were also under Mr. McMicking's care and supervision, and in the treatment of them, oftimes with scant appliances (being naturally an adept in mechanics, and having acquired a full and complete practical knowledge of every detail in telegraphy from personal application in every office from the lowest to the highest in the gift of the proprietary) he displayed a large amount of tact, judgment and skill, as might reasonably have been expected in one so thoroughly tutored: and consequently he very soon came to be recognized as exceedingly expert in the management of submarine telegraph cable work, as well as in all other branches of electrical business and a reliable practical authority; so much so indeed that the late Dr. T. T. Minor, of Seattle, president of the Puget Sound telegraph line, which embraces a number of submarine cables, engaged him to overhaul, test and place both the land line and cables of that company in thorough working order at a daily cost

(18)

for personal services of fifty dollars ($50), the president afterward remarking that considering the distance traversed, the enormous amount of work got out of the steamer and land parties, and the more than satisfactory results obtained in the possession of a good working line, where for some years the company had been battling with a very poor one, the money had been judiciously expended, and the company had large value. With the ingenuity of a Yankee —he came within half a mile of being born one—he possesses the faculty of always managing to accomplish work with the means at hand, suiting the appliances to the work, without exhibiting any desire to create impressions upon an unsuspecting public through the introduction of a variety of electrical devices, bearing high-sounding names, little understood and of doubtful utility, except perhaps to create ostentatious display. On one occasion when working in Rosario channel, San Juan Archipelago, upon a damaged cable which required testing, he discovered that the porous cells of the electropoion battery, then much used, had been left behind at Victoria. To have returned for them would have cost at least $150.00 besides losing much valuable time. On the other hand a battery was essential to the detection of cable faults. What was then to be done? The missing cells were of special composition and size, suited to the filtration of fluids and occupation of a position inside the zinc pole, and having within a cavity sufficiently large to receive the carbon and a small quantity of electropoion fluid. Was it reasonable to suppose that anything to make shift, would likely be discovered in a moderate time, on so desolate a coast? To most persons the difficulty would have appeared as simply insurmountable, and perhaps without a thought of overcoming the difficulty, the order would have been given to hasten to Victoria, and if necessary send on to New York should the cups not be obtainable nearer, and let the work lie over until they were received, as they could not be done without. Not so, however, with Mr. McMicking, it is in just such emergency that his ingenious mind seems to take on renewed impulse. Thoughts crowd in upon the mind in rapid succession, and the determination to overcome takes firm hold. On this occasion, while the vessel was crossing the channel, he retired to the after part of the ship for a moment's quiet, wherein to think out a release, and it was not long in coming. Upon the deck lay a bamboo pole which some of the party had picked out of the

DAVID OPPENHEIMER.

water and cast there. When his eyes fell upon it he saw there the essentials of the absent porous cups, and obtaining a saw the work of cutting off suitable lengths was soon accomplished. Over the lower end of each a course canvas was tied the carbon and fluid inserted and by the time the steamer reached the place for active operations, he had as good an electropoion battery for practical use of eight elements as could have been obtained anywhere, and one of which a few years previous a Siemens or an Edison might have been proud. A number of similar expedients, similar as exhibiting a characteristic determination to be self-reliant, and " work out" could be chronicled among events transpiring during the nine years of his superintendency of the cable system, but we refrain for the present, though the familiar lines of the poet are ringing in our ears:

> What use for the rope if it be not flung
> Till the swimmer's grasp to the rock has clung?
> What help in a comrade's bugle blast
> When the peril of Alpine heights is past?
> What need that the spurring paean roll
> When the runner is safe within the goal?
> What worth is eulogy's blandest breath
> When whispered in ears that are hushed in death?
> No! no! If you have but a word of cheer,
> Speak it, while I am alive to hear.

In 1873 Mr. McMicking was commissioned by the government as a justice of the peace for the Province, which commission he has since held with credit to himself and the administration of justice in the land. During the two years following the issuance of this commission, and while residing in Yale he performed the duties of police magistrate with marked ability. His high sense of man's equality before the law irrespective of social station, his independence of character, regard for the right and love of peace at once gave him a place in the hearts and confidence of the people, and it is safe to say that fully as many of the pending serious difficulties arising between the people by whom he was surrounded were averted, and kept out of court by his timely counsel, as were allowed to enter in, during his administration. He was enabled to discriminate between written law and justice, and to interpret law as found on our statute books as aiming at—desiring justice, rather than the mere fulfilment of the feeble decrees of fallible men. About the same time he was also commissioned a coroner for Yale district, and acted in that capacity during his residence in the district. He was commissioned as well to receive affidavits in matters pending in the Supreme court. From 1875 to 1880 he continued in the government telegraph service with headquarters at Victoria. In 1878 he received the two first telephones imported into British Columbia. These he placed in circuit, on a short line leading out to his residence a mile distant. The capabilities of the instruments as a means of transmitting intelligence soon became apparent, and Mr. McMicking's mature electrical experience enabled him to realize something of the vast possibilities in this new field of electrical development, and consequently in 1880 on quitting the telegraph service he busied himself with the formation of what has since been known as the "Victoria and Esquimalt Telephone company," which he has continued to be manager. This company has enjoyed uniform prosperity under his management, while giving to the citizens of the capital an excellent service. The subscribers of the company now number 345, being, we understand, the largest number in proportion to population, of any city on the continent. Always eager to advance the interests of his much-loved profession, and with an enterprising disposition Mr. McMicking sought and obtained from the corporation, a franchise in 1883 to introduce the Arc electric lights for street illumination. And three towers of 150 feet in height, having clusters of lamps at top were erected, and have since continued to do service. To these additional lights have been added from time to time. In 1887 he managed the formation of a company for the production of the incandescent electric light for domestic lighting. The step proved a veritable boon to all, but especially to those having occasion to use artificial light in large quantities, being the prime factor in causing a reduction of the price of gas from $4 to $2 per thousand feet. And not alone are we to understand was it a boon to light consumers, but, paradoxical as it may appear, we are assured it proved such also to the gas company itself, for we are informed that in consequence of the largely increased consumption by reason of the great reduction in price, the profits to the gas company have actually increased. The introduction by Mr. McMicking of the sub-divided Arc light for commercial purposes, followed in 1889, when a 50-light plant was set in motion from the Victoria electric illuminating company's station in October of that year. In 1881 he built the first electric fire alarm in British Columbia for Victoria City, which consisted of a striker to the large tower bell operated by a water motor, which in turn was controlled electrically by an ingeniously devised repeater, set at the central telephone office from which point fires telephoned in were signalled by striking upon the large bell the number of the telephone which gave the information. This primitive system was replaced by the direct acting Gamewell fire alarm telegraph in 1890, the work being carried out by Mr. McMicking with completeness in every detail. All the electric bell and annunciator services in private and public houses throughout the Province, some of them large systems, have so far been supplied and set up by him. Mr. McMicking may be regarded as the father of electrical enterprise in British Columbia, and at the time of writing is recognized as the central figure in the electrical arena of the Province, where he continues to carry on a general electrical business, besides being manager of the Victoria and Esquimalt Telephone company of Victoria; city electrician, Victoria; general western representative of the Ball Electric Light company of Canada; sole agent of the Gamewell fire alarm, etc., etc. Beyond doing faithful service upon the committees of his aspirant political friends, Mr. McMicking has taken, so far, but little active part in politics. He served one term of two years upon the school board of Victoria city school district, being elected to the position by a sweeping majority. Although his first impressions in political ethics were formed in the William Lyon McKenzie school, we believe him to be anything but a "party" man, having lived too long and thought too deeply to believe that either or any political party or faction is the source of all good or all evil, or to be found willing to sacrifice national needs to party greeds. His religious training was received under the auspices of the Presbyterian church, of which church he has long continued to be an active, and we believe consistent member, always taking a leading place in the work of the church and Sabbath school, and having been a familiar figure in the church choir for the past twenty years. At present writing Mr. McMicking is in the prime and vigor of manhood, enjoying robust health, and we predict for him with his mature and thoughtful mind and even habits, a life of further great usefulness to his kindred and the state.

McMillan, James E., (Victoria), was born at the town of Niagara, Ontario, on the 25th of July, 1825. His father James

McMillan, native of Dublin, Ireland, was engaged in the land agency business at Niagara. His parents removed while he was still in his infancy to Toronto, then known as Little York, and there Mr. McMillan was educated at the grammar school conducted by John Spragge. At the age of fourteen years he was indentured to the printing business, serving his five years apprenticeship partly in the office of Charles Fothergale, who was proprietor of a weekly paper called the *Palladium*, and partly in the office of Rogers and Thompson, who published the *Commercial News*. In 1844 he removed to the town of Galt to take charge of the Dumfries *Courier*, which was about to be established. He was foreman in this office during that year, and in 1845 he went to Oshawa, where he conducted the *Christian Luminary*, the organ of the sect called the Christian denomination. He remained there till 1854 when he removed to Bowmanville, and in conjunction with Mr. Alexander Begg established the Bowmanville *Messenger*. In 1858 he disposed of his interest in this journal and purchased the *News*, a journal published in the same town, which he conducted for one year, selling out in July, 1859, to come to British Columbia. After his arrival in Victoria he obtained employment on the *Colonist*, first as a compositor and then as assistant-editor under Hon. Amor DeCosmos. Some ten months later he went to New Westminster to take charge of the *British Columbian*, then edited by Hon. John Robson and in a short time became a partner in the concern. In 1863 he returned to Victoria, having disposed of his interest in the *Columbian* and in conjunction with Mr. D. W. Higgins started the Victoria *Chronicle*, of which Mr. McMillan assumed the editorship. He continued on this paper for a year and sold out to start the *Morning News*, which in the second year of its existence became an evening paper. A year later Mr. McMillan sold his plant to Hon. Amor DeCosmos, who established the *Standard*, Mr. McMillan becoming superintendent of the mechanical department. In 1871 Mr. DeCosmos was elected to the House of Commons and Mr. McMillan became editor of the paper, a position he held till 1875 when he resigned his position. Six months later he was appointed Government assessor and collector and continued to fill this office till 1877, when he established a job printing business. At this he remained till 1884, when he was offered and accepted the position of sheriff of the county of Victoria which then became vacant. He has continued to fill that office since that time. Mr. McMillan was a member of the city council during 1872 and 1873, and filled the position of mayor in 1874. He is a justice of the peace, a member of the Oddfellows' order and an adherent of the Methodist church. In 1850 he married Miss Spragge, eldest daughter of Mr. Jacob Spragge, of Oshawa, Ont.

Nason, Dethiel Blake, M. P. P., (Barkerville), was born in the town of Lemington, Kennebec county, Maine, U. S. A. His father, who was of English origin, married Miss Anna Elwell, a lady who was also of English descent. Mr. Nason was educated in his native town and left home early in life. He came to British Columbia in May, 1858, at which date the capital city was merely a trading station of the Hudson's Bay Company. Directly after his arrival at Victoria, Mr. Nason went to the mines on the Fraser river and delved for gold, but meeting only with ordinary success returned to Victoria in the fall staying there two months. During the winter of 1858-9, Mr. Nason, in company with five others, ascended and explored the Fraser river in an open boat searching for gold, often dragging their boat over long fields of ice (sometimes two or three miles in extent) and rapids of foaming water. An incident which occurred during the above mentioned expedition will give some idea of the generosity and bravery of the mining pioneers of those early days. Mr. Nason and his companions had journeyed up the river with another party of six men who travelled in a large flat bottomed boat,—sharing hardships and dangers, until they reached a point between Boston Bar and Lytton where there is a long succession of foaming falls and rapids. Mr. Nason's boat had already ascended one rapid and Mr. Nason and his crew were assisting from the shore to haul up the other boat by means of a tow-line, when the immense power of the water turned it round and the boat with its occupants was whirled down the deadly current. It seemed as if all who had been in the second boat must meet with certain death, and Mr. Nason and his party saw their boat fill with water and were powerless to hold the tow-line which flew through their hands like a red-hot bar of iron. During this fearful scene Mr. Nason preserved his presence of mind, and calling to some men on the bank to jump into his boat, he cut loose the tow-line and with the other volunteers was whirled down the frightful rapid after the other boat to which two men were clinging desperately. Mr. Nason guided the rescuing boat and followed the other which he saw disappear in one of the awful whirlpools for which the Fraser river is noted. When it came up again one man had disappeared, and the other was so exhausted that but for the timely arrival of the rescue party he would certainly have succumbed in the fearful torrent. With the greatest danger to their own lives, Mr. Nason and his crew succeeded in rescuing both men, one of whom they picked up far away from the boat in a semi-conscious condition, and brought them ashore. The unfortunate men were now in a perfectly destitute condition having lost not only all their mining outfit but their provisions as well. The rough miners, however, made their loss good by contributing each one something from his store, and the rescued men were sent on their way rejoicing. The expedition not being very successful Mr. Nason sold out and went to California, where he remained twenty months. On his return to British Columbia he found his way into the Cariboo mountains where he engaged in mining till 1867. At Barkerville, Mr. Nason, in partnership with a Mr. Meacham, erected a saw mill and until the present time has been engaged in the lumber trade. Since his arrival in the Cariboo region he has spent more than $110.000.00 in prospecting for gold. Over sixteen years Mr. Nason served as Trustee of the Royal Cariboo Hospital and during eight years was a member of the board of school trustees, besides being president of a number of corporated mining companies. In 1885 he became a British subject and three years later was elected a member of the Legislative Assembly at a bye-election. The worthy member for Cariboo is an adherent of the Church of England of which he is a staunch supporter. In 1875 Mr. Nason was married to one of Victoria's fairest and best daughter's and has six children. The residence of Mr. Nason is at Barkerville, a little town situated in the heart of the Cariboo mountains, which, we may venture to say, is one of the richest mining districts in the world. At the present time Mr. Nason is using every effort in the Provincial Parliament to promote railway enterprise in that region, and has every reason to believe that his labors will, at no distant date, be crowned with success. He is universally esteemed and is considered one of the best mining experts in the Province, while as a sawyer he stands at the top of the tree.

HON. C. E. POOLEY.

Nelson, Hon. Hugh, Lieutenant-Governor of British Columbia, (Victoria), is the son of the late Robert Nelson, Esq., of Shire Cottage, Inagheramore, county Antrim, where he was born on May 25th, 1830. He was educated at his native place, and in June of 1858, during the early period of the gold excitement, came to British Columbia. Unlike the majority of those who were attracted to this country at that time Mr. Nelson did not propose making a fortune rapidly in the gold fields with the intention of going elsewhere to enjoy it. He had come to settle in the new country and assist in building up the English Dominions on the shores of the Pacific. He accordingly chose a more permanent and worthy occupation than gold mining. He engaged in commercial pursuits, and in 1866 became a partner in the lumbering firm of Moody, Deitz and Nelson, on Burrard Inlet, where Moodyville now is. He was also engaged in many other enterprises, and his business shrewdness and enterprise was such that he carried through with success all his commercial ventures. He early became a leader in politics, but did not stand for the legislative council till he came forward as one of the principal promoters of confederation with the Dominion. He was a member of the Yale Convention, and was one of the committee in whose hands the resolutions, passed at that convention, were placed to be carried into effect. He was a member of the last Legislative Assembly of the colony of British Columbia, and after confederation he was one of the first representatives of the new province in the Dominion Parliament, having been elected by acclamation for New Westminster district in November, 1871, and again in the general elections of 1872. He continued to occupy this seat till 1879, when he was appointed to the Dominion Senate. In 1882 he withdrew from business entirely. In February, 1887, he was appointed Lieutenant-Governor of British Columbia, which position he now holds. On September 17th, 1885, he married Emily, daughter of the late J. B. Stanton, Esq., of the civil service of Canada. He is a member of the Union Club, Victoria, and is an adherent of the Episcopal Church.

Norris, George, (Nanaimo), son of the late William George Norris, merchant, was born at London, England, on the 20th of April, 1845. Shortly after his birth his parents emigrated to Canada and Mr. Norris was educated at the Model School, Toronto.

In 1863, at the age of eighteen years, he left Ontario for British Columbia, coming by way of Panama. When he arrived at Victoria he obtained a position on the *Chronicle*, a newspaper conducted by Messrs. Higgins & McMillan. The *Chronicle* was finally merged into the *Colonist* and he then secured a position on the *Colonist*. In 1874 he left Victoria and went to Nanaimo where he established his present newspaper the *Free Press*. Until 1888 the *Free Press* was issued semi-weekly but on September 4th of that year it was changed to a daily. Mr. Norris is Liberal-Conservative in politics, but has not apart from his position as editor of his paper taken an active part in public matters. Through the columns of his journal he advocates what is for the best interests of Nanaimo and the welfare of the Province at large. He occupies positions on the boards of several corporations and is regarded as a shrewd business man. He is a member of the Order of Oddfellows, the Ancient Order of United Workmen, and the Fire Brigade. In 1869 he married, Miss Gough, eldest daughter of Mr. Edwin Gough, of Nanaimo.

Nowell, Reuben, (Chilliwhack), was born at Hermon in Penobscot county, Maine, U. S. A., on November 22nd, 1829. Mr. Nowell went to school in his native town and early in life commenced business as a tinsmith and cornice manufacturer. After spending several years at his trade in the east, Mr. Nowell "pulled up stakes" and went to California where he spent several years at the mines. Not being very successful he travelled northward as far as British Columbia, and settled at Chilliwhack. In this Province also he tried his fortune at the mines, but without success. Mr. Nowell, therefore, decided that for the future he would devote all his attention to agriculture, and as the result of his labor possesses one of the finest farms in the Province. For many years Mr. Nowell has served as councillor and school trustee at Chilliwhack.

Oppenheimer, David, (Vancouver), was born in the kingdom, of Bavaria, Germany, in 1834, and educated there. In 1848 in company with his brother Isaac he left home and came to America, settling first in New Orleans, U. S. A. In 1853 the brothers removed to Lafayette, where they engaged in business. After remaining a short time there they came west to the Pacific coast and settled in Sacramento where they resumed business. In 1860 they came to British Columbia and opened a business in Victoria with branch stores at various places in the Province. There warehouse in Yale was destroyed during the big fire there, and shortly afterwards they established their wholesale business at Vancouver at which place they then centered all their interests. Mr. Oppenheimer was interested largely in real estate in Vancouver, having purchased it before the decision to extend the railway to Coal Harbor had been arrived at. Since he settled in Vancouver his name has been connected with that city more intimately than that of any other citizen. He has given up his entire time almost to civic business in his position of chief magistrate, and under his far sighted management and judicious direction the city has grown to its present large proportions on a basis financially sound. In 1887 he was elected alderman for ward No. 5, and during that term acted as chairman of the finance committee. He was elected mayor by acclamation for 1888 and again for 1889 and stood for office for 1890, defeating his opponent with ease. Mayor Oppenheimer is connected with nearly every enterprise which is calculated to advance the interests of the city or the Province at large. He is a member of the Board of Trade and was president of that organization. He is president of the British Columbia Agricultural Association and of the British Columbia Exhibition association. He has done a great deal to advertise the Province by compiling pamphlets, showing the extent and resources of the country and distributing them in Europe and America.

O'Reilly, Hon. Peter, (Victoria), born in Ireland and educated there. Subsequently entered the civil service and was appointed a lieutenant in the revenue police. Came to British Columin in 1858 and in April, 1859, was appointed assistant gold commissioner and stipendiary magistrate, and later in the same year was appointed high sheriff. He sat in the Legislasive Council of British Columbia from 1863 till confederation. In 1864 he was appointed chief gold commissioner, and in 1881 Indian reserve commissioner, which latter office he still holds.

Pemberton, Joseph Despard, (Victoria), was born in Ireland, near Dublin, and educated at Trinity College, Dublin. Studied the profession of civil engineering and served his time with

G. W. Hemans, M. I. C. E., M. R. I. A. Mr. Pemberton was assistant engineer on part of the Great Southern and Western Railway, was employed for some time by Sir John McNeill, L.S.D., F.R.S., M.I.C.E., M.R.I.A.; was also employed on the East Lancashire Railway, and Manchester, Bury and Rosendale Railway Company; was resident engineer on the Dublin and Drogheda Railway; and resident engineer on the Exeter and Crediton Railway. He was for several years professor of engineering at the Royal Agricultural College in Cirencester and left that place in 1851, to come out to Victoria as Surveyor-General of British Columbia, under the Hudson's Bay Company. In 1850 he was awarded a medal by the late Prince Consort for his design for the Crystal Palace. He was elected to the first Legislative Assembly of Vancouver Island, and from 1863 to 1866 sat in the Executive Council. In 1858 he laid out the townsite of Derby the proposed capital of the colony of British Columbia. On January 1st, 1860, he married Miss Theresa Jane Despard Grantoff. Mr. Pemberton is a strong Conservative and an adherent of the Church of England.

Phillips, Alexander Aaron. (Victoria) was born in London, England, April 19th, 1818, and received his early education there. When he was eleven years of age his father removed to Australia, taking him with him. The family settled in Sydney, New South Wales, and Mr. Phillips lived there till 1849, when, hearing of the discovery of gold in California, he left for the Pacific coast of North America in a fore and aft schooner in company with eleven other passengers. He spent some time mining in various parts of the state, and then returned to San Francisco, making the trip from Humboldt Bay to the Golden City, a distance of 375 miles, in an open whaling boat. He reached 'Frisco the day the first victim of the Vigilance Committee met his merited fate. In 'Frisco he embarked in the bakery business and manufacture of soda water. He subsequently sold out his bakery business and started a grocery business. In April, 1858, he came to British Columbia on the steamer Panama, settled in Victoria and started a business on Yates street. Towards the end of 1858 he established the soda water manufactory he now conducts, in partnership with his son, Phillip Aaron Phillips. Mr. Phillips has been solicited, but has refused to stand for the office of alderman for Victoria. He is a member of the Oddfellows' order and Masonic fraternity, and was instrumental in establishing the first Oddfellows' lodge in Victoria. He is a member of St. George's Society and the British Columbia Benevolent Association. He married Miss Rebecca Phillips when living in San Francisco.

Pimbury, Edwin. (Nanaimo), son of the late Samuel Cosburn Pimbury, was born at Hyde, near Minchinhampton, Gloucestershire, England, in 1834. Educated at Minchinhampton, and at the age of fifteen years left school and was apprenticed to the drug business serving his apprenticeship with John Walker, of Tilbury. After the required five years had been finished he entered into negotiations for the purchase of a business, but not coming to terms he determined to go abroad. He accordingly left England and in the autumn of 1855 he landed at Portland, Maine. From there he went to Wisconsin and for a time was in the drug business in Portage city. In 1856 the great financial crash came and business flattened out. Mr. Pimbury remained during that winter in Wisconsin and in the following spring he went to California with the intention of going into vine culture. He found on his arrival that the country which had been represented to him as a paradise, was an arid waste. He was not therefore encouraged to attempt this business. He was attracted by the gold mining in Arizona and with his brother, who is now farming in Cowichan district, he went to the Colorado river, where he remained for some time searching without much success for the precious metal. From there he went to the Pino Alta Mines, situated east of Tuscon, but he met with no better fortune there. He then heard of the immense riches of Cariboo and at once left, in company with his brother, for British Columbia. On arriving in this country, however, he found matters different from what he had been led to expect. He found that not only were the mines difficult of access but they were very expensive to work. He went up the country some distance but meeting a large number of disappointed men who were returning he went back to Victoria, where in 1863 he met two of his brothers. The four brothers went farming at Cedar Hill, near Victoria, where they remained for about twelve months. At the end of this time Mr. Pimbury took a position in Mr. Langley's drug business in Victoria, while his three brothers purchased a farm in Cowichan. Mr.

Pimbury remained for eleven years with Mr. Langley, and then left to join his brothers in the management of their farm. He was elected at this time as representative of Cowichan in the local Legislature and was again elected in 1878. In the meantime he had established a drug, book and stationery business in Nanaimo, and as his private affairs demanded all his time he refused to stand for the Legislature in 1882. His business steadily increased and before long he put up the handsome new structure which he at present occupies. He has recently taken a partner into his business in the person of Mr. Earnest McGregor Van Houton. Mr. Pimbury is interested in many of the enterprises of Nanaimo and is a director of the Water Works Company. He is a Justice of the Peace for the Province, a member of the Ancient Order of Foresters and an Episcopalian in religion. In Dominion politics he is a Liberal-Conservative.

Prior, Edward Gawler, M. P., (Victoria), second son of Rev. Henry Prior, rector of Dallowgill, near Ripon, Yorkshire, England, was born at Dallowgill on May 21st, 1853 and educated at Leeds Grammar School, and subsequently studied the profession he afterwards followed, that of mining engineer, with J. Tolson Whyte, C. E., at Wakefield. He practised his profession in England till 1873, when he left to come to British Columbia. He arrived at Victoria on December 12th, 1873, and first settled in Nanaimo, where he was appointed assistant manager of the Vancouver Coal Mining & Land Co., Ld. He occupied this position till August, 1878, when he resigned and was appointed Government Inspector of Mines for the Province of British Columbia. He continued in this office till May, 1880, when he resigned and bought in with Alfred Fellows, iron and hardware merchant, Victoria. In 1883 he bought out Mr. Fellow's interest, and has since followed this business. In the general election of 1886 he was returned at the head of the poll to represent Victoria city in the Provincial Legislature. He occupied this seat till January 16th, 1888, when a large requisition was presented to him asking him to resign and stand for the House of Commons in place of Mr. N. Shakespeare. He consented and was elected by acclamation. He has since continued to represent Victoria city in the Federal Parliament. Mr. Prior is a member of St. George's Society and the Masonic fraternity. In 1876 he was lieutenant in

E. G. PRIOR.

the Rifle Co. at Nanaimo; was captain of No. 4 Battery (at Victoria), British Columbia Garrison Artillery, in 1884; was major in 1886, and in 1888 was promoted lieut.-colonel, which rank he still holds. In 1889 he was appointed extra aide-de-camp to His Excellency, the Governor-General, Lord Stanley of Preston, and still holds that rank. In 1890 he went to England in charge of the Canadian Wimbledon team. Mr. Prior is a life member of the North of England Institute of Mining and Mechanical Engineers; he is president of the Liberal-Conservative Association of British Columbia, and is connected with many mining, railroad and other companies. On January 30th, 1875, he married Lizette, youngest daughter of the late John Work, of Hillside, and has three chilren. Mr. Prior is a member of the Episcopal Church.

Rand, Charles David, (Vancouver), son of Edwin and Maggie Rand, was born on August 26th, 1858, at Canning, Nova Scotia. He was educated at Acadia college, Wolfville, N. S., and graduated in arts on June 5th, 1879. Immediately after graduating he removed to British Columbia, arriving in Victoria on September 14th, 1879. For some time after his arrival he followed the occupation of school teacher, five months on Salt Spring Island, one year in Victoria and one year in New Westminster. In 1882 he started a real estate business, and has been engaged at it since that time. He was one of those who had shrewdness to foresee the future of Vancouver and with energy and promptness he took the tide at its flood, and his career has since been one of uninterrupted success. His name is intimately connected with the progress of the Terminal city of which he has, since it came into existence, been one of the most enterprising citizens. His business connections are the most far reaching of any in British Columbia and through his efforts the resources of the Province have been brought before the capitalists of Europe, and English capital has been brought into the country to assist in developing it. On November 15th, 1888, he married Miss Clute, daughter of Mr. J. S. Clute, collector of customs, at New Westminster. In religion Mr. Rand is a member of the Presbyterian church.

Redfern, Charles Edward. (Victoria), was born on the 23rd of October, 1839, in London, England, where his father, Charles Edward Redfern, had a large business as a watch and chronometer maker. Mr. Redfern was educated at Brewer's School, London, and then served an apprenticeship of seven years in his father's establishment to the business of watch and chronometer making. On June 9th, 1862, he left England on the steamer Tynemont for British Columbia, via Cape Horn, and arrived at Victoria on the 17th of September. Shortly after his arrival he went into the jewellery business in Victoria and has continued at it since that time with unvarying success. In 1864 he paid a visit to the Leach river mines. In 1875 he purchased the business of Mr. J. L. Jungermann which had been established in 1858. In 1877 and 1878 he was a member of the City Council as representative for James' Bay ward, and in 1883 he was elected to the position of Mayor of the city. He has never been a candidate for political honors but has taken an interest both in Provincial and Dominion matters. In Provincial politics he is a supporter of the Robson Government and in those of the Dominion he is an Independent. He is a member of the British Columbia Pioneer Society of which he was president in 1886. He has been a member of the St. George's Society since its inception and at present time occupies the position of president. In religion Mr. Redfern is an Episcopalian and an attendant of St. John's Church. He was married in 1877 to Eliza Arden Robinson, daughter of Rev. W. A. Robinson, a native of Ireland and at the present time resident in the Orange Free State, South Africa.

Redgrave, Stephen. (Donald), was born at the small town of Crick, near Rugby, in Northamptonshire, England, and is the son of Thomas Redgrave, esq., of the same place. His father's family, the Redgraves of Crick, rank amongst the oldest and most respected country gentry in the county, having lived in the same place for many hundreds of years. Mr. Redgrave being the youngest of ten sons, his parents educated him at home, employing private tutors for that purpose, among whom may be mentioned the late celebrated Drs. Arnold and Tait. At the completion of his education, Mr. Redgrave studied law in Birmingham. In 1849, Mr. Redgrave was united in marriage to Martha Susan, eldest daughter of Benjamin Lincoln, esq., of Hendon, Middlesex, and of the firm of Lincoln & Lincoln, hatters, Sackville street, London, England, and niece of Robert Cocks, of New Bond street, printer and publisher to H. M. the Queen and the Prince of Wales, etc. In 1852, Mr. Redgrave renounced the study of law and left England for Australia. Like many others Mr. Redgrave tried his luck at the mines but not being very successful he managed to procure an appointment in the government service as a cadet in the "City Mounted Cadets" in Melbourne. In 1859 Mr. Redgrave resigned his position on the force and sailed for Cape Town, where he formed a company whose object was to open up trade between Cape Colony and the interior of the Dark Continent, but, owing to sickness in his family, he was obliged to leave Africa for England and arrived in London during the same year. After a short stay in the "old country" Mr. Redgrave left with his family for Canada, arriving in Quebec in the fall of 1859, whence he proceeded to Kingston staying some time there as guest of Sir Henry Smith. A new police force being formed at that time for the City of Toronto, Mr. Redgrave received a position on it, which however, he soon resigned, and formed an expedition to travel overland to the British Columbia gold fields. Leaving Toronto on April 24th, 1862, the different parties met at old "Fort Garry," now the populous City of Winnipeg. After fitting out for the journey, the whole expedition consisting of about three hundred persons—all told—travelled over the vast plains to Fort Edmonton, and thence to Yellow Head Pass, at which place they separated into two parties, the one travelling down the Fraser in boats, while the other struck out overland till they reached the Thompson river at Kamloops,—the weary marches and immense difficulties having been overcome in six months. Mr. Redgrave spent the winter in Victoria and early in 1863 travelled back via Panama to Toronto on private business, at the completion of which he returned to the mines in Cariboo, working all the summer on Lightning creek. Not meeting with much success Mr. Redgrave abandoned his claim and left Cariboo for Victoria, whence he went to San Francisco where he spent the winter. In 1864, Mr. Redgrave returned again to Cariboo where he was appointed Provincial constable, which position he afterwards resigned and entered the service of the Western Union Telegraph Co. The work of that company being abandoned in 1866, he, in connection with his brother (John Redgrave, Esq., solicitor of Birmingham, England,) purchased estates in Virginia, but the climate proving unhealthy Mr. Redgrave returned with his family to British

(19)

Columbia in 1875. At the commencement of the construction of the Canadian Pacific Railway in British Columbia, Mr. Redgrave was Mr. Onderdonk's commissary until 1884 when he received his present appointment of Registrar and Sheriff of the County Court of East Kootenay. Mr. Redgrave is also Mining Recorder and Stipendiary Magistrate for the East Kootenay District, resident at Donald. Mr. Redgrave was one of the first in the East Kootenay to interest himself in minerals and has materially assisted in their development. In Mr. Redgrave the Government has a competent and excellent official, and the public a strict and reliable officer.

Reece, Jonathan. (Chilliwhack), was born May 1st, 1831, in the county of Oxford, Ontario. His father, Henry Reece, (a native of Germany), and his mother, (nee Elizabeth Kipp of Pennsylvania, U. S. A.) were both United Empire Loyalists. Mr. Reece was educated in Burford school and in the winter of 1854 journeyed to California were he mined three years. On 15th of April, 1858, Mr. Reece arrived in Victoria and spent his first year in British Columbia in mining on the Fraser river, but met with little success. From 1859 to 1870, Mr. Reece carried on an extensive and remunerative stock dealing trade in the Yale district at which latter date he settled at Chilliwhack on a farm preempted by him in 1859 and on which he now resides. At the time when Mr. Reece first landed at Victoria, in the spring of 1858, there were only three small houses (not counting the Hudson's Bay Company's stores) where the large City of Victoria now stands, although about 5,000 white people were camped around the Hudson's Bay Companys fort. Fresh water could only be obtained on payment of 10c. per bucket and Mr. Reece had to pay the Hudson's Bay Company $15 for the privilege of digging a well at the head of James Bay. After remaining three weeks at Victoria, Mr. Reece bought a large canoe (for which he paid $200 in gold) which he loaded with six tons of provisions and together with five others started for the gold fields of the Fraser. At the mouth of the river they were hailed by the British gunboat and were not allowed to proceed till they had paid their license—which Mr. Reece still possesses. There were no signs of civilization to be seen until they reached Fort Langley,—not a branch being cut where New Westminster City now stands. At Fort Langley many miners' tents were to be seen, and also at Hope. When they arrived at Yale the news reached them that an Indian rebellion had broken out above the Fraser canon, and as they journeyed along they picked up the dead bodies of no less than seventeen white men, some of which had arrows sticking into them, whilst many others were headless. The news of the rebellion reaching the Government, troops were sent up and a treaty was made with the Indians, but as the latter broke the treaty four days afterwards the miners settled the matter themselves by killing every red man they came across. Mr. Reece is an adherent of the Methodist Church, and in 1866 married, Lucinda, daughter of Edwin Lewis, of East Oxford, Ontario. He is one of British Columbia's earliest pioneers and has an intimate knowledge of the Province.

Reid, John, (New Westminster), was born at Carrick-Fergus, county Antrim, Ireland, on March 28th, 1852, where his father, Ezekiel Reid, was engaged in farming. Mr. Reid was educated in his native town, and on leaving school assisted his father on his farm until he was twenty-one years of age. In 1873 he left Ireland and sailed for Quebec, and on his arrival in Canada settled at Ottawa, where he at once commenced learning the iron-founding business. While he was at Ottawa he was employed in the construction of the city water works and also in that of the Parliament Buildings. In 1877 he left Ottawa and travelled direct to Victoria, British Columbia, where he only remained one month. On leaving Victoria he settled at New Westminster, where he at once got employment with Mr. W. R. Lewis, who at that time was the proprietor of the business Mr. Reid now owns. After working two years as a journeyman and seven years as foreman, he bought out Mr. Lewis and taking Mr. Curry as a partner continued the business himself. Since that time he has greatly increased the business and has transformed it from a simple blacksmith's shop and carriage factory to an iron foundry. Since coming to British Columbia, Mr. Reid has taken a great interest in Dominion, Provincial and Municipal politics, and is a supporter of the present Government. In 1887 he was elected alderman for St. Andrew's ward. In 1888 he was again elected, but owing to a slight informality the election was declared void, and on his again presenting himself for election was defeated owing to his firm stand on the

Sunday Closing By-law. In 1889 he was elected alderman under the new charter. While in the City Council he was chairman of the fire and light committee. On April 4th, 1883, he married Jessie, daughter of Adam Irving, Esq., of Maple Ridge. He is a member of the Rifle Corps and the Knights of Pythias, and an adherent of the Methodist Church.

Renier, Peter Sidney, (Kamloops), was born in Quebec, on January 29th, 1861. His father, the late Mr. Peter Renier, a native of the Island of Jersey, was for many years military tailor to the garrison of the Citadel of Quebec. His uncle, the late Mr. Charles Leon Renier, edited "*Courten's Modern Encyclopedia*" and in 1870 was created a Commander of the Legion of Honor. Mr. Renier was educated for the merchant tailoring business at Watford, Ontario, and in 1885 came to British Columbia and settled at Port Moody where he worked at his trade one year. When the Canadian Pacific Railway decided to make Vancouver their western terminus, Mr. Renier removed to Kamloops. He soon managed to secure a thriving business in the then young and growing city, and at the present time occupies a prominent position in that community, in which he has a large and ever increasing patronage. On April 16th, 1889, Mr. Renier married Miss Lilian Alexina Tuff. He is a Presbyterian and a member of the Ancient Order of Foresters.

Richards, Francis Gilbert, Jr., (Victoria), was born at Dodgeville, Iowa county, Wisconsin, U. S. A., October 8th, 1855, and is the son of Francis Gilbert Richards, esq., of Victoria British Columbia. In 1862 his parents moved to New Westminster where they lived seven years and in which city he was educated at Brother College. In 1871 Mr. Richards went to Victoria and studied at the Collegiate College until September, 1871, when he entered the Provincial Government service as assistant draughtsman. Mr. Richards served in that capacity till 1878 when he was promoted to the position of chief draughtsman. In 1886 Mr. Richards resigned his position in the Government service for the purpose of entering into business, and opened the Clarence hotel as a first-class establishment. In 1888 Mr. Richards sold out and entered into the real estate and insurance business, and at

E. S. SCOULLAR.

the present time is one of Victoria's best known and most reliable estate agents. Mr. Richards belongs to the Ancient Order of Foresters and in 1876 was elected secretary of the district. Mr. Richards is also a member of the Ancient Order of United Workmen, a lodge of which he formed at Victoria, filling the office of treasurer for two years, when he was elected Master Workman. In 1889 Mr. Richards was elected representative to the Grand Lodge which met at Seattle July, 1889, and was appointed District Deputy Grand Master for Victoria. At present Mr. Richards holds the position of Grand Guide to the Grand Lodge. Mr. Richards is also a member of the Independant Order of Oddfellows. In Dominion politics Mr. Richards is a supporter of the present Government and in Provincial and Municipal politics, a supporter of any measures which tend towards the development of the Province and improvement of the capital city. On May 31st, 1879, Mr. Richards married Elizabeth, daughter of Thomas Davey, esq., a native of Cornwall, England, who for several years filled the position of city clerk of Dodgeville, Iowa county, Wisconsin,—his birth place. Mr. Richards is largely interested in many public and private enterprises and is looked upon as one of Victoria's most trustworthy and energetic citizens.

Richards, Hon. Albert Norton, (Victoria), son of the late Stephen Richards, of Brockville, Ont., was born on December 8th, 1822, at Brockville, and educated at the district school, Brockville. He then studied law and was called to the bar of Ontario in 1849. He practised his profession at Brockville. He was created a Q. C. in 1863 and paid a visit to British Columbia in 1868. When the Dominion Government, in the autumn of 1869, appointed the Hon. Wm. McDougall lieutenant-governor, to organize a new government in the Northwest Territories at Fort Garry (now Winnipeg), Mr. Richards accompanied him as attorney-general in that provisional government, but as Mr. McDougall was prevented by Riel and his armed force of French half-breeds from proceeding farther than the international boundary line at Pembina, the whole party was obliged to return to Ottawa. On May 15th, 1871, Mr. Richards was called to the bar of British Columbia, and in 1875 removed to Victoria to reside. He was admitted as an attorney of British Columbia on July 23, 1875, and practised for one year. In 1876 he was appointed lieutenant-governor of British Columbia, and continued in this office till 1881. For the three years following 1881 he was absent from the Province, but returned in the fall of 1884 and resumed practice as a barrister. On March 1st, 1888, he was appointed police magistrate for the city of Victoria, which office he now occupies. He still continues to practice as a barrister and is considered the best authority in the Province on questions of constitutional law. Mr. Richards was elected twice to the House of Commons as representative for South Leeds, Ontario. He has been twice married; in Brockville on October 13th, 1849, to Miss Francis Chaffey, fourth daughter of Benjamin Chaffey, of Somersetshire, England, who died in April, 1853; and in Pittsburg, Penn., on August 12th, 1854, to Miss Ellen Chaffey Chislett, second daughter of John Chislett, formerly of Somersetshire and latterly of Pittsburg. Mr. Richards is an adherent of the Presbyterian church.

Robins, Samuel Matthew, (Nanaimo), superintendent of the Vancouver Coal Mining Company's Works, was born in Cornwall, England, on the 7th of July, 1834, and educated partly in Cornwall and partly at Plymouth, Devonshire. His father was engaged in business in connection with a number of large mining and manufacturing enterprises and Mr. Robins was for a time associated with him. Prior to the formation of the Vancouver Coal Company he went to London and while there in 1868 was appointed secretary to this company. In 1884 he undertook the charge of the company's business and came to British Columbia. Mr. Robins on arriving at Nanaimo found the Company's business in a poor condition owing to incompetent management. He at once set to work to place the mines on a paying basis and and succeeded not only in doing this but in making them extremely profitable. The work of development has gone on steadily since he took charge and new seams have been opened. During the past five years the yield of coal has been in excess of that of the previous twenty-three years. In 1863 Mr. Robins married Miss Maria Slape, daughter of C. Slape, Esq., of London England, for many years underwriter of Lloyds.

Robson, Hon. John, M. P. P., (Victoria), Premier of the Province of British Columbia, Provincial Secretary, Minister of

Mines and Minister of Education, was born on the 14th of March, 1824, at Perth, Ontario, of Scotch parents, who emigrated to Canada in the early part of the present century. He was educated at his native place and in April, 1854, married Susan, daughter of the late Captain Longworth, of Goderich,. He was engaged in commercial pursuits till 1859, when, in consequence of the discovery of large deposits of gold on the Fraser river, he came to British Columbia. After visiting the mining bars along the river he settled at New Westminster, and early in 1861 established in that city the *British Columbian*, the pioneer newspaper on the Mainland. This journal, which was the leading newspaper of the colony, Mr. Robson edited, and through its columns he fought the battle for constitutional government, for which he was hounded, waylaid, and unmercifully beaten and finally imprisoned by the minions of the administration. Persecution, however, failed to break his spirit or change his tone. He sat in the Council of New Westminster during 1864-5, and during the last year occupied the position of president of that body. In 1867 he was elected to represent the district of New Westminster in the Legislative Council of British Columbia, the Mainland and Vancouver's Island having by that time become one colony. He continued to represent this constituency during four sessions till 1870, in the last of which the terms of confederation with the Dominion of Canada were formulated and adopted by the Legislature. Mr. Robson was one of the most active workers for confederation, both within and without the walls of Parliament, and recorded his protest when the executive council attempted to burk the scheme of union. He was a member of the Yale convention and one of the committee appointed to carry into effect the resolutions adopted at that convention. He removed to Victoria in 1869 and was editor of the *Colonist* for nearly six years. He was elected to represent Nanaimo in the Provincial Legislature in 1871, and sat for that constituency till the spring of 1875, when he accepted the federal appointment of paymaster and commissary of the Canadian Pacific Railway surveys west of the Rocky Mountains, which position he continued to hold until it was abolished in 1879. Mr. Robson returned to New Westminster in 1879 and resumed publication of the *British Columbian*, and at the general election of 1882 was elected to represent the district of New Westminster in the Provincial Legislature. Upon the defeat of the

Beaven administration, on the 26th of January, 1883, and the formation of the Smithe administration, he was appointed Provincial Secretary and Minister of Mines and Minister of Finance and Agriculture. Upon the death of Premier Smithe in March, 1887, Mr. Robson took a similar position in the Davie cabinet, and upon the death of Mr. Davie in 1889 he was called upon to form the cabinet of which he is now Premier. In the general election of 1886 he was re-elected for New Westminster district, and again in 1890. Mr. Robson is president of the Y. M. C. A., Victoria, and is a prominent and uncompromising advocate of temperance and moral reform. He is a justice of the peace for the Province and holds a lieutenant's commission in the militia. He is a vigorous and logical writer and a powerful speaker. His views on all public questions are liberal, progressive and statesmanlike, and his name stands prominently associated with the history of British Columbia. His residence is at Birdcage Walk, James Bay, Victoria.

Ross, A. W., M. P., (Vancouver), was born March 25, 1846, at Nairn, county of Middlesex, Ontario. Educated at Nairn village school, Wardsville Grammar School, Toronto Normal School, University College, and graduated as B.A. at Toronto University. He was inspector of public schools for the county of Glengarry, Ontario, from September, 1871, until November, 1874, when he resigned to study law in Toronto. He settled in Winnipeg, Manitoba, in June, 1877, was called to the bar in February, 1878, and entered into partnership with his brother, the late W. H. Ross, under the firm of Ross & Ross, afterwards Ross, Ross & Kilam, later Ross, Kilam & Haggart. The firm were solicitors for two chartered banks and four loan companies, besides which they soon took the lead in the real estate business of the Province. Mr. Ross was elected a bencher of the newly formed Law Society of Manitoba, in 1880; and after the death of his brother, became the largest operator and owner of real estate in the Northwest, and soon acquired the reputation of being the most successful operator in Canada, his name extending to England, as well as over this continent. As he was considered to be thoroughly posted, and thus able to anticipate an increase in values, his every movement was watched by other real estate men and speculators. Inside of one year during the boom in Winnipeg in 1881-2, he cleared over $500,000, which was all reinvested, while during six months of this period his monthly cash deposits in the bank from receipts of sales made by him ran from $200,000 to 490,000, and everything he touched was a success until the "boom" burst in April, 1882, when he lost everything through his unbounded faith in the natural resources of the Northwest, and its rapid development. In 1881, when the C.P.R. highway was built with remarkable energy, there was a rush of capital and enterprise to Winnipeg, and it was not the visionary ones alone who went thither, but sober, experienced and thoughtful men. Through a variety of causes the rush came to a standstill, banks and monetary institutions, which had hitherto encouraged the wildest of speculation, suddenly tightened and called in their loans, then followed almost a panic with the strewn wrecks of the "boom." All suffered, the oldest and wisest as well as the rest being covered in the wreck; and had the "boom" not burst when it did, Mr. Ross' success would have been pointed out as one of the most marvellous on the continent; but after all the experience and lesson have their value, and Mr. Ross has already to a great extent, retrieved the past. In Manitoba he was connected with nearly every project that had for its object the development of the country, and was chosen to represent the Great Northwest in the "Howland Syndicate" to construct the Canadian Pacific Railroad. In 1884 he came to British Columbia to commence life again, having some interest at Port Moody, the then terminus of the C. P. R. On a visit to this place as well as to the present site of Vancouver he immediately decided the latter only could be the place for the permanent terminus of the great transcontinental railway; and at once declared it was one of the finest natural town sites in the world, which is every day becoming more patent through the energy and enterprise of its citizens. He then assisted very materially in having the change of terminus made to its present site; and has unbounded faith in the great future of Vancouver. He entered politics in 1878, being elected to represent Springfield in the Legislative Assembly of Manitoba, and on a general election being held in 1879 was re-elected, and had only three votes polled against him. He resigned in 1882 to contest Lisgar for the House of Commons and was elected, defeating Dr. Schultz, at present Lieutenant-Governor of Manitoba, a very strong man, and the oldest member for the county. At the last general election, although residing in British Columbia for three years, his constituents returned him by acclamation.

During his term in Parliament Mr. Ross has made two speeches, especially dealing with the future of the great Northwest, which at once gave him a strong position in the House. These speeches were printed by the Government and the Canadian Pacific Railway Co., and scattered broad cast as immigration literature. He is a thorough Canadian in its broadest sense, as distinguished from parochial or provincial; and from an intimate knowledge of the country, considers the hope of the future greatness of Canada rests upon the development of the unlimited natural resources of the region from Lake Superior to the Pacific Ocean. His principal traits of character are geniality, indomitable will, energy and perseverance.

Rudge, George. (Victoria), was born on the 7th of April, at St. Stephen's, New Brunswick, where his father, William Rudge, was engaged in the marble business. Mr. Rudge was educated at his native place and at the age of fifteen years went to work in his fathers business. In 1875 he left New Brunswick and went to San Francisco. After a brief stay there he came to British Columbia and resided for a time in New Westminster. He then went to Seattle where he formed a partnership with Mr. J. Carkeek, and carried on a marble business for three years, when their establishment was burned and their property entirely destroyed. He returned to British Columbia and settled in Victoria, where he established the business he at present conducts and which is now the largest of its kind in Victoria. He has also a branch establishment in Nanaimo, and until recently had one in New Westminster. Mr. Rudge is a member of the Ancient Order of United Workmen.

Scott, Robert Henderson, (North Field), was born on the 27th of April, 1834, in Lanarkshire, Scotland, where his father was engaged in mining. He was educated at the parish school and at an early age began work in the mines. He rose rapidly after he had obtained a thorough knowledge of the work and was engaged for some years prior to leaving Scotland, in contracting and looking after mines in Lanarkshire and Linlithgowshire. He left Scotland in February, 1865, and went to Jackson county, state of Illinois, U. S. A., where he took charge of several large mines. He remained there till 1875, when he came to the Pacific coast. He was engaged in the mines on Puget Sound for a short period. He removed to

Nanaimo in 1876 and was engaged for two years with the Vancouver company. He then took a position at Wellington in Mr. Dunsmuir's mine and continued here for ten years. He was in the mine when the explosion occurred at Wellington in 1876, but was uninjured and rendered effectual assistance in the work of rescue and repair. He then took charge of the mine. He also aided the Vancouver company when the explosion occurred id their mine. He resigned his position last year with the intention of returning to Scotland, but the shaft at North Field was opened and tenders for the work of development were called for. Mr. Scott tendered and was successful. He accordingly took charge and has since that time been pursuing the work vigorously. He is a member of the Oddfellows' society, the Knights of Pythias, the Encampment and the Good Templars. In July, 1855, Mr. Scott married Miss Mary Rowan, daughter of Wm. Rowan, of Lanarkshire.

Sears, Joseph. (Victoria), was born on the 8th of May, 1852, at Rio Janiero, Brazil, whither his parents had gone on a visit. His father was a resident of Boston, Massachusetts, where he was engaged in the plumbing business. In 1858 his father removed to San Francisco, whither Mr. Sears and his mother went to join him in the following year. They found on their arrival that his father had died and his mother was forced to earn a living for herself and child. After a year's residence in San Francisco Mr. Sears removed with his mother to Astoria, then to Salem and finally in 1862 to Victoria, where they remained for three years. During these five years he had been kept constantly at school, and while in Victoria he attended Mr. Jessop's school on Fort street. In 1865 he went to Port Townsend with his mother, but after a year's residence there they returned to Victoria. In 1867 Mr. Sears decided to learn the bakery business, but gave it up after a short time and went at the painting business. He served a four years' apprenticeship with the firm of Lettice and Mitchell, and then went to Portland, Oregon, for a year where he worked at his trade. He returned to Victoria, and in 1876 he opened a business for himself on Government street. Three years later he formed a partnership with Robert Lettice, one of his former employers, the firm of Lettice and Mitchell, having by that time been dissolved. This partnership continued for five years. In 1885 Mr. Sears drew out of the firm and established his present business, which is a large and profitable one. For a year his premises were near Government street on Yates street. He then leased the land on which he is now situated and erected his large shop. Mr. Sears was a member of the volunteer fire department and acted as foreman of the company for several years. He was also one of the trustees when the department was dissolved, and assisted in the management and distribution of the funds. He is an enthusiastic Oddfellow, having joined the order when twenty-two years of age. He has filled every office in the subordinate lodge and encampment, and at the present time fills the office of D. D. G. P., of Victoria jurisdiction,

Shakespeare, Noah. (Victoria), was born at Brierley Hill Staffordshire, England, on the 26th of January, 1839. His family trace their descent from the Shakespeares of Warwickshire, of whom the great poet was a member. After receiving what instruction was obtainable at the public school of his native place, Mr. Shakespeare, being of an independent and ambitious turn of mind, set about making his own way in the world. The lessons which he thus early gained from experience, served him better in climbing the path to distinction than any long scholastic course would have done. He did not, however, as is too often the case with lads leaving school, especially at an early age, abandon his books, but on the contrary after his hours of daily toil he employed his evenings in study. In September, 1862, having become impressed, by favorable reports, of British Columbia as a country in which a young man might make fame and fortune, Mr. Shakespeare took passage for Victoria, which place he reached, after sailing round Cape Horn, on the 10th of January, 1864. As his purse was scantily lined he did not hesitate to accept the first position which offered and which was in the Vancouver collieries. Here he remained for several years performing efficiently and faithfully the work intrusted to him to do. He then removed to Victoria, and shortly afterwards became recognized by the community as a rising man. The workingmen looked to him as their exponent and champion in all matters which affected them, while the citizens generally regarded him as one having at heart the best interest of the community at large. The first public office he accepted was that of councillor and this position he retained for four years. Shortly after arriving in

Victoria the evil which was being occasioned to the Province and which was then more immediately felt by the working man, through the immigration of large numbers of Chinese, impressed itself strongly on Mr. Shakespeare's mind, and he at once began to cast about for some means of mitigating or removing what threatened, at no distant date, to render British Columbia the dumping ground for the worst class of Asiatics. He pointed out to the citizens the dangers which were so apparent to himself, and the result was a general agitation in favor of preventing the entry of Chinese into the country. In 1876, Mr. Shakespeare's name headed a petition signed by fifteen hundred workingmen which was presented to the Dominion Parliament, praying that an act similar to the Australian act, restricting the immigration of Chinese be passed. The petition was presented by Hon. Amor De Cosmos, who at that time represented Victoria in the Federal House. No immediate steps were taken by Parliament in answer to this petition but the agitation was kept up and an Anti-Chinese society formed for that purpose, of which Mr. Shakespeare was elected president in 1879. In 1882 he was elected to the position of chief magistrate of the city by a large majority of the voters and discharged the important duties which this office entailed so much to the general satisfaction that he was, at the expiration of his term, presented with an illuminated address. It was during his incumbency of the Mayoralty that Governor-General Lord Lorne and Princess Louise paid their visit to the Pacific Coast and upon Mr. Shakespeare devolved the duty of entertaining the distinguished guests. In the general election of 1882 he was chosen in conjunction with Mr. E. Crowe Baker to represent Victoria in the Federal Parliament. He was now able to urge in person for restrictive legislation in regard to Chinese immigration and with the assistance of his colleague he succeeded in the session of 1884 in having the present act passed. In 1882 Mr. Shakespeare was elected president of the Mechanics' Institute and in 1885, president of the British Columbia Agricultural Association which latter institution he assisted in organizing. In 1883 he took a trip to England and while there he gave several lectures at his native place and neighboring towns which influenced a large number of people to emigrate to British Columbia and the Northwest Territories. At the general election of 1887, Mr. Shakespeare was again elected to represent his adopted city in the Dominion House. At the conclusion of the first session of this

Parliament he accepted the position of Postmaster at Victoria and retired from the political arena. Throughout his career in Parliament, Mr. Shakespears worked disinterestedly for the welfare of his Province. He was elected as a supporter of the Macdonald Government and saw no reason to withdraw his allegiance from the Conservative party. In 1886 he accepted the presidency of the British Columbia Mutual Fire Insurance Company, which he was instrumental in organizing. Throughout his career Mr. Shakespeare has been a consistent temperance man and has passed through all the offices in the Good Templars' organization. In 1877 he was elected Grand Worthy Chief of the Grand Lodge of Washington Territory and British Columbia, and during 1878 he filled the same position. In 1886 he was elected president of the Young Men's Christian Association of Victoria. In every sense Mr. Shakespeare is a man who has grown up with the country and given his best thought and work to the development of her resources. His career is an example of what may be accomplished by men of sound abilities, who make devotion to duty and unswerving honesty their guides through life. In religion Mr. Shakespeare is an adherent of the Methodist Church. In 1859 he was married to Miss Eliza Jane Pearson and has five children.

Shannon, William. (Vancouver), was born in county Sligo, Ireland, on 19th February, 1839. His father, a native of the North of Ireland, settled in Ontario in 1845, where he engaged in farming. His maternal grandfather, John Lytle, was one of the seventeen young men who welcomed John Wesley to Ireland when he came to introduce Methodism into that country, and subsequently became a preacher under him. Mr. Shannon was educated in the public school of Lindsay, Ontario, and intended to follow agricultural pursuits. In 1862 he visited California and in the following year came to British Columbia, settling at New Westminster. The first years of his life in this Province were spent by him in road contracting in partnership with his brother, Mr. Thomas Shannon. In 1865-6 he mined with varying success at Big Bend, Columbia river, Gold Stream, McUllis, French and Camp creeks and subsequently visited the mining locations in the Cariboo district. He also carried on an extensive packing business and brought the first large freight wagon into Williams' creek. During his long residence in the Province Mr. Shannon has been engaged in all kinds of farming and stock-raising and also in the lumber trade. He has been one of the greatest explorers of the Province, having hunted in it and travelled through it for many years. At present Mr. Shannon, in conjunction with Mr. Charles McLachlan, has a large real estate and insurance business in Vancouver and finds that his knowledge of the Province and his great experience are now bearing good fruit. He helped to form the first rural municipality on the mainland — that of Chilliwhack, but as far as possible has avoided a political life. He married Miss McIndoo, eldest daughter of Wm. McIndoo, esq., a land owner of Victoria county, Ontario. He is a prominent member of the Methodist church.

Shorts, Thomas Dorlan. (Okanagon), was born in the Province of Ontario on June 14th, 1837. His father, Mr. William Shorts, who came of U. E. Loyalist stock, married Miss Ruth Dorlan. Mr. Shorts came to British Columbia in the Fall of 1869, and in 1871 settled in the Peace River District. He spent six months in the Cassiar region where he erected a saw mill, which worked by hydraulic power. He also mined in this Province and in California, meeting with moderate success. In 1882 he removed to Okanagon Lake, where he took up land known as the "Fell Creek Ranch," which he afterwards sold to Mr. Scott Montague, and then commenced carrying freight on the lake. Mr. Shorts first used a row-boat of $2\frac{1}{2}$ tons capacity, and afterwards ran the first steamer which ever ploughed the waters of the Okanagan Lake. Since that time he has been continually adding to his fleet of steamers, and at present is constructing one of over sixty tons capacity and thirty-two horse-power. Mr. Short is a Wesleyan and one of the most enterprising men in the Okanagan district.

Shotbolt, Thomas. (Victoria), was born at Pinchbeck, Lincolnshire, England, in June 1842. He received his elementary education at his native place and then went to Horncastle, Lincolnshire, where he studied the drug business. At the age of twenty years he took his diplomas as a chemist and druggist, and immediately after left for British Columbia, which he reached by way of Panama. He came from Panama to Victoria in the steamer Golden Gate which was lost during her return trip. After spending one month in the employ of Wm. Searly, now of San Francisco, Mr. Shotbolt established the business which he has conducted ever since, and which has increased with Victoria's growth. Mr. Shotbolt is a justice of the peace for the province of British Columbia and is a member of the Masonic order, St. George's society and other friendly societies. In religion he is an adherent of the Episcopal church.

Sinclair, Temple Frederick. (Victoria), was born at Dunbeath, Caithness, Scotland, on February 3rd, 1853. His father, F. A. Sinclair, Esq., was engaged in the fish-curing business. Mr. Sinclair was educated at his native town, and previous to his arrival in British Columbia was engaged in railroad construction in Great Britain. In 1873 Mr. Sinclair came to this Province, and at first settled at Victoria. Mr. Sinclair spent five years in the Cassiar district, during which time he was engaged in mining enterprises, and alse lived one season in the Skagit country. On leaving Cassiar he worked at railroad construction under Mr. Onderdonk and was engaged in tunnel construction. In 1882 he commenced contracting for the construction of parts of the C. P. R., building the road west of Lytton and also on Kamloops lake. Mr. Sinclair also made the entire line on the Shuswap lake, built the Kootenay canal and removed the rocks in Cotton Wood canyon, generally considered the most difficult work on the C. P. R. For more than five years Mr. Sinclair was engaged in improving the bed and banks of the Fraser, and aided materially in making the river better for navigation. At the present time he is engaged in dock construction for Rithet and company at Victoria. Mr. Sinclair is largely interested in the brick yards, salmon fishery and general business at Port Haney and is opening up slate quarries for roofing purposes at Golden on the C. P. R., which he located in 1889, and for which he is importing the best machinery from England and the east. Mr. Sinclair was at one time reeve of the municipality of Maple Ridge. He is a Presbyterian, a member of several Caledonian and friendly societies, and on the 24th May, 1883, married Teresa, eldest daughter of L. D. Loring, Esq., of Lytton.

Smith, Bedford H., M.A., (Nanaimo), son of Daniel Smith, farmer, of New Brunswick, was born at Blissville, Sunderland county, N. B., on June 1st, 1849. By both sides of his house he is descended from United Empire Loyalists. His father's family were in possession of large estates in Connecticut, and the then representative of the house made himself conspicuous by the active part he took on the side of King George. The maternal ancestor, Hartt, was a relative of Endicott, the British Governor of Massachusetts. At the close of the war both families abandoned their estates and transferred themselves to New Brunswick. Mr. Smith was educated at the Baptist Seminary at Fredericton, and subsequently at the University of New Brunswick. He took an art's course at the University and graduated with honors in science. Two years later he took his degree of Master of Arts. After graduating he took charge of a school at Victoria Corners, Carleton county, N. B., where he remained for one year. He then accepted the principalship of Sunbury Grammar School, formerly known as Sheffield Academy. He remained there one year and then, in 1877, came to British Columbia. In this Province he first engaged in the fishing business on Queen Charlotte Islands, and when the company, of which he was a member, amalgamated with the Skidegate Oil Company he became a member of the new company. He was actively engaged at this business for three years, when he severed his connection with the company and removed to Victoria. He then took charge of the school at North Saanich, where he remained for four years, when he was appointed Collector of Customs at Nanaimo, which position he now occupies. Mr. Smith is a member of the Ancient Order of United Workmen, and treasurer of the American Legion of Honor. He was the first president of the Nanaimo Building Society, and is now treasurer of that institution. In July, 1882, Mr. Smith married Annie Brethour, daughter of the late Samuel Brethour, of North Saanich.

Smith, James McBraire, (Victoria), was born at Pownal, P. E. I., in 1838 and came to British Columbia in 1865. Probably few men in British Columbia have a more general knowledge of the Province than Mr. Smith. Although prominent neither in business nor in politics he has been continuously identified with the "ups and downs" of the country during a period of twenty-four years. Like most of our young colonists he cast his lot with the explorers of the gold fields of the interior, and soon after his arrival in the Province proceeded to Cariboo, where he remained seven years.

During the gold excitement in Omineca in 1872 he embarked in mercantile pursuits,—the firm of Smith and Stirling (of which he was a partner) being among the first to establish in the then promising town of Germansen. Surmounting many risks and difficulties, occasioned by the costly means of transport, this enterprising firm established the largest and most complete supply-depot in that region. In the spring of 1873 they had on the portage between Babine Lake and Lake Tatla, about three hundred Indians employed in packing;—the largest train of native packers at any one time engaged in the Province. The Omineca mines not proving as successful a speculation as was anticipated, Mr. Smith returned to Victoria in 1874. Having received in his younger days a good business training, as well as being a first class accountant and correspondent, he readily obtained a position in one of the leading wholesale houses of that city, where he remained five years, during which period he was associated with the Skidegate Oil Works and other enterprises. In 1876 he married the eldest daughter of the late William Bowden, Esq, and in 1869 received the appointment of Government Auditor which he has well and ably filled and which he now occupies. By actual residence in different parts, as well as personal inspection during his journeys in the interior, he has acquired a fund of information of the Province, its resources, requirements and geographical delineations, which is extremely useful and almost indispensable to anyone holding the position he occupies in the Government service. He is an enthusiast regarding the mineral wealth of the country, and, so far as his means allow, is always ready to engage in any of the ventures to develope the hidden treasures in the mountains—it being his firm belief that British Columbia is the richest mineral country on the Pacific slope.

Smith, William John, (Victoria), the third son of Thomas Smith of Kempstone, Bedfordshire, England, was born at Kempstone, on December 26th, 1859. He received his education in his native town, and previous to his arrival in British Columbia was engaged in contracting and in the manufacture of bricks at Orillia, Ont., where he learnt his trade. On February 22nd, 1884, he came to Victoria, and has since been engaged in brick manufacture and contracting. In partnership with Mr. Elford he has erected some

W. B. TOWNSEND.

of the finest blocks in the capital city, and among them the new Presbyterian place of worship—St. Andrew's Church. He is a member of the Masonic and Foresters Orders, and on the 14th of June, 1881, married Mary Duncan, third daughter of Alexander McDonald, Esq. He is an adherent of the Baptist Church. Mr. Smith is a thorough master of his trade, and is one of the best business men in Victoria.

Saunders, Henry, (Victoria), was born January 28th, 1837, in Essex, England. He was educated in his native place and in January, 1862, came to British Columbia. He settled in Victoria and in 1866 managed the business he now owns, for P. Manetta. He subsequently bought out Manetta and entered into a partnership with E. Promin. After two years he purchased the entire business and has since conducted it himself. He is a member of the Pioneer Society of British Columbia.

Sayward, William Parsons, (Victoria), born December 9th, 1818, at Thomastown, Maine, U. S. A., where his father James Sayward, was a shipmaster. Attended Thomastown grammar school till seventeen years of age, when he learned the carpenter trade. In 1838 he went to Florida where he resided for three years and then returned to his native place. He subsequently spent three years in Boston, Mass., and in 1846 again went to Florida and till March, 1849, lived in Key West. In 1849 he removed to California and settled in Sacramento, where he passed two years. In 1851 he removed to San Francisco and engaged in the lumber trade there till June, 1858, when he came to British Columbia and settled at Victoria. He established his lumber business at Victoria shortly after his arrival and has since continued to conduct it. He was married in Victoria to Miss Chambers. He is a member of the Oddfellows' Order and has twice been president of the Pioneer Society.

Seabrook, Roads, (Victoria), was born on May 19th, 1838, in Middlesex county, Ontario, where his father, Joseph Seabrook, was engaged in farming. He was educated at Caradock Academy which institution he attended till he was sixteen years of age, when he left school and assisted his father in the management of his farm.

In 1857 his father died and Mr. Seabrook took charge of the farm and continued to manage it until April, 1862, when the Cariboo gold excitement reached Ontario and drew hundreds of people to British Columbia where they thought to make their fortunes very rapidly. Mr. Seabrook was among the number who came at this time, travelling by way of Panama. He arrived in Victoria in May, 1862, and went direct to the Cariboo mines where he remained during the summer. In the autumn he returned to New Westminster without a cent in his pocket, but with mining experience sufficient to last him a life time. During the winter he was engaged at a number of different occupations and in the spring of 1863 he went back to Ontario for his wife and child whom he had left there. He then returned to British Columbia and until 1869 settled at New Westminster, where for the greater part of the time he was engaged in teaming. He removed to Victoria in 1869 in the employ of Sproat and Co., whose business was on Store street. He subsequently engaged with Welch, Rithet and Company and has continued since that time in their employ. In Mr. Rithet's absence Mr. Seabrook is manager of this extensive business. Mr. Seabrook married Miss L. A. Holloway of Ontario.

Scoullar, Edwin, Sayre. (New Westminster), was born at St. John, New Brunswick, May 7th, 1856. His family which is of Scotch extraction, settled in Canada in its early days and played no unimportant part in the history of the country. His great grandfather, Rev. John Sayre, the first Episcopal minister who preached in Mangerville, Sunbury county, N. B., was one of those old Loyalists who preferred the hardships of life amid what was then the wilds of Canada to abandoning his fealty to the British Crown, after the close of the war of independence. His great-granduncle was Sir John Beverley Robinson, Chief Justice of Canada, and his grandfather William Scoullar, and his uncle Henry Partelear, represented the county of Sunbury in the House of Assembly of New Brunswick in 1845. In 1870 Mr. Scoullar removed with his parents to Windsor, N. S., where he received his education. In 1878 he left home and after visiting many of the leading cities in the United States he arrived in British Columbia on July 1st, 1878. After residing for one year in Victoria he removed to New Westminster and established the store and general hardware business there which he conducted successfully for eleven years. When Vancouver came into existence Mr. Scoullar established a branch business there, the first of the kind in that city. This was prior to the great fire which swept the city out of existence and destroyed his establishment and stock leaving him poorer by $20,000. He immediately started again however, and has now one of the largest stocks in this line in Vancouver. Mr. Scoullar was one of the promoters and is a director of the New Westminster Woollen Mills Co., having taken hold of this enterprise when it was in a languishing condition and about to be removed to Victoria and thus he and the other patrotic citizens who joined with him saved this industry for the Royal City. Together with five others of the Masonic brethern of New Westminster he was the means of erecting the Masonic and Oddfellows' block, by advancing the funds for that purpose. He was one of the promoters of the New Westminster Southern Railroad, has been a director since its inception and was appointed with others to negotiate and carry out the provisions of its charter which was done successfully. Mr. Scoullar is one of the four provincial directors of the New Westminster and Vancouver Short Line. He was elected a member of the city council in January, 1889. At this time the city, working for the first time under its new charter, and not being in a very prosperous condition there was an enormous amount of work to be accomplished to place it in the front rank of the cities of British Columbia. The progress of New Westminster dates from that period and that Mr. Scoullar had a large share in bringing about this happy state of things, the records of the council will prove. He has been gazetted captain of the New Westminster Rifle Company and has always taken a great interest in millitary affairs. He is one of the best shots of the Province, having in one year carried off the Governor-General's medal for the best shot at long range shooting. He has during his residence in New Westminster identified himself with every enterprise of any importance and has taken a deep interest in furthering the best interests of the city. He is senior partner of the firm of A. Turnbull & Co., contractors, who built the Provincial Court House and Central School House in Vancouver and who are now erecting the new Court House at New Westminster. This firm also owns and operates the New Westminster brick yard which has a capacity of 4,000,000 bricks per year. Mr. Scoullar was married,

October 8th, 1883, to Helen McColl, step-daughter of Geo. Turner, esq., C. E. Mr. Scoullar was one of the founders of the New Westminster Board of Trade; he has been a member of the council of that body since its inception, and has been vice-president of the Board.

Seghers, Charles John, born in Ghent, Belgium, December 26th, 1839, died in Alaska, November 28th, 1886. He studied for the priesthood in the ecclesiastical seminary at Ghent, and afterwards in the American College, Lourain; was ordained a priest at Mechlin in 1863, and went to Vancouver's Island as a missionary, rising to be vicar-general. In 1871 he was made administrator of the diocese and on June 29th he was consecrated Bishop of Vancouver's Island. He was the first missionary of the church who attempted the conversion of the Alaskan Indians. In 1878 he visited that territory and all the adjacent islands. Towards the end of the year he was appointed coadjutor to the Archbishop of Oregon and reached Portland on May 1st, 1879. He spent a year in exploring Washington Territory, Idaho and Montana, and published a series of letters in Roman Catholic periodicals in the Eastern States, describing his adventures. In 1881 he succeeded to the Archbishopric, but for several years had been anxious to resign his see to convert the Alaska Indians and he visited Europe in 1883 to obtain permission from the Pope. His resignation was at length accepted and he was re-appointed Bishop of Vancouver Island, retaining his title of Archbishop. On his return in 1884 he started re-establishing the Missions that had come to a standstill. He left Victoria in July, 1886, for Alaska in company with two Jesuits and a guide named Fuller. They arrived at Chilcat and then travelled north along the coast until they reached the station of the Alaska Trading Company at the head of Stewart's river. Leaving the Jesuits to establish a mission among the Stikeen Indians, he started with Fuller and some Indians for Muklakajet, a village near the mouth of the Tamanah river, which he reached on 24th October. He spent a few week in missionary duty among Indians of this trading post and then decided to push on to Unlata, two hundred miles down the Yukon river. Travelling on sleds, the party arrived at a deserted village about 30 miles from their destination. They entered a hut and making a fire lay down before it.

At daylight next morning Fuller, who had several times exhibited anger at being drawn farther and farther into those desolate regions, levelled his rifle at the Archbishop and shot him. The murderer subsequently expressed remorse but gave no reason for the crime. Archbishop Seghers was a man of great erudition and an effective pulpit orator. The body was taken to St. Michael's Island where it was packed in ice and remained two years, it was then brought to Victoria and interred under the church there.

Stelly, George, (Victoria), was born in February, 1829, in canton Solothnan, Switzerland, where his father Joseph Stelly, resided. He was educated at his native place and on completing his studies worked on his father's farm. At the age of twenty-three he left Switzerland, and in 1852 landed at New Orleans. After a short stay in that city he journeyed to Illinois, where he farmed for some time, and later on proceeded to Iowa, where he remained one year. He then crossed the plains to California with ox teams, via. Salt Lake, the time occupied by the journey being five days less than six months. On reaching Placerville, in Eldorado county, he decided to remain, and resided there till 1858, during which time he was fairly successful at the mines. In the Fall of 1858, after having sold out all his interests in California, he came to Victoria, and soon after his arrival went to the British Columbia mines. He mined for fourteen months at Hill's Bar, Emory's Bar and several other places, but meeting with no success, and having expended all his capital, he went back to Victoria. After his return to the capital he commenced business as a contractor and transfer agent, his place of business being the same he now occupies, and he has ever since been very successful. In March, 1863, he married Miss Merkley, a German lady. He is a member of the Pioneer Society and also of the Oddfellow's Order.

Semlin, Charles Augustus, M. P. P., (Cache Creek), was born in the province of Ontario. His ancestors on his mother's side came from Yorkshire, England, to the New England colonies in 1838; his father came from Kent, England. Mr. Semlin was educated at the public schools and by private tuition. At an early age he chose the profession of teaching which he followed until the spring of 1862, when under the influence of the Cariboo gold fever he came to British Columbia by way of New York and Panama; stopping a few days in San Francisco and arriving in Victoria on the 12th of June, 1862. The summer's of 1862, 1863 and 1864 were spent in Cariboo, after which he settled at Cache Creek where he has since resided, and where he is extensively engaged in agriculture and stock raising. At all times taking a lively interest in public matters he became, in 1871, a candidate for the representation of the Yale district. He was elected and served for the four years for which the Parliament was elected. He was defeated at the next general election, and in the next year again when he opposed the re-election of the Hon. F. G. Vernon. In 1878 he was again defeated; at the general election of 1882 he was a candidate and was elected at the head of the poll and sat through the term. At the general election of 1886 he was again elected at t' e head of the poll as an opponent of the present Government. In the autumn of 1889 he was elected president of the Inland Agricultural Society of British Columbia. He is also vice-president of the Ashcroft and Lillooet Pioneer Society, and has been for many years a trustee of the Boarding School and for some years a Notary Public for British Columbia.

Spring, Charles. (Victoria), son of Captain William Spring, was born on February 16th, 1860 at New Westminster, then Queensborough, and educated in the Collegiate and James Bay schools, at Victoria. After completing his education he learned the trade of carpenter, but, after continuing at it for about a year and a half, found that it was too severe on his health, and he abandoned it and entered the employ of the Hudson's Bay Company and remained in that service for seven years. In June, 1884, he resigned his position and went into the sealing business, at which he has since continued. After the death of his father he formed a partnership with Mr. Peter Francis, and since the death of Mr. Francis he has carried on the business himself. He now possesses three vessels. In 1887 his schooner "Onward" was seized in Behring sea by the United States revenue cutter, and he lost $12,000. He is a member of the Pioneer Society, the Board of Trade and the Presbyterian church.

Spring, Captain William, was born at Lisbau, in Russia, near Riga, on the Baltic Sea, October 7th, 1831, and died at Victoria, B.

C., 1886. His father was a Scotchman, who, in his capacity as a civil engineer, visited Russia in 1827 in the employ of a company of railway contractors operating there and who married a Russian lady. While in Russia Captain Spring was born, and shortly afterwards the family removed to Scotland. At an early age Captain Spring entered the mercantile marine, and after visiting various quarters of the world and sailing in nearly every sea, he arrived at Sooke, Vancouver Island, in 1853. In 1861 Captain Spring and Mr. C. B. Young formed a partnership and opened a general store at Bella Coola to supply the miners. They also possessed a schooner, of which Hugh McKay was appointed master. In 1862 Captain Spring was stricken with small-pox and his life was saved by the care and attention bestowed on him by a miner, Daniel McCallum. When Captain Spring recovered the company sold out its interest at Bella Coola and returned to Victoria. They found the west coast business was becoming brisk and in 1863 they (Captain Spring and Mr. C. B. Young) worked up a trade with the Indians in fur and oil, and the same year they started a station at Beachy Bay for salting and curing salmon. They worked up a lucrative business, finding a market for their fish in California and the Sandwich Islands, and continued in partnership till 1864, when Captain Spring joined Peter Francis and in conjunction with him started a trading station at San Juan, on the west coast. From that time till 1870 Captain Spring was engaged in this trade, and during that time purchased and lost quite a number of schooners. In 1870 the seal fishing began to assume importance, and Captain Spring formed a partnership with Mr. Hugh McKay and Mr. Peter Francis to engage in this industry. The company purchased three schooners, the "Surprise," the "Alert" and the "Favorite." They continued this business with increasing success till 1880, when Mr. Theo. Lubbe, now of Esquimalt, joined the firm, which was now known as Wm. Spring & Co. Prior to 1884 the seal fishing had been off the coast of Vancouver Island, but in that year the firm fitted out the schooner "Mary Ellen" with a crew of white hunters, under command of Captain Dan McLean and sent her to Behring's Sea. In 1885 the "Favorite" was also sent north under command of Mr. Charles Spring. From this time forward the company's business prospered and they continued to add to their fleet of schooners, owning six at the time of Captain Spring's death. After his decease his large business was conducted by his son, Mr. Charles Spring, in conjunction with Mr. Francis, and since the death of Mr. Francis, Mr. Spring has had the sole management. Captain Spring was a member of the Pioneer Society, the Ancient Order of United Workmen and the Oddfellows' order. He was an adherent of the Presbyterian Church. He was married and had a family of seven children, two of whom predeceased him.

Springer, Benjamin, (Vancouver), eldest son of the late Benjamin Springer, esq., C. E., lieutenant-colonel of militia, of Middlesex, Ontario, and Eliza Green, was born in Middlesex, Ontario, February 2nd, 1841. His family on the father's side were United Empire Loyalists who removed to Canada after the war of independence rather than renounce their fealty to the crown. Mr. Springer received his elementary education at the public schools of his native place and then attended Caradock Academy, at that time a noted place of learning in Western Ontario. He subsequently studied civil engineering with the intention of following that profession but abandoned it for commercial pursuits. In 1862, during the period of the Cariboo excitement, he left Ontario for British Columbia, coming by way of the Isthmus of Panama. He remained over for one year in California and engaged in mining on American river with indifferent success. He then came on to British Columbia arriving at Victoria in April, 1863. He went direct to Cariboo travelling by the Douglas portages to Lillooet and from there on horseback to the forks of the Quesnelle, and then on foot over the Bald Mountains to Williams creek. He remained in Cariboo engaged in mining for nine years and during that time he developed claims on Williams, Antler, Lowhee, Keithley and Mosquito creeks. He spent the greater portion of his time on Williams creek. On the whole he had fair success in this work, although he did not at any time make a large strike. He had during this period the usual rough experience of the early miner. In the pioneer days he endured hunger and privations and dangers of all kind, and in later years the laborious and unhealthy work connected with developing large claims. In 1872 he abandoned mining and came to the coast where he became connected with the Moodyville company's saw mill, in which in 1882 he took the position of manager. With this institution he remained connected till 1890 when he resigned his position. Mr. Springer has not taken an active personal interest in politics but is in principal a Conservative. He has been a Justice of the Peace for the district of New Westminster for the past eighteen years; a trustee on the school board since 1872, and a pilot commissioner since 1879. He is a member of the Masonic fraternity and takes a lively interest in all matters connected with the order, being a past master and a member of the Grand Lodge.

Stemler, Lewis. (Victoria), was born at Wiesbaden, Prussia, in October, 1845. His father, Frederick Stemler, left Prussia and settled in California during the mining excitement there; came to British Columbia in 1858, and established the business known as Stemler & Co., and in 1867 returned to San Francisco. Mr. Stemler first engaged in the furniture business with Weiler & Co., and remained at this for six years. In 1873 he went to the Cassiar mines, where he became interested in one claim which he worked for some months. He then left a man in charge of it and took a position as toll collector. Shortly afterwards he obtained an interest in the business of H. Gerke & Co., general merchants of Cassiar, where he remained until the following autumn, when he sold to H. Gerke and returned to Victoria. Here he established a coffee and spice business in partnership with G. Leizer, under the firm title of Stemler & Leizer. In the following autumn he purchased Mr. Leizer's interest and conducted the business in his own name until August, 1881, when he removed his business to Wharf street and formed a partnership with Mr. Thomas Earle. Four years ago the firm removed their place of business to Government street, where they are now located. The business has continued to flourish and they now do the largest trade in their line in the Province. In politics Mr. Stemler is a Conservative but he does not take an active interest in public matters, his private business taking up all his time. Mr. Stemler is a Protestant and an adherent of St. John's Church, Victoria.

Stevenson, Arthur. (Lytton) was born near Ottawa on January 5th, 1840. His father, Thos. Stevenson, emigrated from the North of Ireland to Canada about the year 1835, and settled in the Province of Quebec, where he located a bush farm, which has been since improved from year to year, and where he still resides, surrounded by numerous descendants. Mr. Stevenson landed in Victoria in April, 1862, and eventually settled at Lytton. In the summer of the same year Mr. Stevenson went to Cariboo, and, together with Senator James Reid, took up a claim on a creek which they named "Canadian Creek," working it for a considerable time, but gaining nothing more valuable than experience and suffering great hardships. During the fall Mr. Stevenson went to Westminster, where he remained during the winter. For the next two years Mr. Stevenson mined, but, fortune not favoring his efforts, he bade farewell to Cariboo, like many others considerably wiser, but by no means wealthier, than when he first went there. In June, 1865, Mr. Stevenson was appointed Government Road Inspector for the district of Yale, which position he has occupied ever since, and in 1883 was made a Justice of the Peace for the same district. Mr. Stevenson is an adherent of the Presbyterian Church, and is a member of the "Mainland Pioneers' Benevolent Society." On September 21st, 1877, Mr. Stevenson was united in marriage to Agnes, daughter of Frank Lanmeister, esq., one of the earliest settlers in the Province.

Stirtan, Josiah Walter. (Nanaimo) was born on the 18th of December, 1848, in Edwardsburg township, County of Granville, Ontario. He is the eldest son of George Stirtan, who left England in the early part of the present century and settled on a farm in Granville. Mr. Stirtan was educated at his native place, and after leaving school remained on the farm with his father till he was twenty years of age. In 1869 he went to the territory of Wyoming, where he was engaged for two years in bridge building and constructing cars. He then came to British Columbia. Upon his arrival in this Province his attention was attracted to the Omineca mines, and he went to that district, where he spent a season in gold mining, with very fair success. He returned to Victoria in the autumn and went into business at Belmont, opposite Esquimalt, as a contractor, millwright and merchant. He had a boot and shoe manufactory and a tannery here. He continued to conduct this business with successful results for four years, when he disposed of his interests and removed to Nanaimo. At this time, 1875, Nanaimo began to build up rapidly, and Mr. Stirtan has been identified with the history of her progress. He began business as a

JOHN WEILER.

contractor, and during the subsequent ten years he constructed most of the large buildings which Nanaimo now possesses. In 1885 he obtained a right from the city to lay a system of water works, and he accomplished this work with remarkable success, boring the wooden pipes he used with machinery formed after his own design. He brought the water used from native springs. He conducted this system of water works till the demand became too great for the supply, and then, in conjunction with a number of others, he secured a charter to bring the water from Nanaimo river. This charter was subsequently amended to bring the water from Chase river instead of Nanaimo river. A system of waterworks was then built for the new company under the special supervision of Mr. Stirtan and after his own design. For two years Mr. Stirtan occupied the presidency of this company, and then he resigned from the board of directors to take the position of manager. The system constructed by Mr. Stirtan worked, or rather still works admirably and is equal, in point of perfection, to any system on the coast. Mr. Stirtan still occupies the position of manager of the company. He has large interests in Nanaimo city and district, is a director of the British Columbia Tanning Company and a justice of the peace for the district. He has also large interests in Vancouver city and New Westminster district and in coal mines on Vancouver and Texada Islands. He has not hitherto taken an active personal interest in politics and has declined to stand for the Legislature. Mr. Stirtan is a member of the Masonic fraternity. In April, 1880, he married Elizabeth, daughter of Matthew Hall, of Sumas.

Teague, John, (Victoria), was born in Cornwall, England, in June, 1833, and was educated at Clifforth. He left England on the 19th of May, 1856, intending to go to San Jose, Central America, to join his uncle on a coffee and indigo plantation there, but when he arrived at New York he learned that General Walker, who was then on his filibustering expedition, was in possession, and, after waiting for some time he left for San Francisco. When he reached that city he found that the Vigilance Committee was clearing the town of the murderous gang which had made living there so undesirable. After travelling about the state for some weeks he settled down in Grass valley, Nevada county. His first undertaking in Grass valley was a contract to take out quartz rock. This he soon abandoned and took a number of contracts to put up buildings, among them being a ten-stamp quartz mill. He performed the work so well in connection with this mill that its capacity was twice that of a rival company's mill with twenty-one stamps. He remained connected with this institution long enough to obtain a thorough knowledge of the process of extracting the metal from the ore. In the autumn of 1857 he opened an office as a mining broker and remained in this business till May, 1858, when he left Grass valley to come to British Columbia. He took shipping from San Francisco on the steamer Constitution and landed at that point on Bellingham Bay now known as Sehome, it being the intention of the American Steamship Company to create a rival town to Victoria at this place. Mr. Teague remained at Sehome for some days and then crossed to Victoria. At that time the now handsome city was a collection of tents clustered about the old Hudson's Bay fort and there was no hotel accommodation, the first public house being in course of construction. Mr. Teague had not brought his tent from Sehome, and he accordingly returned there. He was very anxious to get to the mines, but was disinclined to venture in a canoe, and he waited until he was able to get over to Victoria again on one of the steamers. He took his tent and outfit with him on this occasion, and when he pitched his tent at Victoria it was on the spot where the entrance to the Methodist church now is. Mr. Teague purchased a mining license from the Hudson's Bay Company and secured passage to Fort Hope on the 4th of July. He visited all the bars on the river as high up as Boston Bar, and finally settled at Murderer's Bar, where he decided to mine. He had to wait till the tide, which was very high, fell, but as the prospecting was good he decided to remain. When the mining began Sir James Douglas, Mr. Young, the Colonial Secretary and Captain Prevost visited the bar, and Sir James tried to influence the miners to settle on land. In this, however, he was unsuccessful. About the middle of February, in consequence of the intense cold, it was decided by the miners to go to Langley. One of their canoes, in which there were about a dozen persons, ran on a snag and split from bow to stern shortly after they had started, and while all succeeded, fortunately, in getting to shore, they were in a rather deplorable condition, having lost pretty nearly everything which they had in their canoe. They started, however, to tramp to Langley over ground covered with snow, encountering swamps every now and again, to cross which they were compelled to construct rafts. They suffered greatly through lack of food, want of sleep and cold. Their clothing was frozen to their limbs, and their pathway through the forest gave them no opportunity of getting the benefit of the sun or the wind. One of their company gave out when nearing their journey's end, and when he was missed Mr. Teague and another went back for him. They found him lying in a hollow log and had to employ force to take him with them. His mind had become impaired from the hardships he had endured. They finally reached camp in safety and Mr. Teague immediately went to Victoria, where he remained till the following Spring, when he again started for the mines. He took the Harrison-Lillooet route to the Quesnelle river, where he remained during the summer prospecting. There was a great deal of destitution in the upper country in that year, owing to the scarcity of provisions, which could not be got through to the camps except at great trouble and expense. Mr. Teague was literally starved out. He returned to Alexandria, where he found about seventy-five men rendered irresolute from hunger, and who had neither the hope of succor by remaining there nor the courage to face the dangers and difficulties of going down the country. Mr. Teague took in the situation and decided that he could accomplish the journey back. He accordingly started out with a companion named John Simpson. Simpson had no provisions and Mr. Teague only six pannikins of flour. They concluded, however, that they could reach the fountain on this, estimating the journey at six days. When they reached Williams' lake they encountered an Indian with fish, but he refused to sell at any price. Before reaching the fountain they thought to save a day by crossing the river and passing over the neck of land half enclosed by the bend in the river. They lost their way, however, and when they again reached the river they were utterly without food. When they reached the big slide they had been two days and two nights without food, and it took them another day to reach the fountain. There they were unable to get anything but a can of oatmeal, but with this they continued their journey down the river. In due course they reached New Westminster and Mr. Teague, after a short rest, crossed to Victoria, where he has since been engaged in business. For several years he was engaged as a contractor in H.

M. naval yards. When he began practice as an architect he at once obtained a large patronage and all the naval work, and his business has since continued to increase. In 1885 he was elected to the City Council for Johnson street ward, heading the poll, but next year he refused to stand, on account of the pressure of his private business. He has taken no active part in politics.

Templeman, William. (Victoria), son of Wm. Templeman of Pakenham, Lanark county, Ontario, was born at Pakenham, on the 28th of September, 1845 and attended school in his native place until he was seventeen years of age. He was then indentured to the printing business for four years serving his apprenticeship in the office of the Careleton Place *Herald*. He then spent three years in different cities in the United States, among them Oswego, New York, Chicago, Memphis and Tennessee, working in offices there. He returned to Canada, and in partnership with a Mr. Northgraves established the Almonte *Gazette*, which is still in existence and regarded as one of the best weekly journals of Ontario. The *Gazette* was conducted in the interest of the Liberal party. Mr. Templeman bought his partner's share at the end of six months and conducted it himself till 1882 when he took two of his employees, Messrs. McLeod and McEwen in with him. During a considerable portion of this time he had acted as clerk for the municipality and also served as the first clerk of the town of Almonte, and for some years as secretary-treasurer of the North Lanark Agricultural Society. In 1884 Mr. Templeman disposed of his interest in the *Gazette* and after a six months trip to the Southern States he came to British Columbia over the Northern Pacific Railway. He arrived at Victoria in the autumn and accepted a position on the *Times*, which had then been in existence for six months. In 1886 he accepted the management of the *Times* which he enlarged and in every way improved and which under his guidance has become one of the leading papers of the Coast. In Dominion politics the *Times* is independent and in local politics in opposition to the present Government. Mr. Templeman is a member of the Oddfellows order, the Ancient Order of Foresters, and the Ancient Order of United Workmen. In religion he is an adherent of the Presbyterian Church.

Thomson, George, (Nanaimo), was born at Waterside near the town of Ayr, Scotland, in 1855, and came to British Columbia in 1873. He took a great interest in the organization of the militia in the Province and was acting as senior sergeant in that force at the time of the disbandment of the Nanaimo corps. During the enforcement of the Dominion Liquor License Act he acted as chief inspector for Vancouver district until it was declared *ultra vires* by the Privy Council. In 1886 he was elected by a large majority to represent Nanaimo in the Provincial Legislature serving in that capacity till the general election of 1890.

Tilley, Seth Thorne, (Vancouver), son of George and Elizabeth Tilley, of Gagetown, Queen's county, New Brunswick, was born there on August 25th, 1836. His family was among the earliest settlers in America, having been of that small and heroic band of seekers after civil and religious liberty who came over in the Mayflower. One branch of the family and that from which Mr. Tilley is descended, settled in New Hampshire and continued to reside there until the close of the war of independence, when they sacrificed their possessions and removed to Canada rather than renounce their allegiance to Britain. They settled in Queen's county, N. B., where many of their descendants still continue to live and among the number the noted Canadian statesman Sir Leonard Tilley. Mr. Tilley received a sound grammar School education at his native place and in 1855 left for California to join an elder brother who had gone there in 1849. He joined his brother in Grass Valley, Nevada county, where he remained mining till 1858 when the excitement over the discovery on the Fraser broke out when he came to British Columbia. He reached Victoria in May and went immediately to the Fraser where he took up a claim on Strawberry Island, above Hope. He was not very successful owing to his ignorance of the peculiarities of the river. He had to abandon his claim for a time owing to flood and when he returned he found it had been "jumped" by a man who took a great deal of gold out of it. Mr Tilley then went to Fort Hope, where he opened a small stationery store at which he continued till 1859, when he removed to New Westminster and opened a book store in that city. He remained in New Westminster till 1863 and was very successful in his business, making a great deal of money. In

1863 he sold out his business, placed his affairs in the hands of an agent and went for a trip to his native place. He returned in 1864 to find that his agent had betrayed his trust and left the country with all Mr. Tilley's money. He then formed a partnership with Mr. D. Witherow in the furniture business which continued till 1866. During 1864 Mr. Tilley acted as city clerk for the New Westminster municipal council and in 1865 he sat at the council board as a member. In 1866 he went to the Big Bend mines where he remained one year with poor success. On his return to New Westminster he decided to go to California. During the next few years he was in business, at different times in California, Arizona and Utah. He carried on business for six months in Salt Lake City. In 1869 he went to San Joaquin to represent a brother in a large business there. In 1870 he was married to Jeannie M. Bracken, daughter of John Bracken, a celebrated mining expert of Wisconsin. He continued to reside in San Joaquin till 1874 when he removed to Santa Barbara and established a book and stationery business there. This business he subsequently disposed of and started a wholesale grocery business, which he conducted till 1879, when owing to his wife's continued ill health he sold out and returned to British Columbia. He was appointed Government commissary between Port Moody and Kamloops and subsequently filled the same position for Mr. Onderdonk. He was then appointed by Sir Joseph Trutch on the Dominion Land Survey and occupied this position till he saw an opening for his old business of books and stationery in Vancouver. He established the first book business in Vancouver, occupying a store on Carrall street, and made a great deal of money. The fire of 1885, which destroyed the town, consumed his stock and left him once more without a dollar in the world. He started again, however, and was soon able to pay off his liabilities and was about to build a store on Cordova street when he was again burned out and $8,000 worth of goods destroyed. These repeated misfortunes did not utterly discourage him. He opened up business again and is once more on the high road to success. He is among Vancouver's most energetic citizens and although he has never sat in the council, having refused to stand for the position on account of his business cares, he takes a strong interest in everything affecting the city's progress. He is an Oddfellow and Knight of Pythias though not a member of the local lodges. He has two children, Charles, manager of the Telephone Co., and a daughter. Mr. Tilley is a member of the Church of England.

Todd, Charles. (Victoria), was born in Carleton county, Ont., on January 12th, 1842, his parents being of Scotch descent. Mr Todd was trained in the county school for the pedagogic profession, which he afterwards followed in his native province. In May, 1862, Mr. Todd arrived in British Columbia and resided at Victoria. During eleven years he was engaged in mining, staying three years at Cariboo, three years at Big Bend, one year at Leech river and four years in the Kootenay district. During four years he represented Kootenay in the first Parliament formed after the confederation. Mr. Todd was superintendent of Provincial Police for over eight years, during which time he did much to increase the efficiency and discipline of the force. He also acted as Indian Agent for three years. In 1873 Mr. Todd was married in Victoria. He is a member of the Independent Order of Oddfellows and the United Workmen.

Tolmie, William Fraser. The late William Fraser Tolmie, L. F. P. and S. G., died on the 8th December, 1886, after an illness of only three days, at his late residence Cloverdale, Victoria, B. C. The deceased was born at Inverness, Scotland, on the 3rd February 1812, and was educated in Glasgow. He left Scotland for America in 1832, in the service of the Hudson's Bay Company, coming around Cape Horn in a sailing vessel, calling at the Sandwich Islands and arriving at Fort Vancouver on the Columbia river, then the chief trading post of the company, in the spring of 1833. In 1834, he joined the expedition under the late Mr. Ogden which traded along the north west coast as far as the Russian boundary, establishing trading posts at different points for the Hudson's Bay Company. In 1836 he returned to Fort Vancouver and assumed his former position as surgeon. In 1841 he visited his native land returning in the following year, overland via Fort Garry, the plains and the Columbia river, and was placed in charge of the Hudson's Bay Company's posts on Puget Sound. He took a prominent part during the Indian war of 1855-6 in pacifying the Indians, being an excellent linguist. He had acquired a knowledge of the Indian tongues and was instrumental in bringing about peace between the

Indians and the Americans. In 1850 he married the eldest daughter of the late John Work, then chief factor of the Hudson's Bay Co. at Victoria, Vancouver Island. The deceased, W. F. Tolmie, was appointed chief factor of the company at Nisqually in 1855. After the company had given up their possessory rights to the Americans in 1859 he removed to Victoria, Vancouver Island, still remaining in the service of the Hudson's Bay Company, and as agent of the Puget Sound Co. until 1870, when he retired and took up his residence on a farm of 1100 acres which he had purchased in the early settlement of the then colony. He took great interest in farming and stock raising and continued to do so up to the day he was taken ill, and was the first who imported thorough-bred stock into the Province of British Columbia. He was a member of the Local Legislature for two terms, representing Victoria district until 1878, and also a member of the first Board of Education for many years, exercising a great interest in educational matters. He held many offices of trust and was always a valued and respected citizen. Many will remember with gratitude his kindly counsel, encouragement and unostentatious charity. Dr. Tolmie was known to ethnologists for his contributions to the history and linguistics of the native races of the West Coast, and dated his interest in ethnological matters from his contact with Mr. Horatio Hale, who visited the west coast as ethnologist to the Wilkes exploring expedition. He afterwards transmitted vocabularies of a number of the tribes to Dr. Scouley and to Mr. George Gibbs, some of which have been published in contributions to American ethnology. In 1884 he published in conjunction with Dr. G. M. Dawson a nearly complete series of short vocabularies of the principal languages met with in British Columbia, and his name is to be found frequently quoted as an authority on the history of the Northwest Coast and its ethnology in the works of Bancroft and other authors. He was at all times ready to place his extensive and accurate knowledge on these subjects freely at the disposal of inquirers. He retained up to the day before his death, accurate recollections of the stirring events of the early colonial days, and there was no one so intimate with the Indian affairs of the Province. He frequently contributed valuable matter and sound ideas to the press of the city upon public questions and events now historical. His wife pre-deceased him on the 23rd June, 1880. They had seven sons and five daughters, two of the latter being dead.

Tolmie, James, M. P. P., (Cloverdale, Victoria), son of William Fraser Tolmie, C. F. Hudson's Bay Company, and Jane Work, was born at Fort Nisqually September 9th, 1855. He was educated at Victoria, and was subsequently engaged in business for five years. He then entered a law office with the intention of studying law, but abandoned this at the end of one year, and has since resided on the farm at Coverdale, which he now manages. In 1888 he was elected to represent Victoria district in the Local Legislature. He is a conservative in politics and friendly to the present Government. He is second vice-president of the St. Andrew's and Caledonian society and is an adherent of the Episcopal Church.

Townsend, William Berridaile. (New Westminster), was born February 28th, 1839, at Battersea, near London, England. Educated at the grammar school in that place, known as the "Sir Walter St. John Bolinbroke School." Having an inclination for a seafaring life he left home at a very early age without the knowledge of his parents, and went to the Baltic with the squadron under Admiral Dundas in 1855, and was at the storming of Seaborg, for which he carries the silver medal, presented by the nation when the Russian war was over. He then visited Madeira, and Bermuda, and later on the Cape Verde Islands. He subsequently remained at home for a year but could not settle down. He accepted an engagement in the Hudson's Bay service and arrived at Fort Victoria in January, 1858, a few months before the gold excitement which broke out in that year and populated the Fraser river, but which Mr. Townsend did not hear of till he reached England again. In 1860 he again landed in Victoria and settled there for two years. He was then smitten with the gold fever and spent the summers of 1862 and 1863 in Cariboo with varied success. In 1864 he returned to England, and was married in September of that year to Eliza, eldest daughter of Mr. John Ridley, of his native village. After spending a few months at home Mr. Townsend and his wife started for the long voyage round the Horn, in a new ship called the Mindoro, but she was run down in the channel and the passengers were landed on the beach near Dover, with scarcely clothing enough to cover them. They got home again, however, and, after a delay of a few weeks, started again on a ship called the Ann Adamson. Misfortune seemed to follow them for the ship was eight months making the voyage, voyage, and when they arrived inside Cape Flattery there was not a man left on board able to pull a rope; five or six had died, and the rest were lying helpless with the scurvy. They soon recovered, however, after landing at Victoria in August, 1865. Mr. Townsend staid there with good success until October, 1875, when his wife's health failed, and Dr. Helmcken ordered her away to some climate more like her native air. Mr. Townsend accordingly removed to New Westminster, and, finding his wife was benefitted by the change, has resided there since. He has no reason to regret having done so, as he has grown up with the place and prospered with its prosperity. Mr. Townsend has important interest in New Westminster and is regarded as one of its most enterprising and loyal citizens. He has served a number of years on the council board of the city, and in 1889 on the resignation of Mayor Hendry was elected to the position of Mayor of the city. He has been a school trustee and takes a lively interest in educational matters. He is a member of the New Westminster Board of Trade, vice-president of the Provincial Exhibition Association of British Columbia, and connected with a number of other organizations, which have for their object the building up of the city and district of New Westminster. Mr. Townsend is a coming man in the politics of the Province. At the last by-election he stood for the House of Commons and was defeated by a bare majority in favor of Mr. Corbould, the elected member. He is an Oddfellow of 25 years' standing.

Tronson, Edward J., (Vernon), son of the late J. Dudley Tronson, esq., inspector of police, and Catherine Briscoe Tronson, of Wellmouth county, Kilkenny, Ireland, was born in October, 1842. During his early childhood both his parents died and he lived with his uncle and guardian Geo. Briscoe, esq. In 1860 on the death of Mr. Briscoe, he went to London and resided with his uncle Colonel Tronson until 1863, when together with his cousin H. H. Horsford, Prior Symon and C. N. Young, (the latter of Departure Bay) he set sail for British Columbia. They left London docks in the "Sea Snake" and after a terrible voyage of seven months, and encountering heavy seas round Cape Horn which obliged them to put back to the Falkland Islands for repairs, they arrived at Victoria in February of the same year. After his arrival in British Columbia, Mr. Tronson farmed some time at Cedar Hill with a cousin, the late Mr. Edward Jackson, and at a later period he held a position in the Bank of British Columbia. During the gold excitement at Big Bend, Mr. Tronson left for that region, but meeting Captain Houghton at Kamloops was persuaded by that gentleman to go to Coldstream, Okanagon, where he and the Messrs. Vernon Bros. had just started the now celebrated Coldstream Ranch. Mr. Tronson made his home for some years at Coldstream, until he pre-empted his present farm at Vernon, which is now in a high state of cultivation. He is a Justice of the Peace and a trustee of the Vernon School Board and takes a great interest in politics, being a strong Conservative. Mr. Tronson is one of the best agriculturists in the Province, and has great faith in the future of the Okanagan district.

Trutch, John, (Victoria), son of the late William Trutch, was born on the Island of Jamaica, W. I., in 1828. He was educated in England, and studied the profession of civil engineering and surveying. In 1851 he came to the Pacific coast, and till 1858 practised his profession in Oregon In 1858 he came to British Columbia and settled in Victoria, where he has resided almost continuously since, and identified himself with the progress and advancement of the Province. He is a member of the Pioneer society and occupies the position of land commissioner of the Esquimalt and Nanaimo Railway Company.

Trutch, Sir Joseph William, (Victoria), son of the late William Trutch, esq., solicitor, of Ashcot, Somerset, England, and afterwards of St. Thomas, Island of Jamaica, where he was clerk of the peace, was born at Ashcot, England, in 1826. He was educated at Exeter, Devonshire, and was articled as a pupil to Sir John Rennie, C. E. In 1855 he married Julia Elizabeth, daughter of Louis Hyde, esq., of New York. In 1849 he came to the Pacific coast of North America, and until 1856 he practised his profession as a civil engineer in California and Oregon. He was subsequently assistant engineer on the Illinois and Michigan canal, and on the Illinois river improvement works. In 1859 he came to British

Columbia and settled in Victoria. From that time till 1864 he was engaged in the construction of public works, and among other well-known works, which he completed, was the Grand Trunk road from Yale to Cariboo, including the Alexandria suspension bridge over the river Fraser, built by him on terms of toll charter. He was chief commissioner of lands and works, and subsequently surveyor-general of British Columbia and a member *ex officio* of the executive and legislative councils of British Columbia until the union of the colony with Canada in 1871. He was one of the delegates to Ottawa in 1870 to arrange the terms on which British Columbia should enter confederation, and in 1871 he went to London to settle finally the details of union. When the union was consummated he was appointed first Lieutenant-Governor on July 1st, 1871, and occupied this office until July 1st, 1876. Since that time he has taken no active part in politics. He was Knighted for his services in 1887.

Tunstall, Simon John. (Kamloops), was born at Ste. Anne de Bellevue, P. Q., on September 19th, 1854. He is the son of Gabriel Christie Tunstall, esq., who married Janet, daughter of Simon Fraser, esq., chief factor of the North West Company, a gentleman of U. E. Loyalist family. He received his primary education at a preparatory school and the high school at Montreal, and afterwards studied at McGill University, his career as a student being a brilliant one. During his third year at the University he commenced the study of medicine and graduated in arts taking first class honors in English literature. In 1874 he took the primary prize in medicine, and in 1875 graduated in medicine, taking the Holmes gold medal. After graduating he went to Papineau-ville where he acted as medical officer during the small-pox epidemic. Four years later he returned to Montreal where he practised successfully for two years, and in 1881 left for British Columbia, arriving at Lytton on 28th July of the same year. He practised at Lytton till July, 1883, when he removed to Kamloops, receiving a bonus from the Provincial Government for so doing. In 1884-5 he had full medical charge of all the men employed in the construction of the C. P. R. from Savonas to Craigellachie. Ever since that time he has practised his profession at Kamloops, being chief C. P. R. medical officer for the Thompson, Shuswap and Selkirk

BIOGRAPHICAL SKETCHES. 313

sections of the Pacific division, besides having a large private practice. Though a strong and consistent "mainlander" and Conservative he has taken no active part in politics, his time being fully occupied by his professional duties. He is a member of the Masonic Order, an Oddfellow, and vice-president of the St. Andrew's and Caledonian Society of Kamloops. He is an adherent of the Church of England and on September 22nd, 1885, married Marianne Lawson, third daughter of James H. Innes, esq., H. M. Naval storekeeper at Esquimalt.

Turner, Hon. John Herbert, M. P. P., (Victoria), son of John Turner, esq., of Ipswich, England, was born at Clayden, near Ipswich, Suffolkshire, England, in 1834. He was educated at Whitstable, near Canterbury and left England in 1856 for Halifax, Nova Scotia. After residing at Halifax for two years he removed to Charlottetown, Prince Edward Island, and commenced business there. While living in Charlottetown he took a principal part in the organization of the first volunteer rifle corps in that Province and continued to be an active member thereof until he left Charlottetown for British Columbia in 1862. This corps in conjunction with other county corps turned out the number of a thousand to receive his Royal Highness the Prince of Wales on his visit to the Island in 1860. It was in 1862 that the reports of British Columbia's marvelous richness had their greatest influence in Eastern Canada and hundreds of the choicest and most energetic young men from all the provinces abandoned established businesses, assured prospects and unsurpassed opportunities for the dream of untold wealth to be gathered from the gold fields. On July 2nd, 1862, Mr. Turner arrived in Victoria on the steamer Oregon in company with a large number of young gold seekers—many of whom, disappointed and discouraged, left the country within a month of their landing and are now scattered all over the globe. A few, however, with more of that combative quality and that indomitable energy and perseverance so necessary in the citizens of a young state settled in Victoria, and stuck to her through good and evil report, sharing their portions of her troubles and triumphs and helping to build up the city to its present prosperous condition. Mr. Turner went into business in 1865, and has continued at it uninterruptedly since that time. During the long period of twenty-five years, since that time he has increased his business until it now has connections in every quarter of the world, and wherever the merchant princes of Canada have commercial dealings, his house is known for its enterprise, its shrewdness and its business probity. As in Charlottetown so in Victoria, Mr. Turner was one of the original promoters and members of the Volunteer Rifle organization and was enrolled in the first corps that was formed there for the defence of the island during the great Fenian excitement and threatened raid in 1865. This corps wore as uniform the celebrated white blanket coat trimmed with black fur. Mr. Turner passed through the ranks from private to sergeant, then into the commissioned ranks and through the various grades, finally retiring at confederation into the Canadian reserve militia with the rank and commission of lieutenant-colonel in June, 1881. He was elected a member of the city council of Victoria in 1876 and again in 1877 and 1878, and in 1879 was elected by acclamation mayor for that year, serving the city during three terms in that position. He was chairman of the British Columbia Benevolent society and also of the Royal Hospital from 1879 to 1882, and chairman of the British Columbia Agricultural society for 1881-2. In the general election of 1886 he was elected to represent the city of Victoria in the Provincial Legislature, and joined the government of Hon. A. E. B. Davie in 1887, being re-elected in August of that year, after having accepted the portfolio of Minister of Finance. At the last general election in June, 1890, he was again returned for the city of Victoria, and now occupies in the government of Hon. John Robson the position of Finance Minister. Mr. Turner has ever since his arrival in British Columbia taken an active interest in and been a steady promoter of the mining and fishing interests of the Province, and is still largely interested in them. He is connected with many of the large enterprises, which have had their origin in Victoria, and while his business is centered in that city he has also large commercial interests in other parts of the Province. In 1860 Mr. Turner was married to Miss Eilbeck, of Whitehaven, Cumberland, England, and has one son.

Vair, James, (Kamloops), a Canadian of Scotch descent was born at Coburg, Ontario, in 1859 and educated at his native place. Came to British Columbia in 1879, arriving at Victoria on March 30th. He first began business at Spence's Bridge and from there removed to Kamloops. He started a branch store in Vancouver but was burned out during the big fire of 1886. He rebuilt his store at Vancouver and after conducting it for one year, sold out and confined himself to his business at Kamloops. Since that time he has resided at the inland capital where his interests have largely increased. He is a director of the Royal Inland Hospital at Kamloops; chairman of the board of managers of the Presbyterian Church; director of the Inland Agricultural Association. He is a member of the Independent Order of Oddfellows, and of the St. Andrew's and Caledonian Society.

Vedder, Adam Swart, (Chilliwack), was born at Schenectady, in the state of New York, on 27th July, 1834. His parents, who were of English and Dutch origin, were descendants of the first settlers of that state. Mr. Vedder received his education at his native place, and previous to his arrival in British Columbia was engaged in a general transportation business. Mr. Vedder arrived in British Columbia on 2nd May, 1860, via Panama, and resided at Hope and Yankee Flat (North Bend) during the two following summers. Mr. Vedder spent several years as a trader and butcher, and had the misfortune to lose all he possessed in a snow storm on Bald Mountain in 1863. Since 1870 Mr. Vedder has been engaged in dairy-farming and stock-raising in Sumas and farming at Chilliwhack, and was warden at the latter municipality. Mr. Vedder built the first house ever erected by a private individual and occupied the first pre-emption recorded, in either Sumas or Chilliwhack. He is one of the best agriculturists in the Province and takes an active part in politics. In 1877 he married Miss Althea Sicker. He is a Presbyterian.

Vernon, Hon. Forbes George, M. P. P., (Vernon), third son of J. E. Vernon, esq., D. L., of Clontarf Castle, Dublin, Ireland, was born at Clontarf Castle in 1843. He is descended from one of the oldest and most illustrious families of England, which took its name from the town of Vernon in Normandy and was established in England by one of the companions in arms of William the Conqueror. In the fifteenth century a branch of the family was established at Clontarf and acquired the large estates there, which are at present in the possession of Mr. Vernon's father. The

Castle on the estate which is historically celebrated was founded by the Knights Templars in the twelfth century and has been rebuilt after the original design by its present owner. Mr. Vernon was educated in England for the royal engineers and in 1863 he received a commission from the Imperial Government. He resigned this however, shortly after it had been granted, and in the same year, 1863, in company with his brother and Col. Houghton, now Deputy-Adjutant General, of Winnipeg, came to British Columbia. Mr. Vernon and his companions engaged in commercial pursuits and ranching and mining in Yale district and the upper country and by reason of business shrewdness, enterprise and hard work were successful in there undertakings. After a time Mr. Vernon took over the management of the entire business having purchased the interests of his partners and has since confined himself almost entirely to ranching, possessing one of the most extensive and finest farms in the Province. In 1875 he first offered himself as a candidate to represent the important district of Yale in the Provincial Legislature and was returned by a large majority. In February, 1876, he accepted the portfolio of Chief Commissioner of Lands and Works in the Elliot cabinet, and on returning to the people for confirmation in this position was re-elected by an overwhelming majority. This position he retained till the general election of 1878, when he was re-elected by his constituents, but in consequence of the defeat of the Elliott administration, Mr. Vernon was in opposition. In 1882 he was not a candidate for re-election but in 1886 he was again returned and on the death, in 1887, of Hon. Mr. Smythe, he accepted office in the Davie Government as Chief Commissioner of Lands and Works. At the last general election in June, 1890, he was again returned by his constituents and now occupies the chief commissionership of lands and works in the ministry of which Hon. John Robson is Premier. Mr. Vernon from his intimate acquaintance with the mining and farming industries of the Province in which he is very largely interested personally, makes an excellent commissioner. He is a hard worker and an able administrator. In 1877 he married Miss Branks, who died in 1885 leaving two children.

Vowell, Arthur Wellesley. (Victoria), son of the late Richard Prendergast Vowell of Clonmel, county Tipperary, Ireland, was born in Tipperary, September 17th, 1841. He was educated at his native place and subsequently served in the Irish militia, doing garrison duty, from 1858 to 1860. He came to British Columbia in 1862 and went direct to Cariboo where he engaged during that season in mining but without much success. He returned to Victoria where he resided till 1866, when he went to Big Bend during the excitement there. At Big Bend he was appointed chief constable and continued to occupy this position till 1872, when he took charge of the Kootenay district as gold commissioner and stipendiary magistrate. In 1873 he was removed to Omineca where he acted in the same capacity, and in 1874 he was ordered to Cassiar where gold had but lately been discovered. In the autumn of 1874 he resigned his position in the Government service. In 1875 at the request of the Government he went to Kootenay to meet Major General Selby Smith and party, when that distinguished officer made his first trip overland to British Columbia. Mr. Vowell was returned at the general election of 1875 to the Provincial Legislature as senior representative of Kootenay district. In the spring of 1876 he resigned his seat in the House and re-entered the Government service, taking charge of the district of Cassiar as gold commissioner and stipendiary magistrate. He remained in charge of Cassiar district until the spring of 1884. At that time in consequence of the largely increased population in Kootenay district, owing to the construction of the Canadian Pacific Railway and the necessarily increased responsibilities attached to the offices of gold commissioner and stipendiary magistrate in that region, Mr. Vowell was ordered to take charge in Kootenay. He discharged the important duties of his offices in Kootenay until 1889 at which time he resigned his position in the Provincial Government service and accepted the appointment under the Dominion Government of superintendent of Indian affairs for the Province of British Columbia. He is a member of the Royal Arch Chapter of the Masonic Order; a member of the Pioneer Society and an adherent of the Church of England.

Wadhams, Edmund Abraham (Ladner's Landing) was born on March 28th, 1833, at Wadham's Mills, Essex county, N. Y., and is the son of Abraham E. Wadhams, esq., of the same place. Mr. Wadhams was educated at Wadhams' Mills and the Bakerfield

Academy, Vermont. In 1858 Mr. Wadhams arrived at Victoria on the steamship Sierra Nevada. He mined with moderate success on the Fraser river in 1858-59 and on Keithley's Creek in 1860. From 1861 to 1868 Mr. Wadhams traded in the Cariboo district and at Victoria and Clinton from 1869 to 1872. He engaged in the salmon-canning business in 1873 and ten years later built the Wadhams cannery, near Ladner's Landing, and, with the exception of the first year, has done a most successful business from the outset. Mr. Wadhams employs in all about 116 fishermen, 160 men about the cannery and 20 overseers and others employed about the more important branches of the business. In 1864 Mr. Wadhams married Bertha Rosamund, daughter of John Wilson, Esq., of London, Eng., by whom he has five sons and two daughters. He is an Episcopalian.

Walkem, Hon. George Anthony, (Victoria), Justice of the Supreme Court of British Columbia, is the son of the late Charles Walkem, esq., chief draughtsman on the Royal Engineer staff in Canada, by Miss Boomer, sister of Rev. Dr. Boomer, dean of Hedon. His family has lived for generations on the border of Devon and Cornwall, England. Mr. Justice Walkem was born at Newry, Ireland, in November, 1834. He was educated at the High School and McGill University, Montreal. He subsequently studied law with the late Sir John Rose and was called to the bar of Lower Canada in 1858, and to that of Ontario in 1861. In 1862 he came to British Columbia and was called to the bar of the colony in 1864. In 1864 he was elected to the Legislative Council of British Columbia to represent the east district of Cariboo and continued to occupy a seat in the Council till 1870. He was one of the most active workers for confederation with the Dominion and when the union was consummated he entered the Provincial Legislature as member for Cariboo. He was appointed a member of the executive council on January 12th, 1872, as chief commissioner of lands and works. From December, 1872, to January, 1876 he was Attorney-General of British Columbia, and on the resignation of Hon. Amor De Cosmos in February of 1874, on him devolved the duty of forming a new administration of which he was premier till January, 1876. Between 1876 and 1878, Mr. Walkem was in opposition, his government having been defeated. In 1874 he was appointed a delegate to go to England, to present to the Imperial authorities the differences between the Province and the Dominion in the matter of the construction of the Canadian Pacific Railway. In 1878 he was returned to power and again assumed the Attorney-Generalship which he continued to hold till 1882, when he was appointed to the bench. During the time of his last administration the question of the construction of the Canadian Pacific Railway gave a great deal of trouble. The undecided policy of the Dominion Government was such that it seemed as if the construction of the road had been abandoned and it was largely through the firm stand taken by Mr. Walkem's Government that the Dominion Government at length decided to proceed with the building of the line. Mr. Walkem was president of the Law Society of British Columbia; is a fellow of the Royal Geographical Society, and a member of the special committee of the British Association for the advancement of science.

Webb, Horatio. (Chilliwhack), son of John and Caroline Webb, was born at Marston-Moretaine, Bedfordshire, England, April 28th, 1852. His family was an old and long established one at Marston and had been in possession of the one farm for eighty-five years. His father was a leading man in all public affairs in Bedfordshire. Mr. Webb was educated at his native village and intended to follow his father's occupation. Shortly after leaving school, however, he came to British Columbia, landing at Victoria on October 5th, 1869. He spent his first winter in British Columbia at New Westminster with his brother-in-law, Mr. G. R. Ashwell, and then settled in Chilliwhack where he engaged in farming. He has since continued to live in Chilliwhack. He is deputy-sheriff, assessor and collector for the municipality. He is a strong supporter of the present Government. On October 15th, 1875, he married Lucy Ada Hopkins, of Norwich, Chenango county, State of New York. Mr. Webb is a member of the Oddfellows' Society, and an adherent of the Church of England.

Weiler, John. (Victoria), was born August 26th, 1824, at Nassau, Germany, and educated there. In 1846, when twenty-two years of age, he left his native country and came to America. He landed at New York and from there went to California in 1850.

In California he was engaged in mining and subsequently in stock ranching. In 1861 he removed to Victoria, British Columbia, and started the furniture factory and crockery business he now owns and which has continued to increase in dimensions to the present time. He has now the largest business of the kind in British Columbia. Mr. Weiler is a member of the Masonic and Oddfellow's Orders. His five sons are engaged with him in the business.

Westwood, William Joseph, born in 1817, died 29th January, 1872, at East Wellington. Mr. Westwood was born at the Lye, near Starbridge, Worcestershire, England, and was educated at Red Hill school, Starbridge. After leaving school he was apprenticed to the blacksmithing business and followed that trade for some time in England. He also opened a grocery store, and, possessing good musical abilities which he had cultivated, he turned them to account and took pupils. In 1849 he left England and with his wife, nee Elizabeth Tilley, came to America, settling in the city of St. Louis, where he commenced business as a blacksmith. His prudence and hard work had their reward and his business prospered so well that he was in a short time able to open another shop, which he conducted concurrently with the first. He also went into the manufacture of nails which brought him in good returns. In 1849 his wife died and in 1850 he married Miss Fanny Tilley, daughter of Mr. Benjamin Tilley, of Starbridge, England. He remained in St. Louis till 1853, during which time two children were born—William Joseph, who died in his infancy, and Elizabeth, now Mrs. Dick, of Nanaimo, born in June, 1852. In 1853 Mr. Westwood was attracted to California, intending to go to the gold fields. He settled in Valao city and opened a blacksmith shop, having changed his determination on the question of going to the mines. He remained in Valao for one year after which he purchased and settled on a farm of 350 acres, between three and four miles from Valao. Here he continued to reside for six years, during which period he increased his farm by leasing first three hundred and fifty acres and and then one thousand and three hundred acres. His ranch was the finest in that part of the state and was greatly admired for the excellence of its stock. While on the farm in California four children were born to him, who are now prosperous citizens of British Columbia. Carlo Novello, born on September 11th, 1854, who is now residing at East Wellington, is a mechanic in the employ of the coal company, and married to Beulah, daughter of Captain Butler; Benjamin Ira, born March 27th, 1856, is also in the employ of the East Wellington Coal company as blacksmith and is married to Miss Abbie Williams, of Wellington; Cicero Ciprao, born July 7th, 1858, is engaged in farming and cattle raising at Wellington, and Milton Tilly Charles, born June 27th, 1859, is engaged in the same occupation. In 1860 Mr. Westwood decided to come to British Columbia with his family. He took passage for Victoria on the steamer Pacific. After having been in Victoria for about a year he purchased the Lion brewery, which he conducted for one year, and then disposed of it. During his residence in Victoria Mr. Westwood made considerable money by investments in real estate and at one time he owned a very large quantity of land on Fort street. He also lost heavily in Goldstream during the mining excitement there, which turned out so badly for everybody who invested in it. In Victoria Mr. Westwood's family was increased by three children born there; George Milfred John, B.A., born April 22nd, 1861, who is now taking a post graduate course at Cobourg University; Rebecca, born February 22nd, 1862, who died in infancy, and William Thomas Paul, born February 4th, 1863, who is now engaged in business as a general merchant at East Wellington and who is married to Miss Kate Garrison, of Blessington, Ontario. In 1864 Mr. Westwood removed to East Wellington, where he had purchased six hundred and fifty acres of land, which he proposed to farm and make a home for his family. He went into stock-raising and dairy-farming, and his venture turned out successful. He was aware that his land contained coal deposits, but he did not make any effort to test their value, and it was not till after his death that a test was made and the mining property, now owned by the East Wellington Coal company, was sold by the family to Mr. Chandler. Mr. Westwood largely increased the extent of his farm during the following five years. During that period two children were born to him, Joseph Arthur Henry, on January 21st, 1866, who is now engaged with two of his brothers in stock-raising and farming; and Fannie Anna Dora Rebecca Henrietta, born October 28th, 1867, now married to Mr. W. J. McKeon, of Victoria. In 1872 at the age of 54 years Mr. Westwood died. His widow who survived him still lives at East Wellington among her children.

Whetham, James, M. D., (Vancouver), was born in Wentworth county, Ontario, on the 1st of February, 1854, and passed his boyhood years in that county. He received his early education at the public school of his own district and subsequently at Waterdown, N. S., and Hamilton Collegiate Institute. His father George Whetham, was, as a young man, a member of the long established firm of S. Whetham & Sons, extensive flax and hemp manufacturers in England, but moved by the same restless and enterprising spirit which afterwards characterized his son, he emigrated to America, selected Wentworth county as his home, there married and started business as a general merchant but unfortunately died, while his family was still young—the subject of the present sketch being then only eight years of age. The English branch of the family is numerous and some of its members have been highly honored by their countrymen. Sir Charles Whetham, Dr. Whetham's uncle, was for many years alderman and director of various corporations in London, and was elected sheriff and finally in 1879 was Lord Mayor of London. Dr. Whetham while still at school was attracted by the glowing accounts of the Canadian Northwest and after teaching school for some time in his native county he started for Manitoba in 1878 and invested a few hundred dollars there in farm lands. But his eyes were still turned westward and he soon set out through the Western and Pacific States. Of all points visited, Spokane Falls consisting then of only a few houses impressed him most favorably and he located some desirable corners there, transferring his Manitoba interest to that city a year before the disastrous boom. Meanwhile he was spending his winters in the study of medicine. Three sessions were passed at Trinity Medical School, Toronto, another session at the Medical School in Portland, Oregon, during one of his visits to the Pacific Coast, and subsequently two sessions at the College of Physicians and Surgeons in New York. With the exception of a short time in Spokane Falls Dr. Whetham has never practised his profession, his attention since graduation being directed mainly to real estate and kindred interests. He was one of the earliest visitors to the future site of Vancouver and soon decided to take a substantial interest in its development. For a time his interests were about equally divided between Spokane Falls and Vancouver, but in 1887 he resolved to make Vancouver his home and both his heart and his treasure are now located there permanently.

Wolfenden, Richard Lt.-Col., (Victoria), was born in Rathwell, Yorkshire, Eng., on 20th March, 1836, and is the third son of the late Robert Wolfenden, esq. Col. Wolfenden was educated at Arkholme and Kirkby Lonsdale, Westmoreland, Eng., and at the age of fourteen entered the printing office of the late John Foster, of Kirkby Lonsdale. In 1855 Col. Wolfenden joined the Royal engineers and acted as an instructor of musketry from 1856 to 1858, when he volunteered for service in British Columbia, under Col. Moody, R.E. In 1859 he arrived at the camp at New Westminster and was employed as accountant in the Lands and Works Department from the date of his arrival till 1862. In 1860 in addition to other duties Col. Wolfenden established the present Government printing office and in 1863 was appointed (on the disbanding of the Royal engineers) superintendent of printing, which position he has filled ever since. He was one of the first to join the volunteer movement in British Columbia and received his commission as ensign and adjutant in the New Westminster rifle volunteers on their enrollment in 1864, which appointment he held until his resignation in 1868 on his removal to Victoria, the capital of the newly-made colony of British Columbia. In 1858 Col. Wolfenden joined the Victoria rifles and received his commission as ensign (No. 1 company) on the enrollment of the active militia of the Province (after the Confederation) in 1874. He was appointed lieutenant in 1876, captain in 1878, captain and adjutant of the British Columbia garrison artillery in 1883, major in 1885, lieutenant-colonel in 1886 and retired, retaining rank, in 1888. Col. Wolfenden is a member of the board of school trustees, of which he is secretary, is president of the Victoria rifle association and vice-president of the Provincial rifle association. He is a member of the Victoria club and the order of United Workmen, and is an adherent of the Church of England. He has been twice married: in 1865 to Kate, daughter of the late George Corby, esq., of Canterbury, England, and in 1879 to Felicte, daughter of the late John Bayley, Esq., of Victoria. Col. Wolfenden is the oldest member of the civil service of British Columbia, having served under the Governors Douglas, Seymour and Musgrave before confederation and since that event under Lieutenant-Governors Trutch, Richards, Cornwall and Nelson. He has published the proceedings of Parliament since the first legislative council in 1864 and the British Columbia *Gazette* since 1863.

Wood, Robert, (Spallumcheen) was born on March 11th, 1841, in the township of Walpool, Ont., and is the son of the Rev. William Wood, of Port Row, in Norfolk county, Ont., and grandson of the late Rev. John Wood, of Swanwick Hall, North Derbyshire, England, now owned by his cousin, Mr. Christopher Wood, and one of the finest county seats in the Midlands. Mr. Wood was educated at the Norfolk County Grammar School. As a lad he had a great wish to learn engineering, but that not meeting the wishes of his parents, he remained at home assisting them with their farm for three years. On March 16th, 1862, Mr. Wood landed at Victoria and during the same year proceeded to Cariboo, where he acquired experience but met with no success. Returning in the fall of the same year to Victoria, Mr. Wood journeyed to Washington Territory, where he farmed during three years, but finding his life there as a vigilante not according to his taste, he settled on one of the, at that time, disputed islands of the straits, where he for several years, was engaged in stock-raising and dairy-farming. In 1872 Mr. Wood settled on the North Arm of the Fraser river, where he remained ten years, during which time he greatly improved his farm by dyking and draining, but finding his health failing he sold out in 1882 and struck out for the Okanagan district, and, after having secured land, settled in Spallumcheen. In 1884 Mr. Wood, in partnership with Mr. D. Rabbitt (a gentleman from Nova Scotia) started a trading store, but was, unfortunately, burnt out the next year, losing a large quantity of valuable goods. After that disaster Mr. E. C. Cargill joined the firm, which now carries on business under the name of E. C. Cargill & Co., and is doing an extensive and remunerative trade in that district. Mr. Wood is a broad-minded man, belongs to no particular political party and is greatly respected by all who have met with him. He is a bachelor and a member of the Free Masons' society. Mr. Wood was one of the first councillors of the North Arm municipality. He has seen all the dangers and passed through the excitement and hardships inseparable from the life of a pioneer settler, and is a loyal and devoted citizen of the British Empire.

Woods, Edward Montague Nelson, (New Westminster), third son of Venerable Archdeacon Woods was born at Victoria on May 1st, 1862. At the age of eleven he was sent to the Old Country to receive his education, and attended Middleton college, county Cork, Ireland. He then entered Queen's university college, Ireland. After completing his university course he returned to New Westminster in 1883, and was articled as a student-at-law to the firm of Corbould and McColl. He was called to the bar of British Columbia in July, 1888, and in the same month was admitted as solicitor. He has practiced in New Westminster since that date. In politics he is a Conservative and a supporter of the Robson government.

Yates, James, was born on January 21st, 1819, at Linlithgow, Scotland. While he was still a child his parents removed to Fifeshire where Mr. Yates grew up to manhood and was educated. In 1849 he came to British Columbia as an articled clerk of the Hudson's Bay Company. He was stationed at Victoria for eighteen months and on the arrival of the company's ships from England Mr. Yates had the work of superintending their discharge and freighting. At the end of eighteen months he applied for the cancellation of his articles and was successful. He then started in business as a trader. He had seen the opening there was for a man of energy and intelligence and he decided not to lose the opportunity. He was very successful in all his ventures and made a great deal of money. He was elected to the first Legislative Council of Vancouver Island in 1855 to represent Victoria city. In 1860 he took his family home to Scotland where he left them and in 1862 returned to British Columbia. Here he put his affairs in order and in 1864 returned to Scotland where he settled. He now lives in retirement at Porto Bello, a suburb of Edinburgh, but keeps himself informed regarding the progress of Vancouver Island in which he is greatly interested.

Yates, James Stuart. (Victoria), eldest son of James Yates, was born at Victoria in 1857 and in 1860 was taken to Scotland. In 1862 his father returned to Vancouver's Island taking him with him. In 1864 he nearly lost his life through an accident in St. Dennis Hotel, New York, by falling several stories down the well of a circular stair case. Both legs were broken and the American physician pronounced him as good as dead, but his father took him to Liverpool, where he placed him under the care of a celebrated bone-setter of that city, Evan Thorn. After three months under Thorn's care he was pronounced recovered. He then went to his family in Scotland. He was educated at Porto Bello and then at the Edinburgh Collegiate school from which he entered the University of that city. He took an arts course and graduated as M. A. in April, 1878, and subsequently as L. L. B. in August, 1881. He then entered Middle Temple, London, England, as a student at law and passed his examination in Hilary term, 1883. He then went to Denmark for a trip and returned to Victoria, British Columbia in October, 1883, where he has since practiced his profession. He is a bencher of the Law Society, a member of the Board of Trade and secretary of the Royal Hospital.

www.ingramcontent.com/pod-product-compliance
Lightning Source LLC
Chambersburg PA
CBHW022147300426
44115CB00006B/384